SITUATING GLOBALITY

AFRICAN DYNAMICS

Volume 3

SITUATING GLOBALITY

African Agency in the Appropriation of Global Culture

EDITED BY

WIM VAN BINSBERGEN
& RIJK VAN DIJK

BRILL
LEIDEN · BOSTON
2004

This book is printed on acid-free paper.

Library of Congress Cataloging-in-Publication Data

Detailed Library of Congress Cataloging-in-Publication Data
are available on the Internet at http://catalog.loc.gov.

ISSN 1568-1777
ISBN 90 04 13133 7

PRINTED IN THE NETHERLANDS

Contents

Maps vii
Photographs vii

PART I: INTRODUCTION

1 Situating globality: African agency in the appropriation of global culture 3
Wim van Binsbergen, Rijk van Dijk & Jan-Bart Gewald

PART II: GLOBALITY THROUGH APPROPRIATION: ANALYSES AT THE CONTINENTAL LEVEL

2 Global and local trends in media ownership and control: Implications for cultural creativity in Africa 57
Francis B. Nyamnjoh

3 Global media and violence in Africa: The case of Somalia 90
Jan-Bart Gewald

4 Can ICT belong in Africa, or is ICT owned by the North Atlantic region? 107
Wim van Binsbergen

5 'Man will live well': On the poetics of corruption in a global age 147
Sanya Osha

PART III: GLOBALITY THROUGH WORLD RELIGIONS

6 'Beyond the rivers of Ethiopia': Pentecostal Pan-Africanism and Ghanaian identities in the transnational domain 163
Rijk van Dijk

7 Global connections, local ruptures: The case of Islam in Senegal 190
Roy Dilley

8 How is a girl to marry without a bed? Weddings, wealth and women's value in an Islamic town of Niger 220
Adeline Masquelier

PART IV: GLOBALITY AND AFRICAN HISTORIC RELIGIONS

9 The social life of secrets *257*
Ferdinand de Jong

10 The persistence of female initiation rites:
Reflexivity and resilience of women in Zambia *277*
Thera Rasing

List of authors *311*

Maps

Map 2.1 Cameroon *67*
Map 7.1 Senegal *200*
Map 8.1 Niger *223*
Map 9.1 Southern Senegal *260*

Photographs

Internet and computer services in Bamenda *78*
Beyond the rivers of Ethiopia *166*
A new mosque being built in the town of Tivouane *194*
Evening prayers at the Nyas *dahira* in Tiaroye *213*
Calabashes waiting to be transported during the *kan kaya* *236*
Women display decorative items on the shelves of their Formica beds *246*
A *nacimbusa* applying *mpemba* (white chalk) to a novice *283*
A novice dancing during the coming-out part of the initiation rite *294*

Part I: Introduction

1

Situating globality: African agency in the appropriation of global culture An introduction

Wim van Binsbergen, Rijk van Dijk & Jan-Bart Gewald

Background and acknowledgements

From 1997 to April 2002 one of the four theme groups at the African Studies Centre (ASC) in Leiden was devoted to the study of globalization and its local responses in Africa. This 'Globalization and Socio-cultural Transformation in Africa' theme group was made up of some of the ASC's permanent staff members, affiliated and visiting researchers in and from Africa, and research associates from within the Netherlands. It was closely linked with the national research project, which was funded and coordinated by the Netherlands Foundation for Tropical Research (WOTRO), on 'Globalization and the Construction of Communal Identities' that was initiated in 1993 by Peter Geschiere and the theme group's leader, Wim van Binsbergen. This project took its cue from work then beginning to appear on the cultural aspects of globalization especially in the articulation of identities, the dynamics of popular culture under globalizing conditions, and the negotiation of commodification.[1] Through the national research group, the ASC's theme group was incorporated in a worldwide 'International Network on Globalization Research' (ING), whose prominent members included Arjun Appadurai, Seteney Shami, Mamadou Diouf, Partha Chatterjee, Jean and John Comaroff, and Ulf Hannerz.

To mark the end of theme group's life-span, an international conference was convened in Leiden in April 2002 to take stock of the theoretical, methodological and empirical progress that had been made in the study of Africa's globalization. It was hoped that the conference's title 'Globalization

[1] For example, Appadurai (1990), Anderson (1992), Clifford (1992) and Hannerz (1987).

and New Questions of Ownership' would capture the dynamics of appropriation and repositioning which, as the Leiden research had suggested, were central — yet hitherto underexposed — aspects of the globalization experience in Africa. We set out below how this initial theme came to be amended during the conference and in the subsequent editorial process leading to the present book.

The convenors and the editors of this volume, Wim van Binsbergen and Rijk van Dijk, register their indebtedness to the African Studies Centre, Leiden, and to the Trust Fund of Erasmus University, Rotterdam, for funding the conference; to all participants and observers for their contributions to our ongoing debate; and to Marieke van Winden and her colleagues at the ASC for their logistical support.

The present collection is the result of that conference. It is based on the papers presented in Leiden, that have been substantially rewritten in the light of the conference discussions and the editors' suggestions, emphasizing what increasingly emerged as a central theme: *African agency in the appropriation of global culture*. This introduction highlights the arguments of this central theme against the background of achievements and problems in African globalization studies since the 1980s. Thanks to a generous grant from the African Studies Centre, the convenors were able to commission specific library research by Jan-Bart Gewald who explored the literature and produced a provisional report. The editors felt that this report would be put to best use if it were incorporated in this introduction, of which Jan-Bart Gewald therefore features as a co-author. We are grateful to the ASC's Library, Documentation and Information department whose literature surveys and excerpts, freely utilized in the following pages, have considerably facilitated the task of writing this introduction.

Finally, the editors wish to extend their thanks to the following persons and institutions who have been instrumental in the realization of this book: to all the contributors for sharing and inspiring our intellectual explorations on globalization and its African trajectories; to Ann Reeves whose excellent work as copy editor often extended into reminding the contributors and editors of their schedule responsibilities; to Mieke Zwart-Brouwer for preparing the lay-out of this book in her usual careful and efficient manner; to Nel de Vink for the beautifully drawn maps; and to Brill Publishers for professional and supportive cooperation in all stages of the book's production.

Having sketched the context in which the book came into being and thanked those who assisted in its delivery, the remainder of this introduction is structured as follows. In Section 2 we deal with globalization and Africa in broad theoretical terms, taking stock of what our years of research in this field have taught us, including the many major puzzles of conceptualization, theory and interpretation that remain. We formulate, in Section 3, what we see as the main message of this collection, as summarized by our title 'Situating Globality: African Agency in the Appropriation of Global Culture'. Then we briefly introduce the book's constituent chapters from this overall perspective. A bibliography concludes the introduction and is a guide to the understanding of some of the most significant aspects of African transformations today.

Globalization and Africa

Globalization as a concept, a phenomenon and an ideology

> [Globalization constitutes] the dominant international system that replaced the Cold War system after the fall of the Berlin Wall. (Friedman 1999: 7)

Over the past fifteen years, 'globalization' has become the buzzword in both academic as well as popular discourse dealing with Africa, and *a fortiori* with the world as a whole. This is indeed remarkable for a word that, according to Waters, did not exist as a processual term in academic literature prior to 1987.[2] In his presidential address to the Ninth General Assembly of the Council for the Development of Social Science Research in Africa (CODESRIA) in Dakar in December 1998, Akilagpa Sawyerr stated that discussion of the 'globalization process' contained within it 'strong doses' of reality as well as mythology, and that globalization, both as reality and as myth, had had a profound impact on the daily life of people in Africa. Professor Sawyerr's address is a fine introduction to the state of play in globalization and the social sciences in Africa, and emphasizes the ambiguity that has come to be associated with the term 'globalization'. An ambiguity, which Sawyerr charmingly admits, 'is not without its uses' (Sawyerr 1999: 1).

And that, precisely, is the problem: globalization has come to mean all things to all people and in so doing has increasingly run the risk of losing its explanatory meaning. There are a number of fields in which globalization, as a process, is taken to mean something. Yet within and between each field, the meaning ascribed to globalization varies from author to author and from discipline to discipline. That is, the various meanings attributed to globalization within these fields are often not compatible, let alone between fields. Generally though, the term globalization is taken to describe processes that are currently taking place on account of changes in information transfer. Due to the recent rapid advances in information and communication technology (ICT), these

[2] Waters (1995: 2). However, cf. Levitt (1983) and Robertson & Lechner (1985), in whose titles the term 'globalization' features.

processes, which may have been long in the making, have substantially changed the world. The transfer in information is quantifiably different from what it was in the past, and this has led to a qualitative difference. Unfortunately for much of the work dealing with globalization in Africa, the process of globalization in itself is taken as a given and events in Africa are viewed solely from within the confines of an implicit globalization-based paradigm.

It is necessary to provide a narrower definition of terms and to distinguish between the concept, the phenomenon and even the ideology of globalization. Often these three are confused in the application of the term.

For those seeking enlightenment as to what is to be understood by the term globalization, there is a multitude of definitions that all circle around and centre on the ever-increasing compression of time and space in the world. This is directly inspired by the early work of Giddens (1991) who proposed that, in terms of theory, account had to be taken of the fact that modernity entailed the increasing expansion of interconnectedness across social, cultural and class systems. According to Giddens, this in turn redefined the boundaries and interrelationships between these abstract categories and the people within them. Giddens proposed that instead of looking at the integration of bounded systems, people need to deal with the issue of order as one of time-space distanciation — the conditions under which time and space are organized so as to connect presence and absence. Giddens noted that modern social systems 'bind time and space'. They connect local activity with activities a long way away and create links across time and space that are not necessarily defined by local factors. Local temporal and spatial conditions can have an impact on socio-political and economic conditions far away. This is nothing new for there have always been cultural and economic exchanges between people; yet the intensity and centrality of these exchanges have expanded greatly with the onset of modernity, and intensified yet again to simultaneously bind all regions across the globe.

Malcolm Waters, writing on globalization in terms of its perceived cultural impact, has referred to globalization in terms of the phenomena that make for the system that Giddens had indicated and perceives of it as:

> a social process in which the constraints of geography on social and cultural arrangements recede and in which people become increasingly aware that they are receding. (Waters 1995: 3)

Likewise, Geschiere and Van Binsbergen deploy the term globalization

> as a descriptive term to draw attention to the rapidly accelerating circulation of goods, people and images on a global scale, since roughly the 1960s; the emphasis

here is on 'rapidly accelerating' since it is clear that global circuits were much older than this.[3]

There are ongoing debates regarding the origins of the phenomenon of globalization. Here the leading question is: is globalization a process that has been going on since time immemorial, or is it merely contemporaneous with and identical to capitalist development and modernization? Within the social sciences for instance, ideas relating to what has become known as globalization have a long antecedent. The work by Peter Worsley (1957) on 'cargo cults' in Melanesia and Terence Ranger (1975) on the Beni Ngoma in East Africa[4] heralded the later work of others, Arjun Appadurai (1990, 1991, 1996, 2000) and Ulf Hannerz (1987, 1996) in particular, on the manner in which concepts, ideas and material objects, once introduced into societies from the outside, can come to be used and deployed in ways that appear to be incompatible and illogical to the societies from whence they came. Whatever the position taken in that debate, it is generally agreed that the recent spectacular advances in information communication technologies have qualitatively changed the manner in which the world is perceived, experienced and acted upon.

Both inside and outside the ASC's theme group on globalization, much of the Dutch research on cultural globalization (and in this it is in line with globalization research internationally) has elaborated the insight that 'processes of globalization' — the impact of modern communication and transport techniques, the spread of industrial commodities, new styles of consumption and new forms of knowledge on a global scale — do not necessarily lead to greater cultural homogeneity. On the contrary, many authors have recently stressed that these processes often reinforce parochial identities. Far from being subsumed in globalization, parochial identities appear to thrive on the impact of globalization. Furthermore, much of what is presented as being traditional in character could be shown, upon closer inspection, to be shot through with aspects of the modern world — indeed the globalizing world — to such an extent that it would be better to refer to these allegedly traditional identities as 'pseudo-traditional' identities.

---

[3] Geschiere &Van Binsbergen, in press (Introduction).

[4] Cf. Worsley (1957), Ranger (1975). 'Cargo cults' is the technical term for popular 20th-century social movements, mainly in Oceania, and emerged as a result of contact with the West especially in the context of World War II. These movements centred on the expectation of the arrival, by ship or by plane, of loads of valuable goods (including Western consumer goods) made available to the local population by the ancestors or other spiritual forces. The Beni Ngoma are early (pre-World War II) ballroom dance associations in East Africa, exclusive to Africans, whose grooming, style of dress and general comportment revealed Africans' careful adoption of European models current at the time.

In the African context, Forben (cf. 1995) can be seen as working along a very different line, namely the interpretation of globalization as an ideology, or even as a policy directive. He is the director of the newly founded African Centre for Humanities (ACH) that was 'set up in response to the need for alternative and innovative approaches to the current challenges facing both Africa and the world at large'. One such challenge is:

> to devise and implement workable global structures which, while being relevant to all, also take account of regional, communal and individual differences — so that each culture and each individual are able to interpret global norms in a way that is most relevant to them locally, while also being consistent with the broader objectives of such global structures. (Forben 1995: 11)

While he broadcasts the desire to maintain cultural identity in the face of homogenization, his own contribution to the debate is basically a pamphlet meant to advertise his own organization and in a sense making use of the opportunities offered by globalization. But, one might argue, so much seems to apply to all Africanist research, especially if undertaken by non-Africans (cf. Van Binsbergen 2003). In terms of ideology, globalization appears to lead to debates on the pros and cons, and to the exclusion of neutral positions in the defence or rejection of the process. Bauman (1998) has argued in detail and with conviction that globalization divides as much as it unites — an observation that applies not only to the massive proliferation of new identities (of an ethnic, religious, cultural, gender, sexual or consumptive and lifestyle nature) in the face of the cliché of threatening McDonaldization (as in hamburger), but also and particularly to the element of worldwide, regional and local social inequality: globalization means the global availability of objects, services and ideas which on the one hand articulates the exalted class position of some, while on the other hand reinforces the subordinate, deprived and exploited situation of many others. Here we are close to the work of Frederic Jameson and Masao Miyoshi (1998) who situate globalization in the logic of the cultural production of capitalism and attempt to theorize the specific logic of the cultural production of the third stage of capitalism.

Thomas Friedman (1999), columnist for *The New York Times* and far from being an anti-globalist, indicates the dangers that emerge from the global functioning of capitalist financial markets and the unequal access developing countries have to these flows. As Thabo Mbeki, then deputy president of South Africa, noted on 28 September 1998 in a speech delivered at the African Renaissance Conference in Johannesburg:

> The current international financial crisis has brought to the fore, very sharply, the fact of the accumulation of vast quantities of especially financial capital in the

> developed countries of the North. The rapid movements of this capital, from one corner of the globe to the other, in search of immediate profit have contributed greatly to the problems which the world is experiencing today. On other occasions we have made the point that we are subjected to the strange situation that the process of the further reproduction of wealth by the countries of the North has led to the creation of poverty in the countries of the South. There has to be something out of joint where wealth begets poverty!

President Thabo Mbeki is currently a major proponent of African Renaissance, never fully defined by himself as a collection of points, some of which are a desperate call for the inclusion of Africa in the maelstrom and perceived benefits of globalization.[5]

> Even now, we can reel off the list of things that need to be done in this regard, including human resource development, the emancipation of women, the building of a modern economic, social and communication infrastructure, the cancellation of Africa's foreign debt, an improvement in terms of trade, an increase in domestic and foreign investment, the expansion of development assistance and better access for our products into the markets of the developed world. (…) We must therefore insert ourselves into the international debate about the issues of globalization and its impact on the lives of the people and make our voice heard about what we and the rest of the world should do actually to achieve the development which is a fundamental right of the masses of our people (Statement by Deputy President Thabo Mbeki at the African Renaissance Conference, Johannesburg, 28 September 1998).

The prime issue is the qualitative difference which space–time compression has brought. Hand in hand with the instantaneous transfer of massive amounts of money (with disastrous results for local economies) goes the equally instantaneous transfer of information. It has been noted that the 'global context remains an empty abstraction unless mediated and translated towards concrete settings where we can discern concrete actors' (Van Binsbergen 1999: 3).

This leads us to the question of how globalization affects daily life in Africa today. As the phenomenon of globalization appeared to have an impact on the world's economy in particular, its effects on continents such as Africa were first and foremost defined in economic terms. Under the influence of global institutions such as the World Bank, globalization came to mean a desired

---

[5] Mbeki (1998). Although a London and Sussex-trained economist (BA 1962, MA 1966, 1968 in economics), Mbeki here simulates ignorance of classic Marxist economics according to which wealth (in other words capital) has no option but to exploit labour, with poverty being the unavoidable result. For the sake of convincing his audience steeped in liberal economics, he pretends that a causal relationship between wealth and poverty is surprising, theoretically unforeseen, therefore undesirable and repairable.

policy and end-state, a prescription for a failing integration in world markets and a guideline for the interventions of singular states. But to gauge this effect, we must first look at the implications of this ideological and prescriptive thinking for Africa's economy.

The economy and a globalist ideological paradigm

Figures released by the United Nations Conference on Trade and Development (UNCTAD) for the year 2001 indicate that the continent of Africa is a marginal player in the world economy.[6] Global 'Foreign Direct Investments' (FDI) consisted of US$760 billion in 2001, of which US$225 billion consisted of FDIs in developing countries. The upbeat news was that whereas global FDI fell by nearly 50 per cent in 2001, FDI in Africa increased by nearly 20 per cent from €9 billion in 2000 to €11 billion in 2001.[7] On the down side, this investment was overwhelmingly concentrated in Egypt, Nigeria, Morocco and South Africa, and was driven primarily by a series of mergers and acquisitions, as well as privatizations of state-owned enterprises. Furthermore, in terms of global FDI Africa accounted for a mere 1.5 per cent, whilst even in terms of developing countries' FDI Africa accounted only for a mere 5 per cent. What these figures indicate is that Africa is to all intents and purposes cut off from the world economy. The only bright spot might be the implication that, in terms of these figures, Africa is not necessarily directly affected by global economic downturns.[8]

The staggering comparisons vex the minds of many social scientists and economists. The bulk of existing material dealing with globalization and Africa is written from an economic perspective, and its production has been funded by global institutions that seek to regulate the global economy, notably the World Bank, the International Monetary Fund (IMF), the Global Agreement on Trade and Tariffs (GATT), the Organization for Economic Cooperation and Development (OECD),[9] and so forth. A reading of this material is interesting precisely because it underscores the underlying belief in the virtues of the mythical free market, as well as in globalization as an inevitable and necessary condition.

[6] United Nations Conference on Trade and Development, 'FDI Downturn in 2001 Touches Almost All Regions', Press Release, TAD/INF/PR36, 21 January 2002.

[7] To put the figure of US$11 billion in perspective, this is the same amount as the US government wants to spend over two years to protect the nation against biological terrorism (*New York Times*, 4 February 2002).

[8] In effect, an echo of the 'uncaptured peasantry' concept; cf. Hyden (1980) and Geschiere (1984).

[9] Ongoing reports dealing with globalization statistics can be accessed at: www.oecd.org

Thomas Friedman (1999: 104) has coined the term the 'golden straitjacket' as the 'defining political-economic garment of this globalization era'. He notes that countries either adopt the golden straitjacket of privatization, macroeconomic stability, fewer market controls, trade deregulation, small government and the like, or they fall behind. This state of affairs is in effect based on no more than a fundamental belief, albeit a belief that underlies the bulk of material emanating from global financial institutions such as the IMF. *Finance and Development*, the IMF's quarterly magazine, devoted its December 2001 edition to 'Globalization and Africa', and in itself provides a fine introduction to the views and beliefs of this institution. Its editors state in the introduction that the articles it presents examine how Africa can reposition itself to take full advantage of globalization, and they argue that the articles 'sketch a road map that could help make globalization work better for Africa'.[10]

In his contribution, Evangelos Calamitsis, the former director of the IMF's African Department, suggests that:

> most countries will probably need to implement stronger domestic policies and reforms designed to consolidate macroeconomic stability, enhance human resource development, improve basic infrastructure and spur agricultural development, accelerate trade liberalization and regional economic integration, promote a sound banking system, foster private investment, and ensure good governance.

However, much more far-reaching is the contribution by Seyni N'Diaye, National Director for Senegal of the Central Bank of West African States (BCEAO) who argues that African states will have to undertake extensive institutional reforms to facilitate full integration into the global economy. N'Diaye notes that Sub-Saharan Africa is confined to the 'peripheries of globalization', and that this should be met with rigorous action, notably structural and institutional reforms, to allow the region to take full advantage of the benefits of globalization while minimizing the risks. To transform Africa, he calls for the institutional reform and transformation of the state, its civil society and the private sector. He views the state as interventionist and declares that 'this interventionist system, …[which], eventually ran out of steam … did not give way to burgeoning private initiative'.

Having advocated a dramatic reduction in the state, N'Diaye then calls for an expansion in the role of civil society, which, in his view, predictably appears to consist of NGOs. It is described as being a mouthpiece for democracy, it is the chief challenger of the power of the state, limiting deviations from good governance and acting as a regulator in the political arena. It is clear that the role of opposition parties is of no importance, and that instead NGOs should

---

[10] *Finance and Development* can be accessed online at http: //www.imf.org/fandd

serve as watchdogs to contain market excesses and to guard against environmental abuse.

While the state is stripped of its powers N'Diaye sees the private sector as the 'main engine for growth' in the context of globalization. As such, 'its operations must be free of heavy-handed and cumbersome regulatory or bureaucratic procedures that could slow its expansion'. Freed of restrictions the private sector needs to be supported by a sound banking and financial sector within a liberalized institutional context.

N'Diaye's optimistic economistic vision shows him to be co-opted by the North Atlantic hegemonism that is imposed on the African continent. In a similar vein is the work by El Toukhy (1998) that analyses the potential effects of the globalization of trade and finance on developing countries. El Toukhy focuses on the Uruguay Round of the General Agreement on Tariffs and Trade (GATT) and the manner in which this relates to Sub-Saharan Africa. He argues that Sub-Saharan Africa, in seeking to reduce its losses and enhance any possible benefits from globalization, needs to:

> develop and strengthen its competitiveness through expanded and diversified productive capacities and market diversification, improvement in marketing skills, quality control techniques and level of technology. (ibid: 481)

Where the necessary funding for these no-nonsense economic strategies is to be found is not indicated but the socio-political improvements which El Toukhy believes to be essential are listed as being, amongst others: macroeconomic stability, structural reform and good governance.

A reading of N'Diaye's work, and through it the underlying assumptions of the financial institutions that seek to regulate global trade and finance, underscores the analysis of Noam Chomsky in his collection *Profit over People*. This brings together articles and lectures written between 1993 and 1998 and Chomsky presents his views on corporate power, media control and the international economy. He argues that corporate power and the suppression of democracy have led to an increase in the personal wealth of a few in the First World at the expense of the majority. Writing on the new global order, Chomsky (1998) describes neo-liberalism as:

> a set of market-orientated principles designed and propagated by the United States government and international financial institutions with the aim of liberalising trade and finance, setting prices according to market forces, privatisation and the curtailment of inflation. These doctrines are used by the powerful nations and

> institutions to create a global order to serve the interests of the rich at the expense of the poor.[11]

Yet it is this fundamental belief that lies at the basis of much of the advice that is being presented to African states — and many of the regulations that (in the form of Structural Adjustment Programmes) are being imposed upon them by the international financial institutions and bilateral aid partners.

A case in point is Nuwagaba's (2001) analysis of the Ugandan situation, in which he focuses on the interface between globalization and poverty reduction in Uganda. Incidentally, Nuwagaba adopts a very general use of the term globalization. In Africa the most vivid experience of globalization is, he says, 'through slavery, characterised by the exploitation of African labour in the Americas, Europe and Asia' (ibid: 32).

In the early 1980s Uganda adopted structural adjustment programmes (SAPs) with the aim of making the Ugandan economy competitive once again on the world stage. The programmes were meant to correct the structural bottlenecks and economic disequilibria that had arisen due to increased importation and increased government expenditure against the backdrop of declining exports and government revenue. These programmes have, however, contributed to the escalation of poverty among Ugandans. Nuwagaba argues that globalized markets require a much greater competitive capacity than the Ugandan economy can provide. In his opinion, most African countries have globalized through a series of shocks rather than by making use of opportunities. Nevertheless, global competitiveness is inevitable if the Ugandan economy is to catch up with global trends and patterns. Globalization must be cautiously embraced if development is to be sustainable, but in the last analysis African economies do not appear to have much of a choice:

> For decades, there has been [a] massive flow of aid to support poor countries but donor fatigue has set in. Uganda must find its own solutions. … The powerful and invisible forces that have given rise to globalization are impossible to resist. (Nuwagaba 2001: 51)

This is not exactly the position of the economist Yash Tandon (1997), who views globalization as capital's final conquest of the rest of the world. With the end of the Cold War, the movement of capital is no longer hindered by the West's need to compromise on account of communism. This has brought about fundamental changes in the global economic system: the strong can now extract what they will, the weak must surrender what they cannot protect. The case of Africa is ample illustration of this. Globalization has created a chasm between

[11] See also http://www.thirdworldtraveler.com/Chomsky/Noam_Chomsky.html

the North and the South. Even land, one of the few assets Africans still hold, is threatened with being globalized. Ironically, whilst capital-led globalization is at the root of Africa's crisis, it is also suggested as its 'solution'. For in Tandon's opinion, the alternatives for the south are to slow down the process of further integration into the global economy; to strengthen local community-based systems of production and marketing; and to begin to steer local resources away from multinational corporations.

N'Diaye and like-minded powerful actors on the African continent may call for the trimming of the African state in the interests of African integration in the world's globalized economy. By contrast however, Nicolas van de Walle (1999) discusses and assesses a number of arguments about the impact of economic globalization on African democracies, concentrating on the economic dimension of globalization, which is simply defined as the process of integration of national economies. He tracks the progress of economic globalization in the recent past and reviews the reasons given in the literature as to why globalization might be viewed as undermining democratic rule. He argues that the international economy is much less globalized today than is increasingly being suggested. According to Van de Walle, globalization processes in Africa are in fact stagnant, if not in retreat. He further argues that the low levels of private capital flows to Africa serve to set the continent sharply apart from other regions of the world. Africa's increasing marginalization in the world economy means global economic integration has different implications for Africa than for Latin America or Asia. Interestingly, Van de Walle calls for the reintegration of African states into the global economy, believing that to do so would be to promote economic growth and limit the leverage of international financial institutions.

In financial terms, Africa appears to be barely involved in the globalized world. Fosu and Senbet (2001) argue that although the economies of Sub-Saharan Africa have generally been sheltered from the direct effects of financial and currency crises because of this disconnectedness, the indirect effects could be considerable. They refer to Africa's increasingly significant economic relationships with Asian countries and the impact of the crises in global markets on commodity prices. Furthermore, they argue that the crises provide important lessons for the African region, especially those that identify mechanisms for maximizing the benefits of globalization while minimizing its risks.

One commonly heard suggestion relating to what Africa should do in the face of economic globalization is regional economic integration. Here attention focuses on the creation of regional economic blocks as a fortress against international financial institutions. Tanoe and Diouf (1999) deal with the serious limitations of regional trade areas, such as the Economic Community of West African States (ECOWAS), the Common Market for Eastern and Southern

Africa (COMESA), and the Southern African Development Community (SADC). They note that openness to world markets and the removal of barriers to international trade and investment are key characteristics of liberalization, and with it the globalization of world trade. There has been a proliferation of regionalized approaches to trade and economic development, however, in Africa. Tanoe and Diouf (ibid: 45-6) observe that regional integration arrangements leading to free trade areas or customs unions, which could serve as a protective barrier to the rest of the world, are only allowed as an exception to the most-favoured nation rule, in the context of the global multilateral trading system, under certain conditions. The members must also notify the arrangements to the World Trade Organisation (WTO) for assessment and recognition. Thus far only COMESA has been notified.

In other words, it is as individual states and not as regional blocks that African states face immensely powerful regional trading blocks such as the North American Free Trade Agreement (NAFTA) and the European Union (EU). This, needless to say, places African states in a weak bargaining position.

This section discussed how the assessment of the economic impact of globalization on the African continent appears to be producing very different views and positions with regard to the question of how and to what extent African economies should become integrated in global economic systems. Some authors are hopeful in their diagnosis and the prescriptive policies they imagine, others remain pessimistic about the chances of such global integration. The next section shows that similar discussions can be seen to be taking place with regard to the socio-cultural impact of globalization on Africa.

Societal impact and the globalist debate

Much analysis has been devoted to how Africans have been seeking to modernize and participate in the globalized world. This work is tellingly countered by that of James Ferguson (1999) who reminds us that in the recent past there were parts and aspects of Africa that participated in the global world as equal players in ways no longer replicated in today's conditions. In grim detail, Ferguson describes how Zambia, once lauded as the vanguard of an African industrial revolution, has moved into economic decline and been sidelined in the modern globalized world. As Ferguson (1999: 235) notes, 'Zambia, in the good times, had been on the map — a country among others in the "modern world"'. Now, Zambia is just another one of the many African basket cases. Ferguson uses the word 'abjection' to describe 'a process of being thrown aside, expelled, or discarded. But its literal meaning also implies not just being thrown out but being thrown down — thus expulsion but also debasement and humiliation' (ibid: 236).

It is this humiliation of Africans through the forceful termination of African participation in the globalized First World that is part of the focus of Ferguson's work. He cites an article from a Zambian newspaper:

> Car owning remains a dream. A decade ago, young men in gainful employment were able to buy cars of all models. That era is gone, gone never to return again. (ibid: 1)

One of the aspects emphasized by researchers dealing with globalization is the uneven impact it has on African communities and societies. The now fairly dated work of Brecher and Costello (1994) sought to describe the process of globalization and its impact. Although they concentrated primarily on the economic impact of globalization, they coined the term 'downward levelling' to describe a process of cultural and societal homogenization that they argued was brought about by globalization. Similar views have been put forward by Barnett (1994) and Bauman (1998) who seek to highlight the reduction in cultural diversity that has allegedly been brought about by globalization — another version of the spectre of McDonaldization.

Interesting in the work of Brecher and Costello (1994) is the fact that they provide an overview of possible and actual strategies as to how globalization is to be countered. In so doing, they provide a description of the varied forms of resistance that have appeared to globalization in underdeveloped, newly industrialized, former communist, and industrial countries. The formation of transnational movements of opposition to globalization is particularly emphasized in their work. In this their work foreshadows the currently popular bestsellers by Hertz (2001) and Klein (2000).

In contrast to these negative views of the impact of globalization on societies is the work of Friedman (1999: 29) who coins the term 'glocalism' and defines it as follows:

> healthy glocalization (...) [is] the ability of a culture, when it encounters other strong cultures, to absorb influences that naturally fit into and can enrich that culture, to resist those things that are truly alien and to compartmentalize those things that, while different, can nevertheless be enjoyed and celebrated as different.

Friedman argues that societies need to develop glocalism, and that failure to do so will lead to their further marginalization:

> The whole purpose of glocalising is to be able to assimilate aspects of globalization into your country and culture in a way that adds to your growth and diversity, without overwhelming it.

Friedman's point of view would appear to be close to the position that we are defending in this collection and that will be highlighted in Section 3 of this introduction. However, as is often the case, the closer the affinity, the more one notices differences. Friedman appreciates the different forms that the impact of globalization can take upon a society but a weakness of his is that he sees such differential impact as the result, apparently, of pre-existing and more or less immutable features which that society had at the moment when globalization manifested itself there. However well intended, his whole approach to societies and their dynamics in a global context is static, mechanical and prescriptive. How can one speak of 'healthy' glocalisation, without burdening one's argument with a heritage of condescension ('we know what is healthy for you, my good man') that is only an enlightened form of North–South hegemonic subjugation? How could one use the word 'naturally' in the context of socio-cultural dynamics (agreed, by definition, to be learned and not genetically determined, to be 'nurture' and not 'nature'), unless as a slip of the pen? How could one revive the old, originally social Darwinist concept of 'weak' and 'strong' cultures and societies? How could one reproduce, without even a semblance of critical distance, the ideology of the multiculturalism[12] of the mutual cultural 'enrichment' of societies in globalization in the face of massive evidence to the effect that, if left to global market forces, globalization would amount to a process of cultural and class subjugation worldwide, so that any enrichment that took place (for example, the installation of ethnic restaurants and festivals) would merely obscure the real loss of identity, autonomy and participation that goes on underneath in the South and on the periphery in general. And how could one speak of 'truly alien', as if it were at all possible (presumably with state-of-the-art methods of cultural anthropology?) to identify that which is unmistakably proper to a particular culture and that which is unmistakably alien? Identity, self, identification and dissociation have been recognized throughout modern social-science studies of ethnicity and identity as highly selective, eclectic, situational and performative, so that, in a post-modern globalizing world, the 'truly alien' can only appear as a deliberate, situational, strategic construct (on the part of the owners of a particular cultural orientation, or on the part of the ethnographer), or both? Essentializing is inevitably part of the construction of identity in any globalizing context but one would hardly expect the social-scientific analyst to join in the game, as Friedman clearly does here.

[12] Also compare Friedman's use of such evaluative, optimistic expressions such as 'enjoy' and 'celebrate' in this connection, which smack of American popular language use in the (often market-triggered and consensus-driven) exhortative, ideological construction of sociability, but that are out of place in analytical social-scientific discourse.

What we propose to retain of Friedman's view of glocalization is the awareness that the experience and the process of globalization may vary infinitely, due to factors that are related to the internal functioning of societies undergoing globalization. However, instead of looking for immutable features to explain this differential, we ought to be looking at different strategies of agency among members of those societies: modes of selection, appropriation, creation and transgression of boundaries, as applied by specific actors at a specific time and place, and (as we argue when discussing the present collection's project) in the context, not so much of new concerns brought and imposed by globalization, but of ongoing concerns towards whose conflictive realization globalization provides new material, new ammunition and new formats, without initiating these concerns themselves in the first place.

Implicit in Friedman's work is the same critique of societies as is to be found in the work of the prominent Orientalist Bernard Lewis, since 1986 a Princeton emeritus. The American historian Paul Kennedy recounts that in early 1979 as Ayatollah Khomeini returned to Iran from exile in France on 1 February, Bernard Lewis declared in *The New York Times* that the 'Shah's overthrow by Muslim clerics would lead not to social improvement and democracy but to a theocracy, intolerance and clerically controlled mayhem'.

Kennedy (2002) notes that Lewis's statements — which today would be recognized as remarkably insightful or even prophetic by many well-informed people outside Iran — ran counter to popular opinion that held that 'the Iranian people, freed from the Shah's yoke, would join the modern, anticapitalist, freethinking world'.

In essence these statements contain the issue that vexes all those dealing with globalization. Far from inevitably leading to homogenization, globalization can also lead to a rise of theocracies that appear in a traditional guise but that are in their organizational structure and technological resources thoroughly modern entities. Lewis's latest work, *What Went Wrong?* (Lewis 2001), deals with the responses of the Muslim world to the West over time, and would seem to support Friedman's assertion that a society's failure to successfully 'glocalize' will lead inevitably to its further marginalization.

Again Friedman helps us (albeit by inviting our disagreement) to articulate more clearly what globalization amounts to. Marginalization is a perspectival, relative concept. Only in a world that has just one focus, one centre, is it crystal clear where the margins are. It would appear as if the central struggle in globalization is not even any more about scarce resources such as wealth, weaponry and technology. It is also less and less about a recognition of outlying groups and identities by a self-proclaimed and powerful centre. The central struggle is increasingly between unicentrism and multicentrism. The illusion of unicentrism, with the United States as the uncontested focus of the global economy, politics, monopoly over mass destruction weapons, morality, ethics and political blueprints (in such fields as human rights and democracy), is increasingly being contested from within and without Africa's intellectual circles. The Black Athena discussion[13] has been essentially about the inevitability of a perspective global multicentredness for the sake of mankind's global future, yet argued on the basis of millennia-encompassing historical evidence which European/North Atlantic cultural hegemony has long managed to push under the table. Comparative philosophy and, more recently, intercultural philosophy in Africa have struggled to drive the message of the essential multicentredness of human cultural and intellectual achievement home.[14] However, a far more explicit, intransigent, belligerent and violent challenge of (the US, hegemonic) unicentrism is to be found in militant Islamism. What is at stake in the latter is not so much the refusal of proudly self-conscious, militant Islamists to be marginalized *vis-à-vis* the US unicentre, but their rejection of the idea that the United States should be 'the' centre' *par excellence*. Failure to appreciate multicentredness as an essential, positive feature of the contemporary world (and even of human history since the Late Palaeolithic) has brought Samuel Huntington (1996) to interpret its manifestations as the inevitable, religion-based *Clash of Civilizations*, lending a thin intellectual justification to a continued and intensified North Atlantic hegemonic project.

Thus, while Friedman and Lewis see globalization as intrinsically the imposition of North Atlantic hegemony, it would be analytically more rewarding to distinguish between two related processes:

a) the fact that local individuals and communities are increasingly being drawn into global networks of communication, information and circulation; or
b) the fact that such networks are not power-indifferent but tend to concentrate power in local, regional, national, continental and intercontinental centres, with less than a handful of centres aspiring to effective world centrality — with the post-Cold War United States as the most striking example.

Justifiably, most writers on globalization would include (a) in their definition of globalization but only a minority would consider process (b) as more than an

---

[13] Bernal (1987, 1991), Lefkowitz & MacLean Rogers (1996) and Van Binsbergen (1997).

[14] Cf. Raju (1962), Mall (1995) and Van Binsbergen (2003).

accidental, ephemeral, regressive and essentially undesirable aspect of contemporary globalization.

Associated with the perceived decrease in cultural diversity is the ongoing loss of languages. When dealing with the global world and seeking to successfully 'glocalize', a society must of necessity acquire a full working knowledge of a global language among at least a sizeable minority of its members. Rabenoro (1999) argues that, to avoid being totally left behind, developing countries — and African ones in particular — need to rethink their language, cultural and educational policies in the framework of their development schemes. In Africa, the privileged minority are at least bilingual and have at their command both an African language and a language of international (in fact, intercontinental) communication, usually their former colonizer's language. Rabenoro notes that the disadvantaged majority are generally monolingual or, if they are multilingual, their second language is a national, pidginized version of an intercontinental language, one that forces exclusion from rather than access to intercontinental circulation. As a result, these people have limited access to the modern sector. Rabenoro is critical of the propagation of multilingualism and multiculturalism, even though this had become part of the ideological politics of recognition by the end of the 20th century. In his view, linguistic diversity hampers communication and hinders development endeavours. Of particular importance is the question of what language is used as the medium of instruction. As one of the possible ways of bridging the gap between the Westernized minority and the disadvantaged majority that are not proficient in a language of international communication, Rabenoro suggests including the teaching of international languages on African school curricula. Perhaps it would be more realistic to admit that this has been a widespread policy for decades but that it has been fatally thwarted by failing infrastructure, poverty and the intercontinental brain drain.[15]

Francis Nyamnjoh (2000) does not share Friedman's normatively optimistic view and reminds us that global availability does not mean global affordability. He brings to the fore once again the fact that access to the global does not necessarily mean that benefits will accrue. He takes a critical look at globalization from the standpoint of the African experience of the West and discusses 'modernization', 'development' and 'globalization' as different labels for the same basic project or mission. This mission consists of freeing the African of his natural and cultural Africanness, and inviting him/her to partake of a 'standardized, streamlined and global' consumer culture.

Such a freeing, which Nyamnjoh appears to regard with sarcasm, cannot pass without further qualification. It could only be liberation in the positive

[15] For an insightful collection of papers on related issues, cf. Fardon & Furniss (1994).

sense if one considered Africanness as something negative. The aim of the whole project of Afrocentrism is to counter such a negative conception of Africanness. However we understand the liberation which globalization is claimed to entail, granted the level of poverty in Africa, as only an elite few qualify to consume first or second-hand. Global availability is not synonymous with global affordability. The majority of Africans have to content themselves with what trickles down to them from relatives or patrons at the centre of power and resources. They have to be satisfied with what Achille Mbembe has called *lécher les fenêtres*, i.e. impotent window-shopping, with rising desire but without the financial means to actually make a purchase. In the face of such inequities, it is difficult to envisage how ordinary Africans can relate to the global (consumer) culture in any way other than with frustration and disenchantment.

Despite and perhaps as a result of such debates on the pros and cons of globalization at a macro level of interpretation, an increasing need was felt to obtain an empirically based understanding of the impact of globalization on local cultures. How are these processes of globalization, both in economic and cultural terms, situated at the mundane level of everyday existence? While it was evident that in terms of economy and culture globalization was transformative of local societies, the exact nature of those changes has remained a matter for further investigation. It was in the social sciences dealing with the intricate processes of social life that this need was particularly felt. In anthropology, social history, political science, human geography and religious studies, an interest for processes of globalization emerged based on empirical research, which did not *a priori* intend to speak out on the value or relevance of globalization but instead was aimed at a further understanding of the phenomenon, its ramifications and the ideologies and imaginations it fostered. In various disciplines the challenge was taken up of exploring the ways in which globalization has become situated in local communities and social processes in Africa. In the following disciplines specific answers are being formulated with regard to the place of the concept and the process of globalization in academic work, and the ways in which these can or should be studied in local situations.

History

> Sometime around 1760, Britain, then France and America took off to another world, one that was increasingly secular, democratic, industrial and tolerant in ways that

> left many of the other regions gasping at the combined implications of such changes. (Kennedy 2002)[16]

Globalization is an eminently historical phenomenon, one that can only be truly understood in a historical context. Over time it has become increasingly possible for people to come into contact with one another in ever-quicker ways and at ever-diminishing cost. Yet, primarily due to the historical discipline's tradition of writing national histories, historians — with some notable exceptions, some of which we have already mentioned — have generally not dealt with globalization. Heralding what could become another paradigm change in the social sciences, and the timely entry of historians into the field of globalization is the excellent introduction in the collective work edited by Anthony Hopkins (2002), not to be confused with the movie star of the same name! The essays presented in his book indicate that the history of globalization does not follow a linear trajectory but instead shows that 'historically, globalization has taken different forms, which we have categorized as archaic, proto, modern, and post-colonial' (ibid: 3). Tellingly he challenges historians to take up research on globalization.

> Identifying the quantitative and qualitative dimensions of globalization, and exploring the links between them, is a starting point that should appeal to historians who are properly sceptical of definitions that commit them to a particular bias, whether economic, political, social or cultural. (ibid: 17)

At the same time he warns historians of the dangers

> of using the term without also being aware that different claims about its longevity, novelty and significance are frequently founded on variations in the way it is defined. (ibid: 36)

These issues are not easily resolved and, having barely entered the debate, for historians to make hard and fast statements would be, in Hopkins's view, unwise. He ends his overview with a profoundly optimistic call: 'Historians now have an opportunity to cross disciplinary frontiers by engaging in this debate' (ibid: 36).

To be sure, the spread of people and ideas around the globe has a long and convoluted history. Generally speaking, historians tend to be confined to a few decades or, at most, centuries of history. Nevertheless, there are those who would dare to consider the several million years of human presence on earth. One such person is the palaeoanthropologist Clive Gamble (1993), who seeks to

---

[16] For an innovative view as to why this should be so, see Allen (1999).

present an overview of the manner in which our ancestors covered the globe. As he notes, contemporary conceptions of prehistory are still bedevilled by the notion of progress, in that human evolution tends to be understood in terms of a development from inferior to superior. Gamble dispels some of the more persistent myths and distortions that this way of perceiving the human past has produced. He presents a synthesis of the archaeology and palaeoanthropology of the last two million years that concentrates on changes in behaviour and stresses the deliberate human purpose that our ancestors displayed when they encountered variations in climate and environment as they ranged across the world. He demonstrates this new way of looking at human prehistory by a study of global colonization rather than by a conventional reassessment of fossil remains and stone tools. He reconsiders the record of geographical expansion that began with the early hominids of Sub-Saharan Africa whose descendants spread to new continents.

Van Binsbergen (1999) employs the concept 'proto-globalization' in a manner that differs significantly from that used by Hopkins, and defines globalization as 'the social (including economic, political, cultural and religious) effects of dramatic advances in communication technology'. He continues by stating that:

> Given the globular shape of the earth, even fairly rudimentary communication technologies of earlier millennia (those of the footpath, the hand-written text, the horse and camel as mounts, the sailing boat) have given rise to early forms of proto-globalization: globalizing religious projects such as Christianity and Islam; globalizing intellectual projects such as the emergence and spread of philosophy and science. (ibid: 4)[17]

This is to be distinguished from events in the second half of the 20th century when developments in communications technology advanced so

> dramatically as to reduce the costs of time and place to nearly zero. (...) this has produced massive qualitative changes in the world at large — changes for which the term globalization in the narrower sense of the word is appropriate. (ibid: 4)

[17] As far as the spread of science is concerned, this argument is taken up again by Van Binsbergen (2003: Chapters 7 & 15). There too the global history of science turns out to be inextricably connected with the global history of (what we identify today as) pseudo-science, such as astrology and other forms of divination (particularly geomancy), that once – in Ancient Mesopotamia, Egypt, China, Greece, the heights of medieval Islamic civilization, and pre-modern Europe – constituted the very hallmark of science. Van Binsbergen's fascination with proto-globalization springs from his tracing, since the early 1990s, of the world history of geomantic divination.

Van Binsbergen's words are echoed in those of Friedman (1999: xviii) who notes:

> The globalization of the present is not new, but is different in its intensity and interconnectivity, this is the era of globalization as stage two or turbo-charged.

A recent article by Frederick Cooper (2001) makes for interesting reading, if only because of his apparent dislike (not uncommon among historians!) of generalizing blanket terms — of which globalization is clearly one. Indeed, for Cooper, African history reveals the inadequacy of the concept of globalization. He argues that what is missing in discussions of globalization today is the historical depth of interconnections and a focus on what the structures and limits of the connecting mechanisms are. Central to Cooper's work is a desire to seek alternative perspectives to a concept — notably globalization — that emphasises change over time but remains ahistorical, and that seems to be about space but ends up glossing over the mechanisms and limitations of spatial relationships.

What Cooper seems to be searching for is the right mix between transactionalist agency and structural determination — in other words a continuation of the debate on reductionist Marxist 'historiography' (more like historicizing political economy or sociology or anthropology) and its fallacies, back in the 1970s.[18] In this insistence Cooper is justified, both by the one-sidedness of much current globalization parlance and by the inconclusive state in which the original debate was left at the time the Berlin Wall collapsed, in dispelling Marxists in all directions and rendering them inarticulate.

Reading Cooper, one is struck by his insistence on clarity and sharp definition of terms and concepts, which, as he notes, is often the fate of concepts in the social sciences. Particularly galling for Cooper is the 'doing history backwards' of much of the work dealing with globalization and he comes close to formulating, in a nutshell, what could be termed 'the globalization paradigm'. In his view, scholars working within the concept of globalization have two complementary views of the present:

- the present as the latest in a series of globalizations each more inclusive than the last; and

[18] Cf. Thompson (1980). Much of that debate was inspired, indirectly, by Popper's (1957) philosophical attack on historicism, including Marxism. African history also went through a phase when Marxist-inspired structural history was very much in vogue, even temporarily affecting some of the finest historical minds such as Ranger's (1979, 1985).

- the present as a global age as distinct from the past in which economic and social relations were contained within nation-states or empires and in which interaction took place among such internally coherent units.

For Cooper, both views suffer from the same methodological fallacy: writing history backwards, taking an idealized view of the globalized present and showing how everything led up to it, or how everything, up to the arrival of the global age itself, deviated from it.

He notes that colonization does not fit the imagery associated with globalization as implying a condition of unboundedness and maximum access. Instead, Cooper reminds us of what historians of early colonial Africa have stressed all along, that colonial conquests imposed territorial borders on long-distance trading networks within Africa and monopolies on what was then a growing external trade, damaging or destroying more articulated trading systems crossing the Indian Ocean and the Sahara Desert and along the West African coast. He exhorts Africanists not to rely on imposed theoretical models but to investigate, once more, empirically, and with an open mind, what is actually happening in Africa. Cooper (2001: 207) notes that:

> Africa is filled with areas where international investors do not go, even where there are minerals that would repay investors' efforts. To get to such places requires not deregulation, but institutions and networks capable of getting there.

In conclusion, Cooper argues that it would be better to

> emphasize not a 'globalising' (or 'deglobalising') Africa (or China or Russia), but rather the changing *relationships* of externally based firms and financial organizations, of indigenous regional networks, or transcontinental networks, of states, and of international organizations. (ibid)

In other words, from a historical perspective, a politically inspired understanding of the process of globalization is indispensable for interpreting the impact of the spread of global forms such as that of the nation-state for African societies. However, as political scientists discovered at an early stage, this spread of global political forms in Africa certainly did not result in a full and unproblematic embrace.

Politics

Writing on globalization, Thomas Friedman (1999: xxi) notes that 'if you want to understand the post-cold-war you have to start by understanding that a new international system has succeeded it'.

The oft-misquoted political scientist Francis Fukuyama, an exponent of United States triumphalism and unashamedly Hegelian in his ethnocentrism and Eurocentrism, wrote in 1992 that:

> a remarkable consensus concerning the legitimacy of liberal democracy as a system of government had emerged throughout the world over the past few years, as it conquered rival ideologies like hereditary monarchy, fascism, and most recently communism. More than that, however, I argued that liberal democracy may constitute the 'end point of mankind's ideological evolution' and the 'final form of human government', and as such constituted the 'end of history'.[19]

For Fukuyama (1989: 3), economic and political liberalism achieved a complete victory in the Cold War and this signalled:

> the end point of mankind's ideological evolution and the universalization of Western liberal democracy as the final form of human government.

In a different though complementary way, the work of Noam Chomsky provides a healthy counterweight to the triumphalism of Fukuyama and others. In 'Consent with Consent: Regimenting the Public Mind', the second essay in *Profit over People* (1998), Chomsky argues that liberal democracy has been used, through the manipulation of public information, marketing and propaganda, to protect and maintain the position of powerful elites. Chomsky argues that transnational corporations, governments and international organizations manipulate societies in such a way as to manufacture consent.

One of the aspects highlighted by the process of globalization is, therefore, the decline in the importance of the nation-state and of national boundaries. In the African context, the validity of the boundaries of African nation-states, a residue of the colonial era frozen by mutual agreement within the Organization of African Unity, has been an issue of debate prior to and since independence. In the wake of the Cold War, the collapse of many African states has brought home, even more forcefully than the two preceding decades, the lesson of post-colonial African politics: the tenuous nature of the African state.

The fragility of the African state, though not necessarily in the context of globalization, is an issue that was already highlighted in the work of the grand old man in African history, Basil Davidson, in his *The Black Man's Burden* (1992). Following on from Davidson's work, and introducing the adverse effects of democratization on the African state, Naerman (2000) deals with the disintegration of the nation-state in the African context. Naermann's work, in his own words:

---

[19] http: //www.marxists.org/reference/subject/philosophy/works/us/fukuyama.htm

> sets the disintegration of the nation-state in Africa and the disruptive effects of the democratization process within a historical perspective, which takes into account the artificiality of state borders and the ubiquity of crossborder migrations.

He demonstrates that the colonial national pattern is basically an irrational creation — preserved more in the interests of the new African elites than those of the grassroots. He explores local reactions to conditions created as part of the process of intensified globalization, arguing that the African position in this regard is fragile. He then focuses on the internal structures of the modern nation-state, dealing with the relationship between the traditional ethnic (national) groups' territorial domain and the present state set-up. He paints a broad canvas of the new patterns of conflict that have appeared in recent years, giving examples of how various configurations in a diverse spatial pattern are the primary basis for a popular affinity that is far stronger than is identification with a nation-state. Finally, he focuses on the situation in Kenya and the complicated ethnic divisions now structuring political action there. Naermann concludes by claiming that, although the academic discourse has found it difficult to imagine an African situation without the nation-state, it may be possible that new kinds of state structures, cooperation and networks will emerge.

The work of Puplampu and Tettey (2000) deals with the implications of globalization for African agricultural development in a situation in which the state collapses, or 'withdraws' as advocated by N'Diaye, and comes to be replaced by NGOs. Puplampu and Tettey note that, in the past twenty years, the crisis of the state in Africa has been a dominant feature of the continent's socio-political and development discourse. In a region where agriculture is the engine of development and the state plays an active role in agriculture, the crisis of the state (according to the authors) has created a vacuum in the institutional framework required for agricultural development. Consistent with globalization, NGOs have emerged and filled the vacuum as viable institutions for agricultural development.

In a similar vein to Chomsky, but complementing the latter by a specific application to Africa, is the work of Owolabi (2001: 71). He introduces his article by claiming that it belongs to:

> the stream of articles that seek to redress the perceived wrongs of globalization and urge societal transformations which can be attained through political interventions.

Owolabi's essay argues that globalization is essentially aimed at the promotion of the imperialistic interests of Western society. He claims that this hegemony is sustained by propagating the philosophy of liberalism. Liberalism and its defence of individual autonomy necessarily promote self-interest, whether at the level of the individual or the state. To avoid the injustice and possible anarchy that may arise as a result of this, the philosophy of liberalism must be reviewed based on criticisms from a communitarian perspective. The only way that globalization can attain a just integration and global peace is by jettisoning the individualism of liberalism for the altruism and sense of community as advocated by 'communitarianism'. Interestingly, and as a sign of the negative effects of globalization, this African author deploys the term communitarianism mainly with reference to North Atlantic 20th-century political philosophers[20] but largely fails to appreciate that, as an indigenous philosophy, communitarianism has a long (though not uncontested)[21] history on African soil.

Kwame Ninsin (2000) is critical not so much of the post-Cold War democratization project in Africa but of globalization and trade liberalisation, which he believes undermine democracy. He touches on the limits of political reform in Africa and states that the dominant discourse on democratization in Africa is premised on the necessity of establishing the basic institutional elements of democracy. This is why, argues Ninsin, elections and liberal constitutions in which the structure of state power has been crafted to safeguard liberty are the main features of political reforms. However, there is also a strong ethical foundation to democracy, which is embedded in liberty as self-development or progress for both the individual and the group. This presupposes an educated, economically secure and critically conscious citizen. The conflict between this richer conception of democracy and the narrowly defined procedural democracy is at the heart of the failure of the democratic revolution in Africa.[22] More specifically on globalization, Ninsin argues that its forces have eroded the capacity of existing social forces to implement the democratic project. He argues that the liberalization of markets has exacerbated the social and economic weakness of Africa's social classes.

Similar to the views expressed by Ninsin (2000) is the work of Francis Makoa (2001) who notes that one of the key demands of globalization, seen as a North Atlantic economic ideal, is that there should be no political interference in economic activity and investment decisions. Thus, according to Makoa, globalization presents the less-developed countries with what appears to be an intractable conundrum. While touting democracy as a condition for economic

[20] Communitarianism (cf. Bell 2001) emerged as a philosophical challenge to the classical liberal position (the state is primarily to protect individual freedom) as defended by Rawls (1971). Among the contesting authors are MacIntyre (1988), Sandel (1998), Taylor (1985, 1999) and Walzer (1983, 1994).

[21] Cf. Wiredu & Gyekye (1992).

[22] The 2002 general elections in Zimbabwe provide a graphic example of exactly what Ninsin has in mind.

success, the neo-liberal ideology that underpins globalization effectively removes the economy from the political agenda: for it advocates *laissez-faire* economic policies that preclude government involvement in investment decisions. As a result, private capital and the bourgeoisie are shielded from social and political scrutiny. Makoa outlines the broad political implications of globalization in eastern and southern Africa, and reflects on possible strategies that might cushion the regional states against its vicissitudes.

It is, however, not only international institutions, global liberalism or internal (ethnic) strife that should be held responsible for the failure of the introduction of the global political form of the nation-state on the African continent. The disintegration of the state also results from what can be called globalization from below: the urge through which African populations increasingly become involved in transnational movement and migration. Never before has the continent experienced such massive forms of mobility culminating in transnational and intercontinental movements of migration of unprecedented magnitude. They are of a magnitude well beyond the control of many a nation-state.

The spatial dynamics of globalization: Migration and transnationalism

One of the recurrent themes in the context of globalization is the ease and rapidity that have been technologically realized in the field of spatial displacement. These conditions have resulted in the greatly increased mobility of people, images and goods around the world. Initially many believed that this would lead to the disappearance of cultural differences but an ever-increasing bundle of recent research indicates that this has been far from the case. In seeking to come to terms with this paradox, Meyer and Geschiere utilized the concepts of 'global flows' and 'cultural closure'. They note (1999: 7) that:

> There is much empirical evidence that people's awareness of being involved in open-ended global flows seems to trigger a search for fixed orientation points and action frames, as well as determined efforts to affirm old and construct new boundaries. For students of globalization it is therefore important to develop an understanding of globalization that not only takes into account the rapid increase in mobility of people, goods and images, but also the fact that, in many places, flow goes hand in hand with a closure of identities which often used to be much more fuzzy and permeable.

The work of Winston Meso (2000) deals specifically with the negative impacts of migration under the influence of globalization for African societies. Meso argues that the migration of skills and labour — human capital — is one of the key features of the globalization trend. The management of this process, according to him, presents an enormous challenge to the economies of the affected countries.

As the work of Stoller (2002) points out, dealing with West African traders on the streets of New York in the context of globalization, transnationality involves more than only the movement of people across geographical boundaries. It also involves the creation of transnational spaces of cultural interaction and imagination, sometimes created through electronic devices such as the Internet, and in other instances forged through virtual interactions such as Sassen indicates for the financial flows between transnational cities.

Ideas of the transnational city in the context of Africa, as expressed by Ali Mazrui (1996), link in with the 'global city' hypothesis and debate as presented by James White, Saskia Sassen and Michael Smith. The most influential, though inevitably dated, book on the global city is Sassen's *The Global City* (1991), in which she establishes a paradigm for analysing cities in a context defined by post-1970s economic restructuring, and by the growing power of multinational corporations able to move massive capital swiftly around the globe. Cities, according to Sassen, have lost their positions as centres of manufacturing. Instead they have gained a new role as centres of corporate control, with centres of supporting service industries. In conjunction with this change there is, according to her, an ever-growing divide between the rich and the poor in cities. Her work has been challenged by White (1998) who argues that she overemphasizes the economy at the expense of political interventions, and that she follows an ethnocentric approach in believing that all cities will become like London and New York, as contradistinctive to Tokyo and Paris. Michael Smith (1998) rises above the debate between Sassen and White by arguing that the 'global city' does not exist in reality except as a social or intellectual construct, in other words as a space of imagination, cosmopolitanism and global interactions which can thus only be investigated in approximation. Smith argues for a comprehensive analysis of all cities as nodes within a network of relationships that overlap and intersect.

A useful corrective, meanwhile, to the grandiloquence about the global city is offered by Simone (1999) in his study of African cities and globalization. He reminds us that African cities are, at one and the same time, the most underdeveloped and the most contemporary. As they have not coalesced around industrialization, they lack the productive base to provide formal work or infrastructural support to their growing numbers, thus compelling continuous revisions or reinventions of largely rural-informed practices of survival, but they have also fostered socio-economic practices and forms of social organization potentially well adapted to globalized post-industrial economies. How to begin to register increases in urban economic productivity simultaneously with human development gains for urban citizens remains a fundamental challenge facing cities in Africa. Particular challenges for African urban governance lie in the social and cultural domain as a result, amongst others, of the profound fissuring tendencies in urban Africa, increased levels of insecurity and crime, and a progressive dissociation of space within cities and across cities. Rather than pinpointing specific policy frameworks and programmes for urban managers to adopt, the author suggests particular ways of thinking about the city that are important precursors to the generation of specific governance practices.

The study of transnational movement in relation to the global interconnectedness of world cities (see Hannerz 1987, 1992, 1996) brings us in addition to the crumbling nation-state closer to an understanding of the spread and emergence of a range of other phenomena as well. While much of this can be studied in terms of style, fashion and music, the final paragraph of this section looks at the relationship of transnationalism with the emergence of new religious forms. New religious movements are emerging in Africa increasingly as a result, if not the product, of global urban interactions.

Religious studies

A series of articles recently edited by Corten and Marshall-Fratani (2001) deals specifically with issues of global flows, migration and nationalism in relation to Pentecostalism. The editors note that over the past two decades, Latin American and African societies have experienced a phenomenal growth in Pentecostal movements. Describing a 'bricolage' of heterogeneous elements, the editors argue that contemporary Pentecostalism provides a striking example of the paradox of difference and uniformity, of flow and closure, that seems to be at the heart of processes of transnationalism and globalization. The studies in the edited volume reveal the diversity of Pentecostalism in Latin America and Africa, especially in its social composition. The dazzling complexity of the Pentecostal phenomenon in Africa and its globalization overtones are well captured, with chapters on the provenance of African Pentecostal theology in Nigerian Pentecostalism, in the Ghanaian Pentecostal diaspora, in the context of the Church of Assemblies of God in Burkina Faso and in the expansion of Pentecostalism to Francophone Africa (Benin and Brazzaville).

What is noted for these new religious manifestations of Christianity also emerges in the context of another world religion, namely Islam. Ousmane Kane (1997) examines the historical role and structure of Sufi orders in West Africa in relation to transnationalism. In the context defined by globalization, the breakdown of the state, and mass migrations, Kane argues that the network that Sufi orders create functions as a substitute for the state in the provision of social security. At present, with their increased mobility, the Sufi networks have been strengthened over ever-greater distances that extend beyond Africa. Parallels to

Kane's work are to be found in the work of Stoller and Van Dijk, both of whom deal extensively with transnational religious and trading organizations and their significance for African migrant communities. Roy Dilley offers a related argument in this volume.

However, while this interrelatedness between transnationalism and the emergence of new religious movements has been well documented, the explanation for the general public's fascination with these religious forms in a context of globalization has resulted in heated debates. Much research has concentrated on the collective imagination, the fantasies, that globalization brings about especially in the periphery of the global system and the way in which these are translated in religious terms.

In explaining this fascination for new religious movements, it is often pointed out that Africans have developed strands of reasoning that seek to explain and provide solutions to the confrontation with global systems and the feelings of exclusion that commonly result from such an experience. In this connection, Van Dijk (1999: 72) refers to 'the enchanted global economy and the moral perils of involvement with foreign commodities'. Here Africans hit on explanations that seek to deal with the world, and which to observers may appear to be absurd, fantastic and beyond the bounds of the rational. Moreover, these are ideas and explanations that seemingly withered and disappeared in Europe in post-Enlightenment times under the onslaught of rationalism. However, it is worth remembering that the European past and present provide a rich corpus relating to the world fantastic and attempts to control this fantastic world.[23]

Research on the issues of witchcraft and magic in Africa in the context of globalization has come to be dominated by the work of Peter Geschiere. His discussion on the modernity of witchcraft in Africa is best represented in his 1997 English translation of *Sorcellerie et Politique en Afrique* (1995). For Geschiere (1998), the obsession with witchcraft in many parts of present-day Africa is not to be viewed as some sort of traditional residue. On the contrary, it is particularly present in the more modern spheres of society. In the comparative, global perspective, this linking of modernity and witchcraft is not peculiar to Africa and Geschiere notes that in other parts of the world modern developments coincide with a proliferation of what have aptly been designated as 'economies of the occult' (Comaroff & Comaroff 1999). Examples from situations as diverse as 17th-century Sweden and early 20th-century Surinam

[23] Cf. from among an extensive literature, Ginzburg (1966, 1989), Thomas (1978), Clough & Mitchell (2001) and Ellis (2001).

come to mind, both from the work of Thoden van Velzen and Van Wetering.[24] An African example is offered by the events at the Kansanshi copper mine in Northern Rhodesia (now Zambia), a good 100 km west of the later Copperbelt, in 1904. The scene offers one of the first[25] instances of the implantation of industrial capitalist relations of production in South Central Africa.

> Tensions also existed at the Kansanshi mine (...) as became manifest in an 'alarming rate of desertions amongst the African workers, apparently related to an early anti-white religious movement'. As Copeman, the Kasempa district officer, made investigations, he 'learned that the Head Capitao [African foreman] and some of his friends appeared to keep the remainder of the native employees in a state of terror'. The Head Capitao turned out to be in the possession of a gruesome collection of skulls and human bones and all the paraphernalia of a witch doctor. ... The Capitao by claiming supernatural powers had sought to make as many as possible join in a horrible brotherhood of which he was the leader. Those who refused to have anything to do with it he used his position to ill-treat. It came out that he had boasted that he would live for ever, and that presently all the white men would die and he and his friends would take possession of their belongings. Those whom he persuaded to join his brotherhood were promised that they would share these benefits but before they were qualified to do so they had to go to the burial place and dig up the latest buried corpses and possess themselves of certain portions, they also had to break the arm and leg bones and suck out the marrow and indulge in other loathsome practices. (Van Binsbergen 1981: 342 n. 39, quoting from CO 3/4/2 Copeman Papers Box 6, in HM 6 Historical Manuscripts Collection, Zambia National Archives)

Copeman publicly destroyed the Capitao's sorcery kit and humiliated him; with their leader. 'Several of the Capitao's neophytes were sentenced to periods of imprisonment, but the mass desertions ceased from this date.'(ibid)

---

[24] Cf. Thoden van Velzen (1977, 1995, 1998), Thoden van Velzen & Van Wetering (2001).

[25] 'One of the first' because the demarcation between mercantile, agricultural and industrial capitalism is not easy to make in this early period of capitalist expansion in South Central Africa. Arab/Swahili and Portuguese traders had penetrated these lands from at least the 18th century CE onwards (cf. Van Binsbergen 1992: 4f and the wider literature indicated there). The use of the Portuguese term *capitao* suggests that early industrial relations at Kansanshi were at least in part modelled on local Portuguese examples. Moreover, as oral sources from western Zambia (Barotseland) indicate, from at least as early as the 1880s (i.e. before the onset of colonial rule), labour migration had existed from South Central Africa to capitalist workplaces in the south, first to the Witwatersrand, and soon also to the mining enterprises and large-scale farms in Southern Rhodesia, now Zimbabwe. In Northern Rhodesia (now Zambia), in addition to Kansanshi, capitalist, European-initiated mining was soon undertaken in Ilaland and in Broken Hill.

The power of contemporary African discourses on occult forces, according to Geschiere, is that they relate people's fascination with the open-endedness of global flows to the search for fixed orientation points and identities. Both witchcraft and spirit cults exhibit a surprising capacity for combining the local and the global. Both also have specific implications for the ways in which people try to deal with modernity's challenge.

Views similar to Geschiere's are to be found in Michael Taussig's pioneering work on commodity fetishism, in which he investigated the economy, the functioning of markets and the exchange of commodities in terms of culture (1980). Rijk van Dijk has continued this emphasis on the morality of commodities within the global economy (Van Dijk 1999: 71-89). Writing on commodities in the global space Van Dijk summarizes a common analytical approach to this topic in the following terms:

> The penetration of foreign commodities into local societies takes place through their links with the market place; and foreign commodities seem able to elicit a sense of alienation, because the market mediates what is a rupture: between the places and cultures where commodities were produced and those where they will be consumed. Since the previous 'social life' of such commodities is unknown to the local cultures which consume them, (...) commodities appear to be enchanted, and to function in local systems as if they possessed a will of their own. The result is that their local appropriation and use are not considered as innocent, but as ridden with evil and embellished with forces that threaten society and personal identities. Social anxieties express these perils that arise when foreign commodities become objects of local social desire. (ibid: 71).

However attractive as a profound insight into African collective representations, Van Dijk (1999: 72) challenges this view, which in his opinion:

> seems to primitivize the other's capacity to deal with the uncertainties and the porous quality of social life which result from engagement with the global economy.

Van Binsbergen (2001), in his contribution to Bond and Ciekawy's recent collection on African witchcraft, which is fairly independent of Geschiere's work, also seeks to correct Geschiere's presentist approach, advocating instead that witchcraft in Africa today is about the 'virtualized boundary conditions of the kinship order' — an order whose basic format goes back at least to the Neolithic, as does its basic defiance through witchcraft, even though under modern conditions of globalization the specific forms and occasions of witchcraft beliefs and practices have been subject to specific changes. The main advantage, however, of this line of work has been the exploration of the ways in which globalization appears to be refracted on the level of the local in terms other than Western positivist science expected. Situating globality in the world of the unseen and the world of imagination became a field to which anthropology in particular had much to contribute.

Anthropology

The important contribution that anthropology was to make to the field of globalization studies was the acknowledgement of the fact that an important aspect of Africa's economic marginalization is that Africans participate in the globalized world community not so much as consumers of manufactured material goods but as consumers and producers of mere images and ideas concerning the global world to which they seem to belong only marginally — again Mbembe's *lécher les fenêtres*. The anthropological study of globalization therefore came to include much more than the field of religion, spirituality, occultism and the like, but went into the exploration of what came to be known as the deterritorialization of culture. As globalization came to be seen as the process through which *a priori* assumptions about the relationship people-place-culture become problematic, anthropology began exploring the production of culture in other places and spaces. The media, expressions of popular culture in art, music, the theatre and so forth as well as the diffusion of consumptive styles of behaviour were turned into important areas of research. In addition it explored the situationality of the production of intellectual thought and images of the idea of Africa, and as such turned the analytical lens upon itself.

Seen from the North Atlantic, the place of Africa and Africans in globalization often has an even more cynical aspect: Africa and Africans tend to be reduced to mere symbols of extreme otherness by reference to which the Western, North Atlantic identity may be constructed through a process of denial, in facile binary oppositions such as:

North Atlantic, the West	Africa
rich	poor
developed infrastructure	failing infrastructure
law and order	legal and political chaos
democracy	tyranny and civil war
internalized discipline	absence of discipline
technological and organizational know-how	absence of technological and organizational know-how
developed	under-developed
civilized	uncivilized
scientific rationality	magic and superstition

Such illusory and hegemonic self-exultation on the part of the West only works as long as firm boundaries separate it from Africa, in other words and paradoxically, it only works under the very conditions that are increasingly undermined by the undeniable fact of Africa's globalization.

Anthropology, as a dominant mode of intercultural knowledge construction, is a child of (proto-)globalization, as a form of predominantly North-Atlantic scientific endeavour. It is largely part of the project of the West and implicitly may contribute to the West's exalted self-constructions. For these reasons the anthropology of globalization is fraught with contradictions, which cannot fail to be reflected in print. The manner in which researchers are to measure, categorize and represent such consumption and production is inordinately complex and confusing, and can lead, not surprisingly, to work and observations that may well be dismissed as 'glo-baloney'. Nevertheless, seeking to portray, understand and explain these processes is the self-avowed purpose of many researchers in the field of cultural anthropology today.

Brad Weiss, writing on northwestern Tanzania, has attempted to tackle the issue the 'imaginary' and the 'global' (2001: 1). As Weiss notes,

> many of the tangible links through which a global order of relationships is concretised are dependent upon the dissemination of imaginative forms. (ibid: 3)

In addition he argues that

> lived worlds distinctly situated as they may be throughout the globalised world are increasingly constructed through fantasies and fabrications that must first be imagined in order to be realized. (ibid: 4)

In this aspect of his work Weiss concentrated on young men in Arusha who congregate around barbershops. He has attempted to come to an understanding of how these young men imagine the world and structure their lives in accordance with this in the context of globalization. Writing on the recent history of Tanzania, Weiss notes that Tanzanian society was simultaneously opened up

> to media, goods, and ideologies never before available, while the decline of state services and subsidies has led (after a brief flourishing of both the formal and informal privatised economy) to the collapse of a host of employment opportunities. This sudden crash on the heels of unprecedented and exhilarating possibilities — unrealised by the vast majority of Tanzanians as anything *but* possibilities — made it possible for a broad swath of people to desire the signs and styles of a global order, while facing ever narrower means by which to satisfy them. (ibid: 8)

Similar to the work of Weiss is Ferguson's 1999 anthropology referred to earlier in this section. He too has grappled to find words to describe what happens to the African imagination in the face of globalization. Africanist researchers, he observes, see that Africans are turned out of the global paradise but how can this process be described, including what goes on in people's minds and in collective consciousness? In studying the work of imagination and consciousness in difficult situations in the Zambian Copperbelt, Ferguson writes:

> The experience of abjection here was not a matter of being merely excluded from a status [developed] to which one had never had a claim *but of being expelled, cast out* (...) from that status by the formation of a new (or newly impermeable) boundary. It is an experience that has left in its wake both a profound feeling of loss as well as the gnawing sense of a continuing affective attachment to that which lies on the other side of the boundary. (ibid: 237-38; italics added)

The views of Weiss and Ferguson are similar to those informing the work of Andreas van Nahl who attempts to describe the impact of globalization and the resulting marginalization of people in Kenya. Van Nahl (1999: 106) notes:

> Rural [Kenyan] towns are nowadays full of young 'businessmen' who own nothing more than the suit they wear and a self-designed business card. Like consumer lifestyle, it seems that business lifestyle is an — at times, desperate — attempt to maintain the self in a world of disintegrating social ties and economic relations.

Weiss (2001: 4) has noted that there are 'models' and 'projections' that inform the 'modes of domination' which exist within the globalized world. Here he refers to the work of Carrier and Miller (1998) who deploy the term 'virtualism' to refer to such models and projections as have been established in a specific time and place yet inform daily practice in quite a different time and place. The similar concept of 'virtuality' has come to the fore in the work of Van Binsbergen (1997), for whom it is to be regarded as one of the key concepts for characterizing and understanding the forms of globalization in Africa. Van Binsbergen seeks to define virtuality and globalization, and to provisionally indicate their theoretical relationship. For him, virtuality is inspiring because it seems to offer part of the answer to anthropology's problematic heritage, notably the discipline's obsession with locality. Yet what exactly is to be understood by the term 'virtuality'?

Inspired by the earlier work of Korff (1995) and Jules-Rosette (1996), Van Binsbergen (1998a: 878) provides the following definition of virtuality:

> Ultimately, virtuality stands for a specific relation of reference as existing between elements of human culture (A_1, A_2, …, A_n). This relation may be defined as follows: once, in some original context C_1, $A_{virtual}$ referred to (that is, derived meaning from) A_{real}. This relationship of reference is still implied to hold, but in actual fact $A_{virtual}$ has come to function in a context C_2 which is so totally dissimilar to C_1, that $A_{virtual}$ stands on itself; and although still detectable on formal grounds as deriving from A_{real}, has become effectively meaningless in the new context C_2, unless for some new meaning which $A_{virtual}$ may acquire in C_2 in ways totally unrelated to C_1.

In short, the concept of virtuality reminds us that societies live their lives according to charters grounded in a historical past, in such a way that not only the society but also the interpretations of the historical charter change over time. In other words, ideas often outlive the context in which they were first thought up.[26]

Reading over anthropological work dealing with globalization as it is seen today, one is struck by people's attempts to control or understand the world as it is around them. This juxtaposition of historical and contemporary consciousness and imagination is fully elaborated on in a number of the contributions in this volume as is highlighted in the following section.

Situating globality: This volume

Beyond 'Globalization and Ownership'

The conference entitled 'Globalization and New Questions of Ownership', held in Leiden from 26-27 April 2002, intended primarily to explore processes of appropriation of diverse, globally circulating, cultural 'materials' on the African continent and the way in which they are woven into new or emerging social fabrics.

Most of the papers presented either took the issue of ownership in rather concrete terms or choose not to address it at all. Instead, a discussion evolved in which a dichotomized representation of issues surfaced. Globalization appears first and foremost as an arena of polarization suggesting an unavoidable and quite prescriptive formulation of the pros and cons, of perceiving its effects as the latest transformation of capitalist encroachment or as a domain of hybridity from where new cultural forms will emerge, as a process of victimization or as a process leading to greater proximity and vicariousness thus lesser estrangement and exoticism; a process to be studied by either the philosopher or the ethnographer.

---

[26] R. Ross in a personal communication.

The dissatisfaction, uneasiness or complete avoidance of the concept of ownership during the conference may have had two root causes, which now can and should be addressed in a different light. One reason for this apparent unacceptability of the concept may have been the polarized nature of the understanding of globalization: ownership as a Western concept has the implication of disenfranchizing others, creating 'haves' and 'have-nots' in a static and often highly confrontational mode. Africa then appears as the disowned place *par excellence.* Yet not all the conference papers took this position. Wim van Binsbergen's contribution, 'Can ICT belong in Africa, or is ICT owned by the North Atlantic region?', emphasized the fact that the question of ownership creates a dilemma, a tension between the view that in some respects ICT is not owned by Africa but by the North Atlantic region, and that in most respects this is a deceptive way of representing social and cultural realities. ICT was invented by a small intellectual and technological elite and subsequently had to be received — as an alien thing — by the ordinary inhabitants of the North Atlantics, and it has been similarly received, and effectively appropriated, in Africa along lines sketched in some detail in his paper. In his view, the question of ownership evokes the tension between inclusion and exclusion that is a major dimension of globalization, without the possibility of that tension being truly resolved either in the direction of exclusion (as if Africa were invariably and totally disenfranchized by globalization) or in the direction of inclusion (as if Africa were effectively and totally incorporated towards full participation in global processes).

Another cause of unease with the concept may have been the result of a highly individualized conceptualization of ownership, a kind of individuality which Western liberal economies now seem to market around the world, thus the product of a particular cultural and historical perception of personhood and subjectivity. Old, highly stereotyped and ideology-heavy dichotomies may have been at the back of the conference participants' minds in this rejection of ownership: of the West as the place of the individualized self in possession of commodities versus Africa as the communalized place of self, of sharing in gift and exchange economies. This concept of ownership is simply too static, too inert and in a strange way not 'globalized' enough to be of use in what the conference eventually was to pursue: a dynamic common ground between these dichotomies, a productive middle terrain, a place of hybridity in the active voice.

During the conference an awareness emerged that it is no longer viable to perceive of globalization as either producing marginalization or victimization of the African continent, or on the other hand as the domain of unbridled chances and new cultural formations. Instead, a complex dialectic was emerging from the confrontation between these views. Key to that dialectic is the understanding of reflexivity, understanding how people in Africa create specific forms and domains in which particular arenas of reflexivity emerge in which the pros and cons, the marginalization as well as the creativity of globalization are debated, lived and experienced. Forms and domains of such reflexivity are both cultural and historical, shaped by prevalent political and economic circumstances and by aspirations and imaginations of groups even entertaining a Utopian kind of view. And they can only be studied by philosophy and anthropology working in tandem. These forms and domains of reflexivity can range from what Habermas (1989) described as the bourgeois café in European societies to the wedding-bed parades in Niger as discussed in the chapter by Adeline Masquelier; from the site of Pan-Africanist thought in public speeches of engaged Pentecostal churches in Ghana as in Rijk van Dijk's contribution to the private and concealed domains of the inner quarters of family life as in Thera Rasing's chapter. Transformations can occur rapidly as these sites of reflexivity may shift from the inner house to the Internet café as in the chapter by Wim van Binsbergen, from the public newspaper readings to the proliferation of public media as described by Francis Nyamnjoh. None of these forms or domains of reflexivity remain frozen in time and what is at stake is that, through the process of globalization, they change in nature and in quality more quickly that ever before. Basically, we argue, these papers have shown us that the pivotal question tackled in these domains and sites of reflexivity is how globalization is or should be tailored to local needs, circumstances and imaginations. Local debates do not revolve around the question of whether one is either a victim or a conqueror of globalization but whether elements of globalization can be used fruitfully, for whatever purpose.

Interestingly, while only a minority of the conference papers explicitly pinpointed the contradictory innovatory dynamics of the tension relation between the inclusion and exclusion of Africa in globalization, and while some (especially those by some of the African participants such as Sichone, Osha and Williams)[27] instead dwelled at length on the misery and devastation created in Africa as a result of globalization, an unexpected theme emerged in many others and was reinforced in the stimulating discussion during the conference: the theme of resilience.

The papers by Judy Rosenthal, Ferdinand de Jong, Roy Dilley and Jan-Bart Gewald reminded us that, instead of perceiving African societies as creatively appropriating globally circulating cultural material or as being crushed by the political economy of globalization under North Atlantic hegemony, there is a third option: that of societies responding to globalization by the pursuit of at

[27] We regret that the papers by Owen Sichone and Odebayo Williams were not able to be included in this volume.

least two forms of social and cultural resilience. First, there is a form of resilience which emphasizes a proud conscious and innovative return to their own time-honoured resources of spirituality, values, world view, forms of social and political organisation, and secondly, another form of resilience can contradict and contest globalization by resisting it on its own terms and by fighting its influence with its own weapons, so to speak.

The first form of resilience, which in recent years has been noted in the fields of African traditional religion, puberty rites, traditional rulers/chieftainship, and ethnic identity, seems to restore the balance against the overwhelming effects of global cultural imports into Africa, and favours a view in which Africa in globalization is eminently capable of creative responses. This form of resilience is successful not only in the appropriation of alien material but also in so far as the affirmation is concerned of that which has been Africa's own for centuries and which, after a few centuries of colonial and post-colonial suppression and exclusion, now (under the new challenges and the new technologies of communication and organization characteristic of globalization) proves capable of once more showing its true, splendid colours.

The second form of resilience, which is discussed particularly in the context of Jan-Bart Gewald's paper on the use of the Western media by the Somali warlords in their conflict with the United States, demonstrates quite a different feature of Africa's creative response. Here, the appropriation of global cultural imports appears to serve the specific interest of casting globalization back in an attempt to defend that which is considered truly inalienable. Globalization can thus not only be mocked and ridiculed but appears to provide, in its violent arrival, the material, the resources as well as the imagination to contest it on its own terms. Examples abound in the societal reactions to international interventions in Africa, to the spread of the global media and to the global spread of the state and the identities and socio-economic structures it stands for.

These forms of resilience may not be mutually exclusive but in certain circumstances may appear simultaneously or may even work in tandem. Furthermore, the convenors also wish to emphasize that discussions of the various conference papers bring to light the notion that not in all cases can resilience be assumed or taken for granted. Whereas anthropology can help us to understand the conditions that give rise to different forms of resilience, philosophy is invoked to elucidate the processes of reflexivity that produce for every movement a counter-movement and for every discourse a counter-discourse.

What the chapters in the present collection bring out almost unanimously is a specific appreciation of the form in which globalization manifests itself in Africa today. Globalization is not the inescapable, all-encompassing juggernaut that is relentlessly rolling on in its way, crushing everything it encounters. It is not the tyrannical outside force to which Africa and Africans have only to submit passively and without options. On the contrary, in the contemporary African context, the specific form globalization takes appears to be largely determined by local and regional concerns and contradictions that were already in place before the recent intensification of globalization. The new objects, ideas and technologies that have become available in the worldwide circulation under modern technological conditions do not simply penetrate Africa merely of their own accord. They are appropriated and mobilized in concrete African situations through the agency of Africans pursuing concrete goals, which have largely been defined by these ongoing anterior concerns, rather than defining those concerns in the first place. The objects of globalization are locally co-opted to constitute new resources and ammunition in pre-existing local struggles about material and/or symbolic issues. Inevitably, such appropriation cannot fail to have a considerable impact on these struggles, even to the extent of partially redefining their stakes and their very format, yet this is only a secondary aspect. Inevitably, again, such appropriation falls short of the aspirations of the African actors involved, given the fact that their economic power is minimal in the world today. Inevitably, such conscious and deliberate appropriation of globally circulating objects and technologies can only take place within a wider context of a globalized world economy and world politics where parameters are set and reset almost entirely without Africans taking part in the decision-making process, and the outcome of which has devastatingly negative effects on African conditions in the fields of the macro-economy, security and well-being. The objective structural features of globalization cannot be adequately captured from a perspective centring on specific African actors' agency. Yet even so, the message of the present collection is that we will miss the essence and will merely continue to pay lip service to obsolete models of totalising hegemonic overkill until we appreciate the eclecticism and the agency attending the contemporary African experience of 'high globalization'.

With such an approach we hope to advance beyond what Held and MacGrew (2002) recently characterized as the 'transformalist school in globalization studies'. With Featherstone and Hannerz as its main exponents, this school looks at globalization processes from the perspective of what impact they have on local societies. Transformalists, therefore, do not view globalization as a homogenizing factor in the way of Wallerstein's (1974) 'world system', but point to local variations in the impact of globalization processes and in the extent to which (under such an impact) heterogeneity will persist and may even increase. Reversing the perspective from the outside to the inside, the advance in the present collection lies in the points of agency and reflexivity, highlighting African actors as conscious and creative strategic actors whose remaining choice, despite the constraints of objective globalizing conditions, is still considerable. In the following chapters, the African local groups and individuals are *not* what the rhetoric of anti-globalization has often made them out to be, namely passive recipients and victims who, devoid of reflexivity, have been simply forced to adjust for better or worse to the impact of globalization. Instead, we show how these African groups and individuals are displaying remarkable creativity, resilience, flexibility and determination to survive and cope. These features (which incidentally were always indispensable in Africa during the colonial and post-colonial periods) are not being destroyed under the impact of recent globalization but are merely the conditions for a transformation as a result of which local groups and individuals are harnessing globalization for their own purposes.

We have already indicated the tension between such an agency-centred perspective and the wider (and inevitably more compelling) structural context of objective globalization of the economic and political domains. Another tension exists between, on the one hand, the conscious, rationally strategic perceptions and motives that we here attribute to Africans in globalization in the context of ongoing struggles and concerns and, on the other, the likelihood that what we construe to be rational choice may in many situations be clad in the trappings of ritual, apparently irrational beliefs (cf. witchcraft!), short-term perceptions and decisions in the here and now whose ultimate implications in terms of the strategic appropriation of globalization may remain utterly concealed to the actors themselves, in the same way as fundamental processes and collective representations of their society remain, inevitably, concealed to the consciousness of most actors in most societies anywhere and in any historical period. This collection suggests that the African selective appropriation of globalization usually takes place as strategic choices in the context of local and regional conflicts and contradictions. It leaves for further research and reflection the question of whether such conflict is necessary for the selective African appropriation of globalization or whether, instead, there is also room for such processes outside the sphere of direct and open conflict.

The individual contributions

We have structured the contributions to this collection into three parts. Part I contains this introduction, while Part II includes chapters seeking to make pronouncements about globalization and the African continent as a whole. Given the emphasis on religion in the ASC's research programme on globalization, it is understood that our case studies, discussed in Parts III and IV, are mainly derived from the religious field.

In Part II, 'Globality through appropriation: Analyses at the continental level', the emphasis is on the media which, through 20th-century technological advances, has been a major factor as well as product of globalization.

The Cameroonian anthropologist Francis Nyamnjoh deals with 'Global and local trends in media ownership and control: Implications for cultural creativity in Africa' and discusses the crystallization of resistance to the cultural homogenization favoured by global consumer media and cultural production, stressing that, in most of Africa, threats to a free, open and participatory media system and society come as much from repressive governments as from the interests of rich nations, international financial institutions and the global corporate media. Too cautious to take any serious risks, especially in marginal and highly unpredictable zones of accumulation like Africa, global capital needs public support and regulation to insulate itself against the vicissitudes provoked or exacerbated by its tendency to put profit before people. Africa's predicament notwithstanding, and as a convincing example of the emphasis on agency and self-reflexivity which our overall characterization of this collection above brings out, Nyamnjoh is critical of meta-narratives that celebrate victimization at the risk of obfuscating the reality of negotiation and survival strategies, and discusses some of the myriad ways devised by Africans to ensure cultural participation for themselves as active agents in local and global processes.

Just how this may work out in concrete situations is aptly illustrated in Jan-Bart Gewald's chapter entitled 'Global media and violence in Africa: The case of Somalia'. Gewald begins by citing the general opinion — which he shares as little as Van Binsbergen, the author of the following chapter — that Africa has allegedly been sidelined in the global ICT revolution. African societies appear to be cut off from the global flows of information. Nevertheless, the manner in which war was waged in Somalia between 1991 and 1994 indicates that this global revolution has affected not only the manner in which war in Africa is reported but also, and more importantly, the very manner in which war is waged in Africa. African societies may be cut off from owning and controlling the streams of images that reflect their continent but, as Gewald argues, they may at times come to temporarily hijack and divert this stream of images and in doing so, ensure that images that support or reinforce their political aims come to be released into the global flow. In the case of Somalia, the real-time images of dead US soldiers being dragged through the streets of Mogadishu were sufficient to compel the United States to end their involvement in Somalia. Globalization offered Africans the means of defeating an immensely more powerful foe at its own game.

Against this background, the question that Wim van Binsbergen poses in the following chapter on ICT's role in Africa takes on considerable relevance. ICT, as a technological innovation and a major factor in globalization, poses particular problems of ownership and identity with regard to the African continent. What is the place of ICT in Africa, and what is the place of Africa in a world increasingly dominated by ICT? Van Binsbergen seeks to explode the apparent contradiction between Africa and ICT. By confronting African thinkers like Mazrui and Gyekye who have argued the incompatibility of African culture and ICT, and advancing a detailed argument to the effect that ICT is just as much and as little owned by Africans as by any other collectivity in the contemporary world, he highlights some of the ways in which the African appropriation of ICT is taking shape and provides illustrations of the agency and self-reflexivity in the light of pre-existing, ongoing concerns and struggles, which we identified above as the specific form which globalization often takes in Africa today.

Strategic appropriation, but then almost in Marx's literal sense of 'primitive accumulation' (in other words, high-handed theft), emerges again in the following chapter by the Nigerian philosopher Sanya Osha entitled: '"Man will live well": On the poetics of corruption in a global age'. The point of departure is Osha's observation that the difference between philosophical and anthropological practices in Africa is becoming exceedingly glaring, maybe because a dominant tradition in the analytical school of African philosophy is limited by a strain of British empiricism. However, new conditions of existence, which conventional tropes of analysis in African philosophy seem unable to handle, are emerging within the African post-colony. While anthropology has produced a voluminous literature on the issue of corruption in Africa, philosophy has largely remained aloof of this eminently important topic. How then has the problem of corruption been addressed in African philosophical practice? Kwame Gyekye, the Ghanaian philosopher, has tackled the problem of political corruption by employing discursive strategies derived from the Athenian philosophical traditions. Osha argues that Gyekye's conceptualization of the problem does not fully describe the emerging conditions in the post-colony. On the other hand, Jean-Pierre Olivier de Sardan, the French anthropologist, analyses the modes of social organization, forms of sociality and the conditions of contemporary globalization that necessitate a more subtle theorization of the problem of corruption in Africa and the ways in which it can be approached conceptually. A comparison between these two approaches makes Osha conclude that a more acute analysis of the situation in the African post-colony is still required.

Part III brings us to a discussion of (the possibility of) African globality through world religions, notably Christianity (in the first chapter of this section), and Islam (in the other two chapters). Rijk van Dijk's chapter, '"Beyond the rivers of Ethiopia": Pentecostal Pan-Africanism and Ghanaian identities in the transnational domain' provides an excellent transition from the preceding, Pan-African-orientated Part II, in that it combines a Ghanaian case study with a consideration of the Pan-Africanism by which that case study is informed. Rev. Mensa Otabil, the founder of the International Central Gospel

Church in Accra, is considered an influential representative of a new Pentecostal-inspired Pan-Africanist ideology. His book *Beyond the Rivers of Ethiopia* lays the foundations of a Pentecostal Liberation Theology that proclaims a Christianized sequel to Pan-Africanism. Operating from Ghana, his ideas concerning Africa and 'Black Consciousness' have spread to Ghanaian migrant communities worldwide. While Otabil has been successful in transforming ownership of the intellectualist production of Pan-Africanism by tailoring it to the needs of the ordinary Pentecostal believer, it has not been adopted so extensively among all Ghanaian migrant communities in the West. By exploring Ghanaian migrant communities and their Pentecostal churches in the Netherlands, where the staunch identity politics of the Dutch government leave little room for the assertive proclamation of 'Africanness', Van Dijk demonstrates that Otabil's ideas do not act as a main source of inspiration everywhere in the Ghanaian diaspora. The Pan-African ideology crumbles in the face of the internal divisiveness of the contemporary Ghanaian experience.

Islam has occasionally[28] been characterized as a (proto-)globalizing project initiated by the expansion of early Islam beyond the confines of the Arabian peninsula in the course of the 7th century of the Common Era (or rather, and more appropriately, the 1st century of the Hijra Era). Hence the contradiction between local particularisms and Islamic universalisms has been a recurrent theme throughout the history of Islam. With regard to West African caste systems, which captivated scholarly attention throughout the 20th century CE, a particular illustration of this overall contradiction is offered in Roy Dilley's chapter entitled 'Global connections, local ruptures: The case of Islam in Senegal', in which he examines the relationship between Islam and caste in Senegal. He investigates how new meanings of caste identity have been negotiated in view of the differing conceptions of Islam that have taken hold within the country. Twentieth-century CE reformist movements challenged the predominant role of Sufi brotherhoods, bringing about a reassessment of the relationship between caste and Islam. The Nyasiyya brotherhood provides the basis for a brief case study, showing that the popularity of this religious order abroad is not matched by its reception in Senegal. Some of the possible reasons are examined for this disjunction between the global connections that the order establishes on the one hand, and the local ruptures it engenders within the local Muslim community on the other. The chapter traces the dynamics of Sufism and reformist Islam to reveal a double-edged thrust of global connections brought about by an internationalizing Islam, and of local ruptures mediated through caste identities.

---

[28] Cf. Breedveld *et al.* (in press) and Van Binsbergen (1998b).

West-African caste systems were noted in the earliest Arabic sources on that part of Africa and were certainly not a product of the introduction of Islam. Thus Dilley's argument is clearly about the strategic negotiation between the time-honoured local and the more recent global in a West-African setting largely informed by Islam. In this respect the chapter has considerable parallels with that by Adeline Masquelier entitled: 'How is a girl to marry without a bed?: Weddings, wealth and women's value in an Islamic town of Niger'. In Niger, bridewealth has become the target of Izala, a 20th-century CE reformist Muslim organization that condemns ostentatious expenditure and promotes frugality. In the Muslim town of Dogondoutchi, where Mawri residents are increasingly being exposed to Western bourgeois values, the Izala ban on excessive bridewealth and extravagant weddings has angered many for whom gift exchange is inseparable from social worth. Mothers struggling to equip their daughters with the latest trappings of modern domesticity thus reject Izala expressions of Islamic frugality. For them, prosperity is not antithetical to Islamic piety. This chapter looks at a young woman's insistence on receiving a Formica bed from her impoverished mother. In another illustration of this collection's central points concerning agency, self-reflexivity and strategic choice in the context of African globalization, it shows how the acquisition of such a bed is implicated in the reconfiguration of a domestic lifestyle that owes as much to local understandings of matrimony and morality as to Western bourgeois domesticity.

World religions such as Islam and Christianity are, by definition, globalizing projects, offering a myriad of specific contexts in which the subject matter of this book can be subjected to specific empirical research and conceptual reflection. However, the contributions in Part IV take us to as aspect of contemporary African life that would, at first sight, appear to be far less obvious as an arena of globalization strategies: the domain of traditional African religion. However the authors manage to bring out how this collection's central message also works for them in the specific Senegalese and Zambian contexts they describe.

Ferdinand de Jong's chapter 'The social life of secrets' opens Part IV. By looking at initiation rituals, he argues that it is possible to arrive at a better understanding of secrets in a given society in a globalizing world. The secret emerges in a performance of complicity involving both initiates and non-initiates, and secrecy produces a shared subjectivity between initiate and non-initiate. Such complicity is often denied in ethnographic texts that claim authority for a subject (the anthropologist) penetrating the secret of the Other. De Jong claims that these ethnographic poetics make a distinction between subject and object that, in the case of secrecy, seems untenable. Had he been tempted to explore the philosophical implication of such a position in addition to its anthropological application, he would have realized that the whole thrust of post-structuralist modern philosophy (especially Foucault, Derrida, Deleuze & Guattari, and Lyotard) supports this line of analysis; the theory of secrecy on which he bases himself is in essence an implicit, anthropologically appropriated product of post-modernism, and as such eminently in tune with the age of globalization. In the concrete empirical setting of southern Senegal, accepting the untenability of the subject-object distinction as for as secrecy is involved implies recognition of the co-ownership of secrets. The secrets performed in a globalizing world can no longer be localized properties. As ethnographic cases in the chapter demonstrate, secrecy creates a translocal intersubjectivity that requires recognition in ethnographic texts — especially since it provides the anthropologist with a dispensation that appears to be much better founded, as far as the epistemology and the politics of transcontinental knowledge production are concerned, than anything that can be offered by the habitual mystique of fieldwork as a unique penetration into the uniquely Other.

Strategies of agency and self-reflexivity are also manifest in Thera Rasing's account of 'The persistence of female initiation rites: Reflexivity and resilience of women in Zambia'. Rasing focuses on female initiation rites in Zambia today and shows how Zambian women, in the context of a globalized environment, reflect on their culture and religion. She examines how initiation rites, as part of this culture and religion, are so resilient that they can still be performed today, in the same format as centuries ago, by middle-class women in the urban environment of the Zambian Copperbelt. Despite many changes in society, this rite has remained a major institution even in present-day globalized and Christianized urban Zambia. The initiation rights are considered primordial and valuable for all women, even for religious sisters. Women are showing reflexivity and resilience in their performance of these rites and in adapting them to modern urban life.

In conclusion, through the exploration of these case studies we aspire to demonstrate the multifaceted ways in which the appropriation of global forms, ideas, objects and resources is taking place in various African societies — ways that may strike us as infinitely creative and resilient given the marginalized predicament of many of these communities. This diversity in the ways globalism is situated in such local circumstances is at the same time an exploration of the infinitely rich texture of agency, whether individually or collectively defined. While globality appears to create new structures in ways that can often only be interpreted through the chaos theory, the domain of resilient agency in the context of these emergent structures awaits further study, to which this present volume should only be seen as a modest beginning.

References

Allen, S.L. 1999, *The Devil's Cup: Coffee, the Driving Force in History*, Edinburgh: Canongate.

Anderson, B. 1992, 'Long-Distance Nationalism: World Capitalism and the Rise of Identity Politics', Wertheim Lecture, Centre for Asian Studies, Amsterdam.

Appadurai, A. 1990, 'Disjuncture and Difference in the Global Cultural Economy', in: M. Featherstone (ed.), *Global Culture: Nationalism, Globalization and Modernity*, London: Sage, pp. 295-310.

Appadurai, A. 1991, 'Global Ethnoscapes: Notes and Queries for a Transnational Anthropology', in: R.G. Fox (ed.), *Recapturing Anthropology: Working in the Present*, Santa Fe, NM: School of American Research Press, pp. 191-210.

Appadurai, A. 1996, *Modernity at Large: Anthropological Explorations of Globalization*, Minneapolis: University of Minnesota Press.

Appadurai, A. 2000, 'Grassroots Globalization and the Research Imagination', *Public Culture* 12 (1): 1-19.

Barnet, R.J. 1994, *Global Dreams: Imperial Corporations and the New World Order*, New York: Simon & Schuster.

Bauman, Z. 1998, *Globalization: The Human Consequences*, New York: Columbia University Press.

Bell, D. 2001, 'Communitarianism', in: *Stanford Encyclopedia of Philosophy*, at: http://plato.stanford.edu/entries/communitarianism

Bernal, M.G. 1987, *Black Athena: The AfroAsiatic Roots of Classical Civilization, I. The Fabrication of Ancient Greece 1787-1987*, London: Free Association Books/New Brunswick, NJ: Rutgers University Press.

Bernal, M.G. 1991, *Black Athena: The Afroasiatic Roots of Classical Civilization, II. The Archaeological and Documentary Evidence*, London: Free Association Books/New Brunswick NJ: Rutgers University Press.

Bond, G.C. & D.M. Ciekawy (eds) 2001, *Witchcraft Dialogues: Anthropological and Philosophical Exchanges*, Athens, OH: Ohio University Press.

Brecher, J. & T. Costello 1994, *Global Village or Global Pillage: Economic Reconstruction From the Bottom Up*, Boston: South End Press.

Breedveld, A., J. van Santen & W.M.J. van Binsbergen (eds) in press, *Islam and Transformations in Africa*, Leiden: Brill.

Carrier, J.G. & D. Miller (eds) 1998, *Virtualism: A New Political Economy*, Oxford: Berg.

Chomsky, N. 1998, *Profit Over People: Neoliberalism and Global Order*, New York: Seven Stories Press.

Clifford, J. 1992, 'Travelling Cultures', in: L. Grossberg *et al.* (eds), *Cultural Studies*, London: Routledge, pp. 96-116.

Clough, P. & J.P. Mitchell (eds) 2001, *Powers of Good and Evil: Moralities, Commodities and Popular Belief*, New York/Oxford: Berghahn.

Comaroff, J. & J. Comaroff 1999, 'Occult Economies and the Violence of Abstraction: Notes from the South African Postcolony', *American Ethnologist* 26 (2): 279-301.

Cooper, F. 2001, 'What Is the Concept of Globalization Good For?: An African Historian's Perspective', *African Affairs* 100 (389): 189-213.

Corten, A. & R. Marshall-Fratani (eds) 2001, *Between Babel and Pentecost: Transnational Pentecostalism in Africa and Latin America*, London: Hurst.

Davidson, B. 1992, *The Black Man's Burden: Africa and the Curse of the Nation-State*, London: James Currey.

El Toukhy, M.M. 1998, 'Globalization and Developing Countries', *The South African Journal of Economics* 66 (4): 464-491.

Ellis, S. 2001, 'Witching Times: A Theme in the Histories of Africa and Europe', paper prepared for internal seminar, African Studies Centre, Leiden.

Fardon, R. & G. Furniss (eds) 1994, *African Languages, Development and the State*, London/New York: Routledge.

Ferguson, J. 1999, *Expectations of Modernity: Myths and Meanings of Urban Life on the Zambian Copperbelt*, Berkeley: University of California Press.

Forben, A. 1995, *Globalization: The African Perspective*, Bamenda: BCC Publishing.

Fosu, A. & L. Senbet (eds) 2001, *Financial and Currency Crises*, Oxford: Oxford University Press.

Friedman, T.L. 1999, *The Lexus and the Olive Tree: Understanding Globalization*, New York: Farrar, Straus & Giroux.

Fukuyama, F. 1989, 'The End of History?', *The National Interest* (Summer): 3-18.

Fukuyama, F. 1992, *The End of History and the Last Man*, New York: Free Press.

Gamble, C. 1993, *Timewalkers: The Prehistory of Global Colonization*, Bath: Bath Press.

Geschiere, P.L. 1984, 'La Paysannerie Africaine Est-Elle "Captive"? Sur la Thèse de Goran Hyden, et Pour Une Réponse Plus Nuancée', *Politique Africaine* 14: 13-33.

Geschiere, P. 1997, *The Modernity of Witchcraft, Politics and the Occult in Postcolonial Africa*, Charlottesville: University Press of Virginia.

Geschiere, P. 1998, 'Globalization and the Power of Indeterminate Meaning: Witchcraft and Spirit Cults in Africa and East Asia', *Development and Change* 29 (4): 811-37.

Geschiere, P. & W.M.J. van Binsbergen (eds) in press, *Commodification: Things, Agency, and Identities: Social Life of Things Revisited*, Durham, NC: Duke University Press.

Giddens, A. 1991, *Modernity and Self-Identity: Self and Society in the Late Modern Age*, Stanford: Stanford University Press.

Ginzburg, C. 1966, *I Benandanti: Stregoneria e Culti Agrari Tra Cinquecento e Seicento*, Torino: Einaudi.

Ginzburg, C. 1989, *Storia Notturna*, Torino: Einaudi.

Habermas, J., 1989, *The Structural Transformation of the Public Sphere: An Inquiry into a Category of Bourgeois Society*, Oxford: Polity Press.

Hannerz, U. 1987, 'The World in Creolisation', *Africa* 57 (4): 546-59.

Hannerz, U. 1992, *Cultural Complexity: Studies in the Social Organization of Meaning*, New York: Columbia University Press.

Hannerz, U. 1996, 'The Local and the Global: Continuity and Change', in: U. Hannerz (ed.), *Transnational Connections: Culture, People, Places*, New York: Routledge, pp. 17-29.

Hegel, G.W.F. 1992, *Vorlesungen über die Philosophie der Geschichte, Georg Wilhelm Friedrich Hegel Werke 12*, Frankfurt am Main: Suhrkamp.

Held, D. & A. MacGrew 2002, *Globalization/Anti-Globalization*, Cambridge: Polity Press.

Hertz, N. 2001, *The Silent Takeover: Global Capitalism and the Death of Democracy*, London: Heinemann.

Hopkins, A.G. (ed.) 2002, *Globalization in World History*, London: Pimlico.

Howe, S. 1999, *Afrocentrism: Mythical Pasts and Imagined Homes*, London/New York: Verso, first published 1998.

Huntington, S.P. 1996, *The Clash of Civilizations*, New York: Simon & Schuster.

Hyden, G. 1980, *Beyond Ujamaa in Tanzania: Underdevelopment and an Uncaptured Peasantry*, Berkeley: University California Press.

Jameson, F. & M. Miyoshi (eds) 1998, *The Cultures of Globalization*, Durham, NC: Duke University Press.

Jules-Rosette, B. 1996, 'What Money Can't Buy: Zairian Popular Culture and Symbolic Ambivalence toward Modernity', paper presented at the international conference on 'L'Argent: Feuille Morte: L'Afrique Central Avant et Après le Desenchantement de la Modernité', Louvain, 21-22 June.

Kane, O. 1997, 'Muslim Missionaries and African States', in: S. Rudolph & J. Piscatori (eds), *Transnational Religion and Fading States*, Boulder & Oxford: Westview Press, pp. 47-62.

Kennedy, P. 2002, 'The Real Culture Wars: Book Review of Bernard Lewis, *What Went Wrong? Western Impact and Middle Eastern Response*', *New York Times*, 27 January.

Klein, N. 2000, *No Logo, No Space, No Choice, No Jobs: Taking Aim at the Brand Bullies*, London: Flamingo.

Korff, R. 1995, 'The Urban Revolution: Civilisation in the Concrete Jungle?', Paper read at the EIDOS (European Interuniversity Development Opportunities Study network) conference on Globalization and Decivlization, Wageningen, 14-16 December.

Lefkowitz, M.R. & G. MacLean Rogers (eds) 1996, *Black Athena Revisited*, Chapel Hill & London: University of North Carolina Press.

Levitt, T. 1983, 'The Globalization of Markets', *Harvard Business Review* 61 (3): 92-102.

Lewis, B. 2001, *What Went Wrong? Western Impact and Middle Eastern Response*, New York: Oxford University Press.

MacIntyre, A. 1988, *Whose Justice? Which Rationality?*, Notre Dame: University of Notre Dame Press.

Makoa, F.K. 2001, 'Globalization and Democracy with Reference to Eastern and Southern Africa', *Journal of Social Development in Africa* 16 (1): 125-41.

Mall, R.A. 1995, *Philosophie im Vergleich der Kulturen: Interkulturelle Philosophie, eine neue Orientierung*, Darmstadt: Wissenschaftliche Buchgesellschaft.

Mazrui, A.A. 1996, 'Mombasa: Three Stages towards Globalization', in: A.D. King (ed.), *Re-Presenting the City: Ethnicity, Capital and Culture in the 21st Century*, New York: New York University Press.

Mbeki, T. 1998, Statement by Deputy President Mbeki at the African Renaissance Conference Johannesburg, 28 September http://www.anc.org.za/ancdocs/history/mbeki/1998/tm0928.htm

Meso, W. 2000, 'The Brain Drain: Will the Outflow of Skilled People Kill the African Renaissance?', *Africa Insight* 30 (2): 2-74.

Meyer, B. 1999, 'Christian Mind and Worldly Matter: Religion and Materiality in the Nineteenth-century Gold Coast', in: R. Fardon, W.M.J. van Binsbergen & R. van Dijk (eds), *Modernity on a Shoestring: Dimensions of Globalization, Consumption and Development in Africa and Beyond*, Leiden: EIDOS.

Meyer, B. & P. Geschiere (eds) 1999, *Globalization and Identity-Dialectics of Flow and Closure*, Oxford: Blackwell.

Naerman, A. 2000, 'The African Nation State: An Elusive Challenge', in: B. Berner & P. Trulsson (eds), *Manoeuvring in an Environment of Uncertainty: Structural Change and Social Action in Sub-Saharan Africa*, Aldershot: Ashgate.

Ninsin, K.A. 2000, 'The Quest for Democracy', *Africa Insight* 30 (3/4): 10-17.

Nuwagaba, A. 2001, 'Globalization and Competitiveness: Implications for Poverty Reduction in Uganda', *Journal of Social Development in Africa* 16 (2): 31-52.

Nyamnjoh, F.B. 2000, '"For Many are Called but Few Are Chosen": Globalization and Popular Disenchantment in Africa', *African Sociological Review* 4 (2): 1-45.

Owolabi, K.A. 2001, 'Globalization, Americanization and Western Imperialism', *Journal of Social Development in Africa* 16 (2): 71-91.

Popper, K. 1957, *The Poverty of Historicism*, London: Routledge & Kegan Paul.

Puplampu, K.P. & W.J. Tettey 2000, 'State-NGO Relations in an Era of Globalization: The Implications for Agricultural Development in Africa', *Review of African Political Economy* 27 (84): 251-72.

Rabenoro, I. 1999, 'Multilingual Developing Countries Facing Globalization', *Social Dynamics* 25 (1): 70-80.

Raju, P.T. 1962, *Introduction to Comparative Philosophy*, Lincoln, NE: University of Nebraska Press.

Ranger, T.O. 1975, *Dance and Society in Eastern Africa, 1890-1970*, London: Heinemann.

Ranger, T.O. 1979, 'Developments in the Historical Study of African Religion: Relations of Production and Religious Change in Central Africa', in: 'Religion and Change in African Societies: Proceedings of a Seminar Held in the Centre of African Studies, University of Edinburgh', 27-28 April, Edinburgh: Centre of African Studies, pp. 1-18.

Ranger, T.O. 1985, 'Religious Studies and Political Economy: The Mwari Cult and the Peasant Experience in Southern Rhodesia', in: W.M.J. van Binsbergen & J.M. Schoffeleers (eds), *Theoretical Explorations in African Religion*, London & Boston: Kegan Paul International for ASC, pp. 287-321.

Rawls, J. 1971, *A Theory of Justice*, Cambridge, MA: Belknap Press of Harvard University Press.

Robertson, R. & F. Lechner 1985, 'Modernization, Globalization, and the Problem of Culture in World-Systems Theory', *Theory, Culture and Society* 2 (3): 103-17.

Sandel, M. 1998, *Liberalism and the Limits of Justice*, Cambridge: Cambridge University Press, 2nd edition.

Sassen, S. 1991, *The Global City: New York, London, Tokyo*, Princeton: Princeton University Press.

Sawyerr, A. 1999, 'Globalization and Social Sciences in Africa', *African Sociological*

Review 3 (1): 1-19.

Simone, A.M. 1999, 'Thinking About African Urban Management in an Era of Globalization', *African Sociological Review* 3 (2): 69-98.

Smith, M.P. 1998, 'Global City — Whose Social Construct Is It Anyway? A Comment on White', *Urban Affairs Review* 33 (4): 482-88.

Stoller, P. 2002, *Money Has No Smell. The Africanization of New York City*, Chicago, Chicago University Press.

Tandon, Y. 1997, 'Globalization and the South: The Logic of Exploitation', *Internationale Politik und Gesellschaft* (4): 389-98.

Tanoe, D. & M. Diouf 1999, 'World Trade Liberalization, Globalization and Africa's Integration Process', *Cahiers Africains d'Administration Publique* (52): 39-48.

Taussig, M.T. 1980, *The Devil and Commodity Fetishism in South America*, Chapel Hill: University of North Carolina Press.

Taylor, C. 1985, *Philosophy and the Human Sciences: Philosophical Papers 2*, Cambridge: Cambridge University Press.

Taylor, C. 1999, 'Conditions of an Unforced Consensus on Human Rights', in: J.R. Bauer & D. Bell (eds.), *The East Asian Challenge for Human Rights*, New York: Cambridge University Press.

Thoden van Velzen, H.U.E. 1977, 'Bush Negro Regional Cults: A Materialist Explanation', in: R.P. Werbner (ed.), *Regional Cults*, London: Academic Press, pp. 93-118.

Thoden van Velzen, H.U.E. 1995, 'Revenants That Cannot Be Shaken: Collective Fantasies in a Maroon Society', *American Anthropologist* 97 (4): 722-32.

Thoden van Velzen, H.U.E. 1998, 'Windows of Opportunity, Windows of Anxiety: Fantasy Scenarios as Globalization Dreams', paper read at the workshop on 'Media and Mediation in the Politics of Culture', Centre for Studies in Social Sciences, Calcutta, India, 4-7 March, organized jointly with the International Network on Globalization, and the Programme on Globalization and the Construction of Communal Identities, Netherlands Foundation of Tropical Research (WOTRO).

Thoden van Velzen, H.U.E. & W. van Wetering 2001, 'Dangerous Creatures and the Enchantment of Modern Life', in: P. Clough & J.P. Mitchell (eds), *Powers of Good and Evil: Moralities, Commodities and Popular Belief*, New York & Oxford: Berghahn, pp. 17-43.

Thomas, K. 1978, *Religion and the Decline of Magic*, Harmondsworth: Penguin.

Thompson, E.P. 1980, *The Poverty of Theory: And Other Essays*, London: Merlin, first published 1978.

Van Binsbergen, W.M.J. 1981, *Religious Change in Zambia: Exploratory Studies*, London: Kegan Paul.

Van Binsbergen, W.M.J. (ed.) 1997, *Black Athena: Ten Years After*, special issue, *Talanta* 28-29.

Van Binsbergen, W.M.J. 1998a, 'Globalization and Virtuality: Analytical Problems Posed by the Contemporary Transformation of African Societies', *Development and Change* 29 (4): 873-903.

Van Binsbergen, W.M.J. 1998b, 'Islam as a Globalising Project: African Perspectives', paper read at the internal study day on Islam and globalization, ASC, Leiden, 29

April.

Van Binsbergen, W.M.J. 1999, 'Mary's Room: A Case Study on Becoming a Consumer in Francistown, Botswana', in: R. Fardon, W.M.J. van Binsbergen & R. van Dijk (eds), *Modernity on a Shoestring: Dimensions of Globalization, Consumption and Development in Africa and Beyond*, Leiden: EIDOS.

Van Binsbergen, W.M.J. 2001, 'Witchcraft in Modern Africa as Virtualized Boundary Conditions of the Kinship Order', in: G.C. Bond & D.M. Ciekawy (eds), *Witchcraft Dialogues: Anthropological and Philosophical Exchanges*, Athens, OH: Ohio University Press, pp. 212-63.

Van Binsbergen, W.M.J. 2003, 'Intercultural Encounters: African and Anthropological Towards a Philosophy of Interculturality', Berlin/Muenster: LIT.

Van de Walle, N. 1999, 'Globalization and African Democracy', in: R. Joseph (ed.), *State, Conflict and Democracy in Africa*, Boulder, Co.: Rienner Publishers, pp. 95-118.

Van Dijk, R. 1999, 'The Pentecostal Gift: Ghanaian Charismatic churches and the Moral Innocence of the Global Economy', in: R. Fardon, W.M.J. van Binsbergen & R. van Dijk, *Modernity on a Shoestring: Dimensions of Globalization, Consumption and Development in Africa and Beyond*, Leiden: EIDOS.

Van Nahl, A. 1999, 'Market Expansion, Globalized Discourse and Changing Identity Politics in Kenya', in: R. Fardon, W.M.J. van Binsbergen & R. van Dijk (eds), *Modernity on a Shoestring: Dimensions of Globalization, Consumption and Development in Africa and Beyond*, Leiden: EIDOS.

Wallerstein, I. 1974, *The Modern World-System I: Capitalist Agriculture and the Origins of the European World-Economy in the Sixteenth Century*, Orlando: Academic Press Inc.

Walzer, M. 1983, *Spheres of Justice*, Oxford: Blackwell.

Walzer, M. 1994, *Thick and Thin*, Notre Dame: University of Notre Dame Press

Waters, M. 1995, *Globalization*, London & New York: Routledge.

Weiss, B. 2001, 'Thug Realism: Inhabiting Fantasy in Urban Tanzania', *Cultural Anthropology* 17 (1): 1-32.

White, J.W. 1998, 'Old Wine, Cracked Bottle?: Tokyo, Paris and the Global City Hypothesis', *Urban Affairs Review* 33 (4): 451-77.

Wiredu, K. & K. Gyekye (eds) 1992, 'Person and Community: Ghanaian Philosophical Studies', Council for Research in Values and Philosophy, Washington DC.

Worsley, P.M. 1957, *The Trumpet Shall Sound: A Study of 'Cargo' Cults in Melanesia*, London: MacGibbon & Keel.

PART II: GLOBALITY THROUGH APPROPRIATION: ANALYSES AT THE CONTINENTAL LEVEL

2

Global and local trends in media ownership and control: Implications for cultural creativity in Africa

Francis B. Nyamnjoh

This chapter discusses the crystallization of resistance to the cultural homogenization favoured by global consumer media and cultural production, stressing that in most of Africa, threats to a free, open and participatory media system and society come as much from repressive governments as from the interests of rich nations, international financial institutions and the global corporate media. Too cautious to take any serious risks, especially in marginal and highly unpredictable zones of accumulation like Africa, global capital needs public support and regulation to insulate itself against the vicissitudes provoked or exacerbated by its tendency to put profit before people. Africa's predicament notwithstanding, the chapter is critical of meta-narratives that celebrate victimhood at the risk of obfuscating the reality of negotiation and survival strategies, and discusses some of the myriad ways devised by Africans to ensure cultural participation for themselves as active agents in local and global processes.

Introduction

It is commonplace for studies of globalization to focus on the big corporate players and macro-processes, often to the detriment of initiatives or responses at the very local level by individuals and groups on the margins of meta-narratives of bliss and gloom. This chapter attempts to focus on both levels: it examines the double effect on cultural creativity in Africa of global trends in media ownership and control in a context of continuous authoritarian grip by the state on local national media production and freedom of expression in general. It draws on the popular saying 'he who pays the piper calls the tune' to examine the implications of public or private media ownership and control on cultural creativity and political freedom in Africa. Although the argument and insights pertain to Africa in general, particular illustrations are drawn from Cameroon, a context I have researched extensively since the early 1980s.

Current debates on media ownership and control are informed by and largely focused on the effects of globalization of neoliberalism on media scenarios throughout the world. Inspired by narrow, individual-centred philosophies of personhood, agency and property rights, neoliberalism is aggressive in its sacrifice of community rights and group interests, as it pursues profit through the illusion of promoting the interests of the autonomous individual as a consumer and citizen. Old patterns informed by more inclusive philosophies of ownership and control are increasingly giving way to new configurations with a focus on the individual, consumerism and exclusion. National state-owned public service media systems are yielding to commercial pressure and its emphasis on 'profit over people' (Chomsky 1999). Propelled by 'the incessant pursuit of profit', global media entrepreneurs are asking for little short of unregulated commercial exploitation and concentrated ownership of the media (McChesney 2001: 1-4). The trend is clearly towards global oligopolies, and the guiding logic of the media firms is, as McChesney puts it, 'get very big very quickly, or get swallowed up by someone else'. Firms, he argues, 'must become larger and diversified to reduce risk and enhance profit-making opportunities, and they must straddle the globe so as to never be outflanked by competitors' (McChesney 2001: 3-9).

An obvious casualty of this shift in philosophies of ownership and control is the traditional emphasis on public service media that guarantees cultural pluralism and diversity by providing for groups and social categories that otherwise would be ignored or marginalized by the market. This tradition of public service media, while not denying the articulation of individual interests, believed that the greatest good came from a negotiated balance between various individual interests as part of a community. Media conceived in this tradition stressed negotiation, interconnectedness and harmony between individual interests and community expectations. Within the ownership logic that inspired the public service media, the freedom to pursue individual or community goals existed within a socially predetermined framework that emphasized conviviality with collective interests, while simultaneously allowing for individual creativity and self-fulfilment. It was, therefore, a philosophy of ownership and control that sought to marry individual and group or community property rights, rather than seeking to impose the illusion of the autonomous individual.

In Europe, the shift in philosophies has meant that, since the 1990s, the market-driven ideas of public-service broadcasting serving the interests and preferences of individual media consumers have taken precedence over media in tune with the expectations of particular cultural communities such as ethnic minorities, and religious and linguistic groupings (Syvertsen 1999, Søndergaard 1999). With a focus on consumption as the ultimate unifier, a supreme indicator of cultural sophistication and symbol of civilization, individuals are seen and treated as autonomous agents glued together by a selfless market slaving away for their cultural freedom, development and enrichment as global citizens. This development blurs the traditional distinction between public-service and commercial media, and passes for public service even the greedy and aggressive pursuit of profit without people. It also obscures the distinction between national media and world services targeting foreign territories, by emphasizing the 'unregulated flow' and 'transnationalization' of the streamlined, standardized and routinized cultural products of the media industries of the West (cf. Golding & Harris 1997). Not only is the traditional idea of public-service radio and television fast becoming outmoded, calls for some ground rules to protect cultural diversity have simply been greeted with the rhetoric of free flows at worst or with token concessions to cultural minorities at best. What is more, the corporate media are in a particularly powerful position, given their dual role as players and umpires in the game of profit (McChesney 2001: 3-9). They 'enjoy an enormous leeway to negotiate and protect interests from the vantage of prior monopoly positions', and 'do not have to bend over backwards to strike deals. It is generally the case that they decide and the world follows suit' (Thomas & Lee 1998: 2). And if they decide to invest mostly in tastes informed by a narrow understanding of culture, then cultural richness and diversity suffer, as the likelihood of cultural imperialism, trivialization and misrepresentation increases. Given the free hand and caprice of the cultural industries and their investors, the piper may well be undertasked with tunes of little significance as creativity, diversity and variety are downplayed in the interests of homogeneity and profitability.

This implies that, their rhetoric of benevolence and munificence notwithstanding, the global media corporations are more about closures than free flows among the world's cultures. The corporate media promotes a largely one-way flow in cultural products that favours a privileged minority as it compounds the impoverishment of the majority through closures and containment (cf. Golding & Harris 1997). As 'empires of image and of the imagination' the corporate media controls global markets and global consciousness (Murdock 1994: 3), mostly by denying access to creativity perceived to stand in the way of profit, power and privilege. The results are streamlined, standardized, routinized or 'McDonaldized' cultural products devoid of complexity, richness and diversity that command a disproportionate share of the global market. The tendency is to mistake plurality for diversity, oblivious of the possibility that an appearance of plenty could well conceal a poverty of perspectives (Murdock 1994: 5).

This leaves ordinary consumers, marginal communities and whole cultures literally at the mercy of the McDonaldized news, information and entertainment burgers served them in the interests of profits by the global corporate media. Because the global media system 'advances corporate and commercial interests and values and denigrates or ignores that which cannot be incorporated into its mission', content becomes uniform, regardless of the nationalities or cultural identities of shareholders. This is hardly surprising since what is wanted are passive, depoliticized, unthinking consumer zombies more prone 'to take orders than to make waves' by questioning the 'light escapist entertainment' menu presented to them by the chosen pipers (McChesney 1998: 7). In this regard it could be argued, as McChesney (1998: 6, 2001: 13) has done, that the basic differences are not between nation-states as such, but between the rich and the poor (whom I term 'consumer citizens' and 'consumer subjects' respectively) across national borders. However, the fact remains that the investors, advertisers and affluent consumers whose interests the global media represents, are more concentrated in and comprise a significant proportion of the populations of the developed world than is the case in Africa where only an elite minority are involved and hardly any local cultural tunes get chosen for the global pipers to perform.

Among other things, this chapter seeks to further situate Africa in relation to the global trend highlighted above, and to discuss the crystallization of resistance to the cultural homogenization the trend favours. It must be reiterated, however, that in most of Africa, threats to a free, open and participatory media system and society are as much from repressive governments as from the interests of rich nations, international financial institutions and the global corporate media. Cultural production in Africa is caught between control by the greedy and aggressive pursuit of profit by the global media on the one hand, and repression at local levels by states marginalized as global players and reduced to flexing their muscles *vis-à-vis* their own populations. Because 'business does not want to go about its activity totally unprotected', global capital needs public support and regulation as 'an insurance against the full vicissitudes of a turbulent and potentially self-destructive system' (Thompson 1999: 142). This expectation of public support and protection is even higher when capital ventures into marginal and highly unpredictable zones of accumulation like Africa, which accounts for barely 1 per cent of global trade. In Africa more than elsewhere, multinational capital colludes with states at the expense of democracy, equity and social development (cf. Mkandawire 2002), and in favour of sterile profitability and power without responsibility.

Given the weakness of African states in relation to the interests of rich nations, international financial institutions and multinationals, and their peripheral position in the global economy and politics, the only real authority or semblance of power affordable to African governments is towards their own populations, which are often too poor and too vulnerable to organize and mobilize effectively against exploitation and repression. What neoliberalism wants of African governments is national and regional policies in tune with the profitability expectations of global capital, policies that minimize countervailing traditions, customs, world views and expectations of continuity. Once they have guaranteed global capital stability, security and protection from local labour and its needs, African states need do no more than embrace the rhetoric of liberal democracy and the tokenism of its freedoms. All multinational capital really needs of them is not so much a guarantee of democracy and stability, as a dictatorship to ensure that local labour and national interests are kept subservient to the interests and power of big business. Often it is understood, though not openly stated, that they need do no more than embrace liberal democratic rhetoric, since few seriously believe that it is possible, in practice, for African states or governments to be both tolerant of the demands of global capital and of the clamour for rights and entitlements by their own nationals. There is trouble only for governments that, in an effort to please their own populations, begin to claim national sovereignty beyond rhetoric, thereby impairing the interests of multinationals and of Western states.

The final section of this chapter, while acknowledging the predicament of Africans as victims of repressive states and the tendency in global capital to privilege profit over people, argues against the tendency towards meta-narratives of victimhood that obfuscate the reality of negotiation and survival strategies employed by ordinary Africans. The section provides evidence of some of the myriad ways devised by Africans to ensure cultural participation for themselves as active agents in local and global processes, despite the reality of repression and exclusion.

Media in Africa: Between repression and profit

In September 1997, a three-day workshop on 'Media Ownership and Control in West and Central Africa' was held in Cameroon. Funded by the World Association for Christian Communication (WACC) and initially scheduled to take place at the University of Buea where I taught and headed the Department of Sociology and Anthropology, the workshop was moved to Yaoundé at the last minute because the Vice Chancellor of the University of Buea, Dr Dorothy Njeuma, had given the background paper a second reading. In her memorandum of disapproval to me through my Dean, she wrote, *inter alia*:

> It will be recalled that the initial title of the workshop was 'Communication and the Globalization of Poverty'. In his response dated 3 July 1997 to the observations which we made relating to the need to observe instructions requiring prior authorization from the Presidency of the Republic for international meetings and the apparent contradiction in the subject of the workshop, Dr Nyamnjoh underlines that the workshop would be a purely academic exercise and that the new title is a sub-theme of the initial subject.
>
> We regret to inform you that the background paper on media ownership and control as contained in document No. 0111/75-4/UB/SOC of 24 March 1997 carries sensitive political overtones which are inappropriate for the University of Buea to be seen to promote at this particular time. The slant given in the paper is also at variance with the view presented by WACC on the factors which they perceive as contributing to the globalization of poverty; the WACC document faults rich nations, international financial institutions and communication transnationals for the spread of poverty (cf. WACC programme for 1997-2001).
>
> In these circumstances, we regret that we cannot give approval for the University of Buea to host the workshop on media ownership and control.[1]

The background paper in question was what I had submitted to the WACC for funding, in which I blamed the globalization of poverty on global consumer capitalism and on authoritarian governments in Africa. The section, which she objected to, was the following:

> A look at the literature and research on media and mass communication in Africa prior to 1990 reveals a tendency towards centralized broadcast systems and a highly repressed private press. [.... In opting for state ownership and control, these governments sought to justify why mass communication needed to be controlled. They claimed that centralism was necessary for successful nation-building. Government ownership and control was justified as being less wasteful of the limited resources, and as guaranteeing the political stability badly needed for rapid development. .... As development becomes more and more illusive and disillusionment at the grassroots widespread, the question arises whether government ownership and control of the media is an answer to the problem of people-centred development communication in Africa.

The vice chancellor's claim that 'the WACC document faults rich nations, international financial institutions and communication transnationals for the spread of poverty' is basically correct. But it tells only part of the story, one that absolves the government she represents of all responsibility, while blaming external forces personified by global capitalism. This points to the dangers of communication

---

[1] See Memorandum No. 0708/75-4/UB/W000 dated 16-07-97 from the Vice Chancellor to the Dean, Faculty of Social and Management Sciences, University of Buea.

scholars, NGOs and media activists being caught up with the challenges posed by globalization in media ownership and control to the point of trivializing or ignoring the traditional hurdles to freedom of expression and cultural production posed by state repression and undemocratic governments. African governments are all too eager to capitalize upon such concessions or oversights by their critics and to divert attention from their rigid regulation of national media and local cultural production.

What the above example shows is that even in the era of intensified globalization, academic, media and cultural freedoms in Africa may be threatened, not only by the interests of global capital and foreign states but also by zealous local officials and repressive governments seeking political survival beyond the verdict of the ballot box. African governments and global capital are in a partnership of hostility towards any assertion of difference and creativity likely to subvert their respective vested political and economic interests. Such double-barrel deafness to popular cultural production and reproduction points to a collusion between African states and global capital to stifle creative diversity in the cultural sphere. Both state and global capital expect Africans to chew unthinkingly, like grateful consumer zombies, the bland cultural fodder served them nationally and internationally by the *mass* media as vehicles of one-dimensionalism.

Nowhere is this partnership and collusion between state and global capital better illustrated than in the relationship between African governments and the Bretton Woods institutions. Both the World Bank and the IMF have preferred to impose pre-packaged, undomesticated ideals of liberal democracy, civil society and citizenship on Africa to the reality of democracy that embraces both the rights of individuals and those of groups, however constituted or defined (cf. Ake 2000). Keen to see neoliberal projects through, these institutions do more than 'resist punishing companies that patronize tyrants', as 'they fear frightening off businesses that prefer to shop for financing where executive decisions won't be judged' (Fishman 2002: 41). In addition, they have readily provided support for acquiescing governments in order to neutralize opposition to the globalization of poverty through unpopular structural adjustment programmes (SAPs). In this way, SAPs have had highly repressive political consequences as they have tended to ignore popular opinion and to rely on authoritarian regimes for implementation. The negative economic, social and political effects of SAPs have been responsible for the most violent forms of exclusion (Gibbon *et al.* 1992, Mkandawire & Olukoshi 1995, Mkandawire & Soludo 1999). The polarization of power and wealth produced by such neoliberal agencies and global capitalism makes democratic rule in marginal zones like Africa virtually impossible since global capitalism needs autocratic powers to penetrate the peripheries with its inequalities (Amin 1997a: 22). This is well illustrated by the state-condoned violence among the Ogoni minority in relation to entitlements over the oil in the Niger Delta of Nigeria (cf. Obi 2001). Globalization has not significantly corrected this centre-periphery logic (Amin 1997b). If anything, it has compounded the predicaments of most Africans who are reduced to consuming fantasies about the West (cf. Nyamnjoh & Page 2002), even if some do succeed in translating such fantasies into new social identities like the *Sapeurs* of the two Congos, thereby affording themselves 'psychological redemption' from 'social dereliction' while simultaneously making a political statement against the misery imposed on them by the Western illusion of material success for all and the authoritative structures of their own African states (cf. Gondola 1999, Friedman 1990, 1991, 1994).

Global entertainment media and their McDonaldized (streamlined, standardized, routinized, universalized and stop-gap) consumer culture lure or coerce Africans, their cultures and creativity to become consumed by the giant compressors of the West. The ultimate effect is, as Soyinka (1994a: 209) has so aptly observed, that Africans are encouraged 'to develop an incurable dependency syndrome and consume themselves to death' as the consumerist culture propagated in the name of development can only guarantee productivity at home in the West by vigorously exporting itself through encouraging the marginalization of competing cultures. As an ideology of an elite few informing only selected sections of life, consumer capitalism cannot afford African cultures the freedom to be of relevance at home or elsewhere in the world (Amin 1997b: 41). The outcome, as Soyinka notes, is that Africans are inducted into an unequal cultural exchange with the West and are reduced to 'feeding the foreign consumerist machine', despite their own cultural values. Youths, mothers, values and tastes are all victims, ravaged by the elite few of the consumer club (ibid: 209-10).

This perspective, which is popular among African scholars, explains both economic underdevelopment, cultural marginalization and stalling democracy in terms of the assimilation and exclusion logic of global capitalism, according to which only the handful of powerful and economic elite in Africa stands to benefit from its internalization and reproduction. The implication of this situation, paradoxically, is a world where globalization does not amount to the homogenization of entitlements and recognition but rather to an intensification of hierarchies and inequalities among individuals, groups, regions and cultures. If globalization creates opportunities, these opportunities come to some as paradise but to most they come as different degrees of hell. The rhetoric might be one of a bazaar to which all are invited, but the reality is few benefit or are given clear-cut choices. One cannot afford to be insensitive to the hierarchies of inequalities that make globalization less a process of cultural flows than closures, compression than inflation, and enhancement than depletion for most communities in the world.

Despite liberalization and globalization

Mindful of this, it should be of surprise to few that the mediascape in Africa in the age of intensified globalization represents more a degree of continuity in repression than change. Despite the winds of liberalization in the late 1980s and early1990s, it is still common in many countries to charge journalists, academics, musicians, playwrights and other artists simply for creativity that brings the state or any of its officials into disrepute. Equally frowned upon by politicians are cultural producers critical of national or foreign dignitaries in ways perceived to be embarrassing to governments and the vested interests they protect. Although governments may proclaim democracy, freedom of expression and cultural renaissance as is currently fashionable, in practice most do not hesitate to sanction even a cabinet minister, a distinguished academic or a celebrated artist who might express a critical or controversial opinion on an issue of pubic interest. This restricts access to government-held information and imposes self-censorship on the very agents whose creativity is supposed to engender the cultural renaissance of official rhetoric. Concerning journalists and the media as vehicles of cultural content, little room is allowed for them to choose freely among the competing cultural options available. Sometimes African governments would rather trust foreign journalists and the media with important decisions concerning their countries than honour their own local media with scoops. Few books by journalists with intimate, first-hand details of African leaders dead and alive are by African journalists, proof perhaps that foreign journalists penetrate African corridors of power much more easily, regardless of their qualifications and competencies. Similarly, it is much easier for a Western production team to make radio and television documentaries about various aspects of African societies than for African governments to fund such productions by their own local media. The reasons for this are not always inadequate finances, but the consequences are devastating for cultural production and reproduction informed by perspectives sensitive to local cultures and predicaments.

Although certain aspects of the draconian laws of the colonial period, the one-party era and military regimes have generally been replaced since the 1990s by new provisions that are relatively more tolerant of opposition views and criticisms, the selective application of the new laws, together with the use of extra-legal measures, have often been to the detriment of a culture of independence and creativity (cf. M'Bayo *et al.* 2000). There remains a craving to control that leaves little doubt about how the lawmakers see journalists, artists and academics as potential troublemakers who must be policed beyond considerations for cultural survival. The tendency is for new laws to grant freedom of expression in principle while providing, often by administrative nexus, the curtailment of press, academic and artistic freedoms in practice. And although strongest in Francophone Africa, this use of derogatory and claw-back measures by the state to limit the right of expression and press freedom is common throughout the continent. Southern African governments have continued to use 'outmoded legislation inherited from their one-party and colonial predecessors' to criminalize dissent and numb the critical instincts of the press (Lush 1998). Even the Nigerian press, frequently presented as the most vibrant and critical, has had to struggle with a battery of repressive laws by successive governments (Oloyede 1996), and in some cases — especially between 1993 and 1999 — certain newspapers and broadcasters had to adopt 'a guerrilla strategy' against state censorship (Olukotun 2002). In South Africa where the first liberation was only achieved in 1994, the press has yet to break free of its past record of black debasement. The end of apartheid has not necessarily made the newspapers more representative of South African diversities (cf. Pityana 2000). The rhetoric of transformation does not seem to match the realities and expectations as the press continues to practice exclusion, even as it preaches inclusion (cf. Duncan 2000). The same is true of academia, which has still to transform itself significantly from its apartheid heritage (cf. Hugo 1998a), a point well illustrated by exchanges between Mahmood Mamdani and others in the curriculum debate on the teaching of Africa at the University of Cape Town (cf. Centre for African Studies, University of Cape Town 1998, Hall 1998). Such control occasions self-censorship that has led to a crisis of credibility of the press, academia and artists in many countries.

The same arsenal of repressive measures has been used to police cultural production in general. States have sought to institutionalize a definition and practice of culture that provides them with the conceptual noises needed to justify their excesses, promote violence and silence, and foster mediocrity as a strategy for surviving the exigencies of liberal democracy. Since 1967, President Omar Bongo of Gabon has been most adept at manipulating the symbolic sphere of Gabonese society to guarantee his own political longevity (cf. Ngolet 2000). Almost everywhere, the quest for such longevity has implied, *inter alia*, states recruiting the services of pro-establishment academics, intellectuals, poets and musicians, while censoring the creative imagination of those perceived to be critical and/or controversial in their art (cf. Soyinka 1994b: 7-9, Mongo Beti 1993: 77-82, Kom 1996, Shear 1996, Mkandawire 1997, Kagwanja 1997, Hugo 1998b, Ngowet 2001: 118-38; Jua & Nyamnjoh 2002). This tendency is illustrated by the reality in Cameroon — an example with parallels in other countries in Africa as evidenced in a recent collection of essays in a special issue of *African Studies Review* on 'African Universities in Crisis and the Promotion of a Democratic Culture' (cf. Nyamnjoh & Jua 2002).

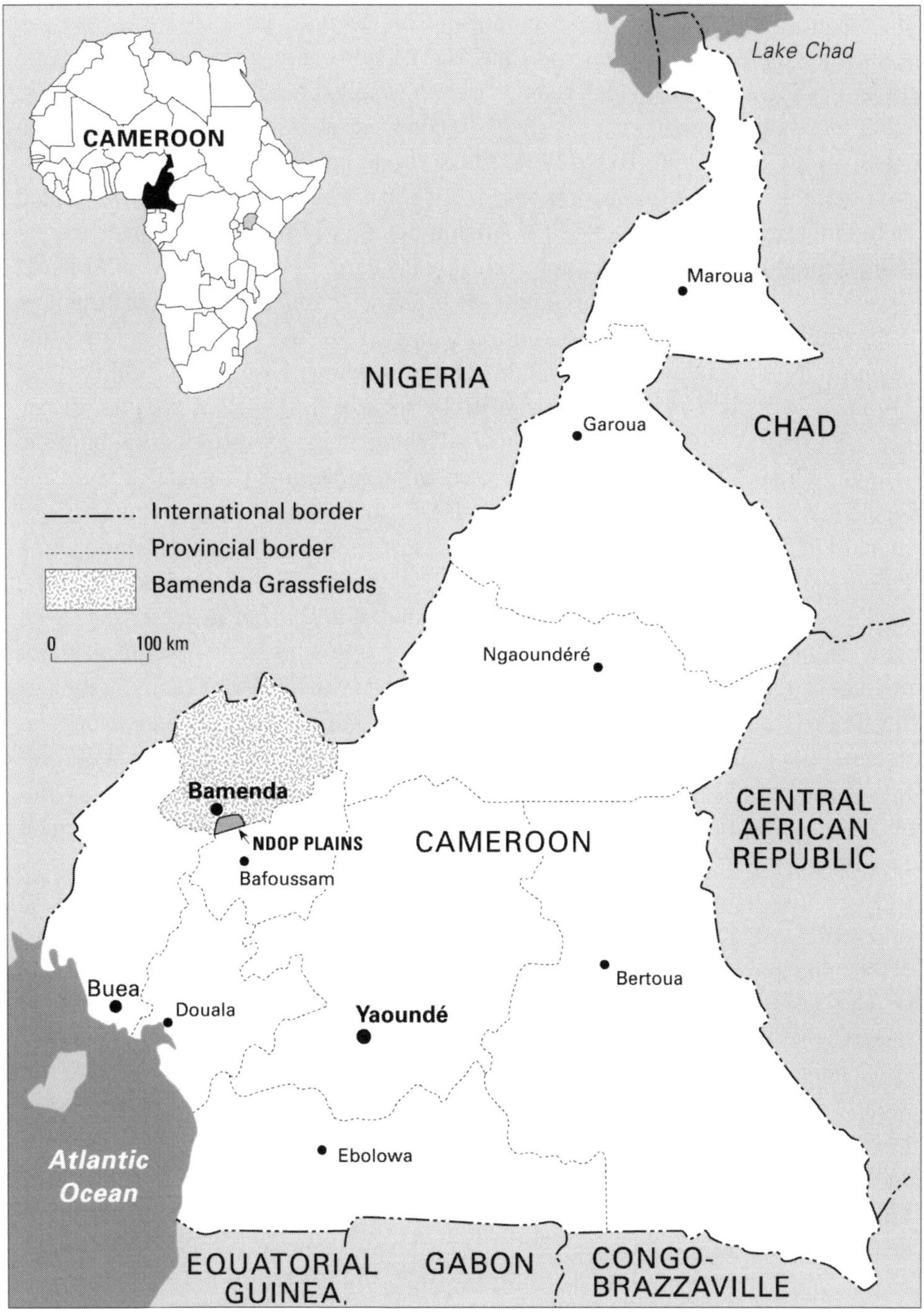

Map 2.1: Cameroon

By way of example: Cultural repression in Cameroon

Academic repression in Cameroon has been extensively documented, not least under President Biya who took over as president following Ahidjo's resignation in 1982 with all the right rhetoric about freedom of expression (Eboussi Boulaga 1993: 30-34, Kom 1996, Tedga 1998, Jua & Nyamnjoh 2002). Under both leaders, the tendency has been to sanction only 'occasional pieces composed by accredited hagiographers' (Kom 1991: 84-88). Among the overtly pro-establishment writers Kom quoted in a 1991 publication were Louis-Marie Pouka M'bague who wrote 'Prière-hommage', a poem in praise of Ahidjo; Samuel Martin Eno Belinga, author of *Cameroun: La Révolution Pacifique du 20 Mai*, a text celebrating the 'high deeds' of Ahidjo; Joseph-Charles Doumba whose *Vers le Mont Cameroun: Entretien avec Jean-Pierre Fogui* was in the same vein; Jos-Blaise Alima, whose *Les Chemins de l'Unité* was 'a glorified account of Ahidjo's nation-building efforts'; Mono Ndjana, whose *L'Idée Sociale chez Paul Biya* made of him 'the ideologue and chief censor of the New Deal'; and Fame Ndongo, Bandolo and Etoundi-MBalla, whose *Le Prince et le Scribe*, *La Flamme et la Fumée*, and *Une Vie à l'Envers* were, respectively, apologies for administrative or conventional thinking. Over twenty titles have since been added to this list in accordance with Fame Ndongo's call in *Le Prince et le Scribe* for a new 'race of writers capable of producing aggressive and conformist works in response to the misguided efforts of "lost" souls such as Mongo Beti, Alioum Fantouré, and Emmanuel Dongala' (Kom 1991: 87). Many academics who initially kept their distance from such pro-establishment scholarship have since yielded to the pressures and bait of co-optation by the regime that has refused to hearken to popular expectations and expressions of legitimacy. These old and new writers — like the government they serve — use selective discrimination in their observations, thus presenting an incomplete, preponderantly positive account of governments that have failed to deliver on nearly all fronts (cf. Nyamnjoh 1999, Jua & Nyamnjoh 2002).

The government has traditionally not hesitated to honour the efforts of researchers who sacrifice critical cultural production for praise-singing quasi-scholarship. Not only was Bandolo named 'Intellectual of the Year' in 1985 by Radio Cameroon following the publication of *La Flamme et la Fumée*, in May 1988 he was appointed Minister of Information and Culture. Two years after the publication of his book that was highly critical of the anti-government press, Valentin Nga Ndongo, a journalist and sociologist, was appointed Director of Press, Information and Propaganda for the ruling Cameroon People's Democratic Movement (CPDM) on July 1 1989. In 1990 Hubert Mono Ndjana became a member of the Central Committee of the CPDM as Press and Propaganda Secretary, and subsequently rewarded President Biya with many more praise-singing volumes, including *Les Proverbes de Paul Biya* (1997). Others, like Jacques Fame Ndongo, were already well placed when they wrote, but still, an additional or a more prominent appointment has usually been the government's way of thanking its 'scribes' or those who, like Fame Ndongo (1985), were charged with training 'les journalistes du Renouveau'. After serving briefly as Rector of the University of Yaoundé I, he was appointed Minister of Communication in 1998 in appreciation of his commitment to the defence of the status quo. For writing *Pour Un Multipartisme Reflechi* (1990) and for showing unconditional loyalty to President Paul Biya — 'the indomitable lion of Cameroonian politics' — as Director of Cameroon Radio Television (CRTV), Professor Gervais Mendoze has earned himself the reputation of being the longest serving general manager of 'the indomitable lion of the broadcast media', a position he has held since October 1988. Most of the establishment scholars share the same ethnic origins as President Biya (who is Beti) and are generally sympathetic to inoffensive cultural production from this ethnic region. This would explain the dominance and prominence of Bikutsi music on national radio and television to the detriment of music from other ethnic regions.

With such an elaborate system of control and selective diffusion of cultural production, critical researchers and creative writers have largely been driven underground or have stayed bottled up by lies and the fear of victimization. When cornered by competing alternatives, the powerful have shown themselves tolerant of limited reform but never a radical '*remise en cause*' of what they stand for — lies, mediocrity, double standards, exploitation and the primacy of the 'politics of the belly' (cf. Bayart 1993). Any change that means sharing their power and wealth with the dispossessed has been resisted, hence the banning of critical publications, music, theatre, art and performances. By thus feeding Cameroonians with falsehoods, the government has compelled everyone to adopt as reality its world of appearances. Convincing people has not been easy, especially as the context and cultures in place suggest that reality is much more than what the sensory perceptions bring home, and that the invisible or hidden hand is very much part and parcel of the order of things (cf. Mbembe 1997, Nyamnjoh 2001).

Economic consequences of rigid state control

The situation of political control has been aggravated by the resilient economic, technical and professional difficulties facing the press and cultural production in nearly all countries. Rigid control means that few serious local investors (never mind the global moguls or oligopolies) have found the press and cultural industry in Africa an attractive option. Financial difficulties have thus compounded the problems of news gathering and news production, and made newspapers in most countries even less credible as they struggle to produce every edition. The situation is little different with the private broadcast media in most countries and even the official media has not always escaped financial difficulties. An obvious consequence of this situation is the lack of research in most news stories, while the electronic media has simply been pushed into the arms of global news and entertainment radio and television corporations for cheap alternatives to locally produced programmes. In some countries, there is no means of encouraging specialized reporting and journalists are compelled to be 'jacks of all trades and masters of none'. Another result is the dearth of trained and experienced personnel: most newspapers have only a skeletal staff, and some are just a one-man show. This has been the case especially since the 1990s when the greater tolerance of press freedom attracted opportunists who saw in the press a window for self-enrichment and the pursuit of other ambitions. Because of such constraints, the press has lost much of its dynamism, vibrancy and credibility of the colonial era. Until recently, only governments have been able to afford to operate daily newspapers, with the advantage of being able to shape public opinion on a daily basis both in the print and the state-owned electronic media which they are reluctant to privatize or to make truly public service in character and content. Forces critical of government have often had to wait for the weekly or monthly publications in which to express their views, no matter how urgent. The ultimate casualty of all this is cultural freedom, diversity and creativity.

Private initiative and globalization in the making

Despite such persistent government control and the continent's inability, as yet, to attract big capital investment by the global oligopolies of the media world, there has been a significant opening-up to private capital and initiative almost everywhere since the 1990s. The ongoing quest for democracy has resulted not only in multipartyism but also in a sort of media pluralism. In almost every country, the number of private newspapers has increased dramatically with the clamour for recognition and representation by individuals and groups. Private FM radio and television stations have mushroomed, with international broadcasters such as the BBC and RFI now readily available locally on FM in certain capitals and provincial cities. The entire continent is experiencing a boom in private, local or commercial radio stations and satellite television (cf. Fardon & Furniss 2000). Malawi launched its first national television station in January 1999 and Botswana followed suit in July 2000. For their part, Lesotho and Swaziland have mobilized a South African commercial broadcaster — M-net — to provide a pseudo-national television system that broadcasts mostly foreign programmes from South Africa and the West.[2] However, the surge in private initiative has not been matched by an increase in the quantity and quality of local cultural production.

Not only has South Africa reformed the South African Broadcasting Corporation (SABC), which served as the mouthpiece of apartheid into the early 1990s (cf. Teer-Tomaselli & Tomaselli 1996, Barnett 1998, Graybill 2000), it has also been opened up to satellite television, with significance for the rest of the continent. The subscription satellite television service M-net that has been operational since 1986 and is owned by a consortium of South African newspaper publishers has rapidly spread its tentacles throughout the continent, and together with Multi-Choice (a subscriber management company whose Digital Satellite Television — DSTV — offers over 23 satellite television channels and 48 audio channels) and Canal Horizon of France virtually dominate the satellite television entertainment scene (Paterson 1998, Banda 2000, Teer-Tomaselli 2001). They have virtually colonized the palates of elite Africans along linguistic and cultural lines, with Canal Horizon harnessing Francophone Africa, and DSTV the Anglophone rest. Canal Horizon, M-net and Multi-Choice specialize in routinized, standardized or McDonaldized international sport and entertainment, which they serve to every subscriber on the continent regardless of region, nationality or cultural preferences, an approach that has occasioned renewed criticisms of Western cultural imperialism through South African and French media outlets. As Teer-Tomaselli (2001) notes, apart from increasing its local programming content and bringing a bit of the rainbow composition of South Africa to reflect on its on-air presentations, M-net has done little to alter its positioning in the new South Africa. Transformation, as Tomaselli and Dunn (2001: 3) point out, should mean more than a mere shift in discourses and demographics; it should entail a change in structures and ethos, something yet to be reflected in the mediascape of the new South Africa. It is hoped that increased local production and programme exchange through organizations such as the Union of National Radio and Television of Africa (URTNA) would correct the dependence on cheap, imported programmes and sports of little direct relevance to Africa.

South Africa has equally witnessed an explosion in community radio stations, with more than one hundred licences having been granted, of which 'some 80 stations were actually on the air on a daily basis' in 1998 (Van Kessel 1998: 12-13). It is estimated that there will be over 200 community radio stations in the near future, although the veteran community broadcaster Zane

---

[2] For an idea of the changing media ownership and control scenarios in West, Central and Southern Africa, see *Media Development*, vol. xlv (4) 1998 & xlviii (4) 2001.

Ibrahim of Bush Radio Cape Town claims that a proliferation of stations is not necessarily a good thing, as those likely to benefit most 'are the "consultants" and the many new broadcast equipment supply companies' who are more likely to be 'laughing all the way to the bank' than serving any community interest. He is equally critical of government involvement in community radio, as it can only be detrimental to 'communities not overly friendly with the ruling party of the day' (Ibrahim 1999: 15). Other countries have also embraced community radio — with and without donor funds — but 'African broadcast cultures' (cf. Fardon & Furniss 2000) are yet to be domesticated in tune with valid critiques of some culturally coloured assumptions about broadcasting and the uncritical internalization of Western media cultures by African broadcast professionals trained in the West or in Western-type schools (cf. Golding 1977).

This modest opening up to and involvement of private capital and initiative in the media can be termed *change* in media ownership in Africa. But control remains largely with government (in terms of laws regulating media ownership and operation) or with the transnational producers of global news and entertainment content on which the continent's media heavily relies. The media in Africa is effectively controlled by government and capital, both of which are keen to feed the public with nothing subversive to their interests and power. If the growing concern in the world is how to mobilize forces to curb or resist the growing concentrated ownership of the media in the service of neoliberalism, in Africa there is the added concern of mobilizing forces to resist government repression and highhandedness to or through the media. Mobilization must be undertaken with the understanding that African governments are in a predicament: they are being compelled by the World Bank, the IMF, the WTO and other institutions of neoliberalism to facilitate the penetration and rape of their markets by multinational capital on the one hand, and are additionally having to face up to the rising expectations and growing disillusionment of their own populations on the other. It is a situation that allows repression and greed to pillage the humanity of ordinary Africans with impunity and callous indifference.

Resisting victimhood in Africa

In a context like that described above in which Africans are finding themselves peripheral to global trends and subjected to the highhandedness and repression of their own governments, it is easy to slip into meta-narratives that celebrate victimhood. While there is genuine reason to be pessimistic and cynical, there is often, on closer observation, also reason to be hopeful. However repressive a government may be and however profound the spiral of silence induced by standardized and routinized global media menus, few people are completely mystified or wholly duped. There is always room for initiative or agency at an individual or group level to challenge domination, exploitation and the globalization of poverty. Histories of struggle in Africa are full of examples in this connection (cf. Mbembe 1992, Gecau 1997, Barber 1997). It is important always to explore how people on the margins of power and wealth strive to survive. The contention here is that Africans have found myriad ways of participating as active agents in national life and global socio-economic processes, their victimhood notwithstanding. This point is further developed below under two subheadings: 'Resistance to state repression' and 'Creative appropriation of ICTs'.

It has been argued that citizenship and globalization are bazaars to which — to use the biblical expression — many Africans are called but few are chosen (cf. Nyamnjoh 2000). Cultural exclusion seems to be the order of the day, even as national and global rhetoric indicates otherwise. Like the rest of the world, Africans are generously invited by capital to partake of the standardized, routinized, streamlined and global consumer culture, of which McDonalds, Coca-Cola, CNN and satellite entertainment television such as DSTV are harbingers (Golding 1994: 7). However, given the level of poverty among Africans, only an elite few qualify (largely through corruption, embezzlement and the abuse of state power and office) to consume first- or second-hand. Global availability is not synonymous with global affordability. The majority have to content themselves with what (if anything) trickles down to them in the ghettoes and villages from relatives and patrons at the centre of power and resources. In the face of such inequities, it is difficult to envisage how ordinary Africans can relate to the global consumer culture in any terms other than the frustration and disenchantment it brings them. To most, globalization is nothing but the 'misery and incoherence of life in the suburbs' and villages; 'the collapse of public transport, state-run educational and public health services; the breakdown of electricity and sewage systems; the serious degradation of ... infrastructure and the sheer abuse of power by self-serving functionaries' (Devisch 1999: 5).

This leaves them and their cultures at the mercy of capital and the elite few in power. As part of a global ecumen for 'the transnationalization of … a supremely local and parochial set of images and values' from the West (Golding & Harris 1997: 9), the power elite in Africa cannot afford to pay more than lip service to local cultural production and reproduction. Their daily activities and behaviour undermine the very doctrine of the importance of upholding African cultural values. The identity and power conferred by joining the global consumer club explains why, despite much rhetoric about cultural renaissance in many African states, the ruling elites continue to acculturate themselves and to 'progressively take on the look of strangers in their own country due to their daily lifestyle, modeled on that of *homo consumens universalis*' (Amin 1980: 175). With a ruling elite whose weakness and marginality *vis-à-vis* global capitalism and its institutions of legitimation have been certified, consuming foreign consumer items becomes a major way of staking claim to power locally and of further mystifying the disaffected populations with whom they have lost credibility. At best, these elites commission 'traditional dances' and 'praise singing' cultural productions which they can use for their personal amusement or to entertain foreign friends and visiting counterparts. Performances that were reserved for solemn occasions in the past have been trivialized and in certain cases commodified for touristic consumption, partly for the gratification of the local elite but also because of the desperate quest by sidestepped cultural communities to survive through feeding consumer tourism.

Resistance to state repression

The processes and effects of co-optation or assimilation of the elite few by consumer capitalism, and how these elite few, in turn, use their consuming foreign as an identity marker and as a source of prestige, status and power have been discussed elsewhere (cf. Nyamnjoh 2000). Here the focus is more specifically on cultural resistance and the creative processes of appropriation underway. As far back as one cares to look, there is evidence that deprived and marginalized voices in Africa refused to celebrate victimhood. Far from giving up in the face of rigid colonial repression, threatened African nationalists eager to communicate their liberation agenda among themselves and with the African masses adopted various strategies: to publish and perish from the repressive axe of the colonial administration; to go underground with the press and its liberation rhetoric enhanced by pamphlets, tracts and word-of-mouth; to turn to or marry with alternative channels of communication such as the grapevine, political rumour and derision; and to use the indigenous media as a substitute or supplement to the shackled press. These strategies were as useful in the Algerian revolution as they were in the radical nationalism of Cameroon's *Union des Populations du Cameroun* (UPC) party, both against brutal French colonialism and racism. Frantz Fanon, as a member of the *Services de Presse du Front de Liberation Nationale* in Tunis, was able to take advantage of *El Moudjahid*, whose articles were not by-lined, to disseminate his revolutionary ideas on colonialism in Algeria and Africa. Thanks to such excessive control and creative responses, the press in Africa has, since colonial times, shared many characteristics with rumour and political derision, including identification with certain values, beliefs and outlooks commonly held by ordinary Africans, some of which may appear bizarre and highly implausible to Western reporters and readers (cf. Ellis 2000).

Faced with post-colonial repression in the 1970s and 1980s, Africans easily drew inspiration from the more muted forms of criticism of colonial times. Excessive control of the established media and other conventional channels of communication helped account for the popularity and importance of *Radio Trottoir*, *Pavement Radio* or *Rádio Boca a Boca*, which proved itself the perfect medium for communicating dissent and discussing the powerful in unflattering terms across the continent. In various countries where dictatorship and repression have thrived over democracy, *Radio Trottoir* has proved effective not only as a vehicle for popular and informal discussion of power and current affairs by urbanites in particular, but also as a counter-power: the 'poor-man's bomb' or the 'weapons of the powerless' in the face of government arbitrariness, water cannons, tear gas and guns. Usually in the form of anecdotal gossip, *Radio Trottoir* in Mobutu's Zaire for example, served the poor as 'a phenomenon of revenge and a rebuttal of censorship' against 'the totalitarian discourse of the Party-State', often through the display of 'an extraordinary verbal creativity', rich in humour, parody and irony (cf. Devisch 1995: 623-24).

In his famous 'Provisional Notes on the Postcolony', now part of his book *On the Postcolony*, Mbembe argues that political derision or humour directed at the autocrat is an attempt by ordinary folk to present the powerful as ordinary mortals with the same appetites and nature as any other person. 'Hence the image of, say, the President's anus is not of something out of this world — though to people's great amusement the official line may treat it as such; instead, people consider it as it really is, capable of defecating like any commoner's.' Through ridicule, Mbembe argues, ordinary people can tame, shut up and render powerless state power. The autocrat, stripped of his aura or magic, becomes domesticated — a mere idol, a familiar friend or a member of the family as much for the ruled as for the rulers (Mbembe 1992: 8-9). Rural pottery on the Ndop Plains of the Bamenda Grassfields thrives by carrying such domestication a step further through the mass production of clay figures of the president, his ministers, gendarmes and military officials for public consumption by the victims of the violence and misery over which they preside. With such banalization and given the fragility of its creation, the pottery contributes towards the neutralization of these otherwise omnipotent symbols of state power and terror.

Rumour, the most distinctive feature of *Radio Trottoir*, defines itself in opposition to official discourse, which it challenges and seeks to replace. The same is true of political cartooning in general, which could be described as the sketched or caricatured version of rumour about the high and mighty in society. Both political rumour and cartooning, it could be argued, are ways of cushioning the hardness of the crushing and stifling official discourse, which monopolizes the public sphere, often claiming to be the sole bearer of truth.

They are an unequivocal confirmation of the truism that withholding relevant information from the public results in desperate attempts by the public to invent that information, and that such inventions are seldom a flattering mirror of the status quo. Cultural vitality in silent spaces is thus the consequence of cultural repression in public spheres. Instead of dying out, repressed creativity reproduces itself in the most unlikely, veiled and often misleading ways. The more repressive the social and political environments, the more metaphorical the forms in which repressed creativity are reproduced.

In Africa today where there is a semblance of democratization, not only has *Radio Trottoir* and political derision become more open and daring, cartooning has joined the bandwagon of political commentary and satire. Caricatures of presidents and their ministers are now uncommon in the press. In Nigerian newspapers — *The Guardian* and *The Times* for example — cartoons in the 1980s and 1990s depicted political leaders and the military — their partners in power — in a very stereotypical fashion. Associated with the Nigerian politician in cartoons are such words as 'rigger, thug, area boy, hidden agenda', lexemes which imply 'a cheating, deceitful, crooked, and corrupt individuality, and emphasize the politician's lack of morals and ignorance and contempt for justice and fair play'. Through cartooning, politicians are stereotyped as 'completely selfish, self-centred, and self-indulgent, lacking in any altruistic thought, action, or motive', and being completely at variance with those they purport to serve. The military, in general, are depicted to be forceful, disdainful of propriety, indifferent to established rules and regulations, and as having 'a tendency towards absolutism and totalitarian control' (Medubi 2000: 200-205). This shows that cartoonists and the ordinary Nigerians and Africans who appreciate their art can 'see beyond the mask or veil of deception worn by the people in power' (Sekoni 1997: 143) and, with ambivalence, 'bring to the fore the challenge of identifying popular understandings of "democracy" that celebrate "the supremacy of the people" over dominant illusions and imposed edicts' (Gecau 1997: 151-59). This in itself is something that could be empowering, even if it does not bring about a revolution or the overthrow of the structures of inequality, mediocrity and cultural control. Increasingly though, in the context of the possibilities offered by increasing technological advances and media plurality, ubiquitous state control of public and private spheres is bound to diminish considerably with time. Hence a future for local and global cultural exchange facilitated by the media outside both the logic of state control and control by global capital may not be that difficult to contemplate.

Creative appropriation of ICTs

Regarding neoliberalism and the globalization of poverty, Africans have been equally creative in their responses, despite their perceived passivism and victimhood. Like other anti-neoliberal forces in the world, African activists have taken advantage of the new information and communication technologies to mobilize and strategize against the multinational corporations and the uncritical support they receive from African states. Prominent African activists such as Dennis Brutus, Trevor Ngwane and Fatima Meer of South Africa are leading members of the anti-globalization coalition that is increasingly becoming a headache for the WTO and the G8. A recent victory by popular forces against the giant pharmaceutical companies in South Africa in connection with the production of affordable generic versions of AIDS drugs locally is equally significant (cf. Bond 2001). Various formal and informal networks are taking advantage of the Internet to promote their agendas in situations where the conventional media continues to blunt aspirations for creative diversity in the global cultural landscape. Web pages and websites have sprung up to celebrate cultural diversity, even if only by elite academics, civil servants, lobbyists and NGOs representing the interests of diverse indigenous minorities such as the Baka Pygmies of the rainforest and the Bushmen of the Kalahari Desert, to the concerns of large cultural entities such as the Yoruba and the Zulu of Nigeria and South Africa respectively. Spokespersons for marginalized groups fighting for cultural recognition and representation have found inspiration, support, accommodation and hope on the Internet, and even ordinary people are benefiting enormously through direct or indirect connectivity.

Although connectivity in Africa is very low compared to other areas of the world (cf. Jensen 2000, Franda 2002), Africa's cultural values of sociality, interconnectedness, interdependence and conviviality (cf. Nyamnjoh 2002) make it possible for others to access the Internet and its opportunities without necessarily being connected themselves. In many situations, it suffices for a single individual to be connected for whole groups and communities to benefit. The individual in question acts as a point of presence or communication node, linking other individuals and communities in a myriad of ways (cf. Olorunnisola 2000) and bringing hope to others who would otherwise be dismissed as not belonging by capital and its excessive emphasis on the autonomous individual consumer.

In the Cameroonian city of Bamenda, for example, where resident telephone lines are grossly inadequate and defective at best, and where Internet connections are difficult and expensive, literate and illiterate people eager to stay in touch with relations, friends and opportunities within Cameroon and in the diaspora flood the few Internet points with messages to be typed and emailed on their behalf. Replies to their emails are printed out, addressed and pigeonholed for them by the operators who can only afford to check for mails twice a day because of exorbitant costs. What is noteworthy, however, is that

Internet and computer services are flourishing in Bamenda.
Photos: Francis Nyamnjoh

the high charges do not seem to temper the determination of those involved to stay in touch with the outside world. The names of some of the Internet businesses (e.g. 'Allied Bamenda' and 'Mondial Computers') reflect their determination to be connected and interconnected.

Through such connections, people are able to exchange news on family, projects, events and developments of a personal and general nature. They are also able to exchange news on different cultural products and to arrange how to acquire the products for one another. It is mainly through this means that Cameroonians abroad manage to stay in touch with local music releases, publications, satirical humour, artefacts and fashion. Each visitor to the home village is armed with a long list of cultural products to take back for him/herself, fellow Cameroonians and friends. Many unmarried young men and women in the diaspora would have given up hope of marrying someone from their home village or country and doing so in accordance with local customs and traditions, had email not been there to facilitate contacts and negotiations with parents and potential families-in-law.

In addition, the cosmopolitan identities of Cameroonians in the diaspora serve as itinerant billboards or as evangelists seeking converts to the cultures of their home villages. Thanks to such advertisements, Grassfields medicine and *ngangas* have been drawn to the West and other centres of modern accumulation where the rising interest in the occult is creating demand and opportunities for *marabouts*, *sangomas, ngangas* and *muti* or magic from Africa. The growing need for magical interpretations to material realities (Moore & Sanders 2001) under millennial capitalism (Comaroff & Comaroff 2000) has meant creating space on the margins for marginalized cultures and solutions. This would explain the back-street shops and dealers in African cultural products ranging from foods to charms and amulets. It also explains the fact that not all the customers visiting these shops and markets are diasporic Africans. The diaspora and the rest of the world are thus connected to the local, and both can work actively to ensure continuity for cultures and communities marginalized at the national and global levels by the big players. Lesson: it does not have to be big to be noticed.

The same creativity displayed in relation to the Internet is true of other technologies as well. The latest technology to be domesticated is the cell phone, which in South African townships and informal settlements, for example, has been used creatively by poor urban dwellers to stay in touch with rural relatives and through them maintain healthy communication with ancestors (cf. Thoka 2001). Under the current structural adjustment programmes, most African states have restructured and privatized parts of their telecommunication facilities, providing for cellular networks that have transformed telecommunications (cf. Ras-Work 1998). A case in point, once again, is Cameroon where 1998 saw the creation of the Cameroon Telecommunication Company (Camtel) by merging Intelcam and the Department of Telecommunications at the Ministry of Post and Telecommunications. Another company created was the Cameroon Telecommunication Mobile Company (Camtel Mobile), an affiliate of Camtel, with the specific duty of installing and exploiting mobile phones in the country. With this initiative, private investors such as Mobilis (or Orange) and MTN-Cameroon have since extended and improved upon the telecommunication services. From a fixed telephone network of around 87,000 subscribers after independence, Cameroon now boasts more than 200,000 cell-phone subscribers for MTN-Cameroon alone. Owning a telephone or being connected by Internet has, since 2000, become much less of a luxury for those who can afford it in the major cities. Even those who cannot afford a cell phone stand to benefit thanks to the sociality and solidarity of the local cultures of which they are a part (cf. Nyamnjoh 2002).

Most cell-phone owners in West Africa tend to serve as points of presence for their community, with others paying or simply passing through them to make calls to relatives, friends and contacts within or outside the country. Thus for example, although Nigerians might actually own fewer phones than most countries in the West, the country generates higher average revenue per user (ARPU) per month. The ARPU of a cell-phone user in Nigeria, with a GDP per capita of US$ 363, is US$ 91, which is five times that of South Africa with six times Nigeria's GDP per capita, and almost twice that of the United States, with close to 1,000 times Nigeria's GDP per capita. For a country with a low level of economic activity relative to G8 countries, Nigeria has a high level of minutes of use (MOU) of 200, compared to 154 in France, 88 in Germany, 149 in Japan, 118 in Italy, 249 in Canada, 120 in UK and 364 in the US (cf. Merrill Lynch Investment Bank 2002). These statistics could be explained by Nigerians receiving more calls than they make, and also by the reality of single-owner-multi-user (SOMU) communities. This suggests that the economic and social value (ESV) of a cell phone in countries like Nigeria and Cameroon with a higher volume of SOMU communities is much higher than the ESV of a cell phone in countries with single-owner-single-user (SOSU) communities. Contrary to popular opinion, sociality, interdependence and conviviality are not always an obstacle to profitability.

By way of further illustration, the Bamenda Grassfields of Cameroon are noted for their 'subversives' and for spearheading the questioning by Anglophones of the political and cultural domination of Cameroon by Francophones and French cultural values (cf. Konings & Nyamnjoh 2003). By using a cell phone, such dissidents or subversives are better able to bypass conventional channels of control with their messages of struggle to one another, and are easily alerted to possible danger by collaborators at the centre of state power. Dissidence can be planned and coordinated right up to the minute of execution by collaborators who do not have to be physically located in their national territories to be relevant and useful to ongoing struggles. At the social level, diasporic Grassfielders or migrants collectively supply a free phone to someone in their home village so they can call to give and receive messages from family and friends. Marriages, feasts, funerals, 'crydie' and village development initiatives can no longer pass any Grassfielder by simply because they are in the diaspora. The cell phone has become the long arm of the village chief or council, capable of reaching even the most distant 'sons and daughters of the soil' trapped in urban spaces with requests for the development of the home village (cf. Geschiere & Nyamnjoh 1998). The dramatic increase in the sales and theft of cell phones is an indication that this technology is welcome among Grassfielders exploring ways of denying exclusion to its smile of triumph.

Bamenda is also an example of how Africans are negotiating their cultures and creativity out of the artificial silence imposed on them by political and economic imperatives. The city has created space for cultural products of diverse origins and qualities. Bamenda has the latest high quality global entertainment television delivered by DSTV (Multi-Choice) and Canal Horizon of France to the elite few in their mansions and offices. It also boasts of poorer consumers seeking to catch up in bars, hotels, lodges, 'resting places' and chicken parlours using the same facilities as bait for customers big and small.

Bamenda is equally full of shops owned mainly by the Nigerian Igbo business community selling at affordable prices Nigerian-made and pirated films from Hollywood and Bollywood. Pirating may be a breach of copyright but it is also an indication of the desire to belong by those denied first-hand consumption of the cultural products in question. Anglophone Cameroonians in general are benefiting from the Nigerian cinema industry that has refused to wait until the time it is able to produce high-quality films with sophisticated modern technology. Using very basic equipment and releasing its products directly on video cassettes, Nigerian filmmakers have captured a large market among West Africans at home and in the diaspora, offering films more culturally relevant than even the most sympathetic Hollywood product. Such creativity has contributed to making Christianity more relevant to illiterate urban and village folks, as it is possible for 'Jesus of Nazareth', his white skin notwithstanding, to be betrayed, crucified and resurrected in Pidgin English and local Grassfields languages and, above all, to be affordable, thanks to dubbing and pirating. The films may flicker and frustrate even the most accommodating viewers but their popularity seems to suggest that a poorly produced culturally relevant film is better than none at all. This is also suggested by the ready availability of such gadgets as camcorders, digital cameras and VCRs that are ready to capture and immortalize the high points in the lives of individuals and communities. Births, marriages, funerals, 'crydies', graduation ceremonies and feasts are all moments to be captured for 'future memories', and not having a camera of one's own is hardly a deterrent given the number of photo studios, roving photographers and cameramen. Sons and daughters of the region working with the state television that is perceived to marginalize the English language and Anglophone culture, sometimes use their initiative and influence to direct the attention of the television camera to people and events from their home areas.

In the domain of scholarly production and creative writing, the climate of repression since independence has meant a dearth of local publishing in general and of quality in particular. Publishers have had to steer clear of all controversial material, which, given the sensitivity of government to anything mildly critical, has forced them out of business or reduced them to printers of inoffensive but unprofitable literature. Little of what is published in Cameroon can boast even an ISBN number. In the 1990s however, a semblance of political liberalization provided some individuals with the opportunity to get into desktop publishing. One of those to have distinguished themselves in this regard is Dr Linus Asong who has taken up self-publishing since the publication of his first novel, *Crown of Thorns*, in Canada. His desktop publishing company — Patron Publishing House — has even expanded to publishing other local writers, including a conversational autobiography of Ndeh Ntumazah, an opposition political leader who has spent the best part of his life fighting for a new political culture in Cameroon. Although the quality of printing and binding leaves a lot to be desired, Asong's hard work may have brought to the limelight novels, poetry and books that otherwise would never have made it into print in a situation where potential authors are either victims of administrative censorship or suffer a high rejection rate at the hands of commercial publishers. If and when there is a breakthrough, this is often on the publisher's terms and the profit motive is never disguised. Asong's efforts may be trivialized and mocked by colleagues with their heads in the clouds but they tell a story of resistance and hope worthy of emulation. Otherwise, much cultural creativity would continue to waste away on the periphery of the global cultural industries.

A similar situation exists in the local music industry. Although Cameroon has had an impressive list of stars with proven track records since independence, budding musicians find it difficult to make a breakthrough, partly because few of those who have succeeded have bothered to invest in the industry at home. Success seems to imply going to live in France, and coming home briefly for concerts or at the invitation of the ruling elite to celebrate a certain anniversary. The Bamenda Grassfields are arguably the region where there has been the least achievement in producing local pop stars. The reasons are not obvious but it is clear that Grassfielders love their indigenous music heritage. Gatherings and occasions at home or in the diaspora are always an excuse for singing, drumming and dancing to local rhythms. Amateur audio and video recordings are easy to come by, and are widely reproduced and circulated. Dedicated performers of dances are not difficult to find in cities where Grassfields elites may want to show off or entertain their guests with a bit of 'our culture'. Not wanting to be totally eclipsed, some elites have attempted to sponsor the production of local Grassfields talent, some of whom (Francis Ndom, Prince Afo-AKom, and 'Bottle Dance' musicians like Richard Nguti, John Minang, Ni Ken and Depipson) have made it to the national scene with music from their home area. These and other up-and-coming artists in the region and elsewhere shop around for sponsors ranging from businesses to NGOs and publicity-seeking elites, through other artists and the national orchestra.[3]

The quest for success does not exclude prostitution in various forms,[4] and the outcome is not always a foregone conclusion. But few give up too readily, even if this means a form of success limited to performing in bars and market places and at private functions like itinerant musicians and for very little pay. However limited the financial rewards, local performers do more than ensure continuity for their home cultures. They often have more space to articulate social criticism than their better-known foreign-based counterparts, and their poverty is in a way a blessing since it compels them to stay within Cameroon instead of migrating to France to celebrate success. Critical music in tune with popular expectations is not limited to the most disfavoured regions of the country. Even among the Beti whose Bikutsi music has been given greater prominence on state television and radio by the sheer fact of its association with President Paul Biya and his ethnic brethren in power, not all voices have been singing their praises. Critical Bikutsi songs have emerged among local performers to challenge complacency and support for President Biya, 'a son of the soil' who has repeatedly failed to deliver on promises even to those of his own ethnic kin (Onguene Essono 1996).

[3] John Minang's album, *Issiah*, carries advertisements for 'L&B', 'Beneficial Life Insurance' and 'PMUC'. Prince Afo-Akom obtained sponsorship from the World Wildlife Fund thanks to his song 'Our Environment', in which the WWF is mentioned positively.

[4] In order to get by, some Cameroonian musicians include in their lyrics the names of individuals seeking greater social or political visibility in exchange for monetary payments.

Conclusion

In most of Africa the threats to a free, open and participatory media system and cultural production are as much from repressive governments as from the interests of rich nations, international financial institutions and multinational capital. The chapter suggests that it is necessary to look beyond meta-narratives of euphoria and victimhood to understand how marginalized individuals and communities are responding to state repression and the global logic of cultural flows and closures.

The creative responses highlighted here and explored by others elsewhere (e.g. Friedman 1990, 1991, 1994, Gondola 1999) are only indicative of the ongoing efforts by ordinary Africans to be part of national and global processes on their own terms, even when clearly excluded by the structures in place. Together with the creative appropriation of ICT and second-hand consumer goods from the West, these responses are evidence that ordinary Africans are refusing to lose hope in the face of disenchantment with neoliberalism. New religions, some no less entrepreneurial than leading multinationals, have developed to capitalize on this resilience in ordinary Africans. They promise 'new hopes' for the 'cheerful givers' (cf. Meyer 1998, Van Dijk 1999) and their popularity is yet another indication of how determined Africans are to fight off exclusion. Together with healing churches informed by a creative marriage of African and Western traditions, the new churches are competing for material and spiritual attention among slum dwellers trapped by 'misery and hardship' in 'tragic spaces' (Devisch 1995, 1996). Pyramid schemes, casinos and games of chance have also fed on the resilience of ordinary folks, by provoking in them 'fantasies of abundance without effort', and leading them to believe in the possibility of 'beating capitalism at its own game by drawing a winning number at the behest of unseen forces' (cf. Comaroff & Comaroff, 2000: 297). Criminal rackets promising effortless immigration and work permits have sprung up to take advantage of the burning desire in ordinary people to succeed. Similarly, Nigerian *4-1-9* and Cameroonian *Feymen* fraudsters have equally used the Internet and cell phones creatively to access more people with their letter scams and fraudulent business deals that have brought some of them dazzling riches (cf. Fisiy & Geschiere 2001: 227-42, Malaquais 2001). Adults and children have been sold into slavery, and magical solutions are being increasingly sought for material predicaments (cf. Comaroff & Comaroff 2000, Moore & Sanders 2001). It is clear that the reality of exclusion in neoliberalism has created its own opportunists but in this opportunism should be seen the determination of ordinary Africans to forge on, victimhood notwithstanding. The creative responses hinted at in this chapter imply that it is hardly the end of the story to acknowledge disempowerment and marginalization, for in process (and often veiled or subtle) are countervailing forces in the service of hope. Because the 'Tam Tam' remains relevant, even as the Internet and the cell phone are being adopted and celebrated (cf. Ras-Work 1998), Africans are able to make the best of all worlds in a context where cultural survival has long ceased to be a matter of course. And thanks to their creativity, sociability, negotiation and conviviality, Africans have refused to endorse the requiem for their way of life. The future may well have much to draw from African world views and cultures, marginalized currently by power and wealth.

References

Ake, C. 2000, *The Feasibility of Democracy in Africa*, Dakar: Codesria.

Amin, S. 1980, *Class and Nation: Historically and in the Current Crisis*, London: Heinemann.

Amin, S. 1997a, 'Reflections on the International System', in: P. Golding & P. Harris (eds), *Beyond Cultural Imperialism: Globalization, Communication & the New International Order*, London: Sage, pp. 10-24.

Amin, S. 1997b, 'L'Afrique et le Développement', *Jeune Afrique Economie* 3 Février (234): 36-43.

Banda, F. 2000, 'Multichoice in Zambian Broadcasting: Choice? Whose Choice?', Paper presented at the Political Economy of the Media in Southern Africa Seminar, University of Natal, Durban, South Africa, 25-29 April.

Barber, K. 1997, 'Introduction', in: K. Barber (ed.), *Readings in African Popular Culture*, James Oxford: Currey, pp. 1-12.

Barnett, C. 1998, 'The Contradictions of Broadcasting Reform in Post-Apartheid South Africa', *Review of African Political Economy* 25 (78): 551-70.

Bayart, J.-F. 1993, *The State in Africa: The Politics of the Belly*, London: Longman.

Bond, P. 2001, *Against Global Apartheid: South Africa Meets the World Bank, IMF and International Finance*, Lansdowne: University of Cape Town Press.

Centre for African Studies, University of Cape Town 1998, *Teaching Africa: The Curriculum Debate at UCT*, Cape Town: University of Cape Town.

Chomsky, N. 1999, *Profit Over People: Neoliberalism and Global Order*, New York: Seven Stories Press.

Comaroff, J. & J. Comaroff 2000, 'Millennial Capitalism: First Thoughts on a Second Coming', *Public Culture* 12 (2): 291-343.

Devisch, R. 1995, 'Frenzy, Violence, and Ethical Renewal in Kinshasa', *Public Culture* 7 (3): 593-629.

Devisch, R. 1996, '"Pillaging Jesus": Healing Churches and the Villagisation of Kinshasa', *Africa* 66 (4): 555-85.

Devisch, R. 1999, 'Mimicry, Parody, and the 'Cannibalisation' of the French Master Language in the Prophetic Healing Churches of Kinshasa', Paper presented at the Department of Anthropology, University of Cape Town, South Africa, 30 April.

Duncan, J., 2000, 'Talk Left, Act Right: What Constitutes Transformation in Southern African Media?', Keynote address presented at the Political Economy of the Media in Southern Africa Seminar, University of Natal, Durban, South Africa, 25-29 April.

Eboussi Boulaga, F. 1993, 'L'Intellectuel Exotique', *Politique Africaine* 51, Octobre, 26-34.

Ellis, S. 2000, 'Reporting Africa', *Current History* 99 (637): 221-26.

Fardon, R. & G. Furniss (eds) 2000, *African Broadcast Cultures: Radio in Transition*, Oxford: James Currey.

Fishman, T.C. 2002, 'Making A Killing: The Myth of Capital's Good Intentions', *Harper's Magazine* August, 33-41.

Fisiy, C.F. & P. Geschiere 2001, 'Witchcraft, Development and Paranoia in Cameroon: Interactions between Popular, Academic and State Discourses', in: H.L. Moore & T. Sanders (eds), *Magical Interpretations, Material Realities: Modernity, Witchcraft and the Occult in Postcolonial Africa*, London: Routledge, pp. 226-46.

Franda, M. 2002, *Launching into Cyberspace: Internet Development and Politics in Five World Regions*, Boulder: Lynne Rienner Publishers.

Friedman, J. 1990, 'Being in the World: Globalization and Localization', *Theory, Culture & Society* (7): 311-28.

Friedman, J. 1991, 'Consuming Desires: Strategies of Selfhood and Appropriation', *Cultural Anthropology* 6 (2): 154-63.

Friedman, J. 1994, 'The Political Economy of Elegance: An African Cult of Beauty', in: J. Friedman (ed.), *Consumption and Identity*, Harwood Academic Publishers.

Gecau, K. 1997, 'The 1980s Background to the Popular Political Songs of the Early 1990s in Kenya', in: R. Zhuwarara, K. Gecau & M. Drag (eds), *Media, Democratization and Identity*, Harare: University of Zimbabwe, pp. 149-76.

Geschiere, P. & F.B. Nyamnjoh 1998, 'Witchcraft in the "Politics of Belonging": Democratization and Urban Migrants' Involvement with the Home Village', *African Studies Review* 41 (3): 69-91.

Gibbon, P., Y. Bangura & A. Ofstad (eds) 1992, *Authoritarianism, Democracy and Adjustment: The Politics of Economic Reform in Africa*, Uppsala: Nordiska Afrikainstitutet.

Golding, P. 1977, 'Media Professionalism in the Third World: The Transfer of an Ideology', in: J. Curran, M. Gurevitch & J. Woollacott (eds), *Mass Communication and Society*, London: Edward Arnold, pp. 291-308.

Golding, P. 1994, 'The Communications Paradox: Inequality at the National and International Levels', *Media Development* xii (4): 7-9.

Golding, P. & P. Harris (eds) 1997, *Beyond Cultural Imperialism: Globalization, Communication & the New International Order*, London: Sage.

Gondola, D.C. 1999, 'Dream and Drama: The Search for Elegance among Congolese Youth', *African Studies Review* 42 (1): 23-48.

Graybill, L. 2000, 'Lingering Legacy: Apartheid and the South African Press', *Current History* 99 (637): 227-30.

Hall, M. 1998, '"Bantu Education?" A Reply to Mahmood Mamdani', *CODESRIA Bulletin* (3&4): 33-36.

Hugo, P. 1998a, 'Transformation: The Changing Context of Academic in Post-Apartheid South Africa', *African Affairs* 97 (386): 5-27.

Hugo, P. 1998b, 'The Politics of "Untruth": Afrikaner Academics for Apartheid', *Politikon* 25 (1).

Ibrahim, Z. 1999, 'What Does "Community" Mean for Community Radio? Reality Check', *Rhodes Journalism Review* December, p. 15.

Jensen, M. 2000, 'Making the Connection: Africa and the Internet', *Current History* 99 (637): 215-20.

Jua, N.B. & F.B. Nyamnjoh 2002, 'Scholarship Production in Cameroon: Interrogating a Recession', *African Studies Review* 45 (2): 49-71.

Kagwanja, P.M. 1997, 'Post-Industrialism and Knowledge Production: African Intellectuals in the New International Division of Labour', *CODESRIA Bulletin* (3): 5-11.

Kom, A. 1991, 'Writing Under A Monocracy: Intellectual Poverty in Cameroon', *Research in African Literatures* 22 (1): 83-92.

Kom, A. 1996, *Education et Democratie en Afrique. Le Temps des Illusions*, Paris: L'Harmattan.

Konings, P. & F.B. Nyamnjoh 2003, *Negotiating an Anglophone Identity: A Study in the Politics of Recognition and Representation in Cameroon*, Leiden: Brill.

Lush, D. 1998, 'The Role of the African Media in the Promotion of Democracy and Human Rights', in: S. Kayizzi-Mungerwa, A.O. Olukoshi & L. Wohlgemuth (ed.), *Towards a New Partnership with Africa: Challenges and Opportunities*, Uppsala: Nordiska Afrikainstitutet, pp. 42-65.

Malaquais, D. 2001, 'Arts de Feyre au Cameroun', *Politique Africaine* (2): 101-19.

M'Bayo, R.T., C. Onwumechili & N.R. Nwanko (eds) 2000, *Press and Politics in Africa*, Lewiston, NY: Edwin Mellen Press.

Mbembe, A. 1992, 'Provisional Notes on the Postcolony', *Africa* 62 (1): 3-37.

Mbembe, A. 1997, 'The "Thing" & its Double in Cameroonian Cartoons', in: K. Barber (ed.), *Readings in African Popular Culture*, Oxford: James Currey, pp. 151-63.

McChesney, R.W. 1998, 'The Political Economy of Global Media', *Media Development* xlv (4): 3-8.

McChesney, R.W. 2001, 'Global Media, Neoliberalism, and Imperialism', *Monthly Review* 52 (10) http://www.monthlyreview.org/301rwm.htm.

Medubi, O. 2000, 'Leadership Stereotypes and Lexical Choices: An Example of Nigerian Cartoons', *International Journal of Comic Art* 2 (1): 198-206.

Merrill Lynch 2002, *Wireless Matrix — 4Q01: Quarterly Update on Global Wireless Industry Metrics*, Merrill Lynch & Co. Merchant Banks.

Meyer, B. 1998, 'Commodities and the Power of Prayer: Pentecostalist Attitudes Towards Consumption in Contemporary Ghana', in: B. Meyer & P. Geschiere (eds), *Development and Change*, Special Issue on 'Globalization and Identity: Dialectics of Flows and Closures', 29 (4): 751-76.

Mkandawire, T. 1997, 'The Social Sciences in Africa: Breaking Local Barriers and Negotiating International Presence. The Bashorun M.K.O. Abiola Distinguished Lecture Presented to the 1996 African Studies Association Annual Meeting', *African Studies Review* 40 (2): 15-36.

Mkandawire, T. 2002, 'Globalization, Equity and Social Development', *African Sociological Review* 6 (1): 115-37.

Mkandawire, T. & A. Olukoshi (eds) 1995, *Between Liberalisation and Repression: The Politics of Structural Adjustment in Africa*, Dakar: Codesria Books.

Mkandawire, T. & C.C. Soludo 1999, *Our Continent, Our Future: African Perspectives on Structural Adjustment*, Codesria/IDRC/Africa World Press: Dakar, Asmara.

Mongo Beti 1993, *La France Contre l'Afrique: Retour au Cameroun*, Paris: La Decouverte/essays.

Moore, H.L. & T. Sanders (eds) 2001, *Magical Interpretations, Material Realities: Modernity, Witchcraft and the Occult in Postcolonial Africa*, London: Routledge.

Murdock, G. 1994, 'The New Mogul Empires: Media Concentration and Control in the Age of Divergence', *Media Development* xli (4): 3-6.

Ngolet, F. 2000, 'Ideological Manipulations and Political Longevity: The Power of Omar Bongo in Gabon since 1967', *African Studies Review* 43 (2): 55-71.

Ngowet, L. 2001, *Petites Miseres et Grand Silence: Culture et Elites au Gabon*, Libreville: Editions Ndze.

Nyamnjoh, F.B. 1999, 'Cameroon: A Country United by Ethnic Ambition and Difference', *African Affairs* 98 (390): 101-18.

Nyamnjoh, F.B. 2000, '"For Many are Called but Few are Chosen": Globalization and Popular Disenchantment in Africa', *African Sociological Review* 4 (2): 1-45.

Nyamnjoh, F.B. 2001, 'Delusions of Development and the Enrichment of Witchcraft Discourses in Cameroon', in: H.L. Moore & T. Sanders (eds.), *Magical Interpretations, Material Realities: Modernity, Witchcraft and the Occult in Postcolonial Africa*, London: Routledge, pp. 28-49.

Nyamnjoh, F.B. 2002, '"A Child is One Person's Only in the Womb": Domestication, Agency and Subjectivity in the Cameroonian Grassfields', in: R. Werbner (ed.), *Postcolonial Subjectivities in Africa*, London: Zed Books, pp. 111-38.

Nyamnjoh, F.B. & N.B. Jua 2002, 'Introduction to a Special Issue: African Universities in Crisis and the Promotion of a Democratic Culture: The Political Economy of Violence in African Educational Systems', *African Studies Review* 45 (2): 1-26.

Nyamnjoh, F.B. & B. Page 2002, 'Whiteman Kontri and the Enduring Allure of Modernity Among Cameroonian Youth', *African Affairs* 101 (405): 607-34.

Obi, C.I. 2001, 'The Changing Forms of Identity Politics in Nigeria under Economic Adjustment: The Case of the Oil Minorities Movement of the Niger Delta', Uppsala: Nordiska Afrinkainstitutet, Research Report no. 119.

Olorunnisola, A.A. 2000, 'African Media, Information Providers and Emigrants as Collaborative Nodes in Virtual Social Networks', *African Sociological Review* 3 (1): 46-71.

Oloyede, B. 1996, *Press Freedom in Nigeria: A Critical Analysis of Salient Issues*, Abeokuta: Kunle Alayande Printing & Publishing Company.

Olukotun, A. 2002, 'Authoritarian State, Crisis of Democratization and the Underground Media in Nigeria', *African Affairs* 101 (404): 317-42.

Onguene Essono, L.M. 1996, 'La Démocratie en Chansons: Les Bikut-si du Cameroun', *Politique Africaine* 64, Décembre, 52-61.

Paterson, C.A. 1998, 'Reform or Re-colonisation? The Overhaul of African Television', *Review of African Political Economy* 25 (78): 571-83.

Pityana, N.B. 2000, 'South Africa's Inquiry into Racism in the Media: The Role of National Institutions in the Promotion and Protection of Human Rights', *African Affairs* 99 (397): 525-32.

Ras-Work, T. 1998, *Tam Tam to Internet: Telecoms in Africa*, Johannesburg: Betam Communications & Mafube Publishing.

Sekoni, R. 1997, 'Politics & Urban Folklore in Nigeria', in: K. Barber (ed.), *Readings in African Popular Culture*, Oxford: James Currey, pp. 142-46.

Shear, M. 1996, *WITS: A University in the Apartheid Era*, Johannesburg: Witwatersrand University Press.

Søndergaard, H. 1999, 'Some Reflections on Public Service Broadcasting', *Nordicom Review* 20 (1): 21-28.

Soyinka, W. 1994a, 'Culture, Memory and Development', in: I. Serageldin & J. Taboroff (eds), *Culture and Development in Africa*, Washington: The World Bank, 201-18.

Soyinka, W. 1994b, 'Democracy and the Cultural Apologia', *Afrika Spectrum* 29 (1): 5-13.

Syvertsen, T. 1999, 'The Many Uses of the 'Public Service' Concept', *Nordicom Review* 20 (1): 5-12.

Tedga, P.J.M. 1998, *Enseignement Supérieur en Afrique: La Catastrophe?*, Paris : L'Harmattan.

Teer-Tomaselli, R. 2001, 'Transformation, Nation-Building and the South African Media, 1993-1999', in: K. Tomaselli & H. Dunn (eds), *Media, Democracy and Renewal in Southern Africa*, Denver: International Academic Publishers.

Teer-Tomaselli, R. & K. Tomaselli 1996, 'Reconstituting Public Service Broadcasting: Media and Democracy during Transition in South Africa', in: M.B. Anderson (ed.), *Media and Democracy*, Oslo: University of Oslo Press.

Thoka, M.D. 2001, 'Cellphones, Ancestors and Rural/Urban Connections. Report of Research Conducted in Monwabisi Park in November 2000', Paper presented at joint conference of AASA and SASCA, UNISA, South Africa, 9-11 April.

Thomas, N.P. & P. Lee 1998, 'Editorial', *Media Development* xlv (4): 2.

Thompson, G. 1999, 'Introduction: Situating Globalization', *International Social Science Journal* LI (160): 139-52.

Tomaselli, K. & H. Dunn 2001, 'Reform and Outreach: Analysing Southern African Media', *Media Development* xlviii (2): 3-8.

Van Dijk, R. 1999, 'The Pentecostal Gift: Ghanaian Charismatic Churches and the Moral Innocence of the Global Economy', in: R. Fardon, W. van Binsbergen & R. van Dijk (eds), *Modernity on a Shoestring: Dimensions of Globalization, Consumption and Development in Africa and Beyond*, Leiden: EIDOS, pp. 71-90.

Van Kessel, I., 1998, 'Mass Media in South Africa: From Liberation to Black Empowerment', Paper presented at 'The Role of Media in Africa' seminar at the African Studies Centre, Leiden, the Netherlands, October 8.

3

Global media and violence in Africa: The case of Somalia

Jan-Bart Gewald

It has been argued that Africa has been sidelined in the global ICT revolution and that African societies appear to be cut off from global flows of information. Nevertheless, the manner in which war was waged in Somalia between 1991 and 1994 indicates that this global revolution has affected the manner in which war has come to be waged in Africa. African societies may indeed be cut off from owning and controlling the streams of images that reflect their continent, but they may, however, at times come to temporarily hijack and divert this stream of images, and ensure that images that support or reinforce their political aims come to be released into the global flow. In the case of Somalia, the real-time images of dead US soldiers being dragged through the streets of Mogadishu were sufficient to make the United States end their involvement in Somalia.

Introduction

Any form of good scholarship dealing with Africa would of necessity place African societies within the context of the wider and thus global world. The bulk of material dealing with Africa in the context of globalization has been dominated by economic studies, many of which fail to take cognisance of, let alone deal with, the social or cultural aspects of globalization. Fortunately, there is also a substantial amount of literature within the social sciences that deals with Africa in the context of globalization. Unfortunately some of this literature is esoteric, and thus generally unintelligible to the majority of readers, or anecdotal in the extreme.[1] It is often forgotten that anecdotes, though they may lead to complementary head-nodding and exclamations from admiring academic audiences, do not in themselves explain why events are taking place. Thus descriptions of Somali or Liberian gunmen bearing their arms in ways copied from US television shows may be interesting but do not explain why these men are taking up arms in the first place.[2] Wars in Africa cannot be adequately explained merely through reference to fashion. This is not to deny that styles and images may influence the manner in which wars are fought. In his work on northern Tanzania, Brad Weiss explicitly states that his focus is on the interplay of 'the imaginary' and 'the global', and it is in dealing with imagination that he makes the following tantalizing remarks:

> Far from (simply) an indulgence in escapist and illusory delusions, imaginative practice becomes essential to the very definition of reality as it is perceived and encountered. Conceived of in this way, fantasy becomes a medium through which to pursue the concrete processes by which consciousness is engaged in the world. A further insistence of many who address 'the imagination' is the recognition that such practices include far more than liberatory exercises in boundless, cultural creativity. Our interests in the imagination *must incorporate the fantasies of ethnic cleansing and other brutalities* as well as educational aspirations, regimes of mass consumption as well as utopian visions of democratic reform (Weiss 2001: 5, emphasis added).

In other words, imagination does not only include the pleasing and desired aspects of life, but can also just as often come to include the darker side of life, fantasies that include the hurt and destruction of others. However, ideas and fantasies in and of themselves are not sufficient explanation as to why violence should occur.[3] This is well presented by Clapham (2001) who, in dealing with developments in Sierra Leone, readily refers to aspects of a globalized popular culture in seeking to explain aspects of violence:

---

[1] To be sure there could be those who would wish to argue that there is no need for academic literature to be intelligible to the majority of readers. However, I do believe that the role of the academic is to seek to explain the world, and to do so in ways that are easily accessible to as large a group of people as possible.

[2] For an extreme example of this sort of material, see Amina Mama (2001), 'Gender in Action: Militarism and War' at: http://www.uct.ac.za/org/agi/papers/military.htm.
For an overview of some of these perceptions to be found in the popular media, see Ottosen (1994) and Kennedy (1993).

[3] Regarding the human mind, evil imagination and destructiveness, interested readers may wish to see Erich Fromm (1973) *The Anatomy of Human Destructiveness*, New York: Holt, Rinehart and Winston.

> The products of an alienated American youth culture, notably the Rambo film 'First Blood' and gangster rap music, were readily reinterpreted in local terms as symbolising and legitimising resistance against a repressive official structure. (Clapham 2001)[4]

Equally disturbing to the work that seeks to explain violence in terms of fashion, is that of the widely read and respected American commentator, Robert Kaplan (2001), who writes:

> As anybody who has had experience with Chetniks in Serbia, 'technicals' in Somalia, Tontons Macoutes in Haiti, or soldiers in Sierra Leone can tell you, *in places where Western Enlightenment has not penetrated* and where there has always been mass poverty, people find liberation in violence. … worrying about mines and ambushes frees you from worrying about mundane details of daily existence.[5]

For Kaplan, isolated Africa has not attained a 'certain economic, educational, and cultural standard' that would 'tranquillize' physical aggression that he sees as a part of being human. In other words, African primitives need to be civilized and, until this occurs, wars and violence will be the natural way of things in Africa.

There is a burgeoning literature that shows that the wars being fought out across the length and breadth of Africa are intimately connected to international global flows of weapons, drugs, diamonds and other trades. The work of Christopher Clapham, Stephen Ellis and Paul Richards on the wars in Sierra Leone and Liberia provide insight into the manner in which these wars take place within a global setting in which Africa is not an isolate. The genocide committed in Rwanda, and the subsequent Congolese wars, took place within a global context in which ethnic cleansing and crimes against humanity could be imagined — a context in which horrific examples of success are accessible and available to allow the imagined successful implementation of similar crimes against humanity. Yet to describe the violence committed in Rwanda, as the high priest of globalization studies Arjun Appadurai (1998: 905) does, as a vivisection of the body politic is assuredly poetic but far from explanatory.

> … bodily violence may be viewed as a form of vivisection, and as an effort to resolve unacceptable levels of uncertainty through bodily deconstruction. This approach may cast light on the surplus of rage displayed in many recent episodes of inter-group violence. … such extreme and intimate violence may partly lie in the

[4] http://www.ippu.purdue.edu/failed_states/2001/papers/CLAPHAM2.pdf
[5] Kaplan's view of Sierra Leone is countered by Richards (1996).

> deformation of national and local spaces of everyday life by the physical and moral pressures of globalization. [6]

It is generally accepted that the process of globalization has been in progress for decades, if not centuries. What is truly new in the last twenty years though has been the introduction of the electronic ability to compress space and time in a manner that is accessible to the majority of people on earth.[7] The major difference with the past is the amount of information and the speed with which both information and real-time images can be transferred from one point on the globe to another. In the whole globalization discussion, it is this issue of space-time compression that is the most important for our work. Having said this, it is necessary that examples as to how space-time compression has affected violence in Africa be presented. How has space-time compression qualitatively changed violence in Africa?[8] An example of violent conflict in Africa is examined here and the role of space-time compression discussed therein. It is in effect an argument about a specific form of space-time compression, namely the local and highly contested use and appropriation of features of the global spread of mass media and mass communication.[9]

Globalization and Iraq

In 1991 Peter Arnett, CNN's reporter-at-large, became the face and voice of the world's first globalized war. Standing on the roof of the Intercontinental Hotel in downtown Baghdad, Arnett covered the first air raids of the American-led Allied forces against Iraq. Television viewers around the world saw Operation Desert Storm unfold. At 3 a.m. in Baghdad, 1 a.m. in Amsterdam, and the

---

[6] See also Appadurai (1998: 906) 'Yet, to my knowledge, no single work has sought to explore the precise ways in which the ethnic body can be a theatre for the engagement of uncertainty under the special circumstances of globalisation'.

[7] Certainly telegraph and later telephone and even later wireless have been available from the 1860s onwards, but only for a limited audience and only within specific settings. The major transformation is the availability of real time mass-media images and mass communication.

[8] It has been in seeking to deal with the impact of globalization on Africa that the entire WOTRO globalization project was established in 1994.

[9] In his discussion of the information age, specifically in relation to questions of ownership, Castells (1997: 309-352) argues that the media, or rather access to media, has become the essential domain for politics. In this domain the most important issue is the (visual) image that puts a specific message across. In this struggle for images the most effective political message to be found is the image that conveys a negative message. Politics has, according to Castells, become the domain of images of spin.

beginning of prime time, 5 p.m. Eastern Standard Time in New York, anti-aircraft fire streamed through the air, the streaks of tracer bullets clearly visible on television screens around the world. Surface-to-air missiles rocketed into the sky, their thunderous blue-to-orange exhaust trails sporadically dominating television images. Approximately half an hour after the anti-aircraft barrage had begun, the first incoming cruise missiles and other ordinance launched miles away began exploding in and around Baghdad. Explosions lit up the Baghdad skyline, and seconds later the rumbling sound of the same explosions reached Peter Arnett and his CNN news crew standing on the hotel rooftop in the centre of Baghdad.[10]

Drinking bourbon and nibbling anchovies, I, along with the rest of the modern world, watched on TV the opening stages of the world's first truly globalized media war. For 17 hours, thanks to the services of CNN and Peter Arnett, the world could see, live before their very own eyes, the unfolding of an allegedly new era of warfare, in which media, smart bombs and the near total absence of Allied casualties on the Alliance's side were the order of the day. This did not mean that there was no carnage.[11] As the war progressed, Alliance forces killed tens of thousands of Iraqi conscripts. Iraqi soldiers came to be buried in their trenches by American bulldozers, Iraqi troops and Iraqi and Palestinian refugees fleeing Kuwait were strafed and killed,[12] and the world's largest conventional ordinance, euphemistically known as the 'daisy cutter',[13] was dropped on Iraqi positions. For all its extensive media coverage, this, the seedier reality of war, was not transmitted to the world's television audiences. Instead, they were presented with what became known as the 'Incubator Scam'.

---

[10] Peter Arnett no longer works for CNN but those interested can contact him directly via his personal website: http://www.peterarnett.com/

[11] For an excellent first-hand view of the Gulf War by an American marine, see Swofford (2003).

'We fire and fire the AKs, a factory of firepower, the fierce scream of metal downrange and discharged cartridges and sand flying everywhere, now all of us shooting in the air, shooting straight up and dancing in circles, dancing on one foot, with the mad, desperate hope that the rounds will never descend, screaming, screaming at ourselves and each other and the dead Iraqis surrounding us, screaming at ourselves and the dead world surrounding us, screaming at ourselves, at the corpses surrounding us and the dead world. . . . And I know we'll soon carry that mad scream home with us, but that no one will listen because they'll want to hear the crowd-roar of victory.'

[12] For a report on the 'Highway of Death', see URL: http://deoxy.org/warcrime.htm. This site contains a report compiled by Ramsey Clark who served as Attorney-General in the Johnson administration. Clark was convenor of the Commission of Inquiry for the International War Crimes Tribunal that presented the report in New York on 11 May 1991.

[13] For technical details and gung-ho views on the 'daisy cutter', see: http://www.fas.org/man/dod101/sys/dumb/blu-82.htm.

In it, the audience of the US television programme *Sixty Minutes* was presented with a bereft and distraught Kuwaiti nurse who stated that she had personally witnessed Iraqi troops throw new-born babies out of incubators in a hospital in Kuwait City. It was only later that this turned out to be a propaganda hoax, and the nurse none other than the daughter of the Kuwaiti ambassador to the United States. [14]

It is a truism, but the first casualty in war is indeed the truth. However, it has also been said that reality is what you can get away with. From the very beginning, the Gulf War was the mother of all media wars. Every evening for the duration of Operation Desert Storm, Allied commanders presented the world with clinically clean videogame images of missiles thudding into buildings and bunkers — and never any bodies. Norman Schwarzkopf, Colin Powell and others gloated at the Iraqi driver who failed to look in his rear-view mirror. Live, real time, in our living rooms, bars and workplaces, we watched beleaguered Israeli citizens collecting government-issued gas masks and sealing their apartments against imminent Iraqi attacks. American Patriot missiles rocketed into the night sky above Tel Aviv and allegedly intercepted incoming scuds, whilst crack British SAS teams sought out and destroyed mobile scud launch sites in Iraq. But, was it the truth? When Peter Arnett, now a well-known name, reported on the bombing and destruction of a baby-milk factory in a US bombing raid, CNN was put under pressure to ditch him.[15] When journalists began reporting on the Highway of Death, the war was over, and nobody wished to entertain the suggestion that Alliance soldiers could ever have committed war crimes.[16]

The Gulf War, which ended with American forces being feted in a ticker-tape parade through New York City, was — from the beginning to the end — a global media event.[17] Live, the citizens of the world could see how the United States overcame its Vietnam syndrome and pounded home the truth that henceforth the United States of America was the Lone Ranger, the sole superpower answerable to none.

In the aftermath of the Gulf War, American military strategists, when analysing their total and devastating victory, took on board the concept of the 'Revolution in Military Affairs' (RMA), otherwise known as the 'Military Technical Revolution' (MTR). RMA is a concept that, interestingly enough,

---

[14] For a report on this fabrication and others like it, see http://www.fair.org.

[15] In 1995, when Arnett returned to Baghdad, the baby-milk factory was back in production.

[16] This even though RAF pilots refused to take part in the carnage that was taking place.

[17] With regard to the first Gulf War, see, in particular, Baudrillard (1995). For a further interesting and humorous view on these issues, see Castells in discussion with Harry Kreisler: http://globetrotter.berkeley.edu/people/Castells/castells-con4.html

developed out of what had initially been dubbed 'military technical revolutions' by Soviet military planners. In the 1970s, Soviet military theorists identified periods of fundamental change in military affairs, and sought to theorize these changes. By the early 1980s, Soviet military theorists recognized and began considering 'the implications for future war of technological advances in microelectronics, sensors, precision-guidance, automated control systems, and directed energy' (Watts 1995). In 1988, Discriminate Deterrence, the American commission of inquiry on long-term defence strategy, submitted a report suggesting amongst other things:

> Dramatic developments in military technology appear feasible over the next twenty years. They will be driven primarily by the further exploitation of microelectronics, in particular sensors and information processing, and the development of directed energy. These developments could require major revisions in military doctrines and force structures. ... [T]he Soviet military establishment is already engaged in a major effort to understand the military implications of new technologies, and appears to have concluded that revolutionary changes in the nature of war will result. The much greater precision, range, and destructiveness of weapons could extend war across a much wider geographic area, make war much more rapid and intense, and require entirely new modes of operation. (Iklé, Wohlstetter *et al.* 1988)

Seen in this light, particularly with its emphasis on ICT, RMA is very much part and parcel of the process referred to as globalization.[18] The work of Ajay Singh (1995-96), which emphasizes the changes that have been brought about in what he refers to as the 'Space-Time Paradigm' is particularly relevant here. In March 1993 the Center for Strategic and International Studies (CSIS) published a report entitled 'The Military Technical Revolution: A Structural Framework', in which it was declared that MTR was 'a fundamental advance in technology, doctrine, or organization that renders existing methods of conducting warfare obsolete' (cited in Watts 1995: 4). It was with this doctrine in mind that the United States prepared to wage war in Somalia.

---

[18] There is a fair amount of literature available on RMA and MTR. However readers seeking a finely written and strident introduction are directed to read, M.J. Mazarr (1994), *The Revolution in Military Affairs: A Framework for Defense Planning*. The publication can be accessed at:
http://carlislewww.army.mil/usassi/ssipubs/pubs94/rma/rma.pdf

Somalia

'We know you better than you know us.' (Hassan al Tourabi)[19]

Of late, al hadji Osama Bin Laden has appropriated a substantial amount of airtime on the world's various media networks. In his ever-extending fifteen minutes of fame, Bin Laden has been wont to state that events in Somalia proved to him that the United States of America could be beaten.

The end of the Cold War had serious implications for states in Africa.[20] In the Horn of Africa, Somalia and Ethiopia were countries that had vacillated between Soviet and US support. In both instances the withdrawal of superpower support for their respective regimes had major implications. Ethiopia came to be divided into two separate states, and Somalia collapsed into anarchy. In March 1991, US Assistant Secretary of State Herman Cohen declared Somalia to be a civil strife disaster, after which the Office of Foreign Disaster Assistance began funding relief efforts there.

Immediately after the Gulf War, the position of George Bush Sr. as president of the United States of America appeared unassailable. However, the substantial public support that Bush had enjoyed evaporated by the middle of 1992. In the immediate run-up to the presidential campaign, the Bush administration attempted to shore up the president's ever worsening position. On 14 August 1992, a month prior to the start of the presidential campaign, the Bush administration turned its attention to Somalia again and ordered a major airlift of relief supplies (Operation Provide Relief).

Operation Provide Relief, like other attempts to provide relief to the starving in Somalia, ground to a halt and in the absence of a centralized authority, relief workers were unable to transport goods to their intended destinations. In keeping with the logic of a scarce market, a situation had developed in Somalia in which a multitude of armed factions demanded taxes prior to allowing the transportation of food aid through their territory. Without protection, food convoys were unable to move and calls for solid and sustained military intervention in support of the food convoys were voiced. In November, with the presidential elections over, US aid agencies and members of Congress lobbied to have the US take greater action in Somalia. Undoubtedly, George Bush Sr, who had just been crushingly defeated in the presidential elections by Bill Clinton and had seen his stature fall from all-conquering world leader to

---

[19] Dr Hassan al Tourabi is a graduate of the University of Oxford and the Sorbonne, founder of the Sudanese National Islamic Front, and a former friend and colleague of Osama Bin Laden.

[20] Regarding the ending of the Cold War and its impact on Africa, see, amongst others, Akinrinade (1998), Oyebade & Alao (1998) and Furley (1995).

unpopular president, saw in the situation that was developing in Somalia an opportunity which could allow his presidency to end with a positive flourish, and ensure his entry into the proverbial history books as a good and benevolent president.[21]

To the world's sole superpower, the assorted and factious gunmen scattered across the former state of Somalia appeared to be a walkover. Having overcome their Vietnam syndrome in the Gulf War, the United States of America proceeded to walk slap bang into the Somalia syndrome.

At the end of November 1992, the outgoing Bush administration decided to commit 28,000 US troops to spearhead an armed intervention in Somalia in support of UN relief efforts. On 4 December, the United Nations Security Council voted to support US intervention, and George Bush went live on television to address the nation:

> There is no government in Somalia. Law and order have broken down. Anarchy prevails. ... It's now clear that military support is necessary to ensure the safe delivery of the food Somalis need to survive. ... And so, to every sailor, soldier, airman, and Marine who is involved in this mission, let me say you're doing God's work. We will not fail. Thank you, and may God bless the United States of America.[22]

From the very beginning, Operation Restore Hope was a major media event. Work conducted elsewhere indicates that it was only following Bush's decision to intervene that media coverage of Somalia truly expanded. In other words, contrary to voiced opinion, media attention had in itself not been responsible for the president's decision to intervene (Robinson 2000, 2002). Though printed media coverage increased substantially, it was specifically in the sphere of live television coverage that truly absurd situations developed. In the days immediately after Bush's announcement, media teams from the competing networks scurried around the various possible landing sites that might be used by the intervention force. Camera crews, some with portable generators, set up camp at what appeared to be the most likely landing sites. In the event, the US Joint Chiefs of Staff did not disappoint the many and varied media concerns. In the early hours of 9 December 1992, heavily armed US marines and Navy Seals

[21] To be sure there is another far more sinister line of reasoning that relates US intervention in Somalia to the machinations of Bush and his staff to further support oil prospecting rights on Somali territory. See 'The Oil Factor in Somalia', an article by Mark Fineman in the *Los Angeles Times*, 18 January 1993:
http://www.netnomad.com/fineman.html
A similar view can be found at: http://www.casi.org.uk/discuss/2001/msg01143.html

[22] President Bush's address to the nation on 4 December 1992, cited in Robinson (2001).

landed on the beaches around Mogadishu in a blaze of flashbulbs and live worldwide television coverage.

Live, real time, those preparing evening meals for their loved ones in New York City could watch as, halfway round the world, US forces — who were the epitome of Hollywood's finest soldiers — stormed ashore. In the nights prior to the US forces' landing, camera crews had anxiously peered out to sea, providing their worldwide audiences with expansive shots of an empty sea accompanied by newspeak debating and announcing the imminent arrival of American forces. When the forces did finally arrive, irate Defence Department spokesmen chided the media crews for being there, not realizing the apparently precarious and dangerous nature of their position. If anything, the landing of America's finest on the shores of Somalia in a blaze of publicity served to emphasize to all observers the importance of publicity and media in the modern world. Andrew Purvis, a journalist currently working for *Time* magazine, recently wrote:

> I was on the beach when US troops arrived in Mogadishu in 1992, and the feeling around me that tempestuous night was a mixture of euphoria and awe. Most Somalis genuinely welcomed the US deployment, waving as Navy Seals in face paint and black camouflage waded ashore. They believed the US would help rid them of the anarchy and famine that had already left tens of thousands dead. AK-47-toting militiamen in their cloth wraps and rubber sandals were also impressed by the military show, not knowing what the US colossus was capable of. Within a few months, all that had changed. (Purvis 2002)

Prior to becoming involved in Somalia, the US National Security Council commissioned think tanks in the United States to submit reports recommending what was to be done should the United States choose to intervene in Somalia. An operational concept plan, 'Military Intervention in Somalia', was drawn up by Frederick C. Cuny on behalf of the Carnegie Endowment for International Peace and the Center for Naval Analysis, and submitted to the US NSC.[23] Apart from listing recommendations with regard to the operational concept — Objectives, Force Structure, Security Zones, Exclusion Zones, and so forth — the eleven-point plan included the following final paragraph:

> The most troublesome element is the likelihood of sniping. There will undoubtedly be some individuals and possibly groups who will find cause to fire upon US or allied troops. The terrain outside the city is not suitable for ambushes or sniping; it is flat and open. The most likely place for sniping will be Mogadishu since it alone

[23] A copy of this report is to be found at: http://www.pbs.org/wgbh/pages/frontline/shows/cuny/laptop/somalia.html.

> offers concealment and escape possibilities. For this reason, it is strongly recommended that US and allied forces stay out of the city.[24]

Three days after landing in Somalia, American forces were in combat. From then onwards, with intermittent periods of relative calm, they became drawn ever deeper into war. After being initially overawed by the intervention force, Somali combatants came to challenge American forces increasingly openly. Within a month of their arrival, American forces had identified Mohammed Farah Aidid as their primary opponent. On 12 January 1993, the first marine was killed whilst on patrol in Mogadishu and from then onwards, slowly but surely, Somali combatants gained in confidence, and the American forces were constantly harassed by snipers operating in the city. Time and again, even though gun ships attacked Somali positions, American forces were subjected to surprise attacks. Eventually, after seven months of bungling, many wounded and a number of dead, members of the 3rd Battalion 75th Ranger Regiment and the 1st Special Forces Operational Detachment (DELTA) were deployed to Somalia with orders to capture Aidid. In conjunction with this deployment, Operation Eyes Over Mogadishu was started. It entailed round-the-clock surveillance of Mogadishu by Lockheed Orion surveillance planes and helicopters supported by helicopter gun ships, and helicopter troop carriers.

America's involvement in Somalia was predicated on a positive media image: American forces guarding food-aid convoys and aiding the starving and needy. This image changed completely when Wild West 'wanted' posters bearing Aidid's image appeared throughout Mogadishu.[25] In support of these posters, and in an attempt to minimize American casualties:

> The U.S. launched its campaign from the air, using attack helicopters and AC-130 Specter gun ships to carry out what military analysts confidently described to the world's media as 'surgical' strikes. They were not. In the most notorious incident — to Somalis, anyway — Cobra gun ships blasted a tall white stucco building in central Mogadishu in July 1993. The target was a well-publicized meeting of clan elders loyal to Aidid, but the victims, some 70, included innocent civilians. Word of the strike spread quickly through Mogadishu's alleyways and coffee houses. When a

[24] The Operational Concept Plan justified its recommendation that American forces refrain from entering Mogadishu by referring directly to the costly lessons learnt by the Indian army in its failed operations in Jaffna Town in Sri Lanka, and suggested that, should Mogadishu be included, the British should be encouraged to 'commit an experienced force ex Northern Ireland to manage the irregular urban warfare threat'.

[25] Robert Oakley, US Ambassador to Somalia between November 1992 and May 1993, noted that the reward of US$25,000 was an insult.
http://www.pbs.org/wgbh/pages/frontline/shows/ambush/interviews/oakley.html

> handful of foreign journalists arrived at the scene, Somalis, including women and children, turned on them and beat four to death. (Purvis 2002)

The killing of the four western journalists unleashed a storm of protest in the West, and must have provided Aidid and his planners with an indication as to how they could strike back at the 'Lone Ranger'.

But who was Mohammed Farah Aidid, the man so anxiously sought and vilified by the Americans? Aidid had been a general in the Somali national army, and as such had enjoyed military training in both the East and the West.[26] In the late 1980s Aidid was instrumental in deposing the Somali dictator Mohammed Siad Barre and in the ensuing chaos in which Somalia came to be torn apart, Aidid became president of what remained of Somalia. Even so, American forces treated him with the utmost contempt, placed a price on his head and declared him a bandit, a thug and a warlord. To be sure, this view of Aidid was reinforced every time militiamen allied to Aidid demanded payments and prevented food convoys from moving through areas under their jurisdiction. Nevertheless, the truth remains that he was simply dismissed as a serious opponent, yet he — more than any other general since Giap — defeated American forces at their own game.

Aidid was effectively trapped in Mogadishu, yet to all observers it was clear that the United States was reluctant to commit forces on the ground in the city. Instead, as was noted above, US forces preferred to attempt to reach their objectives by pounding their alleged opponents with cannon fire from the air. Dropping specialized units from helicopters into the city complemented this strategy. In keeping with Operation Eyes Over Mogadishu, helicopters continually flew over the city, aircraft that — as Aidid's forces so capably showed — could be shot down with the simplest of weapons. On 3 October 1993 an American helicopter attempting to 'exfiltrate' an American unit was shot down by a RPG 7, a simple shoulder-fired rocket-propelled grenade. The aircraft crashed and was immediately surrounded and attacked by Aidid's soldiers. When another American helicopter attempted to provide support for the downed aircraft, it too was shot down, also by an RPG 7. With two of their aircraft shot down in the city, American forces attempted to reach them overland but to do so they too had to enter the city — terrain held by Aidid's forces. American armoured personnel carriers sent into the city ran into ambushes.[27] In this single event, an estimated 1,500 to 2,000 Somalis, including

---

[26] Mohammed Farrah Aidid's son and successor, Hussein Mohammed Aidid, possessed American citizenship and returned to Somalia as a US marine in 1992. See: http://news.bbc.co.uk/hi/english/world/africa/newsid_1146000/1146654.stm.

[27] For a profoundly disturbing view of these events: http://www.angelfire.com/ne2/somalia/enter.index.html.

non-combatants, were killed and wounded, whilst 18 US servicemen were killed and no less than 78 wounded.[28]

American forces had effectively flown, driven and crashed into a terrain in which all of their high-tech communications equipment counted for nought. Citations for 'Medals of Honor', posthumously awarded by the US army to two of its snipers killed in the events of 3 October, clearly indicate the nature of the terrain:

> When debris and enemy ground fires at the site caused them to abort the first attempt, Sergeant First Class Shughart and his team leader were inserted one hundred meters south of the crash site. Equipped with only his sniper rifle and a pistol, Sergeant First Class Shughart and his team leader, while under intense small arms fire from the enemy, fought their way through a dense maze of shanties and shacks to reach the critically injured crew members. Sergeant First Class Shughart pulled the pilot and the other crew members from the aircraft…[29]

The pilot, Chief Warrant Officer Michael Durant, survived the engagement but was captured by Aidid's forces.

Immediately after the battle, on the morning of 4 October, jubilant Somalis dragged the body of an American soldier through the streets of Mogadishu. CNN broadcast these unedited images live to the world. Abdullahi Hassan, who acted as Aidid's propaganda minister, arranged for CNN to receive a copy of the video footage of the captured pilot stating: 'Innocent people being killed is not good'. Durant was held captive for eleven days by Aidid's forces during which time Abdullahi Hassan allowed the competing media networks access to Durant and the world received images of a frightened young American being held captive and being cared for by the followers of Aidid. He told Mark Huband, a journalist with *The Guardian*:

> Too many innocent people are getting killed. People are angry because they see civilians getting killed. I don't think anyone who doesn't live here can understand what is going wrong here. Americans mean well. We did try to help. Things have gone wrong.

Within a month of Durant's capture, all American servicemen had been withdrawn from Mogadishu. Aidid had defeated the world's sole superpower

[28] Malaysian and Pakistani soldiers assisted the American forces that entered Mogadishu. Many of them were also killed and wounded. Robert Oakley (US Ambassador to Somalia) estimated the number of Somali casualties in an interview with PBS: www.pbs.org/wgbh/pages/frontline/ shows/ambush/interviews. See also Hirsch & Oakley (1995).

[29] http://www.army.mil/cmh-pg/mohsom.htm.

and, as Osama Bin Laden has been happy to point out, Somalia proved that America could be defeated.

In Somalia, Mohammed Farah Aidid hijacked the weapons of the powerful and used them for his own aims. The US intervention in Somalia was determined and defined by the media and in the aftermath of the Gulf War, the US public had come to expect and anticipate clean real-time live images of their men doing 'God's' work. That this medium could also provide them with real-time live images of mangled American bodies and frightened captured young men had not been anticipated, and no amount of spin-doctoring could prevent it. In Somalia, Aidid took control of, if only for a short period of time, part of the arsenal of ICT superiority that the US had, and used it against them. Hungry for their media ratings, international media companies struggled with one another to scoop the images that would terminate America's involvement in Somalia, and subsequently Rwanda. Direct real-time images of death and destruction, a development that had been made possible by the rapid advances in ICT, spread around the world. From Tokyo to Johannesburg, Sao Paolo, New York and San Francisco, audiences heard the words and saw the face of the frightened young pilot urging America to withdraw, and within the space of a month America withdrew.

> There was no longer any support for the US to engage Somalis in combat as far as the US public was concerned. The impact of Americans being dragged through the streets, a large number of Americans killed and wounded without any real explanation by the White House, in advance, of why we were there. The fact that the mission was no longer a humanitarian mission. That we were somehow engaged in a war and why this war was worthwhile meant that there was no support whatsoever for any sort of active operation, other than self-defense military operations in Somalia.[30]

The reaction by the United States to events in Somalia had wide-ranging repercussions. Bosnian Serbs publicly celebrated developments in Somalia, secure in the knowledge that they would never have to face US troops in face-to-face combat (Power 2002). With events in Somalia in mind, Rwandan extremists planning to commit genocide developed a plan of action that would guarantee the withdrawal of foreign European troops from Rwanda. On 11 January 1994, Major General Romeo Dallaire, the Canadian officer commanding the United Nations Assistance Mission of Rwanda (UNAMIR) contacted UN headquarters in New York and transmitted a coded cable via satellite. The cable proves that by as early as January 1994, the world had knowledge about the impending genocide. In his cable Dallaire referred to a

[30] http://www.pbs.org/wgbh/pages/frontline/shows/ambush/interviews/oakley.html

Rwandan informant, a 'very very important government politician. ... is a top level trainer in the cadre of interhamwe'.

> He informed us he was in charge of last Saturday's demonstrations whose aims were to target deputies of opposition parties coming to ceremonies and Belgian soldiers. They hoped to provoke the RPF BN to engage (being fired upon) the demonstrators and provoke a civil war. Deputies were to be assassinated upon entry or exit from Parliament. Belgian troops were to be provoked and if Belgians soldiers resorted to force a number of them were to be killed and thus guarantee Belgian withdrawal from Rwanda.[31]

Hijacking the powerful

Castells has noted that one of the prime constraints on the fighting of wars for rich countries is the flow of information:

> It's not just that people no longer feel there are values worth dying for, but their ability to get information about what's happening on the battlefield is the kind of information flow that leaders who want to engage in war have to respond to, and are therefore forced to get out of the war quickly.[32]

That this is the case has been clearly brought to the fore by what happened in Somalia and later Rwanda. In both cases, the weapons of the powerful — here the media — could and can be hijacked for a short period of time and then released again. This temporary ownership has effects and results that are totally unintended on the part of the powerful. In and of itself there is nothing new about the images being presented, yet what is new is the speed, pervasiveness and quantity of the material being presented. When the Germans were defeated in battle in Namibia in the late 19th century it took at least four months before the defeat could be avenged, yet when Aidid shot down a helicopter above Mogadishu, the change was immediate. The example of Somalia indicates that there is a struggle for access to media streams. It also highlights the need for further study on how local actors use international media streams to advance their own aims that is a move away from the anecdotal and a move into the concrete. In essence, the case of Somalia is a further example of the struggle, on the part of Africans, to develop ways and means with which to divert and hold,

[31] A copy of this cable is to be found at:
http://www.pbs.org/wgbh/pages/frontline/shows/evil/warning/cable.html.

[32] http://globetrotter.berkeley.edu/people/Castells/castells-con4.html

even if for only a limited amount of time, the streams of information and goods that flow around the globe.

References

Akinrinade, S. 1998, *Africa in the Post-Cold War International System*, London: Pinter.

Appadurai, A. 1998, 'Dead Certainty: Ethnic Violence in the Era of Globalisation', *Development and Change* 29 (1998): 905-25.

Baudrillard, J. 1995, *The Gulf War Did Not Take Place*, Bloomington/Indianapolis & Sydney: Indiana University Press & Power Publications.

Castells, M. 1997, *The Power of Identity: The Information Age — Economy, Society and Culture*, Oxford: Blackwell Publishers, pp. 309-52.

Clapham, C. 2001, 'Sierra Leone: The Global-local Politics of State Collapse and Attempted Reconstruction', Paper prepared for the Failed States Conference, Florence, 10-14 April.

Furley, O. 1995, *Conflict in Africa*, London: Tauris Academic Publishers.

Hirsch, J.L. & R.B. Oakley 1995, *Somalia and Operation Restore Hope: Reflections on Peacemaking and Peacekeeping*, Washington: United States Institute of Peace.

Iklé, F.C. & A. Wohlstetter *et al.* 1988, 'Discriminate Deterrence', Washington DC: US Government Printing Office, p. 8, cited in: B.D. Watts, *What Is RMA, What Is the 'Revolution in Military Affairs'*, Northrup Grumman Analysis Center 703 (351): 3.

Kaplan, R.D. 1994, 'The Coming Anarchy: How Scarcity, Crime, Overpopulation and Disease are Rapidly Destroying the Social Fabric of our Planet', *Atlantic Monthly* February.

Kennedy, F. 1993, 'In Somalia, Machiavelli vs. Rambo', *New York Times*, 22 July.

Mazarr, M., J. Shaffer & B. Ederington 1993, 'The Military Technical Revolution: A Structural Framework', Washington: CSIS.

Ottosen, R. 1994, 'Rambo in Somalia? A Critical Look at the Media Coverage of Operation Restore Hope', Paper presented to the 6th MacBride Round Table, Honolulu, Hawaii, 20-23 January.

Oyebade, A. & A. Alao 1998, *Africa After the Cold War: The Changing Perspectives on Security*, Trenton, NJ: Africa World Press.

Power, S. 2002, 'Genocide and America', *The New York Review of Books*, 14 March.

Purvis, A. 2002, 'One Lesson Worth Remembering', *Time*, 20 February.

Richards, P. 1996, *Fighting for the Rain Forest: War, Youth & Resources in Sierra Leone*, Oxford: James Currey.

Robinson, P.G. 2000, 'The News and Intervention: Critical Media Coverage, Policy Uncertainty and Air Power Intervention During Humanitarian Crisis', Paper for the Political Studies Association UK 4th Annual Conference, London, 10-13 April.

Robinson, P.G. 2001, *Operation Restore Hope and the Illusion of a News Media Driven Intervention*, Oxford: James Currey.

Robinson, P.G. 2002, *The CNN Effect: The Myth of News Media, Foreign Policy and Intervention*, London: Routledge.

Singh, A. 1995-96, 'Time: The New Dimension in War', *Joint Forces Quarterly*, Washington DC: National Defence University, Winter.

Swofford, A. 2003, *A Marine's Chronicle of the Gulf War and Other Battles*, New York: Scribner.

Watts, B.D. 1995, *What Is the 'Revolution in Military Affairs'*, Northrup Grumman Analysis Center 703 (351): 2.

Weiss, B. 2001, 'Thug Realism: Inhabiting Fantasy in Urban Tanzania', *Cultural Anthropology* 17 (1): 1-32.

4

Can ICT belong in Africa, or is ICT owned by the North Atlantic region?

Wim van Binsbergen

ICT, as a technological innovation and a major factor in globalization, poses particular problems of ownership and identity with regard to the African continent. What is the place of ICT (Information and Communication Technology) in Africa, and what is the place of Africa in a world increasingly dominated by ICT? This chapter seeks to explode the apparent contradiction between Africa and ICT. In the first part the author confronts African thinkers like Mazrui and Gyekye who have argued the incompatibility of African culture and ICT. Having advanced an argument to the effect that ICT is just as much and as little owned by Africans as by any other collectivity in the contemporary world, the second part of the chapter sets out, with a more empirical argument, some of the ways in which the African appropriation of ICT is actually taking shape.

Introduction: Two worlds?

Until well into the 1970s when computer terminals were still scarce and the microcomputer unknown, academic computer use in the Netherlands was mainly restricted to main frames that today we would consider hopelessly antiquated. Usually we ran our jobs at night, in our absence, as the computer was slow and the queue of rival jobs was virtually endless. The supreme moment came the next morning when we grabbed our batch of output from the counter assistant who ran the printer to which we had no direct access: The output consisted of enormous quantities of A3 fanfold paper full of barely legible printed lines of 80 characters in caps. Walking away from the counter, we would hold the wide and hopefully heavy batch of output at eye height, and with pounding heart would start to skip through the output to see if the computer had brought us the outcomes we had hoped for.

Ten years later, when doing cultural anthropological research into the psychotherapeutic practices of local oracular priests in the mangrove woods of the West African country of Guinea-Bissau, I was struck time and again by the similarity between our tense and hopeful scrutiny of computer output back in the 1970s and the stance that these priests (often practising in groups of two or three at a time) adopted when administering the frequently-resorted-to 'chicken oracle'. In local Manjak society,[1] sacrifices to spirits and ancestors were the order of the day. Each sacrifice's acceptance or rejection by the spirits had to be ascertained by a one-bit decision device: in a swift movement the belly of a chicken was cut open, and the unexpectedly long, cream-coloured string of guts was held high in the sunlight to be scrutinized professionally so that the priestly colleagues could decide on the presence or absence of unnatural darker stains on the outside of the guts. The outcome could be *black* (unfavourable) or *white* (favourable). The priests wore no outward signs of their professional status but they stood out unmistakably as servants of the supernatural — privileged with extraordinary power and knowledge — by the combination of their tense technical attention; their fond deliberations on details absolutely invisible to lay outsiders; their relentless and triumphant final judgement that for the client held the greatest possible significance (for they were supervising sacrifices, no Manjak will sacrifice unless driven by despair, and each sacrifice involves very great costs of time, money and frustration); and the studied neglect with which the disfigured dead animal was cast away.

The choice of these two opening vignettes, one Dutch and one African, purposely conjures up the compartmentalized world image from which I want to step back in this chapter. 'Africa', 'Europe', 'the North Atlantic region' — these are not neutral descriptive categories and certainly not distinctions underpinned by scientific analysis but merely geopolitical programmes serving to designate the hegemonic relationships in the contemporary world:

- The North Atlantic region as characterized by material technology in which the interaction between man and machine (i.e. a conglomerate of highly heterogeneous material part objects functioning on the basis of a rationally composed and empirically underpinned coherent complexity) entails, in addition to social effects, an interference with nature that is explicitly

[1] See Van Binsbergen (1984) and (1988).

intended as well as demonstrably effective, and that may be conducive to some social utilization of natural forces.
- Africa as characterized by socio-ritual technology ('magic') in which machines in the above sense do not feature, and in which man only produces a social effect by merely the *illusion* of an interference with nature, through interaction with objects that are either naturally given (the chicken), or that may be produced with the aid of simple technology (the priest's knife slitting open the chicken's stomach).

According to such a conception of the world, ICT (Information and Communication Technology), as eminently typical of the technology of North Atlantic modernism and postmodernism, would be alien to Africa. Accordingly, it would — allegedly — merely do violence to African people if material technology were to occupy just as much of a central and taken-for-granted part of their lives as has come to be the case in the North. By such a postulated development, the most beautiful, most essential contribution of Africans to the global achievements of mankind would — still allegedly — be destroyed, given the constraints imposed by this world view. But this would be unlikely to happen anyway for, because of their own 'culture', 'Africans' would (so this conception of the world maintains) be scarcely capable of developing the various specific skills necessary for contemporary computer use. In accordance with the essentialism characteristic of geopolitical constructions, the division of labour between North and South is conceived of as perennial and immutable: to us the computer, to them the chicken oracle — as presumably it has been since the beginning of time, or certainly since the late 19th century, when British colonial expansion in Africa took place to the tune of the following late 19th-century popular couplet that in its emphasis on the Northern monopolization of the technical achievements of that time and age (including advanced weaponry) implies the essence of a not-yet-globalized world:

> *Whatever happens,*
> *we have got*
> *the Maxim gun*
> *and they have not.*

One of the principal tasks of intercultural philosophy is to explode precisely this world view, and to replace it by a model more in accordance with the contemporary global reality that is characterized by immense diversity, the international interconnectedness of cultural orientations, and the virtually unlimited global availability of state-of-the-art technologies.

The problem as seen from the perspective of intercultural philosophy

Intercultural philosophy investigates, as its central theme, *inter-culturality*.[2] It does so by means of a theoretical reflection on such concepts as culture, cultural difference, cultural diversity, cultural relativism, identity, multiculturality, power, hermeneutics and dialogue. With the use of such concepts, intercultural philosophy critically explores the conditions under which we might speak of interculturality. What are the units between which the interaction takes place that is presupposed in the concept of '*inter*'-culturality? On what grounds (and are these valid grounds) do we distinguish between such units? What nature, permanence, boundedness *vis-à-vis* each other, internal structure or internal consistence can we attribute to these units? Is it meaningful to speak of a plurality of cultures (in line with well-established contemporary language use) in such a way that we attribute to each culture out of which that plurality consists, such features as internal integration, boundedness *vis-à-vis* other such cultures, association with a specific part set of humanity, and association with a part of the earth's surface as the historical habitat of that part set? Or is such a use of 'culture' and 'cultures' too much a reflection of such self-evidences as have established themselves in the socio-political structure of contemporary society — self-evidences that the philosopher ought to critique rather than take for granted? Is it meaningful to speak of an African 'culture' or 'cultures', and to attribute distinctive features to it or to them? The world appears in our experience as a complex of contradictions, foremost among which is the contradiction between existing inequalities in terms of power and resources, on the one hand, and the appeal to a shared humanity regardless of these inequalities, on the other. What is the relationship between (a) such underlying inequalities, and (b) thinking in terms of culture and cultural differences? Is (b) simply the masked, oblique expression of (a)? Are intercultural knowledge and intercultural communication possible? Or will such knowledge always remain invalid, to the extent to which it is incapable of escaping from the distorting effects produced by the hegemonic subjugation of one subset of humanity to the language, power, productive interests, world view and values of another such subset? Is it possible for cultural mobilization initiated by the local actors themselves, and by philosophical reflection by intercultural philosophers, to rise above these limitations? Can such mobilization and reflection even be a means to redress inequalities and to enhance the validity of intercultural knowledge? These are some of the themes of intercultural philosophy.

---

[2] Cf. Mall (1995), Mall & Lohmar (1993), Kimmerle (1994), Kimmerle & Wimmer (1997) and Van Binsbergen (2003: Chapter 15 and *passim*).

With specific application to ICT this yields two central questions:

(1) Is ICT to be viewed as the specific and characteristic achievement of only a subset of humanity (notably the North Atlantic part)? and
(2) Is ICT therefore not really at home in Africa?

I will answer these questions in a largely negative way. This allows us to situate Africa within a globalizing world, and to admit that in such a context Africa has unmistakably and self-evidently access to essentially metalocal elements such as ICT. Next, we can pose the more empirical question as to how such access takes shape in concrete terms. In other words, how does the enculturation of ICT in Africa manifest itself by means of a transformative localization — often a virtualization — of whatever is available worldwide in the ICT field?

ICT as North Atlantic and therefore as not really at home in Africa?

Several African philosophers have concerned themselves with the question of the retention or loss of cultural identity under conditions of contemporary information and communication technology. Does electronic ICT in Africa lead to creative and liberating cultural appropriation by Africans? Is it leading to the annihilation of the African cultural heritage? Or do both propositions apply somehow? Is the computer in Africa to be taken for granted or does it remain an alien element? Way back in the late 1970s, the prominent political philosopher Ali Mazrui (hailing from Kenya and now at the State University of New York, USA) regarded the computer as a 'cultural transplant' from the North, alien to the societies and cultures of Africa and only capable of having a devastating or subjugating effect in the African context (Mazrui 1978). Jules-Rosette (1990) summarizes Mazrui's view in the following terms:

> [the] imported nature [of the computer] might badly fit the tasks and orientation of non-western workers, and as a result it may form a source of socio-cultural disruption, increasing economic dependency and introducing modes of thought which are alien to the working environment in which the computer is being used.

Mazrui was recently supported in this point of view by the Ghanaian philosopher Kwame Gyekye (1997: 37), who stated that:

> Ideally, technology, as a cultural product, should rise from the culture of a people, if it is to be directly accessible to a large section of the population and its nuances are to be fully appreciated by them.

But by contrast, Paulin Hountondji from Côte d'Ivoire maintains a relativizing distance from any attempt to claim an absolutely distinct African identity and culture, including an African philosophy. He invites his African colleagues to recognize the fact that contemporary African expressions are increasingly linked up with a global cultural, philosophical and technological mainstream. Here Africans, provided the intercontinental inequalities attending the material conditions for the production of knowledge are lifted and on the basis of the African historical background of what Hountondji calls 'endogenous knowledge production', may very well prove able to make a contribution, which then is to converge with, rather than deviate from, widely accepted formats and achievements.[3] For Hountondji, ICT is the answer to Africa's lagging behind in academic knowledge production, and the African Institute for Advanced Study, which Hountondji is now in the process of setting up in Benin (based on Princeton's model for such institutes), will rely on electronic ICT and not on such time-honoured African means of communication as the talking drum).[4]

Open debate on these questions is severely impeded by the fact that it is situated in global and national arenas where social control favours the public production of politically correct statements, or of statements that reflect the parochial collective interests of a particular group of participants in this debate. Many philosophical positions on the issue of the transcontinental reception of ICT are possible, and among them are socially privileged geopolitical points of view, entrenched by the effects of societal power distribution, ideology and media coverage. The latter points of view may have become installed in the collective representations of large sets of people in such a way that these viewpoints can hardly be explicitly discussed and confronted any more without prejudice or without inviting bitter controversy. These collective representations also tend to invade the philosophical discourse, to the extent to which philosophers, too, are children of their time and of their wider society.[5] The naïve geopolitics of everyday North Atlantic parlance, such as the evocation of a particularly negative othering of African conditions and people, is often replicated in what are otherwise sophisticated specialist philosophical arguments.

Let us seek to sketch, by means of a few rough distinctions, the fields of tension that are encountered here.

In the times of mercantilism, imperialism and colonialism, 'the African' was constructed, in North Atlantic thought, as the *other par excellence* — an other to whom the philosophical achievements of the Modern Age (insights in the

[3] Cf. Hountondji (1996, 1988, 1990, 1994).

[4] Hountondji (personal communications, 1997-1998).

[5] Cf. Van Binsbergen (2003: Chapter 15).

human condition, and such human rights as derived from such insights), scarcely applied, even though Europeans insistently claimed these insights and rights for themselves. Subsequently, after decolonization, the second half of the 20th century witnessed two almost opposite movements seeking to redress — with the mobilization of a good deal of emotion — this racialist exclusion of Africans:

(a) On the one hand, in a modernist Enlightenment-derived frame of mind, and largely in the context of development cooperation, and its underlying philosophies, there is the attempt to reclaim things African under the heading of allegedly universally applicable, and originally North Atlantic, categories (such as 'world religion', 'democratic constitutional arrangements', 'modern health care', 'formal education', 'the formal organization' as the dominant format for social and economic life, 'modern technology', 'economic planning', 'literature', 'philosophy', 'art'). From this perspective, being 'African' would be an irrelevant category, under which more essential universal categories become manifest.

(b) On the other hand, there is the particularism projected onto fragmented African identities as an aspect of the ethnicization process in which (under postmodern conditions such as the erosion of the modernist world view of the Enlightenment, of the centralist nation state, and of the illusion of the autonomous subject) the contemporary world as a whole is involved. This process consists of the fact that politics is no longer primarily experienced as a struggle for scarce material resources but for public recognition of a particularistic group identity. Once such recognition has been extended to the group, it will successfully claim material resources as a matter of course. From this perspective, 'being African' is a quality in its own right, not to be relegated to any more universal category.

From the perspective of movement (a), things African dissolve as a slight ruffle amidst so many others within the great flow of world culture and world history. Movement (b) however battles against such a blurring of distinctions and stresses the construction and presentation of an identity of one's own at the local, regional, national and continental level. The tension between these two movements produces a torsion that lends confusing double binds to much of the contemporary thinking about Africa, North Atlantic hegemony, and universality. From the ethnicizing perspective (b), African identity appears as the emphatic politicized condition for participation in intercontinental processes of communication, knowledge production, cooperation and intervention. From the development perspective (a), however, African specificity has been underplayed in favour of universalism in science, economics and social-organizational and constitutional matters. These two simultaneous movements (a) and (b) each lead to a different appreciation of such cultural programming as structures everyday life, political organization, forms of production, world views and religious practices. According to movement (a), each cultural ordering (even if recognized to be unmistakable, comprehensive and difficult to escape from) is yet a more or less ephemeral, superficial orientation under which more fundamental intercultural communalities lurk — communalties that are claimed to be universal but that in fact are conceived primarily in accordance with North Atlantic models. This view implies the possibility that culture does not produce a total experience encompassing an individual's entire life, and therefore also implies the probability that each individual is simultaneously involved in a plurality of different cultural orientations. It would not, thus, be meaningful to speak of a 'culture' or of 'cultures' in the sense of integrated, bounded, distinct human modes of being that encompass life as a whole and that are shared by large sets of people.[6] The surface fragmentation of 'cultures' would be taken to dissolve into comprehensive spatial and temporal communalities and continuities at a deeper level. By contrast, the ethnicization movement (b) invites us to let the many concrete cultural orderings coincide more unequivocally with the identities that we construct for ourselves within contemporary political arenas, and to attribute to these orderings, in this context, a permanence and a discrete distinctive nature that are commensurate with the severity of the contradictions and with the seriousness of the struggle within these arenas. The South identity or identities, from a development perspective (a), would ultimately appear to be contingent and unessential, yet from the ethnicization perspective (b) would appear to be reified and essentialized. Since the greatest, most conspicuous inequality in our time is that between North and South on a global level, from the ethnicization perspective (b) it would amount to a treacherous attack on the most important resources available for improving the conditions and enhancing the empowerment of people in the South, if as under (a) one were to take a relative view of any Southern, for instance any African, identity. Thus perspectives (a) and (b) lead to utterly contradictory positions, neither of which could be said to be more justified than the other. *Interculturality is invariably characterized by the puzzle of contradicting positions between which we cannot choose* unless we are prepared to destroy the equality of these positions and forfeit interculturality for the sake of a one-sided alternative of hegemony, subjugation, objectification or ethnocentrism.

[6] Cf. Van Binsbergen (2003: Chapter 15).

This goes some way towards sketching the complex context in which we may explore, from an intercultural perspective, the strained relationship between, on the one hand, 'Africa' (i.e. African identity), and contemporary ICT, on the other.

We have to admit that 'Africa' is not a fixed and firm reality. When Mazrui and Gyekye see 'Africa' as being penetrated by the computer, then their concern is not so much with a land mass that extends between certain latitudes and longitudes, one on which hundreds of millions of people move in a gaudy interplay of cultural and social organizational varieties — partially rural and in accordance with historically specific local patterns, partially urban and increasingly in accordance with patterns that are either recent local innovations, or transformed borrowings from elsewhere in the contemporary world. In the debate surrounding ICT, 'Africa' is primarily an identity construct: the issue is 'African culture' or 'African cultures' that are alleged to be negatively influenced by the supposedly alien computer and the latter's capabilities of communication and information.

To what might such a possibly negative influence be attributed? Here at least three answers would be possible:

(1)(1') ICT is Northern culture, and hence (1'') ICT is irreconcilably opposed to African culture;
(2)(2') ICT is metalocal world culture, without local specificity and local validity, and hence (2'') ICT is, in principle, devastating for any localizing cultural identity such as the African one; and
(3)(3') ICT is inimical to culture, and hence (3'') ICT is inimical to the African culture or cultures.

At first glance something could be said in favour of each of these three theses but none entirely passes the test of closer scrutiny. This is partially due to the dual nature of each of these theses: each starts with a global cultural appraisal of ICT, followed by a claimed effect of the global characteristic on the African situation. Even if either of the two parts were true, their combination might still be false.

ICT inimical to any culture?

Only in the case of thesis (3) is the derivation of (3'') from (3') evident: whatever is inimical to culture is inevitably inimical to African culture or cultures. Technological pessimism has been part of the recent continental philosophical mainstream with its principal exponent being Heidegger (1977), who has claimed that technology is by its essence perpendicular to any culture and does not constitute an integrated part of it. But even so, thesis (3) can hardly be defended. Whatever definition we offer of culture, in continuity with widespread established language usage, we are likely to prefer to describe culture as something that has a collective nature — in other words, something that is the attribute of a set of people, of a subset of total humanity. In addition, our definition is likely to include an aspect of spatial extension, since even the smallest set of people inevitably occupies a certain space. Regarding the time dimension, our concept of culture is likely to include a certain permanence, supported by interpersonal learning processes to bridge the gap between generations and to guarantee cultural continuity in the face of the individual mortality of a culture's human bearers. In other words, culture is likely to be considered as being subjected to processes of regulated transfer between people whose cultural competence is initially unequal: people belonging to different generations, classes, genders, linguistic groups, local outsiders versus local insiders, etc. And our definition of culture is also likely to include an aspect of recognizable patterned ordering that allows culture both to be specifically recognized as a transferable collective attribute and to be actually transferred to those who adopt patterned cultural specifics as their distinctive collective attribute.

Information and communication are implied in most of these aspects of our definition of culture. Information and communication are thus essential aspects of culture, and they always take place via a specific medium — a specific technology. The face-to-face communication[7] by which culture is predominantly transferred in family settings constitutes a technology of speech and rhetoric — in other words a technology of information and communication. Another such technology of information and communication has been formed — ever since the earliest imperial times of the Assyrians, Persians, Chinese and Romans — by the technologies of the mail road with its shunting points where horses and couriers were replaced, or in the last thousand years (if we go by the Chinese invention of block printing, rather than by the West European variety of detached type) the technology of printing, and in most recent times the technologies of movies, radio, television, video and the Internet. These have all amounted to technologies of information and communication constitutive of culture. Instead of being inimical to culture, ICT constitutes a central element in everything we would prefer to call culture. There seems to be little reason to

[7] Even here though the role of non-spoken representations – in sacred emblems, images, writing, photographs, videos, email, telephone conversations, etc. – must not be underestimated or restricted to the most recent times.

exclude present-day electronic ICT from this general picture. However, we must point out the tension between:

(i) the ethnicization perspective on culture (according to which culture is bounded, specific and integrated, and comprises and defines specific part sets of humanity); and
(ii) communication as a fundamental aspect of *any* culture.

The former (i) is conducive to demarcation, the latter (ii) to extension, which in principle may be unlimited and may comprise mankind's entire world. In other words, communication that is constitutive of culture may spill over beyond that one culture and thus assault its specificity. The fact that language is one of the principal means of communication for constituting culture works to the advantage of demarcation: language is highly structured and specific in terms of its lexicon, phonology and syntax. Languages are in principle not mutually intelligible and each specific language therefore effectively limits the part set of humanity and (to the presently rapidly decreasing extent to which languages are neatly distributed across the globe in the way of geographical language areas, each of which is tied to a specific section of the earth's surface) the spatial radius within which communication takes places and culture consolidates itself. Not for nothing is language the main stable indicator of ethnic identity. But regardless of how language is acquired,[8] many (probably most) people in the world are multilingual to a greater or lesser extent, and thus it is possible to step out of the limitations imposed by merely one language. Moreover, language is by no means the only method of communication, by no means the only factor constituting the communication element in culture. One example may make this clear. Anyone who makes a transcontinental trip across Africa in an old car will meet people along the way with whom they can barely converse, if at all, but who are able to repair their car should the need arise. Obviously communication about that type of technological knowledge (and many other types of knowledge) is language dependent only to a very limited extent. Through communication processes culture is both consolidated and continually spread outside the space that was initially defined as that culture's proper domain. Moreover, by communication processes, culture is continually invaded from

[8] Most anthropologists would claim language mastery to derive exclusively from a learning process, but reasons have been advanced from various sides to qualify this statement, for example, from Chomsky (1968, 1986) postulating the innate nature of language ability to Sheldrake (1981, 1988) suggesting that the acquisition of an unknown language is made easier the more speakers that language has, as if an intangible supporting network – a 'morphogenetic field' – would add to individual learning achievements.

outside within the proper domain it has initially claimed for itself. As a result, the localization of culture and the close link between culture and identity in the process of ethnicization tend to be continually threatened and destroyed. On these grounds one might argue that ICT is both constitutive of, and inimical to, culture, but one might as well maintain that the very conception of culture as localized, bounded and identitary, is inimical to culture! Exit thesis (3).

ICT as Northern culture

Thesis (1) is considered to be true by the early Mazrui and by Gyekye. Our example of African car repairs is doubly instructive, for it also shows that many forms of cultural programming (such as knowledge of transport technology, specifically of the internal combustion engine), that we would initially be inclined to situate in a particular area of the contemporary world (notably in the North Atlantic), have not confined themselves to that region, and have in fact gained worldwide distribution. Not only the silly clichés of globalization, such as jeans, Coca Cola and the McDonald hamburger, but also globally trendy styles of clothing, of cosmetics and bodily hygiene, means of transport, organizational forms, world religions, and globally circulating forms of time reckoning, of music and its reproduction, of dance, recreation, sports and sexuality, have gained an absolutely metalocal distribution. Africa takes part in this distribution, not so much because Africans can afford actual consumption out of this global supply (most of them cannot) but vicariously: to the extent to which representations of this metalocal culture, via TV, video, radio, the printed press and people's own observations across class boundaries, have reached contemporary Africans and inform their desires. Africans today seek to partake of *Modernity on a Shoestring* (cf. Fardon *et al.* 1999). All this amounts to the cultural aspect of globalization. By globalization we mean, in general, the process through which local contexts in the world are more and more dissolving into a worldwide network of interaction under the influence of technological innovations that have reduced to virtually zero the costs (in terms of time and money) of communication and information. Globalization was, in the first instance, observed with regard to transnational movements of capital along electronic media but now turns out to have important cultural dimensions.[9]

[9] A selection from the rapidly growing literature in this field includes Bauman (1998), Beyer (1994), Featherstone (1995), Friedman (1995), Hannerz (1992), King (1991), Meyer & Geschiere (1998), Robertson (1992), Van der Veer (1996), Warnier (1999), cf. Van Binsbergen (1999), the English version of which appears as Chapter 12 of Van Binsbergen (2003).

In this situation, appealing to 'African culture' or 'African cultures' implies the risk that we dissimulate the problematic, constructed, virtual nature of these concepts. One of the main themes of the contemporary African experience has been the revival, often even the militant reconstruction, of the 'authentically African' despite, and often with the aid of, prominently installed metalocal contemporary technologies: the printing press, music, recordings, film, radio and television, the Internet, cultural festivals with electronic sound technologies. There is no empirical support for the claim that historical African culture may still be captured, entirely intact and self-evident anywhere on the African continent today, by any means. Whatever passes for African culture today has become to a lesser or greater degree *virtual*: in name it harks back to historical cultural material (world views, norms and values, religious symbols, institutions deriving from the local past), but in fact it appears in contemporary representations as fragmented, as produced under a new globally influenced format, and as having lost its coherence with a more integrated and persistent local cultural framework. It has become redefined and hangs in the air (Van Binsbergen 1997b, 1998).

In this context, to speak of ICT as a cultural transplant is misleading to the highest degree. Such a claim denies the continuity between North Atlantic and African manifestations of globalized metalocal culture and suggests instead — in a nostalgic re-enactment of the redeeming mysticism of things African — a geopolitical separateness between continents in the cultural domain, and in general a purity and authenticity of cultural domains that in our day and age is certainly nowhere to be found. I reserve for another argument the question of whether such purity and separateness *at any moment in the past* would have been adequate terms to describe the actual situation within Africa and the relationship between Africa and the North Atlantic. The fact that Mazrui and Gyekye pursue cosmopolitan forms of knowledge production (philosophy, political science) in an originally European language (English), and that they do so effectively and with great success and appeal especially outside their African country of origin, is in itself sufficient proof of the point I wish to make here with regard to the present lack of separation and of purity.

Would it even be anachronistic to claim, in our time and age, a specific local or regional origin and identity (for example 'North Atlantic', 'American', 'European') for technologies that at present have a metalocal distribution, including electronic ICT?

It is characteristic of modern times that technological innovation has expressly become an industry, a collective, explicit and rationally organized production process. Technology has loosened itself from the more comprehensive socio-cultural frameworks that produced it, and has for a long time largely ceased to be an expression of the local socio-cultural forms which such frameworks have assumed. In other words, apart from minor and immaterial embellishments, there is nothing remarkably Dutch any more about Philips ('the inventors of the CD', as their advertising slogan claims) CD equipment, nothing remarkably American about Macintosh computers, nothing remarkably Japanese about Fuji cameras. Patent law regulates the appropriation of forms of technology that generate so much productivity and on which products for such lucrative markets are based, that restrictions on the circulation of that type of knowledge are worth enforcing, at least in the immediate future. Of course, these restrictions on the circulation of knowledge only serve to ensure the greatest possible circulation, with the greatest possible profit, of the products made on the basis of that knowledge in line with the general trend of globalization.

The spatial imagery surrounding innovation is often deceptive. Typically, innovation tends to be imagined as coming from the outside, from a different domain from one's own, even if in fact that origin is far more continuous with one's own domain. For the Dutch farmer who has taken to monitoring his cattle by computer, this is a 'town' technology, initially alien to his own rural environment but his very appropriation of this technology, as of so many others, has already rendered relative the entire contradiction between town and country. To the Dutch academic who in the last fifteen years has totally transformed his/her style of writing, research and teaching following the arrival of the microcomputer and the Internet, the latter may have appeared as an alien 'American' technology, but again its very appropriation renders relative the distinction between the European home and the no-longer-faraway United States.

But is there any way of denying that the computer is originally North Atlantic? Some readers may know that the Internet was originally a specifically American military innovation in the 1960s, long before the advent of the microcomputer. The computer in general undoubtedly originated in specific accumulative cultural achievements of North Atlantic culture. The computer testifies to this state of affairs in many ways: in its internal design; in its external design and aesthetics; in the principles according to which the user interface has been conceived to readily appeal to the most likely, North Atlantic users; in the iconography and syntax informing the communication between computer and user, and between users; and in the illusion of an absolutely individual autonomy in ownership, access, financial and legal responsibility of the owner — whereas in reality that user tends to be blindly dependent on systems that are inaccessible as black boxes and that owe no accountability to anyone. The Microsoft empire and the negative stereotyping it generates among the more conscious users is a case in point. Even the built-in conflicts, ironies and humour in the computer domain may be relegated to the specific types of cultural programming attending the scientific, technological, military and entrepreneurial milieus — strongly North Atlantic and predominantly US — in which this technology has realized its rapid development. The language aspects of the computer are in the first instance American English. And without the inventive mathematics of Von Neumann, Turing and the members of their generation from the North Atlantic region, there would have been no computer.

Does this mean that the computer and ICT in general are eminently at home in the North Atlantic world? That is admittedly where they have been received for years with great rapidity in all kinds of successive phases of their innovation. But this reception in itself already shows that, even in the North Atlantic world, computers are not in the first place at home — the environment in which they originated is scarcely the standard North Atlantic environment but something far more limited and specific. The most adequate description of this process of reception may be one of globalization, for instance in the following terms.

Older formations of culture were made possible by older technologies of communication and information technology (from the footpath and the talking drum to writing, the mail coach and the sailing ship). At the same time these older cultural formations were breached by communication spilling over (by virtue of the same older technologies of communication and information) outside the localizing frames of identity. The double effect of both constituting culture and spilling over beyond the boundaries of cultural specificity has been a general feature of technologies of information and communication. Also, in the technologies of the computer (and of ICT in general), the local specificity of a cultural orientation has transcended itself by creating a medium that by its very nature is communicative and informative, and that is so even to a far greater extent than the older technologies by which older socio-cultural formations were supported. Far from being anathema to culture, contemporary ICT displays the typical dramatic relation *vis-à-vis* culture that technology has always had: facilitating and destructive at the same time.

Electronic ICT may, on the one hand, be a product of Northern culture but, on the other hand, it puts paid to this very type of localized culture. It is capable of supporting historical cultural identity constructions and is admittedly used for that purpose (see, for example, Anderson 1992), but of far greater significance is its ability to breach identitary boundaries and to render thinkable and to support new forms of identity (like communities of emailers, electronic discussion groups, etc.) that are exclusively ICT based. This new medium has turned out to be communicative and informative, and thus it claims its place among the instruments not for the destruction but for the perpetuation of culture.

Even if it were only for this metalocal nature inherent in electronic ICT, the computer in Africa cannot justifiably be called a North Atlantic cultural transplant — for its North Atlantic nature has been too much transcended to make 'North Atlantic' a fitting characterization any longer. Moreover, as we have seen, the globalizing metalocal domain extends to include contemporary Africa where the 'authentically African culture/cultures' have at best survived, if at all, in the form of carefully maintained virtual enclaves, geared to the annual production of a harvest festival, a chief's ceremony, a dancing performance, all of which have been partially reshaped in accordance with global models of media production, and thus have been virtualized.[10] Nobody who takes an overview of contemporary socio-cultural life in Africa can escape the conclusion that in most places globalized elements are present and are even taken for granted, are no longer seen as alien but have been successfully appropriated in order to end up as local and indispensable even though they may still stand out as sources of prestige. Nowhere in Africa do the jeans, the bra, the car, canned food, formal organizations in education, health services or religion give rise to surprise anymore — they demonstrate that in many respects life in Africa has ceased to be 'African' but — just like life in Western Europe — has become metalocal, not to say global. Often, but not always, African Christian churches turn out to play a major role in filtering the market supply of modern consumption items, and in selectively validating and rejecting these: for example, accepting ladies' underwear and the maxi skirt but rejecting women's trouser suits and miniskirts; accepting the video but rejecting the disco; accepting Coca Cola and Fanta but rejecting bottled beer; accepting — from the images of fast North Atlantic life seen on videos and TV — the expensive and prestigious car but rejecting the open admission of the practice of sexual promiscuity, etc.[11]

This non-authentic Africa, however inefficient and unpredictable in its details, is also for Africans a much more tangible reality than the mythical 'authentic Africa'. And in this tangible non-authentic Africa, ICT is not an alien transplant but an increasingly important aspect — taken for granted and no longer dispensable — of a socio-cultural milieu (notably that of the African elites) that, while geographically situated in Africa, has since the 19th century (if not earlier) closely followed North Atlantic technological developments and participated in these developments as a matter of course.

---

[10] Cf. my 1992 Amsterdam inaugural lecture: Van Binsbergen (1992a = 1994b). On the same problematic, cf. De Jong (1994, 2001) and Van Binsbergen (1994a).

[11] On these church practices in the context of the global market, cf. the contributions by Meyer and Van Dijk, both on Ghanaian Pentecostal churches, in Fardon *et al.* (1999) and Van Binsbergen (1997b: Chapter 1).

ICT as metalocal global culture

What remains is thesis (2):

> (2)(2') ICT is metalocal world culture, without local specificity and local validity, and hence (2'') ICT is, in principle, devastating for any localizing cultural identity like the African one.

This argument contains sufficient elements to render plausible the first part (2') of this thesis but what about the second part (2'')? Localizing cultural identities in Africa, as elsewhere, exists in a state of tension *vis-à-vis* the globalizing elements (including electronic ICT) that have spread so abundantly all over Africa. This tension is, in principle, not necessarily destructive because, as argued above, the new technologies may also serve to support historical identities. The apparently alien transplant may yet turn out to further in unexpected ways that which is local and identitary, *pace* Mazrui and Gyekye. But to be able to serve that purpose, these technologies must in the first place be *available* and must also — as a further condition — have undergone some degree of local acclimatization. In Africa, these conditions are by now met for such communication techniques as the written press, radio, the telephone, television, cassette recorders and video, and in many places these technologies demonstrably support and inform identity constructions. However, in most places in Africa this is not yet the case with regard to the Internet: there are far too few user computers and providers, electronic network connections are unreliable, and the costs of Internet use are prohibitive for most Africans. Yet in the urban centres, around universities, and in the interplay with intercontinental migrants residing in the North Atlantic where Internet access is a matter of course, the computer is beginning to play an important role in the articulation of ethnic, cultural and religious identities. A large and ever-increasing number of African expressions are now available on the Internet, often as a result of Africans in the diaspora building websites largely for consumption at home, in Africa.

But the majority of the African population has, as yet, hardly any access to this medium so that it is not available as a direct expression of local identity. Whatever manages to present itself, and to maintain itself, under such conditions of scarcity, does so usually by virtue of non-local inputs in terms of interests, means and formats, and therefore would produce only the most misleading representations of what may yet pose as a local situation.

This state of affairs was particularly driven home to me with regard to the rural district of Kaoma in the heart of western Zambia. I have conducted anthropological and historical research there since 1972 but it was only in 1994 that I could for the first time make an international telephone call from the district; and only a year later could I, from the Netherlands, have my first e-mail contact with someone residing in the district capital.

Anyone who searches the Internet for 'Kaoma' with any of the usual search machines, does admittedly find a number of hits that unmistakably apply to this district.[12] But if one tries to construct an image of Kaoma District on the basis of these hits, one gets absolutely lost in the fog — the kind of fog that hangs over North Atlantic polders or prairies, not the kind that in the early morning hangs over Kaoma's *dambos* (wetlands) at the bottom of its shallow, wooded valleys where duiker antelopes and wild pigs (and until the 1980s even buffalo and elephants) are startled by local hunters; some of whom are in the employ of local princes, and some of whom still wield Portuguese muzzle-loading guns from the 19th century. Kaoma's representation on the Internet is a misleading travesty of the actual local situation, not a form of valid knowledge but a form of ignorance. The Kaoma District that speaks to us via the Internet is merely a reflection of the intercontinental presence in the district, including a Dutch development project parading on its website an exceptionally successful local woman farmer (but one belonging to the locally hated, non-local immigrant group of the Lozi). There is also the US-controlled evangelical parent body of the Evangelical Church of Zambia that operates a major hospital in the district and its matron shares her unmistakably Southern States spirituality with visitors to her website.

---

[12] 'Kaoma' is only a very short word and is likely to exist in several other languages and contexts than that of western central Zambia, where it has been the name of a district since 1969 (previously called Mankoya District), and the name of a stream since time immemorial. It is likely that the word 'Kaoma' has also penetrated the Internet from some of these other contexts, e.g. in Bemba, a major Zambian language, which however is not a *lingua franca* anywhere near Kaoma District, 'Kaoma' is one of the names of the High God. In a government move directed at Lozi rebelliousness, President Kaunda replaced the older district capital's name Mankoya with Kaoma in 1969. 'Mankoya' was based on the Nkoya ethnonym, while 'Kaoma' is derived from the nearby Kaoma river and therefore was considered to be ethnically neutral. *Likota lya Bankoya*, a collection of Nkoya oral traditions from the first half of the 20th century, proposes an etymology for the hydronym Kaoma in terms of the destruction of a king's ceremonial drums (in Nkoya called *mawoma*) in the 19th century (Van Binsbergen 1992b: 389). However, hydronyms are notorious for their tendency to immutability over long stretches of time, which makes this recent etymology of Kaoma somewhat suspect.

ICT between the local and the global in an African context

The specific case of Kaoma suggests a situation around African ICT which I would deem eminently capable of generalization: when it comes to knowledge production concerning Africa, the Internet only renders to the outside world what that outside world has put into the Internet in the first place. In this light, there would seem to be little reason for the euphoria that generally attends discussions about ICT in African intellectual circles.[13] For the time being, we should look anywhere except on the Internet for valid and representative knowledge production on Kaoma District and its inhabitants.[14] And Kaoma District is representative of very many districts in Africa where, despite the virtualization and globalization of life, the traces of older historical socio-cultural forms can still be discerned so that people may yet entertain the illusion — although it is an illusion and nothing more — that these forms have braved the decades or even the centuries.[15]

A new field of tension arises here: that between the medium-specific format (in which inevitably the North Atlantic cultural origin of ICT shines through) and the contents, that in principle may be derived from all knowledge systems of all times and from all over the world. From the extent to which ICT is metalocal, it is valid to say that this medium — irrespective of its North Atlantic origin — may display great flexibility as far as its specific cultural context of use is concerned. Sharing the cultural orientation, the mathematical rationality, the iconographic and aesthetic principles of the makers of ICT, is by no means a condition for the effective appropriation of this medium, and for the subsequent use of this medium for purposes and from the perspective of a world view that in itself would be rejected by that very same mathematical rationality: many divination systems including African ones such as Ifa and Hakata, 'voodoo' (which has now become a globalized term without any meaningful referent to any specific ritual practice in any specific time and place but which originally referred to the West African indigenous concept of *vodun*), recently invented or

---

[13] Cf. Nkwi (1995), Nyamnjoh (1997), Ras-Work (1998). Also cf. the central role that Thabo Mbeki (1999), Nelson Mandela's successor as president of South Africa, attributes to ICT.

[14] My own texts, which often mention Kaoma District, have only been available on the Internet since March 1999, and apart from a few exceptions do not carry the catchword 'Kaoma' among their metatags. In mid 2001 an initiative arose among young Nkoya intercontinental migrants now in the United Kingdom to create a Nkoya website that would enhance the visibility of Kaoma District on the Internet. This is another example of how new technologies of globalization may help to articulate local identities.

[15] Remarkably, one may also critique the Internet, not because it offers incorrect but because it offers correct information in Africa and therefore disturbs Utopian identity constructions; cf. Okigbo (1995).

re-invented traditions such as the *wicca* witch cult, and forms of oriental systems of thought such as Taoism — all of these are well represented on the Internet. But when they appear there, it is almost invariably in a format (that of short written texts in a North Atlantic language, supported by visual material largely conceived in accordance with North Atlantic modernist or postmodernist aesthetic conventions as mediated by popular graphics computer programs) that implies a subjugation, domestication, of these non-Western forms of knowledge to North Atlantic models, at least at the formal and iconographic level. What is more, they often appear in the form of irritatingly gratuitous pseudo-knowledge, without critical apparatus — as sub-intellectual instant food, as a globalized and virtualized product (usually with a strong New Age element) that has only its name and superficial appearance in common with the original knowledge system that is claimed to be thus represented.

It appears as if ICT strikingly manifests the themes of unity and diversity, localization and globalization in the modern world. An analysis of ICT, as attempted here, forces us to discard the illusion of sharp distinctions between cultures and between continents; such illusions make up the widespread but distortive geopolitical, ideological mind-set concerning the structure of the modern world. Instead it advocates a view based on a plurality of fields of tension and a plurality of kaleidoscopically superimposed and counteracting contradictions, between which the intercultural philosopher has to pick his or her way, just as prudently and falteringly as does the contemporary world citizen at large.

Let us now assess how the enculturation of ICT is taking place in Africa itself as an aspect of globalization.

How is the African enculturation of ICT taking place?

The expansion of ICT in Africa

Since the 1960s the use of the computer has continuously expanded, not only in the North Atlantic region but also in Africa. The first move was the rise of in-house computing by the transition from the main frame to the microcomputer, and the transition from input by means of punched tape or punch card to input via the computer screen. In government institutions and universities, and in successful, capital-intensive sectors of commercial life, a total transformation of the administrative workplace has occurred. Previously the workplace was characterized by forms that hailed from the colonial era: authoritarian relationships, over-staffing, defective competence, and ritualization. New forms of management, cooperation (or, due to the fixation of everyone to his/her individual computer screen, the absence of cooperation!), the personal exercise of power, and career mobility have come within reach due to the microcomputer. Computer specialists have taken the place of accountants and other administrative personnel with an intermediate-level training, women have gradually gained their own place in this new set-up and professional organizations have been formed in order to guard over the new power and privileges to which computer skills have given access. Wherever the microcomputer has been introduced, it has tended to lead to a marked increase of responsibilities and competences of first-line administrative personnel. This has resulted in fundamental changes in labour relations within bureaucracies and enterprises; moreover, *vis-à-vis* the public, the individual civil servant, now armed with a computer screen, can even more convincingly than before conjure up and exploit the image of the omnipotent state answerable to none — one of the most intransigent heritages of the colonial state in post-colonial Africa. Private training institutions have begun to exploit the new market generated by such expectations of professional upward mobility, steep rises in income, consumptive opportunities and security as have been associated with computer-training certificates. Thus the collective technological Utopia that has been noticeable in the affected sectors of African urban life has been mirrored by a personal Utopia.

One of the few researchers to have carried out richly conceptualized empirical research on ICT in Africa has been the prominent African American anthropologist Benetta Jules-Rosette in her book *Terminal Signs* (1990). Although the path of her analysis is somewhat hampered by a social-contract view of national societies in Africa, and by her rather humourless unconditional loyalty *vis-à-vis* the African computer workers featuring in her research, Jules-Rosette (1990: 10f) offers nice examples of the kind of contradiction that one may encounter in the field of African ICT:

> A senior programmer at a Kenya wholesale outlet attempts to manage the transition from a labor-intensive NCR keypunch computer to a new electronic multi-user system while increasing the number of employees for whom he is responsible. If he increases the number of employees, although their individual work tasks have diminished, he will obtain the title of data processing manager and double his salary. Government administrators in Ivory Coast strive to develop a computer policy that will limit the activities of multinational computer vendors such as IBM, BULL, and UNISYS, while simultaneously encouraging these companies to invest in the country. The Kenyan government organizes the computerization of key government ministries but imposes stringent restrictions on public access to computers. These cases are not merely management conundrums. They share a common theme. Each case illustrates an effort to manipulate the narratives of public discourse in order to delimit everyday practices that constitute the adoption of new technologies. Computer policies project a specific representation of development and change.

The pattern of expanding ICT differs greatly between African counties. Government policy (as enshrined in national five-year development plans and in import tax legislation) varies between the consistent furthering of ICT as a recognized precondition for post-industrialization in Côte d'Ivoire, via a restrictive and contradictory government policy in Kenya that slowly but surely is achieving automatization, and via countries with a slow and vague take-off in ICT like Mali and Sudan, to countries that are barely ready for ICT like Niger and Angola due to their stagnant economies or civil wars. Until recently South Africa formed a case apart. This country has for 150 years boasted an advanced industrial and scientific infrastructure that became tributary to the apartheid state in the second half of the 20th century resulting in ICT imports being prohibited by an international boycott until 1990. This boycott, however, was only consistently observed by Scandinavian countries, and as a result South Africa has been, and remains, by far the most computerized African country (Slob 1990). South Africa is also the only African country that scores high (20th position) on the international list of Internet implementation and use.

Not only international enterprises but also continental African institutions, research bodies, UNESCO,[16] North Atlantic governments and development agencies are active in the field of enhancing ICT in African countries. For instance, the proceedings of the Second African Colloquium on Information Research, held in 1994 in Ouagadougou, the capital of Burkina Faso, were made into a prestigious book (Tankoano 1994) of close to a thousand pages filled with formulas, diagrams, tables and bibliographies. Publication was made possible by an eloquent combination of national and international organizations: the University of Ouagadougou, the Burkinabé Ministry of Development, the University of the United Nations, the National Institute for Research in Information and Automation of Burkina Faso, ORSTOM (the French Institute for Scientific Research in the field of Development and Development Co-operation), PII-IIP (UNESCO's intergovernmental information programme), CIMPA (the International Centre for Applied Mathematics) and the Association of African Universities. About half of the many authors contributing to the book were Europeans either in Africa or in French ICT institutions, but African researchers make up the other half. The entire world is involved in ICT in Africa, and ICT demonstrates that Africa is indeed part of the wider world — as an unmistakable aspect of the globalization process into which the countries and societies of the African continent are increasingly being drawn. Despite the abundance of ferrous dust (the African continent is one large tableland whose surface is coloured red by ferrous minerals), power failures, the permanent risk of ritualization, the constant threat of burglary and theft of hardware, and the

[16] Cf. UNESCO (1980).

unmistakable class formation and poverty which means that for the time being only a happy few can effectively participate in ICT in Africa, ICT is, in principle, just as much (or as little) at home in Africa as elsewhere in the modern world.

The tension between ICT euphoria and the negative assessment of African globalization

There is no lack of lengthy arguments that sing the praise of the potential of today's ICT, especially the Internet, for Africa. These arguments discuss technical limitations (defective infrastructure, for example the telephone network, the number of ICT connections, the low quality of the servers available), economic aspects (poverty and the fact that many Africans operate economically outside the formal sector of the government and commerce and hence have no access to the Internet), the transformation of bureaucracy as discussed above, and the possibilities of generating an innovating flow of information via the Internet in the rural areas of Africa.

The euphoric thought that ICT could mean a bright future for Africa is widespread, not only among intellectuals[17] but also among politicians. Here it is significant that Thabo Mbeki, the president of South Africa, has attributed a decisive role to the ICT revolution in his blueprint for an African Renaissance (Mbeki 1999).

The euphoria is surprising. No doubt we must situate the spread of ICT in Africa in a context of globalization but where Africa is concerned globalization is, in general, not a reason for euphoria but for profound concern. For Africa, economic globalization has been synonymous with an ever-increasing marginalization: the intercontinental proceeds from Africa's products have declined in spite of increasing productivity, and today Africa is involved in no more than one per cent of transactions in the world economy. Under post-colonial governments, the continent's national economies have been disrupted due to mismanagement and the erosion of bureaucracies. These national economies have moreover been plundered by national elites who have appropriated the state. In most African countries the citizens have long since learned not to count on essential government bodies such as the police, the judicial powers, health services, educational services and public works. Because of the hideous debt burden, more money leaves the African continent in the form of interest payments than it receives in the form of development aid, including balance-of-payments aid. Such Structural Adjustment Programmes as have been intercontinentally imposed upon African countries have brought neither political stability nor economic rationalization but have produced an

[17] Cf. Nkwi (1995), Nyamnjoh (1997), OAU (1995) and Ras-Work (1998).

increasing impoverishment of large sections of the African population. Yet, at the same time, the increased communicative aspects of the globalization process have led, in the most frustrating way, to the installation of new consumptive targets and desires among that same population. Incapable of effectively protecting (let alone actively taking care of) their citizens, many post-colonial African states have been the scene of violent struggles involving regional and ethnic groups and political adventurers during the last few decades. Under the heading 'development cooperation', prolonged and many-faceted interventions from the North Atlantic region have yielded incidental local successes. This has contributed to the formation of a comfortable local point of address in the form of an NGO-based, servile, loyal and affluent local sub-elite with good organizational and technical skills (including ICT). But all this has not been able to redress the overall miserable situation prevailing in Africa today.

It would appear as if the expansion of ICT in Africa has coincided with the disintegration of African societies. Does this mean that Jules-Rosette's title *Terminal Signs* has (despite the optimistic positioning of its author) a *double entendre*: does the title not just refer to the social and semiotic interpretation, by Africans, of the signs that appear on computer terminals? Do these very signs testify to the destructive contradictions, the almost terminal illness, of Africa today? Could Mazrui (1977, 1978) be right after all and is ICT, as an unmistakable aspect of globalization in Africa, establishing the conditions for the further economic subjugation of the continent? Do we have to add to this economic subjugation, a cultural subjugation in this sense, that African ways of interacting between fellow-humans and between man and world (ways whose praises have been sung so frequently in African ethnographies and African philosophies) are — as argued by Gyekye — miles apart from those social and cosmological models that are necessary for the successful use of computers? To answer this question we must assess the cultural dynamics that surround ICT in Africa.

An empirical context of ICT enculturation: The Francistown cybercafé

If in principle, as argued above, ICT is just as much at home in Africa as elsewhere in the world, then let us go and visit it in Africa. In Southern Africa (not only in South Africa as mentioned above, but also in Botswana, Swaziland, Lesotho and Zimbabwe), ICT is expanding faster than elsewhere on the African continent. A sign of the increasing accessibility for a substantial proportion of the population is the proliferation of cybercafés in these countries in recent years. But before becoming too optimistic about conclusions based on this phenomenon, let us take a closer look at one such café as a place of ICT enculturation in Africa.

In April 1999 I spent a week working in a cybercafé in Francistown, Northeast District, Botswana. Francistown was founded a hundred years ago as a result of European capitalist interests. In the following decades, Africans came to constitute the majority of the population, and in the 1980s the town underwent rapid demographic and economic growth. Seen from the North Atlantic, Francistown (Botswana's second largest town with about 70,000 inhabitants in 1999) is an unpromising place: an ugly agglomeration of endless rows of identical small houses grouped around two veritable shopping streets with traffic lights and modern buildings of up to two floors (malls, banks) flashing the logos of world brands: Adidas, Nashua, Texaco, Toyota, IBM, British Airways, etc. Seen from the villages that still house half the population of the African continent, Francistown is a baffling world city. This is where, in the late 1980s, I made my acquaintance with the fax machine, which until then did not play a role in my Dutch academic life. I thus had high expectations of the cybercafé that was situated on the top floor of one of the newest malls.

I was disappointed. The cybercafé's hardware consisted of five customer-operated computers and one reasonably fast professional computer used as the server for a few hundred Internet subscribers in the region. The front part of the shop was equipped for the sale of current hardware and software, and computer books could be found in amazing abundance in the adjacent general news shop and bookshop that had no links with the cybercafé. Francistown is an important centre of commerce and industry, and the vast majority of Internet subscribers are to be found in these sectors of the economy — as it turns out when we search the Internet for 'Francistown' with one of the current search machines. In the week I was there, the designing of a website for a local bridal fashion shop took much of the attention of the cybercafé's staff of four: the tawny-coloured manageress who was equally fluent in Southern African English and Setswana, the black male assistant with a good basic knowledge of the Internet, the white female graphic designer, and finally the black cleaning woman, a mature slightly corpulent lady whom the manageress and the other staff treated much as though she were an elderly family member to the extent that sometimes the impression given was one of a tightly-knit family enterprise headed by the cleaner! With one or two exceptions, the Internet café's clients used only a minimal selection from the range of facilities offered: in a daily or weekly routine they hastily read and sent a few emails (they were anxious not to exceed the cybercafé's minimum fee of about €1 per 15 minutes). Some asked for help when searching for the many websites that offer free email accounts. Occasionally young black women came in for advice on how to open email accounts, manifestly at the instigation of absent white South African boyfriends, to enable them to stay in touch regularly and cheaply. Only a very few people looked on the Internet for a specific site or cautiously surfed between sites, but after visiting a few sites even these customers vacated their bar stools with an eloquent look at the clock. All bodily and verbal contact between clients was avoided as if they were catching each other in socially discouraged or taboo behaviour. Staff–client contact was limited to a minimum, and nothing of the richly textured personal relationship between the staff was shared with the clients. Interaction in a public toilet could not have been more impersonal. This lack of social exchange contrasts markedly with Francistown public culture, in whose turbulent recreational setting the word 'café' has certainly connotations of sociability, exchange, self-presentation, status-seeking through conspicuous consumption, the experience of identity by associating oneself with a fixed social and physical location in the recreational space. Most of the time, I was the only customer in the cybercafé. Even in a town as developed and dynamic as Francistown, the target group of the cybercafé was obviously only the few people who (to judge by their general appearance) could not afford a state-of-the-art computer (including the subscription to the electricity mains network, the telephone network, and the Internet) and who had no access to such hardware in their place of employment but who nonetheless were coming to explore hesitantly the new information and communication technology. Enculturation, appropriation towards a local cultural programming, was only very partially the case. On the contrary, for the customers, the Internet would appear to form a secluded domain that one might appropriate instrumentally (with considerable monetary cost, effort and frustration), but whose contents were not in line with the socio-cultural programming of one's own life as a Francistonian. The game of social relations was grinding to a halt in the intimidating nearness of the computer. However, the cybercafé's staff had already regained their natural pose and thus manage to incorporate ICT in their everyday lives in a much more natural manner. Preliminary conclusions made after a week in the Francistown Internet café were that if the Internet is to be the hope of Africa, the realization of that hope would take a while in large parts of Africa.

Backgrounds of ICT enculturation

How is ICT appropriated and localized in African environments in the sense of the emergence of practices that amount to an original creative elaboration upon this new technology and in the course of which local symbols and meanings — both old and new — are conferred upon that technology?

Above I sketched a field of tension, one of whose poles was that ICT might be primarily thought of as eminently North Atlantic. In this respect ICT fits in with an ideal of the appropriation, by Africans, of European symbols of power, prestige and success. During the colonial period (which incidentally lasted considerably less than a century in most part of Africa), this ideal spread widely over the continent. It was expressed in styles of clothing, hairstyles, housing and interior design, family life, choice of modes of transport, recreation, religion — not only among the elite but also among a much larger urban middle class and, to some extent, even right out to the remotest corners of urban slums and to the rural areas.

We should not read too much positive submission in the adoption by Africans of North Atlantic cultural models. Here, as always when it comes to the adoption of cultural elements across sizeable distances in space and/or time, a considerable 'transformative localization' occurs:[18] that which was initially alien is encapsulated by more or less altering its form, meaning, use or a combination of these aspects, according to principles that already exist locally. Nowadays, decades after African states gained their independence, the structure of African elites has changed considerably. They have become more inclusively and unabashedly cosmopolitan, global. But the elites continue to search for prestigious lifestyles and symbols of domination, this being what they have in common with socio-political elites all over the world. The exercise of power in contemporary Africa is increasingly taking place within the framework of formal organizations (such as the state, the army, the party, the enterprise, the church, trade unions, universities) but this framework tends to be much looser and less compelling than in the North Atlantic, far more subject to personal and particularistic manipulation. Often the formal organizations in Africa do not work properly, and if they do work to some extent this is due less to effective bureaucratic and legal rationality than to patronage, ethnic manipulation and informal social networks behind the façade of the formal structure. Here virtualized models of social and political power are being mediated that are not rooted in the North Atlantic heritage but instead in pre-colonial forms of leadership and initiative within kinship groups and pre-colonial states. In many parts of Africa, for several centuries before the effective European colonization of the continent, trade goods hailing from afar were both the symbols of an unrivalled power over life and death, and access to the supernatural (for example, firearms and imported liquor — like Dutch gin which came to constitute the preferred libation liquid at local African shrines), and the attributes of incomparable prestige (textiles, Chinese glazed ware, Ancient Egyptian artefacts, European clothing, etc.). The appropriation of ICT as a means of power must also be seen in this light: not as the imitation of the power and lifestyle of Europeans but as a localized means of prestige that, at the same

[18] The term 'transformative localization' refers to the process of local accommodation by which, in the course of diffusion, a geographically displaced item of culture is transformed so as to fit the systematics of local cultural orientations, cf. Van Binsbergen (1997c).

time, constitutes a real means for the exercise of power in the African social environment. It appears to be a common trait in any system of power, no matter where it occurs in space and time, inside or outside Africa, that the effective exercise of power by means of force goes hand in hand with an ensemble of collective representations which draws this exercise of power into the domain of the numinous and the speculative, that projects it into a magic of power, and hence facilitates people's submission to that power without them openly confronting it.[19] In Africa, this magic has of old taken the form of a discourse on sorcery[20] — of evil that is perpetrated by humans in an extrasensory way and that forms one of the major indigenous explanations of misfortune. In many African societies connotations of sorcery have of old surrounded those occupying high status and specializing in the communication with a human, extra-human or supra-human outside world at the boundary of local society: the king, the headman, the diviner-priest-healer, the blacksmith, the bard, the trader. Although the roots of this complex of collective representations lie in a local kinship order that goes back at least to Neolithic agricultural communities, during the last few decades Africa has seen an intensification of sorcery as an idiom *par excellence* for the articulation of the contradictions of modernity — the tension between consumptive desires and (as a condition to fulfil those desires) the breakdown of historic forms of social organization, solidarity, morals and ethics.

The individualized microcomputer fits very well in this cultural framework — in the first place as a new prestige object of elitist power, and as an instrument for the effective exercise of power in the management of social, political and commercial information, processes and contacts. But this is also and particularly so because ICT conjures up the numinous magic of power so strikingly with its flashing, uncannily real images, its high speed and instantaneous access which give the impression that space and time appear to submit to the user/owner of the microcomputer. Thus, especially in the eyes of uninitiated onlookers, old magical dreams such as bilocation, omnipresence and omnipotence appear finally to come true. For instance, in Benin today the computer is known as *grigri yovo*: 'the magico-religious object[21] of the Whites', and the Internet is explicitly equated with *voodoo* (a cult system based on

---

[19] Cf. Taussig (1997). For an African application of similar ideas, cf. Van Binsbergen (1992b, 1993), and for a theoretical elaboration applied to Ancient Mesopotamia, cf. Van Binsbergen & Wiggermann (1999).

[20] Cf. Van Binsbergen (2001).

[21] I avoid the word 'fetish' which without further discussion would only give rise to confusion.

ecstasy and initiation that, next to and in collusion with the post-colonial state, constitutes the major form of social organization in this African country).[22]

The microcomputer and especially the Internet have, therefore, inserted themselves not only in the recreational practices of African elite children and in the scientific data collection of African intellectuals but also in the power strategies of prominent African politicians and entrepreneurs, and of those aspiring to join their ranks. In the practices of these politicians and entrepreneurs this state-of-the-art form of ICT is often seen to occur in combination with:

- modern natural science and business economics;
- more traditional magical practices (diviner-priests are frequently consulted for political and economic success and for protection in that connection); and
- esoteric world views (theosophy, Rosicrucianism) that from an Oriental and/or pseudo-scientific periphery of North Atlantic rational thought are in the process of conquering Africa in the same way as they are spreading in the North Atlantic in the New Age context.

That the African enculturation of ICT is triggered not only by specific technological and career advantages but also by the desire to explore and appropriate a comprehensive new lifestyle, and even new idioms of social and cosmic power, is suggested by a remarkable research finding from Francistown, Botswana.

My research on the urban culture of Francistown as a window on both local rural traditions and on the process of cultural globalization in Africa brought me into close contact with the three highest-ranking local leaders of the cult of the High God Mwali. This cult is a pre-colonial organization that has now superficially reorganized itself, displaying to the state the appearance of an effective modern formal organization (a professional association of traditional healers, and an African Independent Church) that is more in accordance with Botswana civil law. The three priests combine their high office with flourishing therapeutic and herbalist practices, and in addition operate — in line with a widespread Southern African pattern — a bar, a bottle store, a butchery, a transport company and a dancing troupe. Inside their modern, detached houses, designed and appointed according to cosmopolitan standards, their lives centre around the television set crowned with plastic flowers and surrounded by a circle of heavy armchairs with embroidered head covers. Apparently Africa's consumptive modernity (whose aesthetics appear to be somewhat dated and

[22] Personal communications, Elly Reinierse and (via Elly Reinierse) Ulrike Sulikowski.

second-rate from a North Atlantic perspective) can very well be combined with religious leadership of an originally pre-colonial type. The point is that all three of these cult leaders have young adult daughters who, around 1990, were vaguely active in their fathers' cults (for example in some sort of informal receptionist capacity, attending to callers seeking therapy and ritual advice), but who were primarily pursuing introductory computer training. These daughters were thus among the few Francistonian women who at that time could mobilize the financial means and the kinship support for their personal ventures in ICT. As specialists in an old sphere of power, these specialists, through their daughters' computer training, made sure they did not miss out on a new sphere of power.

Of course, the perception of ICT as magical and as kindred to sorcery, in the eyes of political and economic leaders and of those — almost all of them devoid of computers — over whom they hold sway, is only one aspect of the localization of ICT in Africa. I have already mentioned its use in offices and by intellectuals. Here we see a combination of purposeful rational behaviour, on the one hand, characterized by universalist procedures and assumptions (bureaucratic management, information processing), and, on the other, not so much dreams of computer-underpinned power (as among the political and economic elite), but certainly Utopian pondering on personal career success and on the redress of Africa's ICT backwardness as compared to the North Atlantic region. This Utopian aspect constitutes an additional incentive to acquire computer skills, and lowers the threshold of ICT reception.

All this means that within contemporary African societies, an extensive and many-sided discourse about computers has developed which facilitates the further personal and collective appropriation of ICT. Again the situation is not fundamentally different from that in the North Atlantic: one does not need to command, or even to emulate, the mathematical and micro-electronic rationality of the designers in order to use the computer effectively as a black box — the methods of such use are learned, formally or informally, in a circle of equals (secondary school pupils and university students, friends, colleagues, system managers in training), and in a way in which ordinary everyday spoken language turns out to play a remarkably significant role — even if spiced for the occasion with intercontinental computer terms that are preferably left untranslated. Here again we see the tensions between local and global, intracultural and metacultural, which make ICT such an interesting testing ground for the investigation of interculturality.

These two factors together, namely the appropriation (in a colonial, pre-colonial and post-colonial context) of alien artefacts within more or less elitist frameworks of power, magic and Utopia, and the fact that culturally the computer is a user-friendly black box which is serviceable anywhere, globally, metalocally, furnish us with the beginnings of an answer to the obvious question as to why the incursion of ICT into Africa has met with so little resistance and has been so readily accepted — *as if cultures do not exist*.

From book to web in the African context

I suspect that in answer to this last question other factors might be adduced in addition to the two already mentioned. These additional factors refer to the structure of communicative and procedural connections in ICT such as those it has developed globally in the form of hypertext, hyperlinks and the nested and layered criss-crossing structures engendered in that context. Before the advent of computerized ICT, information management and information transmission were largely modelled on *the book*. This implied the model of a large, unique, self-contained and clearly demarcated quantity of information, highly organized and internally consistent, almost exclusively verbal (i.e. not visual, auditive, motoric, etc.), and as such linearized from beginning to end, in such a way that in principle the medium cogently prescribed one, and only one, path through this information. Such a book model has provided the unit of knowledge production for five millennia in the Ancient Near East including Egypt, Graeco-Roman Antiquity, China, India, the world of Islam, and finally Europe. The 'book model' emerged particularly in Ancient Egypt, where from the New Kingdom onwards the papyrus-leaf *Book of Coming Forth by Day* (also known as the *Book of the Dead*) was only one example of the proliferation of books as the central repositories of knowledge, cherished at the ancient temple academies called Houses of Life and further manifested by the usual burial gift of a copy of the *Book of the Dead*.[23] By contrast, the Ancient Mesopotamian books formed conceptual units held together by titles and rubrics but were physically distributed over a considerable number of clay tablets and hence did not contribute physical unity. After the book model, the idea of the human person was modelled.[24] The same model also informed the idea of the formal organization with its legal (text-based) authority; and probably its was also the book model that informed the idea of the distinct culture, each culture being a specific item in a range of a plurality of cultures, and codified by means of a certain genre of books, notably ethnographies. The world's subjugation to North Atlantic hegemony between the 18th and 20th centuries of the North Atlantic era meant the subjugation to the book (including the Bible, in so far as this subjugation took the form of the spread of Christianity) and likewise the much earlier submission of large parts of Asia, Europe and Africa to Islam, following the Prophet Muhammad's departure (*hijra*) from Mecca that marked the

[23] Cf. Budge (1989), Allen & Hauser (1974).

[24] I owe this suggestion to my colleague Jos de Mul.

beginning of the Islamic era, and amounted to a submission to the Book, notably the Qur'an. Not only the colonial subjects' subjugation but also their subsequent assimilation and final emancipation (by appropriation of North Atlantic models of equal rights, socialism, trade unionism, formal education, franchise, etc.) meant an internalization of the book model. In Africa this disciplining in terms of the book model has only partially taken root even though millions of Africans today are closely comparable with the North Atlantic readers of the present book in terms of formal education and employment within formal organizations. However, African societies have never quite turned into book-style cultures in the same way as this process has advanced progressively in the North Atlantic region and especially in the latter's urban centres. In West African English, the expression 'You know book' has become a standard expression for the person who has a formal education, praising him and setting him apart as a relative exception at the same time. Over the last century, the domain of globalization and virtualization has certainly been an expanding aspect of African societies but the size of that domain in proportion to the totality of African life has remained limited. A considerable part of African life has continued to take place outside formal organizations, and whatever was created in terms of formal organization functioned mainly informally, if at all. The linearity and consistency of the book model did fit a North Atlantic modern world characterized by social and political relations that have largely taken on an instrumental nature, have lost many of their former ritual and symbolic aspects, and therefore have lost much of their meaning. The individuals involved in these relations are increasingly atomized, autonomous and competent, living their lives in political and economic security. Most Africans in colonial and post-colonial settings have always lacked such security, and this is one explanation, among several others,[25] as to why the book model — the individuality, the viable and smoothly functioning formal organization, the linear path thorough social, political and symbolic relationships, and the almost total disenchantment (Weber) of the world — has never occurred in Africa on a scale anywhere comparable to that of the North Atlantic. In modern Africa, one has always needed to compensate the insecurities of the modern, urban, state-based aspects of social life by maintaining (as far as possible) old systems of kin-based and ethnic solidarity — orientated toward the village with its centuries-old practices and systems of representation encompassing many domains of life, and with its concomitant, endlessly proliferating and branching networks of social relations. For excellent reasons, the relational *network* has proved to be a very fertile concept in the

[25] Other such factors, having to do with ideological and political processes of the *longue durée*, are discussed at the end of Chapter 8 of Van Binsbergen (2003).

study of African towns, where informal networks turned out to form for the most part the principal format of social structuring (Mitchell 1969). In this African context it is normal to think in web-like structures, which would be dismissed as inconsistent, incompetent and insufficiently bounded from the point of view of the book model. In this connection there are many points for further research on such crucial topics as: what the consequence is of this web-like or rhizomatic,[26] typically African, social structure, for people's orientation in space and time; the local definition (as porous? as ambiguous?) of the person within such a ramifying environment; the nature of the social and physical space. How might this web-like orientation facilitate, in its turn, modern uses of computers? It is not necessary to appeal in this connection (as Afrocentrists are bound to do) to a special vitality of African cultures, to some special innate talent of Africans, or to some special type of 'savage thought' (Lévi-Strauss 1962) that allegedly might characterize informal situations inside and outside Africa. For an explanation of the continued survival in Africa of non-formal, non-booklike practices and concepts that in North Atlantic societies have been largely supplanted by the state and by other formal organizations with their enormous influence on daily life and the everyday experience, we need only refer to the extent to which colonial and post-colonial insecurities attending the formal situations have been created in Africa by North Atlantic initiative.

For as long as the book remained the norm, and for as long as the forms of communication associated with the book predominated, Africa with its un-booklike response self-evidently lagged behind in ways that it would never be able to make up. It is not the computer in itself which constitutes an assault on the formal and the linear in information, and puts an end to the book as the gold standard. Rather, such a revolution is being prompted by the ramifying, rhizomatic forms in which information is being presented and may be managed on the Internet and in the hypertextual structures within microcomputers. 'The stone which the builders rejected, the same is become the head of the corner' (Mt 21: 42). Not of course because they are Africans but because they are in a privileged position to bring out the problem and potentials of the South, of the Third World, in our times (*grosso modo*, to Asia and Latin America the same perspective applies), modern Africans have as a matter of course mastered the skills needed to survive with their families in a social context characterized by the tension between, on the one hand, the insecure, urban, formal environment

[26] Cf. the concept of 'rhizome' with Deleuze & Guattari (1972, 1980, 1991), with which they seek to contrastively pinpoint for contemporary North Atlantic society, the transformation from the book model to a freer form of subjectivity, one which makes 'it possible to let the individual and/or collective instances come to the fore as self-referential existential Territories, adjacent to, or functioning as boundary conditions for, an alterity which in itself is subjective' (Guattari 1992; my translation).

and, on the other, the manifestations — which also to Africans are often ambivalent — of a persisting but eroded system of kin-based and ethnic solidarity with ultimately a rural and historical referent. In such a context one seldom puts all one's eggs in one basket but instead tends to cultivate and operate simultaneously many contacts, many strategies, many obligations, many kin relations along a multitude of alternative genealogical paths, with many compromises, many contradictions between these commitments — with a logic that is inclusive rather than exclusive, and that prefers not to abide by the principle (which has governed the entire Western philosophical tradition) of the excluded third, in the hope that one may be allowed to have one's cake and eat it too. This structural feature permeates all aspects of African life especially in the increasingly insecure post-colonial situation. It is highly manifest in situations where public life is constantly on the verge of total collapse, such as depicted in recent ethnographic studies by René Devisch (1995, 1996) and Filip de Boeck (1996a, 1996b) on Congo (-Kinshasa). Freely translated towards computer practice, the art of living needed for such situations reminds one of practices for hypertext-based Internet use on the modern computer. This would mean that the modern African is someone who is at least as well equipped, if not better, for the mental requirements of state-of-the-art computer use as the North Atlantic adult, whose main handicap in this computer era may very well prove to be his attachment to the gold standard of the book.

But we have not yet reached the stage where Africa can cash in on this apparent advantage in the handling of web-like structures. Inhabitants of the North Atlantic region and of East and South Asia are strongly represented in the world of ICT, and Africans are mere newcomers there. In this connection, Northerners may continue to boast their skills in the handling and improvement of formal systems. For after all, the rhizomatic structure of the actual application of ICT, however far it tends towards the chaotic, requires us to begin with a strictly formal, logical point of departure in the algorithms and technologies used. But also with regard to formal systems, Africans have their own local traditions. It is not impossible that Africans training in ICT may derive some unexpected advantage from their being acquainted with indigenously African formal systems such as mathematical board games[27] and divination methods[28] that are encountered all over the African continent. Hountondji, the African philosopher who has so strongly criticized the construction (in the hands of his African colleagues and their North Atlantic

---

[27] See Zaslavsky (1990), Seidenberg (1960), Schmidl (1915) and Van Binsbergen (1997a).

[28] See Maupoil (1943a, 1943b), Bascom (1980), Abimbola (1975), Akiwowo (1983), Mákanjúolá (1991), Kassibo (1992), Traoré (1979), Aromolaran (1992) and Van Binsbergen (2003: Chapters 5, 6 and especially 7).

supporters) of an African mystique under the pretext of philosophy,[29] considers the exploration of such historic local forms of science, mathematics and technology an important field of research (Hountondji 1996, 1994). The purpose of such research is not so much to help explode racial stereotypes and to gather points in favour of Afrocentrism but to further among Africans a proud and empirically underpinned vision of their own competence and their own birthright to engage with modern technology.

References

Abimbola, W. (ed.) 1975, *Sixteen Great Poems of Ífa*, Paris: UNESCO.

Abiola Irele 1996, 'Introduction', in: P.J. Hountondji, *African Philosophy: Myth and Reality*, Second edition, Bloomington & Indianapolis: Indiana University Press, pp. 7-30 & 184-85 (notes).

Akiwowo, A. 1983, 'Understanding Interpretative Sociology in the Light of Oriki of Orunmila', *Journal of Cultures and Ideas* 1 (1): 139-57.

Allen, T.G. & E.B. Hauser 1974, *The Book of the Dead, or, Going Forth by Day: Ideas of the Ancient Egyptians Concerning the Hereafter as Expressed in Their Own Terms*, Chicago: University of Chicago Press; translated from Egyptian by T.G. Allen; prepared for publication by E.B. Hauser.

Anderson, B. 1992, 'Long-distance Nationalism: World Capitalism and the Rise of Identity Politics', Wertheim Lecture, Amsterdam University, Amsterdam: Centre for Asian Studies.

Appiah, K.A. 1992, *In My Father's House: Africa in the Philosophy of Culture*, New York & London: Oxford University Press.

Aromolaran, A. 1992, 'A Critical Analysis of the Philosophical Status of Yoruba Ifa Literary Corpus', in: H. Nagl-Docekal & F. Wimmers (eds), *Postkoloniales Philosophieren Afrika*, vol. 6, Vienna: Oldenburg, pp. 140-54.

Bascom, W. 1980, *Sixteen Cowries: Yoruba Divination from Africa to the New World*, Bloomington: Indiana University Press.

Bauman, Z. 1998, *Globalization: The Human Consequences*, London: Polity Press & Blackwell.

Beyer, P. 1994, *Religion and Globalization*, London: Sage.

Budge, E.A.W.T. 1989, *The Book of the Dead: The Chapters of Coming Forth by Day*, (3 vols in 1 vol), London: Arkana; first published in 1898.

Chomsky, N. 1968, *Language and Mind*, New York: Harcourt Brace Jovanovich.

Chomsky, N. 1986, *Knowledge of Language*, New York: Praeger.

De Boeck, F. 1996a, 'Domesticating Diamonds and Dollars: Identity, Expenditure and Sharing in Southwestern Zaire (1984-1997)', in: B. Meyer & P. Geschiere (eds) 1998, *Development and Change*, special issue, 29 (4): 777-810.

[29] Incidentally, Hountondji's position has been contested, not only by particularizing and essentializing Africanist philosophers but also by a cosmopolitan African philosopher like Appiah (1992); cf. Abiola Irele (1996).

De Boeck, F. (ed.) 1996b, 'Postcolonialism, Power, and Identity: Local and Global Perspectives from Zaïre', in T.O. Ranger & R.P. Werbner (eds), *Postcolonial Identities in Africa*, London: Zed Books, pp. 75-106.

De Jong, F. 1994, 'The Making of a Jola Identity: Jola Inventing their Past and Future', in: J. van der Klei (ed.), *Popular Culture: Beyond Historical Legacy and Political Innocence*, Utrecht: CERES, pp. 133-50.

De Jong, F. 2001, 'Modern Secrets: The Power of Locality in Casamance, Senegal', PhD thesis, Amsterdam University.

Deleuze, G. & F. Guattar 1972, *L'Anti-Oedipe: Capitalisme et Schizophrénie, I*, Paris: Minuit.

Deleuze, G. & F. Guattari 1980, *Mille Plateaux: Capitalisme et Schizophrénie, II*, Paris: Minuit.

Deleuze, G. & F. Guattar 1991, *Qu'est-ce que la Philosophie?*, Paris: Minuit.

Devisch, R. 1995, 'Frenzy, Violence and Ethnical Renewal in Kinshasa', *Public Culture* 7 (3): 593-629.

Devisch, R. 1996, '"Pillaging Jesus": Healing Churches and the Villagisation of Kinshasa', *Africa* (66): 555-86.

Fardon, R. W.M.J. van Binsbergen & R. van Dijk (eds) 1999, *Modernity on a Shoestring: Dimensions of Globalization, Consumption and Development in Africa and Beyond,* based on an EIDOS conference held in The Hague, Netherlands, March 13-16 1997, Leiden & London: European Inter-university Development Opportunities Study Group [EIDOS].

Featherstone, M. 1995, *Undoing Culture: Globalization, Postmodernism and Identity*, London: Sage.

Friedman, J. 1995, *Cultural Identity and Global Process*, London: Sage; first published in 1994.

Guattari, F. 1992, *Chaosmosis: An Ethico-aesthetic Paradigm*, translated by P. Bains & J. Pefanis, Sydney: Power Publications; translated from French edition 1992, *Chaosmose*, Paris: Galilée.

Gyekye, K. 1997, 'Philosophy, Culture, and Technology in the Postcolonial', in: E.C. Eze (ed.), *Postcolonial African Philosophy: A Critical Reader*, Oxford: Blackwell, pp. 25-44.

Hannerz, U. 1992, *Cultural Complexity: Studies in the Social Organization of Meaning*, New York: Columbia University Press.

Heidegger, M. 1977, *The Question Concerning Technology and Other Essays*, New York: Harper.

Hountondji, P.J. 1988, 'L'Appropriation Collective du Savoir: Taches Nouvelles pour une Politique Scientifique', *Genève-Afrique* 26 (1): 49-66.

Hountondji, P.J. 1990, 'Scientific Dependence in Africa Today', *Research in African Literatures* 21 (3): 5-15.

Hountondji, P.J. (ed.) 1994, *Les Savoirs Endogènes: Pistes Pour une Recherche*, Paris: Karthala.

Hountondji, P.J. 1996, *African Philosophy: Myth and Reality*, Second edition, Bloomington & Indianapolis: Indiana University Press; this English translation first published in 1983; first French edition published in 1976.

Jules-Rosette, B. 1990, *Terminal Signs: Computers and Social Change in Africa*, Berlin & New York: Mouton de Gruyter.

Kassibo, B. 1992, 'La Géomancie Ouest-Africaine: Formes Endogènes et Emprunts Extérieurs', *Cahiers d'Etudes Africaines* 32, 4 (128): 541-96.

Kimmerle, H. 1994, *Die Dimension des Interkulturellen*, Amsterdam & Atlanta: Rodopi.

Kimmerle, H. & F.M. Wimmer (eds) 1997, *Philosophy and Democracy in Intercultural Perspective*, Amsterdam & Atlanta: Rodopi.

King, A.D. 1991, *Culture, Globalization and the World-System: Contemporary Conditions for the Representation of Identity*, Binghamton: Macmillan.

Lévi-Strauss, C. 1962, *La Pensée Sauvage*, Paris: Plon; translated in English, 1973, *The Savage Mind*, Chicago: University of Chicago Press/London: Weidenfeld & Nicholson; first published in 1966.

Mákanjúolá Ilésanmí, T. 1991, 'The Traditional Theologians and the Practice of Orìsà Religion in Yorùbáland', *Journal of Religion in Africa* 21 (3): 216-26.

Mall, R.A. 1995, *Philosophie im Vergleich der Kulturen: Interkulturelle Philosophie, eine Neue Orientierung*, Darmstadt: Wissenschaftliche Buchgesellschaft.

Mall, R.A. & D. Lohmar (eds) 1993, *Philosophische Grundlagen der Interkulturalität*, Amsterdam & Atlanta: Rodopi.

Maupoil, B. 1943a, 'Contribution a l'Etude de l'Origine Musulmane de la Géomancie dans le Bas-Dahomey', *Journal de la Société des Africanistes* (13): 1-94.

Maupoil, B. 1943b, *La Géomancie à l'Ancienne Côte des Esclaves*, Paris: Institut de l'Ethnologie.

Mazrui, A.A. 1977, 'Development Equals Modernization Minus Dependency: A Computer Equation,' in: D.R.F. Taylor & R.A. Obudho (eds), *The Computer and Africa: Applications, Problems, and Potential*, New York: Praeger, pp. 279-304.

Mazrui, A.A. 1978, 'The African Computer as an International Agent', in: A.A. Mazrui, *Political Values and the Educated Class in Africa*, London: Heinemann, pp. 320-42.

Mbeki, T. 1999, 'The African Renaissance, South Africa and the World', in: A. Hadland & J. Rantao, *The Life and Times of Thabo Mbeki*, Rivonia South Africa: Zebra/Southern/New Holland Struik, pp. 170-83.

Meyer, B. & P. Geschiere 1998 (eds), 'Globalization and Identity: Dialectics of Flows and Closures', *Development and Change*, special issue, 29 (4): 601-15; published separately in: B. Meyer & P. Geschiere (eds) 1999, *Globalization and Identity: Dialectics of Flow and Closure*, Oxford: Blackwell.

Mitchell, J.C. (ed.) 1969, *Social Networks in Urban Situations: Analyses of Personal Relationships in Central African Towns*, Manchester: Manchester University Press.

Nkwi, P.N. 1995, 'Electronic Mail: The Experience of the Network of African Medical Anthropology (NAMA)', *African Anthropology* 2 (1): 154-61.

Nyamnjoh, F.B. 1997, 'Africa and the Information Superhighway: The Need for Mitigated Euphoria', paper read at the WAC C-UNESCO Workshop on 'Communication and the Globalization of Poverty: Media Ownership in West and Central Africa', Yaoundé (Cameroon), September 8-10, earlier version by F.B. Nyamnjoh, F. Wete & T. Fonchingong 1996, entitled 'Media and Civil Society in Cameroon', *Africa Media Review* 10 (2): 37-66.

OAU (Organization of African Unity), 1995, 'ICC's Seminar on New Information Technologies in Africa, Yaounde (Cameroon) May 29-31 1995: OAU's Presentation', paper presented at ICC workshop on 'New Information Technology and Standardization of Communication Equipment in Africa', May 29-31, Yaoundé, Cameroon.

Okigbo, C. 1995, 'National Images in the Age of the Information Superhighway: African Perspectives', *Africa Media Review* 9 (2): 105-21.

Ras-Work, T. (ed.) 1998, *Tam Tam to Internet*, Mafube Publishers: Johannesburg.

Robertson, R. 1992, *Globalization: Social Theory and Global Culture*, London: Sage.

Schmidl, M. 1915, 'Zahl und Zahlen in Afrika', *Mitteilungen der Anthropologischen Gesellschaft in Wien* 45: 165-209.

Seidenberg, A. 1960, 'The Diffusion of Counting Practices', *University of California Publications in Mathematics* 3 (4): 215-99.

Sheldrake, R. 1981, *A New Science of Life*, London: Blond & Briggs.

Sheldrake, R. 1988, *The Presence of the Past*, New York: Vintage Books.

Slob, G. 1990, *Computerizing Apartheid: Export of Computer Hardware to South Africa*, Amsterdam: Holland Committee on Southern Africa.

Tankoano, J. (ed.) 1994, 'Actes du 2e Colloque Africain sur la Recherche en Informatique: Ouagadougou (Burkina Faso), du 12 au 18 October 1994', Paris: ORSTOM Editions.

Taussig, M.T. 1997, *The Magic of the State*, London: Routledge.

Traoré, M.L. 1979, 'Vers une Pensée Originelle Africaine: Exposé Géomantique, Critiques de la Négritude et du Consciencisme', Thèse de 3e cycle, Université de Paris-IV.

UNESCO (United Nations Educational, Scientific and Cultural Organization), 1980, 'The New World Information and Communication Order,' Resolution 4/19 of the 21st Session of the UNESCO General Conference, Belgrade, reprinted in: *NACLA Report on the Americas* 16 (4): 32.

Van Binsbergen, W.M.J. 1984, 'Socio-ritual Structures and Modern Migration among the Manjak of Guinea Bissau: Ideological Reproduction in a Context of Peripheral Capitalism', *Antropologische Verkenningen* 3 (2): 11-43.

Van Binsbergen, W.M.J. 1988, 'The Land as Body: An Essay on the Interpretation of Ritual among the Manjaks of Guinea-Bissau', in: R. Frankenberg (ed.), *Gramsci, Marxism, and Phenomenology: Essays for the Development of Critical Medical Anthropology*, special issue, *Medical Anthropological Quarterly* new series, 2 (4): 386-401.

Van Binsbergen, W.M.J. 1992a, 'Kazanga: Etniciteit in Afrika tussen Staat en Traditie', inaugural address, Amsterdam: Vrije Universiteit; English version: 'The Kazanga Festival: Ethnicity as Cultural Mediation and Transformation in Western Central Zambia', *African Studies* 53 (2): 92-125.

Van Binsbergen, W.M.J. 1992b, *Tears of Rain: Ethnicity and History in Western Central Zambia*, London & Boston: Kegan Paul International.

Van Binsbergen, W.M.J. 1993, '"Geef hem dan maar aan de Krokodillen": Staatsvorming, Geweld en Culturele Discontinuïteit in Voor-koloniaal Zuidelijk Centraal Afrika', in: H. Dahles & A. Trouwborst (eds), special issue on state formation, *Antropologische Verkenningen* 12 (4): 10-31; English version: '"Then

Give Him to the Crocodiles": Violence, State Formation, and Cultural Discontinuity in West Central Zambia, 1600-2000', in: W.M.J. van Binsbergen in collaboration with R. Pelgrim (ed.), *The Dynamics of Power and the Rule of Law: Essays on Africa and Beyond in Honour of Emile Adriaan B. van Rouveroy van Nieuwaal*, Berlin & Münster & London: LIT for African Studies Centre, Leiden, pp. 197-220.

Van Binsbergen, W.M.J. 1994a, 'Dynamiek van Cultuur: Enige Dilemma's van Hedendaags Afrika in een Context van Globalisering', contribution to a special issue entitled 'De Dynamiek van de Cultuur', guest editors L. Brouwer & I. Hogema, *Antropologische Verkenningen* 13 (2): 17-33; English version: 'Popular Culture in Africa: Dynamics of African Cultural and Ethnic Identity in a Context of Globalization', in: J.D.M. van der Klei (ed.), *Popular Culture: Africa, Asia & Europe: Beyond Historical Legacy and Political Innocence,* Proceedings Summer School 1994, Utrecht: CERES, 1995, pp. 7-40.

Van Binsbergen, W.M.J. 1994b, 'The Kazanga Festival: Ethnicity as Cultural Mediation and Transformation in Western Central Zambia', *African Studies* 53 (2): 92-125.

Van Binsbergen, W.M.J. 1997a, 'Rethinking Africa's Contribution to Global Cultural History: Lessons From a Comparative Historical Analysis of Mankala Board Games and Geomantic Divination', in: W.M.J. van Binsbergen (ed.), *Black Athena: Ten Years After*, Hoofddorp: Dutch Archaeological and Historical Society, special issue, *Talanta: Proceedings of the Dutch Archaeological and Historical Society* 28-29 1996-97: 221-54.

Van Binsbergen, W.M.J. 1997b, 'Virtuality as a Key Concept in the Study of Globalization: Aspects of the Symbolic Transformation of Contemporary Africa', The Hague: WOTRO, Working papers on globalization and the construction of communal identity, 3.

Van Binsbergen, W.M.J. 1997c, 'Alternative Models of Intercontinental Interaction Towards the Earliest Cretan Script', in: W.M.J. van Binsbergen (ed.), *Black Athena: Ten Years After,* Hoofddorp: Dutch Archaeological and Historical Society, special issue, *Talanta: Proceedings of the Dutch Archaeological and Historical Society* 28-29 1996-97: 131-48.

Van Binsbergen, W.M.J. 1998, 'Globalization and Virtuality: Analytical Problems Posed by the Contemporary Transformation of African Societies', in: B. Meyer & P.L. Geschiere, *Globalization and Identity: Dialectics of Flows and Closures*, special issue, *Development and Change* 29 (4): 873-903; also separately published as B. Meyer & P.L. Geschiere (eds) 1998, *Globalization and Identity: Dialectics of Flow and Closure*, Oxford: Blackwell, pp. 273-303.

Van Binsbergen, W.M.J. 1999, 'Enige Filosofische Aspecten van Culturele Globalisering: Met Bijzondere Verwijzing naar Malls Interculturele Hermeneutiek', in: J. Baars & E. Starmans (eds), *Het Eigene en het Andere: Filosofie en Globalisering: Acta van de 21 Nederlands-Vlaamse Filosofiedag*, Delft: Eburon, pp. 37-52; revised English version incorporated in: Van Binsbergen (2003, Chapter 12).

Van Binsbergen, W.M.J. 2001, 'Witchcraft in Modern Africa as Virtualised Boundary Conditions of the Kinship Order', in: G.C. Bond & D.M. Ciekawy (eds), *Witchcraft Dialogues: Anthropological and Philosophical Exchanges*, pp. 212-63.

Van Binsbergen, W.M.J. 2003, *Intercultural Encounters: African, Anthropological and Historical Lessons Towards a Philosophy of Interculturality*, Berlin & Münster & London: LIT.

Van Binsbergen, W.M.J. & F.A.M. Wiggermann 1999, 'Magic in History: A Theoretical Perspective, and its Application to Ancient Mesopotamia', in: T. Abusch & K. van der Toorn (eds), *Mesopotamian Magic*, Groningen: Styx, pp. 3-34.

Van der Veer, P. 1996, *Conversion to Modernities: The Globalization of Christianity*, New York & London: Routledge.

Warnier, J.-P. 1999, *La Mondialisation de la Culture*, Paris: Découverte.

Zaslavsky, C. 1990, *Africa Counts: Number and Pattern in African Culture*, Brooklyn NY: Lawrence Hill, 2nd paperback edition, Boston: Prindle, Weber & Schmidt; first published in 1973.

5

'Man will live well': On the poetics of corruption in a global age

Sanya Osha

The difference between philosophical and anthropological practices in Africa is becoming exceedingly glaring, maybe because a dominant tradition in the analytical school of African philosophy is limited by a strain of British empiricism. However, new conditions of existence, which conventional tropes of analysis in African philosophy seem unable to handle, are emerging within the African post-colony. How has the problem of corruption been addressed in African philosophical practice? Kwame Gyekye, the Ghanaian philosopher, has tackled the problem of political corruption by employing discursive strategies derived from the Athenian philosophical traditions. This chapter argues that his conceptualization of the problem does not fully describe the emerging conditions in the post-colony. On the other hand, Jean-Pierre Olivier de Sardan, the French anthropologist, analyses the modes of social organization, forms of sociality and the conditions of contemporary globalization that necessitate a more subtle theorization of the problem of corruption in Africa and the ways in which it can be approached conceptually. Perhaps a more acute analysis of the situation in the African post-colony is still required.

Insofar as it is 'philosophical' or 'theoretical', the Greek *corpus* stretches — for Arendt — from Parmenides to Plato and Aristotle, and then to Heidegger. It is characterized by the primacy of truth, *theoria* and the *vita contemplative*. Heidegger's Presocratics, including Anaximander, are modern in Arendt's eyes. The only genuine Presocratic experience is political experience (an echo of which can still be heard in Aristotle), where the focus is not truth but freedom. For freedom, by definition, is not a philosophical concept: it is an exclusively political concept, indeed the quintessence of the city-state and of citizenship. Our philosophical

> tradition of political thought, beginning with Parmenides and Plato, was founded explicitly in opposition to this polis, and its citizenship. (Cassin 1990: 39)

The garb of Kant

The extract above in theoretical terms is at the centre of my subsequent discussion: the irreconcilable tensions between the philosophical and the realm of politics. Since philosophy prides itself on having rigorous methods of inquiry, since its innate sense of wonder compels it to articulate discourse at its margins and beyond its frontiers (*metaphysics*), since as Derrida (1978) states, it poses questions to itself that it cannot answer, then it sometimes shows itself in a bad light. In short, my subsequent discussion would end up highlighting the limits of a particular kind of philosophizing, the exhaustion of *theoria*, of categorical imperatives in the face of overwhelming social dynamics. Evidently, in a context of rapid social flux, gestures of philosophical distanciation never fully describe transgressive social landscapes. Rather, they tend to reify the abstract in social processes to the detriment of the 'real' dynamics that motivate those very processes.

Kwame Gyekye, the Ghanaian philosopher, devotes an entire chapter in his 1997 text *Tradition and Modernity* to the issue of corruption. For him as a philosopher, philosophy serves as a guiding light, as the cognitive apparatus by which to get to the bottom of the matter. A central part of my purpose here is to indicate the limits of his approach and also demonstrate how certain disciplinary markers rather than shedding understanding may engender even more confusion.

One of the grave shortcomings of philosophy as a discipline in Africa seems to lie in the framing of inappropriate questions: 'Does African philosophy exist?' 'What constitutes the being of African philosophy?' Otherwise it adopts counterproductive methodologies such as ethno-philosophy, which has encountered severe criticism.[1] Lately, in my opinion, philosophy in its extreme pseudo-theoretical form, that is, in its anti-sophistical gestures and its

[1] See Mbembe (2001a). The disciplinary conflicts between history and anthropology and between philosophy and anthropology have become even more pronounced under conditions of contemporary globalization. In his essay 'The End of Geography', Arvind Das (2002: 34) writes: 'the idea of "nation", which historians institutionalized over the last few centuries, is also seen to be outdated, like history itself. Instead, the anthropologists seem to prevail over the historians, asserting that it is the a-temporal cross-sectional division of humanity into various ethnicities that is more relevant than the historically evolved nationalities and nations that have hegemonised political-ideological discourse till recently.'

overestimation of its powers, sometimes attempts to describe social processes using the wrong tools.

Gyekye (1997: 193) states that 'political corruption, despite its name, is essentially or fundamentally a moral problem' and continues by saying that 'political corruption is thus an act of corruption perpetrated against the state or its agencies by persons holding an official position in pursuit of his own private or personal profit'. Thereafter, he lists a whole variety of corrupt political practices that do indeed shed light on the broad range of issues surrounding this topic. For instance, he writes that 'graft, fraud, nepotism, kickbacks, favoritism, and misappropriation of public funds are all acts of political corruption' (ibid:). Gyekye does not limit the scope of his definition to political corruption alone. Business executives, public officials, clerks in all sectors and immigration officials all perpetrate corruption.

He also makes several normative statements — as philosophers are wont to do — as he enumerates the conditions under which corruption can thrive:

> Political corruption can flourish under weak political leadership. For political leaders or top public officials who are weak and can hardly be expected to control subordinate officers tempted by bribes and forms of political corruption, either because, being weak leaders, they do not have the nerve or courage to exert control, or, perhaps, being honest themselves, they have compromised their own integrity and moral authority and so cannot discipline others. (Gyekye 1997: 194).

Here, he is attempting to maintain the stance of a philosopher (and a committed one at that) who can make insightful comments on the workings of the polity. That is to be expected in philosophy but philosophers must be cautious about running philosophy down since an element in the nature of the discipline perhaps prevents it from a humble demarcation of its own limits.

Gyekye, in addressing himself to the problem of corruption, not only defines it as a philosopher should but also proposes solutions. In the space between the definition of the problem and the articulation of the solutions we find an entire conceptual region that invites a series of interesting analyses. Has he in fact exhaustively defined corruption? From what context or concatenation of contexts do his definitions emerge? This question is crucial because the African post-colony that constitutes the primary site of inquiry is indeed a most interesting, if perplexing, site. In addressing ourselves to this particular site, not only do we have to interrogate the various configurations of the social processes taking place therein, we also have to debate the nature of the state and its various problematic trajectories, the forms of life and death that now predominate on the continent and how these forms invite fresh methodological categories to describe these new developments and social processes, and finally the nature and status of moral philosophy itself. In relation to the last point, not only do we need to situate instruments of abstraction in their most viable context but we also need to address the political economy of moral philosophy in contemporary Africa in order to be more keenly aware of the appropriateness of our conceptual implements, in other words, the multiple and problematic relationships between theory and society and how they might or might not conceptualize the new. This brings us back to the issue raised in the first quotation in this essay, that is, the apparent irreconciability of philosophy and political practice. In Arendt's corpus there is a sustained focus on the divide between philosophy and political science, i.e. thinking (philosophy) and conditions of activity in the public sphere (politics), and this dichotomy is never quite resolved. The problem is not merely one of theory and practice, it also relates to an evident disciplinary impasse, the running against limits. When a discipline questions itself about something for which it has no answers, what does it then do?

In facing this important question, Gyekye ransacks the inventory of philosophical tools and comes up with a set of established disciplinary responses. Philosophy, being the mother of all other disciplines, ought to have an appropriate response. In putting the final nail in the coffin, Gyekye (ibid: 201) states that 'political corruption is a *moral* problem and should be grappled with from that standpoint'. For him, 'it is a moral pollution of officialdom as well as of the wider society' (ibid: 203). And according to him, 'the next question is to determine a satisfactory approach to dealing with it' (ibid: 205). He does not define precisely what he means by 'moral' but we can assume that his stance on the issue is inflected and overdetermined by classical Western philosophical thought. Let us examine a number of interesting points Gyekye makes along the way.

First, he addresses the nature of political corruption in the politics of traditional Africa. Granted that the institutions of governance and the sophistication of official bureaucracies in traditional Africa are limited, Gyekye agrees that 'it cannot at all be denied that political corruption in the form of receiving and giving bribes or misusing or misappropriating public or communal or lineage goods and resources does exist in the traditional politics and administration in Africa' (ibid: 201-203). In making this assertion, Gyekye has ventured into the historical anthropology of corruption in Africa, a multidisciplinary space into which one would have expected him to expand. Second, he incorporates a sociological perspective when he writes: 'I was once told by a fairly senior public official who was seeking election to a parliament in a country in Africa: If I get elected, I would seek an appointment as secretary of trade. If I get it, *man will live well*' (ibid: 204). Gyekye makes half-hearted forays into history and sociology in coming to grips with the problem of corruption in Africa.

In addition, he discusses the nature of the state, which from an African perspective is a highly contentious issue. On this he writes: 'governments are generally perceived as distant or objective entities whose activities have little bearing on the welfare and the daily lives of the citizens, and to whose activities the citizens, in consequence, have very little ideological and emotional attachment' (ibid: 195).[2] This comment indeed opens up a large discursive space that we cannot afford to miss because it links the superstructure of the state to the moral economy of corruption in intriguing ways, especially within the Africa context. My view here is that philosophy again comes up against its own limits. There will be more on this later.

This question of philosophy's limitations is particularly evident when Gyekye addresses the solutions to corruption.

> One of the central problems of moral life is the problem of moral weakness, that is, the problem of knowing the right thing and yet doing the wrong thing, of acting against our better judgement. (ibid: 210)

In classical philosophy, Gyekye tells us that 'the ancient Greek philosophers called this problem of moral conflict *akrasia*: moral weakness, weakness of will, incontinence' (ibid: 210). Indeed, Gyekye's primary discursive impulse owes much to the ancient Greek tradition, as is evident in the considerable faith he places on rationality. And he deduces that rational human beings would always behave in morally just ways. This opinion commendably tries to break the bonds of exceptionalism, to speak of a problem in Africa in the broadest universalistic terms possible. But this commendable thrust brings us to another problem that lies at the heart of universalism itself. As noted, one of the well-known shortcomings of philosophy in Africa is its project of ethno-philosophy. And some of the conceptual breakaways from this dead-end have been robust espousals of universalism. Mudimbe (1988, 1991), Appiah (1992) and Mbembe (2001a, 2001b) have all, to varying degrees and in various ways, posited forms of universalism in their conceptualizations of Africa and African topics. For Mbembe (2001a), this project encapsulates seeing 'the world as a category of

---

[2] This point has a direct bearing on the question of ownership. Figures of authority in Africa are commonly known to privatize the instruments and powers of public office (see Ake 1996). This phenomenon forces us to consider the genealogy of ownership. In times of corporate capitalism, 'long-distance nationalism', as formulated by Anderson (1992), reproblematizes the notion of the homeland. Writers such as Ayer (2000, 2002) have proffered even more radical accounts of what now constitutes a home. See also Appiah (2002).

thought'. It also includes a rigorous critique of what he terms 'the prose of nativism' (Mbembe 2002).

Thus, philosophically speaking, not all terms of universalism are universal. The universal is always mediated by factors that stem from the particular. By extension, the particular invariably creates the conditions of possibility for the universal and *vice versa*. These complimentary and contradictory logics are always in motion defining both the universal and the particular in a field of dialogics. In Gyekye's particular case, his brand of universalism, in a way, does a disservice to the particular. To be sure, the way in which it does this might in fact be no particular shortcoming of his own but rather that philosophy as a discipline has a lot to answer for.

The next part of this chapter deals with the particular local conditions that Gyekye's mode of philosophising (mis)represents. Again, I stress that in attempting to get to the roots of this shortcoming it might be more useful to interrogate the limits of philosophy itself, to call it to order for transgressing its boundaries and for not discovering new conceptual instruments or annexing better-suited disciplinary boundaries. Perhaps the fact of the matter is that philosophy has a lot to answer for by failing to carry out processes of remapping upon itself and its territories.

Freefall

Interestingly, corruption in Africa can be read and described in other ways. In relation to Gyekye's reading of corruption, Jean-Pierre Olivier de Sardan's essay entitled 'African Corruption in the Context of Globalization' is instructive from both a theoretical and an empirical angle. First, he reminds us 'that anthropology is a discipline concerned with empirical researches and grounded theories' (Olivier de Sardan 1999: 247). This disciplinary signal is, to be sure, important and he agrees with Gyekye that 'the "corruption complex" includes nepotism, abuse of power, embezzlement and various forms of misappropriation, traffic in influence, prevarication, *délits d'iniliés*, abuse of the public purse, etc.' (ibid). There are basically no definitional disagreements between Gyekye and Olivier de Sardan but their conceptual trajectories and methods of discursive articulation are markedly different, and this difference becomes fundamental when viewed from the disciplinary perspective.

Before moving on to differences in approaches let us note that Gyekye (1997: 195) says: 'corruption is common to all human societies, even though the frequency and prevalence of its incidence may differ among societies'. Similarly, Olivier de Sardan (1999: 248) points out that 'corruption is a worldwide phenomenon, but it is not only a modern one; it has existed from the

Roman and Byzantine empires through to communist and post-communist Eastern Europe, and from the political machinery of nineteenth-century American towns to Mediterranean societies'. Perhaps this is why Gyekye disagrees that there is a 'culture of corruption' specific to Africa.

The similarities end there. First, Olivier de Sardan informs us that corruption is related to monetarization and commodification. So theoretically, 'corruption in Africa today is embedded in collective norms, collective logics and collective identities, and that is the reason for its pervasiveness on a continental level' (ibid: 248). For Olivier de Sardan, it makes sense to discuss corruption in Africa on the basis of regionalization and globalization. These conceptual paradigms are absent in Gyekye's discussions. In addition, Olivier de Sardan (ibid: 249) demonstrates why North Atlantic forms of corruption differ from African forms. And even within African forms of corruption there are essential differences. Thus, 'Botswana or Burkina Faso were once said to have very little corruption, while the pervasiveness of corruption in Zaire is unparalleled' and furthermore, he writes that 'there are very different spaces and levels of corruption. I shall distinguish international, regional and local corruption' (ibid: 248). These crucial distinctions are obviously paradigmatic in the way in which they highlight particular disciplinary practices. Let us now examine the various types and distinctions in Olivier de Sardan's analysis of corruption.

There is a difference, for instance, between big-time corruption and petty corruption. Big-time corruption involves presidents, ministers, directors of important offices and heads of public corporations, while petty corruption is practised by policemen, clerks, nurses, customs officers, etc. The fact is that 'everyone in Africa, man or woman, peasant or townsfolk, young or old, has routine experiences of dealing with corruption (and the like), this being a part of the social landscape' (ibid: 250).

In Achille Mbembe's (2000a, 2000b, 2001a, 2001b, 2002) corpus, this routinization of corruption, violence and processes of brutalization assume more dramatic characteristics. We are forced to acknowledge the emergence of an entirely new political economy of violence, exploitation and domination in addition to the construction of new public and private moralities to which they give rise. Again, theoretically, these configurations reverberate strongly on the ways in which we perceive and reconstruct events in everyday life. Our discursive epistemologies have to take these developments into account in order to remain relevant.

Olivier de Sardan notes that in Africa there is often a reluctance to report evident cases of corruption to constituted authorities. Such cases are then left to the realm of rumour and speculation, clearly adding to the moral economy of witchcraft. (In most parts of post-colonial Africa, most things that cannot be explained are attributed to sorcery, especially in places where literacy levels are low and in the continent's various sites of problematic modernities. See the numerous articles by Peter Geschiere and also Wim van Binsbergen on this issue.) In the words of Olivier de Sardan (1999: 251), 'denouncing to the police a relative, a neighbour, the relative of a friend or of a neighbour — anyone with whom one has a personal tie, even a weak one — is unthinkable: the social disapproval would be too great'.

This brings us to the specific forms of sociality to be found in Africa. Indeed certain forms of these social networks have assumed transnational proportions. Migrant francophone trading communities in Johannesburg serve as powerful ethnic and national bases for new immigrants from those communities and assist them with integration into the host city.[3] The same can be said about Nigerian traders of Ibo extraction based in South Africa. Studies have indicated that these migrant communities are becoming increasingly sophisticated in their modes of integration and activities but this is at the transnational level. At the local level, these forms of sociality are no less complex and in fact, they are at the very heart of the social bond. The injunction to be one's brother's keeper is not only biblical in its coloration but is also linked to primordial origins and even in an age of excessive bureaucratization and technological surveillance post-colonial subjects are finding ways in which to bypass complex and advanced social systems to reinscribe the 'filiative' and the 'affiliative' in often intriguing and unexpected ways.

The practice of gift giving is, for example, an interesting area in which to interrogate how African forms of sociality mediate the dynamics of corruption. In this respect, it is pertinent to note that corruption is linked with bargaining, 'a commodified form of negotiation regulating almost all forms of exchanges current in Africa' (Olivier de Sardan 1999: 253). Thus:

> The practice of corruption benefits from this logic of negotiation and bargaining. Not only is corruption in the strict sense of the word an object of bargaining — thus affecting the form of normal, customary commercial transactions — it also takes the shape of a simultaneous negotiation of rules, their pertinence and modes of interpretation. (ibid: 253)

There is verbal sparring involved in the bargaining process associated with corruption just as it is an established practice to employ middlemen in everyday life to protect oneself from aspects of corruption. At this juncture, we have to bear in mind the difference between African forms of sociality and North Atlantic ones. Olivier de Sardan points out that European forms of sociality 'are clearly inferior, diverse factors — including withdrawal of the nuclear family, confinement within limited circles of friends and close acquaintances, absence

[3] See Simone (2000) and also D.B. Coplan (1994, 1995).

of relations between neighbours — have resulted in a weaker sociability in the North than in the South' (ibid: 256). On the other hand, in Africa:

> One cannot refuse a service, a favour, a bit of string-pulling or compliance to a relative, neighbour, party comrade or friend. No more ought one refuse the same to someone 'sent' by any of the above. The circle of individuals to whom one feels obliged to render services is thus astonishingly wide. The other side of the same coin is that one has a great number of people to call upon. The system thus becomes one of a 'generalized exchange' of services, big or small, usually in the shape of an officially illicit favour. (ibid: 256)

By extension, one of the worst fates that can befall an individual in Africa is to be devoid of social capital as its weak forms of governmentality, bureaucratization and economic development, which encourage familial forms of sociality, make chronic patrimonialism inevitable. Social capital in Africa has very distinct forms. A lucrative government appointment is seen as an opportunity not only to enrich oneself, one's immediate family and extended family but also possibly one's local community. Thus, to refuse a position of authority in Africa 'would be a simultaneous show of ingratitude, egotism, pride, naivety and even stupidity' (ibid: 258). Related to this, there is a blurring of the distinctions between the private and public domains. This lack of distinction between the private and public domains in Africa is a feature that can be traced to pre-coloniality where traditional chiefs 'were obliged to make a general show of largesse and thereby attract public praise for their generosity' (ibid: 258) and the transitions in Africa between the colonial state and the post-colonial state are not always very significant because the colonial state was erected on an epistemology of violence that the political elites inherited and hardly modified.

Olivier de Sardan made two other points that are of significance here. First, he points out that: 'in Europe, everyday forms of consumption oblige constant dipping into one's pocket. But everyday forms of sociability shy away from the monetary idiom. In Africa, on the contrary, everyday sociability requires quite a lot of cash' (ibid: 260). This view is quite accurate. House-warming ceremonies, 'freedom parties' for artisans who have completed their training programmes, burials, 'washing' the purchase of a new (today, second-hand) car are all social events that require considerable expenditure. Thus the monetarization of everyday life exerts a lot of pressure on all and sundry.

Given this kind of trajectory, Olivier de Sardan's analysis of corruption in Africa is decidedly more nuanced than that which is to be found in current approaches in African philosophical thought. In his hands, the anthropology of corruption in Africa obviously leads us to a related set of questions. What is the nature of the state in contemporary Africa and how have its colonial antecedents contributed to its present trajectory? I ask this particular question because Gyekye, in his characterization of the state in Africa, casts it in a rational light. But is this really the case? In addressing this question we would be able to get a more representative picture of the political economy of morality in Africa. And finally, in addressing the general economy of conduct it would be useful to note how the crises of the state have give rise to other non-statist technologies of violence and domination and the particular moralities that this development engenders. Both Gyekye and Olivier de Sardan in their analyses of corruption do not do this. One is not saying — especially in the case of Olivier de Sardan — that they ought to have done so *per se*. However, I think it is worthwhile indicating the emergence of social processes, configurations and developments that will definitely compel a rethink of what we mean by the state, law and order, and the common good. If we are able to cast these terms into the vortexes that are currently transforming African social spaces, they might come to acquire the specificity that is often lacking in African contexts.

Jean and John Comaroff draw our attention to what they term 'the metaphysics of disorder' in post-apartheid South Africa (Comaroff & Comaroff 2002). In particular, they observe that:

> Crime, itself ever more global, looms large in the 'new world disorder'. Its forms are becoming increasingly flexible, copying strategies from the legitimate business world as it constitutes an 'uncivil society' that flourishes especially where the state withdraws; hence the ubiquitous role of the mafia in Russia and other post-totalitarian polities which perform, for a fee, services that government no longer provides. These criminal 'phantom states' are an ever more prevalent feature of our time. They exist in relation to transnational crime of increasing sophistication, shading imperceptibly into networks of terror that are rapidly replacing conventional military forces as the prime challenge to 'national' security. (ibid: 3)

This state of affairs is particularly evident in the African post-colony and affects the general economy of conduct in startling and fundamental ways. Thus it means we have to find new conceptual frameworks in which to theorize terms such as corruption, the state and the common good. Gyekye's discussions of these allied matters show the limits of his disciplinary approach. Olivier de Sardan, on the other hand, opens up a space for even more productive discourse. The type of discourse that Olivier de Sardan engenders is now the focus of my attention.

These spaces that Gyekye's discussion excludes and which Olivier de Sardan draws attention to only demonstrate with greater urgency the task facing the human sciences. There is a pressing need for multivocality and multiplicity in (re)presenting the world, in probing the disjunctures and continuities between the abstract and the concrete in modern existence, between the individual and society and between the citizen and nation and how these various configurations are being transformed through impersonal neo-liberal processes of commodification and monetarization. Thus there is the need for us to retool our rhetorical and conceptual strategies in dealing with them.

Let us now turn to the general economy of violence in the post-colony. As already mentioned, the origin of the colonial state is based on violence or what Mbembe (2001b) terms the dictum of the *commendement*. He defines the character of the post-colony in the following terms:

> The notion 'post-colony' identifies specifically a given historical trajectory — that of society recently emerging from the experience of colonization and the violence which the colonial relationship involves. To be sure, the post-colony is chaotically, pluralistic; it has nonetheless an internal coherence. It is a specific system of signs, a particular way of fabricating simulacra or re-forming stereotypes. (ibid: 102)

And in most post-colonies, the violence of the colonial state is usually inherited by succeeding political elites who are prone to the privatization of public authority.[4] In this context it becomes absurd to act and think within either strictly Athenian or modern regimes of rationality. Those alien regimes of rationality must first of all be established on clearly lopsided and violent foundations.

Let us consider a few concrete examples. The often-mentioned 'crisis of the nation', 'the dissolution of the state' and 'the exit of the state' in many parts of Africa have acquired several dramatic forms. In fact, there is now talk about 'the terror of the state'. This general state collapse has given rise to the spread of illicit organizations and 'uncivil' actors that are now usurping the spaces vacated by the state. This has led to the near institutionalization of processes that were formally regarded as informal. Chronic statist disorder and withdrawal have transformed the state in post-colony under neo-liberal conditions into an anomaly or a chimerical phantom overwhelmed by the violence that produced it and also the violence it in turn dispels without a seemingly rational basis. Given this scenario, we have to devise new ways of viewing and conceptualizing civil publics in Africa. If, for instance, it has been noted that 'the South African underworld is peopled not just by the unemployed, but also by the "well-healed and well-educated", suggesting that, for a growing sector of the population — above all, young black men — the gangster lifestyle has a seductive appeal' (Comaroff & Comaroff 2002: 7), then we have rethink the entire constitution of both civil and uncivil society in Africa. In other parts of Africa, the spread and entrenchment of uncivil publics is more or less a way of life.

---

[4] See Ake (1996).

Mbembe describes the instrumentalization of war as a way of life in which lives and bodies are judged on the basis of value, usually monetary, and supposedly valueless lives are destroyed by both statist and non-state formations in the pursuit of gain.[5] The cases of Rwanda, the Democratic Republic of Congo, Liberia, Sierra Leone and even Nigeria bear this out. If the functions and aims of the state have indeed changed this much, we cannot afford to employ unsuited conceptual paradigms to describe the forms of life and death now prevailing in the post-colony. Thus in relation to a particular phenomenon — such as corruption — these new moral and socio-political geographies have to be taken into account.

Conclusion

I began with a discussion of Gyekye's treatment of corruption. Gyekye approaches the issue by employing established philosophical trajectories and, in a somewhat Socratic manner, he concludes that the problem of corruption is basically a moral one. One needs to possess the strength of will to overcome corrupt inclinations and practices. But in arriving at this conclusion, he takes his milieu — Africa — for granted. Thus his discussion and conclusion are, to put it mildly, removed from their essential context.

Olivier de Sardan, on the other hand, situates his discourse within a considerably more graphic and identifiable context, and the social dynamics that activate the construction, perception and dissemination of corruption are more clearly drawn. This project of regionalizing and localizing corruption for analytical purposes is indeed useful. For any discussion of corruption to make sense, the emerging existential conditions on the African continent — the collapse of the state(s), the informalization of most productive sectors and the gangsterization of everyday life — must be taken into account. And when considering these disturbing parameters, it becomes evident that most of our descriptive and conceptual paradigms for the emerging configurations in the post-colony need to be modified. Just as the routinization of supposedly corrupt practices and processes of brutalization have become entrenched, new moral loyalties and geographies are emerging from them. The task now should be to carry out interrogations of these moral geographies in a fairly representative way.

Indeed the challenge is to examine the logics of morality in the post-colony and the related issues to which they give rise without the usual old vocabularies which do not have the capacity to fully describe them. Even a metaphysics of

---

[5] See Mbembe (2000a) and his 'Necropolitics' in P*ublic Culture* (2003, vol. 15, no. 1).

disorder is usually ensconced within a specific dynamic and based on a *modus operandi* that paradoxically allows for the production of life. And the production of life secures its own means of preservation even within the Hobbesian jungle and the violence of its seemingly irreversible logic. Even communities of crime and social disorder (in a country such as Nigeria) have codes of behaviour and loyalty, no matter how rudimentary they may be. In other words, in spite of the overwhelming chaos, violence and decay that mark a significant proportion of African lives in the post-colony, there are still ways and means of bonding that display characteristics of normalcy. The extreme and in some ways oppositional condition would be outright war. How can African philosophical thought account for the widespread institutional failures in the African post-colony? Evidently, it would have to avail itself of rigorous social research, which Gyekye, as we have seen, does not quite succeed in doing. In this case, African philosophy as a disciplinary practice is not adequate until it discovers the usefulness of interculturality (in its anthropological and philosophical combination). At that point, its flexibility and potentialities are bound to increase dramatically.

Finally, the process of narrativizing these developments brings us back to a theme I touched on at the beginning of this chapter — the limits of certain disciplinary enclosures. My response to that important theme is simply this: in coming up against unproductive limits, we not only miss opportunities and the ways in which to describe how the new occurs, we also contribute in no small measure to the closure of discourse, to the end of disciplinary practice itself.[6]

References

Ake, C. 1996, *Democracy and Development in Africa*, Ibadan: Spectrum Books.

Anderson, B. 1992, *Long-distance Nationalism: World Capitalism and the Rise of Identity Politics*, Wertheun Lecture, Amsterdam: Centre for Asia Studies.

Appiah, A.K. 1992, *In My Father's House: Africa in the Philosophy of Culture*, New York: Oxford University Press.

Appiah, A.K. 2002, 'Citizens of the World?', *Biblio: A Review of Books*, special issue, March-April. Also published in *NEXUS* no. 26, issue on cosmoplitanism, Nexus Institute, Tilburg, the Netherlands.

Ayer, P. 2000, *The Global Soul*, New York: Alfred A. Knopf.

---

[6] See Van Binsbergen, (forthcoming) *Intercultural Encounters: African and Anthropological Lessons Towards a Philosophy of Interculturality.* In this ground-breaking book, Van Binsbergen argues for a new disciplinary symbiosis between advocates, nothing short of new disciplinary formation. Mudimbe (1988, 1991) also negotiates the interface between philosophy and anthropology.

Ayer, P. 2002, 'Transit Loungers', *Biblio: A Review of Books*, special issue, March-April.

Cassin, B. 1990, 'Greeks and Romans: Paradigms of the Past in Arendt and Heidegger', *Comparative Civilization Review* 22, Fall.

Comaroff, J.L. & J. Comaroff 2002, 'Criminal Obsessions: Imagining Order After Apartheid'', paper delivered at the Institute for Social and Economic Research (WISER), University of Witwatersrand.

Coplan, D.B. 1994, *In the Time of Cannibals: The Word Music of South Africa's Basotho Migrants*, Johannesburg: Witwatersrand University Press.

Coplan, D.B. 1995, *Lyrics of Basotho Migrants*, Madison: University of Wisconsin.

Das, A.N. 2002, 'The End of Geography', *Biblio: A Review of Books*, special issue, March-April.

Derrida, J. 1978, *Writing and Difference*, Chicago: Chicago University Press.

Gyekye, K. 1997, *Tradition and Modernity: Philosophical Reflections on the African Experience*, New York: Oxford University Press.

Mbembe, A. 2000a, 'An Essay on the Political Imagination in Wartime', *CODESRIA Bulletin* 2, 3 & 4.

Mbembe, A. 2000b, 'At the Edge of the World: Boundaries, Territoriality, and Sovereignty in Africa', *Public Culture* 30.

Mbembe, A. 2001a, 'Ways of Seeing: Beyond the New Nativism', Introduction, *African Studies Review* 44 (2).

Mbembe, A. 2001b, *On the Post-colony*, Berkeley: California University Press.

Mbembe, A. 2002, 'African Modes of Self-Writing', *Public Culture* 36.

Mudimbe, U.Y. 1988, *The Invention of Africa: Gnosis, Philosophy, and the Order of Knowledge*, Bloomington: Indiana University Press.

Mudimbe, U.Y. 1991, *Parables and Fables: Exegesis, Textuality, and Politics in Central Africa*, Madison: University of Wisconsin Press.

Olivier de Sardan, J-P. 1999, 'African Corruption in the Context of Globalization', in: R. Fardon, W. van Binsbergen & R. van Dijk (eds), *Modernity on a Shoestring: Dimensions of Globalization, Consumption and Development in Africa and Beyond*, Leiden & London: EIDOS.

Simone, A. 2000, 'Going South; African Immigrants in Johannesburg', in: S. Nuttall & C.A. Michael, *Sense of Culture: South African Culture Studies*, Cape Town: Oxford University Press.

Van Binsbergen, W.M.J. (forthcoming), *Intercultural Encounters: African Lessons for a Philosophy of Interculturality*.

PART III: GLOBALITY THROUGH WORLD RELIGIONS

6

'Beyond the rivers of Ethiopia': Pentecostal Pan-Africanism and Ghanaian identities in the transnational domain

Rijk van Dijk

Rev. Mensa Otabil, the founder of the International Central Gospel Church in Accra, is considered an influential representative of a new Pentecostal-inspired Pan-Africanist ideology. His book 'Beyond the Rivers of Ethiopia' lays the foundations of a Pentecostal Liberation Theology that proclaims a Christianized sequel to Pan-Africanism. Operating from Ghana, his ideas for Africa and for 'black consciousness' have spread to Ghanaian migrant communities worldwide. While Otabil has been successful in transforming ownership of the intellectualist production of Pan-Africanism by tailoring it to the needs of the ordinary Pentecostal believer, it has not been adopted so extensively among all Ghanaian migrant communities in the West. By exploring Ghanaian migrant communities and their Pentecostal churches in the Netherlands, where the staunch identity politics of the Dutch government leave little room for the assertive proclamation of 'Africanness', this chapter demonstrates that Otabil's ideas do not act as a main source of inspiration everywhere in the Ghanaian diaspora.

Introduction

The emergence in various parts of Sub-Saharan Africa of a thriving literature of religious tracts, booklets and pamphlets — mostly of a Christian nature — has been noted by many authors (see Meyer 1995, 1999, Ellis & Ter Haar 1998, Gifford 1998, Maxwell 1998, 2001, Van Dijk 1997, 2001a). This literature is sold or sometimes handed out for free in bookshops, at market stalls or among the many church congregations that have sprung up particularly in urban areas. Some churches, and certainly not only the established mission churches, have their own printing presses and publishing houses that are responsible for producing many of these publications in addition to their own regular church-related journals. In West Africa, countries such as Ghana and Nigeria are known for the activities of a particular brand of Christianity in this field: the new charismatic Pentecostal churches. These churches represent the fastest growing form of Christianity in this part of Africa and many scholars have observed their dominance in the public sphere and in the public media (Hackett 1998, Meyer 2001, Marshall-Fratani 1998, Van Dijk 2001e) where they actively broadcast their religious messages on radio and television, produce glossy brochures in which their victorious nationwide spread is portrayed and publish books discussing their religious and moral creeds.

These books and tracts comprise several distinct genres ranging from a 'confession' literature of conversion experiences to testimonies of personal journeys into the dark world of evil and occult powers (and the author's victorious re-emergence) to highly theological treatises concerning certain Biblical truths and dogmas. Popular fascination with this literature often focuses on booklets that describe the author's highly mystical and emotional confrontations with a demonic world of witchcraft and evil spirits.[1] Sometimes replete with details about the nocturnal activities of witches and their hideous assaults on the normal order of society or the writer's reputation in daily life, books of this genre tend to reveal a society's nightmares and anxieties in a world full of uncertainties. Particularly in the West African setting, all this literature is transmitting a moral and socio-political message in a context where increasing pressure is being exerted on the legitimacy of the authority wielded by such institutions as the state, chieftaincy, established mission churches or family elders. Although much of this literature is not explicitly political in focus or nature, it is not difficult to see the ways in which it turns matters pertaining to moral authority and power in social life into issues of Christian or even Pentecostal beliefs, truths and points of view. Booklets and pamphlets that speak out against involvement in occultism, witchcraft and moral laxity do so in a West African context in which holders of power have increasingly become suspected of dealing with hidden forces, of being involved in exploitative and self-serving 'crooked' relations and machinations. This literature can, at first

---

[1] The best-known example of this genre is Emmanuel Eni's *Delivered from the Powers of Darkness* (Ibadan, Scripture Union Press, 1987).

sight, be interpreted as religion and Christian morality filling a void that the steadily reducing legitimacy of state and other civil organizations is leaving behind.

In Ghana, many books of these diverse genres have been written by founder-leaders of the new Pentecostal churches that have emerged over the last two decades in the country. Rev. Mensa Otabil, the leader and founder of the highly successful International Central Gospel Church in Accra, is considered one of the most influential representatives of this group of renowned religious leaders. He is considered by many to be the 'Rabbi to the Nation' because of his sharp and moral pronouncements against the Ghanaian government. Like many of his colleagues, he has written a number of booklets dealing with Pentecostal truths bearing such titles as 'Four Laws of Productivity' and 'The Why, What, How, When and Where of Giving', all of which have been published by Altar International, the publishing house connected to his church.[2]

However, he has also published a remarkable piece entitled 'Beyond the Rivers of Ethiopia: A Biblical Revelation on God's Purpose for the Black Race' (Otabil 1992). It is exceptional in comparison with all the other genres of literature that have emerged in these Pentecostal circles in that it represents a relatively new and Pentecostal-inspired Pan-Africanist ideology. In it, Otabil lays the foundations for what has been called an 'Evangelical Pentecostal Liberation Theology' (Larbi 2001: 349) which proclaims a highly Christianized Pan-Africanist sequel to the ideas of Fanon, DuBois and, more recently, Gilroy (1993). In a critique of Mudimbe's *Idea of Africa* (1994), Davies has placed this book alongside Appiah's *In My Father's House* (1992) as works that display a different sensibility with regard to the meaning of present-day African philosophical thought (Davies 1998). The 'cunning aim' (as Davies calls it) of these books is not to replace the white colonial library or the white Bible, nor to glorify 'Egypt' in a Bernalian sense,[3] but to rework them and re-inscribe an essential black presence into these texts. Without such a presence, liberation or messianic hope would never have come into existence.

In the present global context of increasing marginalization of Africa, such notions of 'black pride' appear to be appealing to many. Operating from Ghana, Otabil has been preaching his message for Africa and for 'black consciousness', as he calls it, not only in many parts of the continent but also in the Ghanaian migrant communities in the United Kingdom and the United States where his ideas have started circulating among some of the Black American communities

[2] See Van Dijk (1999) for a discussion of the idea of a Pentecostal economy.

[3] See Van Binsbergen (1997) for an extensive discussion of Martin Bernal's work on the Black Athena hypothesis.

FOREWORD BY LEONARD LOVETT
BEYOND
the rivers of
ETHIOPIA
a
biblical revelation
on God's purpose for the
Black Race
MENSA
OTABIL

in places such as New York. Crucial to an understanding of his popularity is the fact that works such as those of Otabil and Darkwah for instance, offer a Christianized re-appropriation of Afro-centric ideas capable of achieving two things at the same time: a new ownership of longer dating but highly intellectual and secular Pan-African ideals, and a critical confrontation with Western 'book knowledge' as it is often pejoratively called and to which many Africans have become increasingly exposed through the global spread of formal education. In emphasizing divine wisdom and inspiration in the appropriation of Afro-centric ideals, a unity of Africans is proclaimed on the basis of spiritual empowerment by heavenly forces.

In this chapter I explore the significance of this work for and within Ghanaian Pentecostalism, and its spread to various parts of Africa and beyond. The relationship between the Ghanaian diaspora and the global spread of Ghanaian Pentecostalism is evident and has been substantiated by recent research. However, ideas of Pentecostal Pan-Africanism are not equally vibrant among all Ghanaian migrant communities in the West. By exploring Ghanaian migrant communities and their Pentecostal churches in the Netherlands, this chapter demonstrates that these ideas are not considered a main source of inspiration everywhere in the Ghanaian diaspora. It examines the relative success of Mensa Otabil's Pan-Africanist message in Ghana and its marked absence in the life of the Ghanaian diasporic community in the Netherlands. It argues that staunch identity politics by the Dutch government, in this particular case, have left little room for the assertive proclamation of 'Africaness'. Interestingly, the Dutch government has recently celebrated 300 years of diplomatic relations with Ghana and plans to erect a 'slave monument' as a *lieu de memoire* of the Dutch role in the slave trade, but its identity politics appear to be obfuscating Otabil's appeal. Identity has become too much of a contested terrain for Ghanaians, a contestation in which any reference to Pan-Africanist notions is not considered helpful to their community's cause in the multicultural society of the Netherlands.

Pan-Africanism and Pentecostal transnationalism

Historically, Ghana had a pivotal position in the efflorescence of Pan-Africanism. Without going into historical detail here, it is clear that a number of those leading personalities whose contributions to the establishment and worldwide spread of Pan-Africanist ideals and organizations through birth or descent are related to what is present-day Ghana. Accra, the capital city of Ghana, is very much part of what Ebron (2000) recently called the 'memory scape' of Pan-Africanism. It is home to such organizations as the Pan-African

Writers' Association and features, for instance, the George Padmore Library and the W.E.B. DuBois Centre which highlight Ghanaian achievements and contributions to Pan-Africanism. An ever-increasing interest is developing among Afro-American communities into the countries of the former Slave Coast, with Ghana drawing specific attention (see Ebron 2000, Hasty 2002, Davis 1997). Nkrumah, Ghana's first president, displayed an explicit and pronounced interest in maintaining ties with the diaspora, in enhancing the spread of Pan-Aficanist ideals within Africa and in keeping the memory of the slave trade alive for generations to come. Later presidents would follow suit. Nkrumah based his ideas about the African spread of Pan-Africanism on the activities of early Pan-Africanists who saw it as their task to come to Africa, settle in various countries and establish direct links with Pan-African conferences held in the Western world. For instance F.Z.S. Peregrino, a Ga from Accra who had settled in the United States around 1900, was one of these early 'Ghanaian' Pan-Africanists who firmly believed in the need to create unity among the African peoples and nations not only in the diaspora but on the African continent as well (Parsons n.d.). He thus settled in Cape Town and, in line with Pan-Africanist 'tradition', began publishing books and tracts and even a journal, the *South African Spectator*, in which Pan-Africanist ideals were introduced to many in Southern Africa. His work reached as far as present-day Botswana and Zambia.

Later presidents of Ghana, in particular J.J. Rawlings, recognized in the relationship between Ghana and the diaspora, and in Ghana's role in Pan-Africanism, other dimensions in addition to the politically motivated ideals of unity, dimensions that would relate to cultural and economic aspects of the relationship between Ghana and Afro-American communities. As in so many other postcolonial African states, the government — controlled by Rawlings's National Democratic Party (NDC) after it came to power in a coup in 1981 — stepped up efforts to overcome the legacy of colonialism and missionization by using the past as a rich resource for societal renewal, for achieving progress and development in a 'Ghanaian' way. While some of the cultural traditions are approached critically, the state's policy of augmenting the general public's awareness of its cultural heritage has aimed at fostering national cohesion and involving the diaspora in domestic affairs. The NDC government thus created a National Commission on Culture that uses governmental funds for the organization of local, regional, national and international festivals. Furthermore, it gave a high priority to culture on school, college and university curricula (for instance, in the form of music and dance classes), and actively supported organizations such as the DuBois Centre and PANAFEST, a biannual Pan-African festival featuring the cultural variety of Ghana's heritage both in Ghana and its expressions in the diaspora. It has become a widely acclaimed Pan-

African cultural festival with extensive programmes of Ghanaian cultural displays, dance classes, literature and ritual ceremonies. It actively promotes photo, film, video, theatre and musical productions that seek to produce images of Ghanaian cultural life and show its diversity and vibrancy. The PANAFEST festivals reach out to communities of Ghanaian migrants and descendants in the former slave colonies and encourage them to remain in close contact with their cultural roots.

This festival must be placed in the context of other initiatives that seek to engage the diaspora in the life of the nation. There is a great deal of 'roots'-oriented tourism from Black Americans who visit the Slave Coast and places of significant meaning in the history of slavery (for instance, the slave fortresses) (Bruner 1996). The economic interest for Ghana in this specific type of tourism, even defined as a secular pilgrimage by some (Davis 1997, Ebron 2000), has become so substantive that Rawlings once called slavery a 'blessing in disguise' (Hasty 2002). Events such as the state-orchestrated Emancipation Day or the so-called Home-Coming Summits with all their visitors from overseas have acquired a clear economic significance for the local population. On the other hand, visits by presidents and paramount chiefs from Ghana to the overseas diaspora communities have attributed political support to the cause of black communities in the United States and the United Kingdom in particular. It was during such visits that former president Rawlings would emphasize Pan-African ideals in general and point to Ghana's needs in terms of development.

It is in this sense that an overlapping of diasporas has occurred (Lewis 1995, Hanchard 1999, Byfield 2000: 5). The way in which Pan-African ideals feed into the support of Ghana in cultural and economic terms coincides with the way in which revenues are accrued from the migration of Ghanaians. Ghana, as even the present newly elected president Kufuor acknowledges, is dependent for its survival in the modern world on its diaspora. (Overseas revenues are the country's third largest source of income after gold and cocoa.) In the past two or three decades Ghana has become a country of large-scale emigration, a form of mobility focused on places where black communities of former descendants of the Slave Coast already exist. In addition however, shifts have occurred as the search for job opportunities also came to focus on Western countries that featured much less in the production of Pan-Africanist notions, such as Germany, Italy and the Netherlands.

It is estimated that 12 per cent of Ghanaians are presently living abroad (Peil 1995) and the ambition of many young urbanites is to participate in intercontinental labour migration. Many families in Ghana perceive migration to the West of one or several of its members as a strategy of economic success and survival. This is a clear departure from earlier colonial and postcolonial movements of labour migration in and out of the country. Much of Ghana's history in the 20th century can be described as being cloaked in mobility. In the colonial period, lasting until the mid 1950s, a great deal of internal migration occurred from northern groups moving to the southern and central regions in search of paid employment in the emerging sectors of cocoa production, mining and urban industries. Large migrant quarters arose close to cities such as Accra and Kumasi where the northern labour migrants settled, contributing to the growth of the urban areas and their economic success. Experiencing an economic boom during the 1960s, independent Ghana under Nkrumah witnessed an influx of labour migrants of a more regional nature and particularly an unprecedented labour migration by Nigerians (Peil 1979, Sudarkasa 1979). During the 1970s, Ghana's economy, particularly cocoa production and similar export-oriented activities, were hit hard by deteriorating world-market commodity prices. A massive out-migration began of Ghanaian labour migrants seeking their fortune regionally. Nigeria, by then with a new booming economy, attracted and absorbed large numbers of Ghanaian migrants until 1983. During Nigeria's rapid decline in the mid 1980s, the country's rulers, contrary to previous ideals of African unity, developed a new and rather violent policy of mass deportation of those labour migrants that its economy could no longer absorb. Hundreds of thousands of Ghanaian migrants were faced with expulsion from the country while a return to Ghana and its deteriorating economy was no viable option either.[4] It was at this time that the new and massive intercontinental migration began, leading to the establishment of Ghanaian migrant communities in many European cities such as Hamburg, London, Amsterdam and New York. Ter Haar (1998) showed that by 1996 the Ghanaian migrant population had become the largest group among all the officially recorded migratory movements from Sub-Sahara Africa to Europe.

It was in the movement of large numbers of people from Nigeria back to Ghana that a new form of Christianity — known as charismatic Pentecostalism — was introduced into Ghana, inspired by similar religious movements that had already emerged in Nigeria. Pentecostalism has since become the most popular form of Christianity in Ghana over the last twenty years and has become deeply intertwined with the diasporic movement of Ghanaians worldwide. Between 1987 and 1992 the number of Pentecostal churches grew by as much as 43 per cent (see Ghana Evangelism Committee 1993). Although there are many different forms of Pentecostalism and not all are gaining popularity at the same rate, recent figures show a marked increase in the spread of Pentecostalism throughout both rural and urban Ghana. Many of these churches belong to what has become known as the 'second Pentecostal wave' that has swept through

[4] See Aluko (1985) and Yeboah (1986) on the Nigerian expulsion policy and the international outcry that followed.

Africa since the 1970s, and has led to the emergence, particularly in urban areas, of a newer type of Pentecostalism that in contradistinction with other independent churches began to proselytise a highly modernist discourse in which notions of individual self-making strongly prevail. These churches, such as Dr Mensa Otabil's International Central Gospel Church and Bishop Duncan Williams's Christian Action Faith Ministries which were founded in the late 1970s, quickly attracted many members amongst the young and urban middle class in search of success and prosperity in life (Gifford 1998, Van Dijk 1997, 1999).

This popular second wave of Pentecostalism continued a process that can be described as the indigenization of earlier mission-based Pentecostalism (see Meyer 1995, Larbi 2001). Missionary Pentecostalism was introduced to Ghana during the first three decades of the 20th century and took root with the founding of churches from England and the United States such as the Assemblies of God and the Apostolic Church. Though sometimes viewed in anthropology as belonging to the category of so-called spirit-healing churches that emerged at roughly the same time (locally known in Twi as *sunsum asore*), important differences in terms of ritual discourse, practices and modernist outlook have meant that Pentecostalism eventually took a different path to these other independent churches.

In terms of the various forms of Christianity, these Pentecostal churches have engaged in a cultural dialectic on two fronts. They have challenged mainstream Christianity on the perception of evil, on the diabolization of key elements of the African cosmology and on ways of counteracting witchcraft and evil spirits. Mainstream Christianity (Presbyterianism, Catholicism, Methodism and Anglicism) has preferred to deny the existence of witchcraft (*bayiE*) and has rejected the power of spirits (*adze*), amulets (*asuman*) and traditional healing practices as being mere superstition. It has refused to accommodate or absorb any of the elements of African cosmology in order to save the pure faith from being contaminated by devilish and occult forces. The development of independent African Christianity and its diverse forms of spirit-healing churches can be interpreted as a process of coming to terms with the powers that mainstream Christianity denied and ignored, and as a way of providing individual members with healing and protection. Whilst including Christian doctrines, the spirit-healing churches such as the Nazarene Healing Church and the Musama Disco Christo Church have provided healing through a range of objects and substances that clearly originated from ritual practices rooted in the veneration of *abosom* (family and ancestral spirits) and their worship through the shrine priests (*okomfoo*). The use of herbs, candles, oils, baths, concoctions, magical rings and the like was very much a part of this world and was included in the spirit-healing churches' symbolical repertoires.

However, the new Pentecostal churches engaged in a second dialectic here as they could not accept practices that would signal the continuation of a cultural past that would make the church vulnerable to attacks from the Devil and his many demons. Ancestral spirits, witches and ritual practices that related to veneration and protection were consequently classified as demonic and were diabolized (Meyer 1999). A rigid dichotomy was developed distinguishing benevolent from malevolent powers and spiritual forces, leaving no middle terrain for ambiguity. Whereas ancestral deities (*honhom ananom*) can either work for good or bad in the community or particularly in the family, not denying their existence and influence in Pentecostalism is equivocally brandished as malevolent. Healing and deliverance from such powers can only take place through the 'blood of Christ', the laying-on of hands and ecstatic prayer sessions in which the benevolent presence of the Holy Spirit is manifest through speaking in tongues (in Twi *kasa foforoo,* literally 'speaking the new language'). Objects and substances that relate to a cultural past are not allowed within its ritual practice and discourse. In Pentecostal practice attention is paid to fasting, which is primarily perceived as a way to come to a spiritual control and inspection of the belly (*yam*) as the place where the ancestral spirits make their presence felt and influence the reproduction of society.

So while the mission Pentecostal churches started to Africanize around 1950 in terms of leadership and forms of worship, the importance of their own distinctive ways of dealing with evil forces in society grew. This approach contradicted mainstream Christianity that denied the efficacy of these forces and opposed the 'demonic' practices of the spirit-healing churches. It is important to note that while the Pentecostal churches grew in strength, the spirit-healing churches became less influential, less appealing and less able to adjust to the changing fortunes of Ghanaian society as it entered a global system.

Although the older Pentecostal churches were clearly represented in Ghana's urban areas and could claim international links through their overseas branches, the new type of charismatic Pentecostal churches made internationalism their hallmark (Van Dijk 1997, 2001b, Gifford 1998). In Accra and Kumasi, churches were adding terms such as 'international', global' and 'world' to their names, promising religiously inspired access to transnationalism.[5] Furthermore, this new Pentecostalism appears to be inspired by the developments of Pentecostalism in America. Firmly located in the prosperity gospel, it propounds the notion of the individual's combined spiritual and socio-economic

[5] Examples include the well-known International Central Gospel Church, the Global Revival Outreach Ministry, the Harvest Ministries International and the World Miracle Church. In some of these churches, their international approach is represented symbolically by placing flags near the pulpit of each country in which branches have been established.

success. Leaders come across as having charismatic powers and acumen in business relationships.

From the mid 1980s onwards, another salient feature of these churches has been their international self-presentation. The global claim has become a prominent feature, demonstrating that, unlike most spirit-healing churches, they can extend beyond Ghana, and Ghanaian and West African culture. Consequently, they have actively sought to enter other cultural contexts and have ascribed a place for them in their ideology, organization and subsequent religious experience. The claim is not simply that Ghana is 'too small a place for our message', but that entering other cultural contexts deepens, enriches and essentializes the religious experiences of Pentecostal communities (Van Dijk 2001a, 2001b). Operating from Accra or Kumasi, these churches began setting up branches outside Ghana, particularly in Western Europe and the United States. Pentecostalism has connected with the 'new' African diaspora through its message for a mobile urban population eager to participate in transnational movement. Over the last decade, migrating to the West has become increasingly difficult due to the stiff measures taken by most governments to curtail immigration from Africa. While Europe has turned into a 'fortress', large numbers of Ghanaian Pentecostal churches have been able to establish themselves in the continent's major cities, thereby once more adding to the image and promise of success and internationalism that Pentecostalism appears to harbour. In many cities in Western Europe but also in the US and even in Israel and Japan, these new Pentecostal churches have been able to establish satellite congregations, and cater to the needs of the Ghanaian migrant in the diaspora.

Pentecostalism in Ghana feeds into the Occidentalized notions that many young people still maintain of the West, of images that bespeak the West's affluence as a place of desire. These churches have, therefore, developed connections with international Pentecostal circles through modern means of transport and communication and are creating an extensive exchange of people and materials both to and from Ghana. Conversely, some of the Pentecostal churches that were founded in the Ghanaian diaspora have ploughed their way back to Ghana. In other words, alongside Ghanaian-based Pentecostal churches that have been set up among Ghanaian communities in Amsterdam, London or Hamburg, Pentecostal churches with no previous links with Ghana have emerged. Pentecostalism has become a transnational phenomenon that in its modern forms is reproduced in its local diversity through a highly accelerated circulation of goods, ideas and people. In fact it has formed a moral and physical geography whose domain is one of transnational cultural interpenetration and flow as created and recreated through travel and encounter.

In the Netherlands there are approximately 40 Ghanaian Pentecostal churches in cities such as Amsterdam, The Hague and Rotterdam where sizeable Ghanaian migrant communities are to be found. They vary in membership from 50 to 600 adults and include both legal and illegal migrants. In The Hague, which is the location of one half of my multi-sited research (the other being in Accra), eleven Pentecostal churches are currently operating in a community of (officially) 2.000 adults (Van Dijk 2001c, 2002b). They hold an influential position in the community and function as the *de facto* moral authority on a wide range of matters pertaining to birth, marriage, funerals and other rituals and arrangements. Six of these churches have direct links with churches in Accra while the others were founded in The Hague during the late 1980s. Styles of ritual practice, worship, the elements of personalism and international linkage refer to what can be observed in Accra among these churches and create a deep sense of transnational continuity, global unity and exchange, and direct accessibility for the Ghanaian migrant. Despite the ever-toughening border controls and identity politics of the Dutch government with regard to immigration, one of the latest arrivals within the Ghanaian community in The Hague has been a satellite of one of the most remarkable Pentecostal churches in Accra: the International Central Gospel Church of Mensa Otabil.

The Pan-Africanist message of Mensa Otabil

Rev. Mensa A. Otabil, the leader and founder of the International Central Gospel Church (ICGC) in Accra, is by far the most influential, renowned and outspoken of all the Pentecostal leaders who have come forward in Ghana's second Pentecostal wave. His eloquence and innovative style, his command of the public media and his uncompromising public pronouncements have made him an example to be followed by many emerging Pentecostal leaders in the public domain in Ghana. His flamboyance and his public presence have also made him a favourite subject of study in much of the science-of-religion type literature on Ghana. Studies such as those by Gifford (1998), Hackett (1998), Larbi (2001) and Darkwah (2000) emphasize various aspects of his moral and religious message, his theology and the sources of inspiration he has sought in American Pentecostalism, his coverage of the public media and his role in the emergence of what can be called the highly appealing prosperity gospel in Ghana. These authors do not fail to note the elements of political criticism that transpire in many of his messages, which have made him the moral watchdog of the nation, as well as the Pan-African sentiments that come across strongly. It is the tantalizing combination of Pentecostalism, Pan-Africanism and political criticism that explains much of his massive appeal in Ghana, on the African continent, as well as in many parts of the Ghanaian diaspora and other black communities overseas. The peculiarity of this combination is unique and must be explored against the backdrop of the transnational nature of Ghanaian Pentecostalism.

Otabil established the ICGC in central Accra in 1984 in line with the way in which a predecessor, Bishop Duncan Williams, had established his church, the Action Faith Ministries, and who in his turn had imported this form of religious organization into Ghana from Nigeria. Starting with church services in a cinema,[6] the church then decided to move to one of the biggest halls in the city until it finally moved to a newly constructed multi-billion cedi church building in the very heart of Accra in 1996. The success of the church and of Otabil's appeal have coincided with the broad and popular success of Pentecostalism in Ghana at large but is also due to Otabil's charismatic personality and the many services the church renders to the public. It is run on the basis of a modernist and highly liberal notion of religious entrepreneurship which includes the professional proliferation of its basic tenets through the production of cassettes, videos, tapes, printed materials such as books and magazines, television and radio shows and church planting activities throughout Ghana and in other parts of the world. Otabil's messages reach every corner of Ghanaian society and are rapidly spreading across Africa and the diaspora. The books he has written circulate around the world and discussions about his ideas can be found on the Internet. He himself holds two honorary doctorate degrees in the Humanities and Divinity, and the church also moved into academia when in 1998 it opened the first privately owned Pentecostal university in Africa, Central University, with two faculties, namely, Theology and Business Administration. Otabil became the chancellor of the university and as part of this academic effort began publishing his own lectures in a separate series, New Dawn publications.

For ordinary members of the ICGC, however, other and more religious services of the church have remained important, particularly the 'Solution Centre' where people go for spiritual healing and deliverance. The purpose of these rituals is to bring 'divine provision' to every individual in his/her quest for success, prosperity and progress in life. Here people are told they should enter into a covenant with the heavenly forces and be disciplined, diligent and determined whatever that covenant sets forth. This is all dependent on personal free will, choice and ambition and it is for this reason that the so-called Winner's Club was established, a special division of the church with an 'exclusive membership of the highly motivated and dynamic achievers in fields

---

[6] This was the Regal Cinema, Osu. Birgit Meyer attaches specific significance to the fact that so many of these new Pentecostal churches tend to occupy cinemas for their church services. Many of them do so as they cannot afford to build a place of their own.

of business, law, commerce, accountancy who seek to use biblical and secular principles to affect society' (Gifford 1998: 81). It is exclusive particularly in terms of membership fees, which often amount to hundreds of dollars a year.

The overall success of Pentecostalism in Ghanaian society can, in addition to its transnational appearance and globalizing outlook, be explained by this ideology and praxis which strike a responsive chord among the educated English-speaking and upwardly mobile groups in Ghanaian society. In Otabil's case this ritual practice and its public appeal relate to his Pan-African ideas. These are very much based on the Hamitic hypothesis but are largely inspired by Senghor's negritude, and proclaim the worldwide redemption of the Black Race not by a return to traditional African heritage but by an African appropriation of the Bible and the Gospel. They are deeply Afro-centric in the first place. In his book *Beyond the Rivers of Ethiopia* (1992) Otabil develops a specific form of liberation theology, which redefines the position of Black people in the Bible as crucial to God's redemptive and messianic plan for the world. Davies (1998: 130) writes:

> The aim of the book is clear: to retrace within the Bible (the King James version, no less) "the purposes of God for the Black Race". Thus we have an exegetical exercise in which the Bible is rethought in terms of Abraham's third wife, Keturah, of Moses father-in-law, of the Midianites, of the Cushites, of the Cyrenians, of Simon the cross-bearer, of some of the early Church elders.

Whites have distorted the Bible and its message for the future of Africa to such an extent that even Africans themselves have come to believe that the black race has been cursed. Otabil is convinced that his liberating Afro-centric work plays a role in what he calls the breaking of a certain mentality which he finds is prevalent among many Africans: a mentality of 'slavery', 'dependency' and that of a 'begging attitude' as he once called it in one of his public sermons. Through the appropriation of the Gospel, African peoples and descendants of former slaves can look for prowess and pride in being black and of having played such a crucial role in saving mankind in Biblical and present times: 'Whenever the world has been in crisis the black man has always appeared on the scene' (Otabil 1992: 87). The book is a strident rejection of this mental slavery and proclaims a 'breaking' of attitudes that do not confirm this quest of self-esteem and promising initiative and entrepreneurship:

> The most difficult part to break in any situation of addition and dependency is not the physical but the mental, so then mental slavery is more difficult to break than physical slavery. (p. 69)
>
> When I was called into the ministry, one of the things the Lord led me to do was to liberate my people from mental slavery through the preaching of the Gospel and to

> lift up the image of the black man so as to be a channel of blessing to the nations of the world. (p. 18)
> Businessmen, lawyers, inventors, teachers, your time has come.... You may be starting late, but you must run with purpose. (p. 86)

The book, tellingly opening with a foreword by L. Lovett a professor in Afro-American religious studies at the Oral Roberts University in Oklahoma (from which Otabil received one of his two honorary doctorates), has been widely read in Afro-American circles throughout the United States. Internet discussions and readers' reviews can be found acclaiming the book and Otabil's message for as one reader stated:

> This book shatters the myth that we as black people are not in the Bible. God has a plan for us and Christianity is not a white man's religion. We were never cursed. In the light of white America's lies through the years it is time to get the truth. (www.Amazon.com/Beyond the Rivers of Ethiopia/p. 2)

Otabil began receiving numerous invitations to speak at events in America, thereby giving greater circulation to his ideas in Afro-American communities. Beyond the International Central Gospel Church branches that were established across the Atlantic, for example in New York but also in London, his books, tape recordings, video recordings as well as his privately owned magazine *Greener Pastures* received wide circulation in Ghanaian migrant communities and among a great number of the Afro-Americans interested in their roots. His private initiatives, such as the university he established, received material support from these communities and the university has become affiliated to the Council for Christian Colleges and Universities in the US.

He took further measures in Ghana and other African countries to spread his specific Pan-African message by establishing the so-called Pan-African Believers' Conference, an annual meeting of representatives of African and Afro-American Christian communities and churches. The one I was able to attend in 1998 had as its central theme 'Lift Up Your Head, Africa' and in his opening speech Otabil deplored what he called the 'I don't care attitude' and warned all present that:

> We should not make the mistake of copying Western and Asian countries blindly. The Malaysian economy has become a model for Africa, but unfortunately for us their economy is now in crisis. We must demand our rights and must develop our own models by fighting the 'I don't care' attitude of our leaders!

On other occasions he openly criticized African leaders, including President Rawlings, for putting African countries under the yoke of neo-colonialism and under the control of such organizations as the IMF and the World Bank and their structural adjustment programmes (Gifford 1998: 88). Books he published after *Beyond the Rivers of Ethiopia* developed this line of thinking, of combining Afro-centric ideas with economic success and development through the preaching of a change in attitude whereby a promise of progress and prosperity is reserved for those eager to be industrious, studious and willing to sacrifice time, energy and resources to developing their own initiative. In a book entitled *Four Laws of Productivity*, for example, he admonishes the reader: 'Most of the time the reason why people are poor is because of laziness' and continues: 'Make sure you go beyond what everyone else is doing. And that may mean sleepless nights studying. But one day you will come to stand above the others.'

Outside Ghana his visits to other countries in Africa have often left local Pentecostal leaders deeply impressed by his powerful appearance and messages. In Zambia and Zimbabwe his participation in large Pentecostal summits attended by influential leaders from within the region such as Ezekiel Guti (Zimbabwe), Nevers Mumba (Zambia) and Enock Sitima (Botswana)[7] left many baffled and surprised by his messages of black pride, Pentecostal awakening and resistance to oppressive political and economic structures (Gifford 1998: 236-45). This appealing combination of Afro-centrism and Pentecostal liberation theology was unheard of in this region of Africa where political dictatorships continued to rule until the mid 1990s. Preaching fire-and-brimstone messages against the 'African inferiority complex' as he called it, his public sermons became news and were hotly debated in the public media, partly because of their alleged anti-white sentiments, (being expressed in countries with a still considerable 'white' population) and partly because of their overtly political criticism:

> ...your personal individual prosperity is tied up with the prosperity of the nation. We have to think structurally about the economy of the nation. You can't preach in Africa and not be political. If a nation is poor, its people will be poor. Christians can't say 'let's leave politics to politicians'. No, if wrong policies are made, you can pray all you want, and you won't have anything. In South Africa, God has changed the situation. They have a black President, but 98% of the wealth in South Africa is in non-black hands. So you can have a black President, but what's different? Christians have the faith, non-believers have the money. But you can't claim anyone's money by faith — it's illegal. If you want to have money, there is only one way: work. On 6 March 1957 Ghana was the first nation to get Independence. But the economy is not controlled by Ghanaians. The economy is controlled by

[7] See Maxwell (1998) on Guti in Zimbabwe and Van Dijk (2002a) on Sitima in Botswana.

> multinationals. We worked for them to create wealth for them to take it out of the country. We were hewers of wood and drawers of water for them. I prayed to God to prosper, but we have to change economic structures and social structures. If I don't have that opportunity, I can pray all I want and I'll still be poor. When we were colonised, structures were built in our nations. The British came not because they thought we needed the gospel; they came because they wanted raw materials…and impoverish you. You can pray all you want, but it won't help…unless we start looking at the structures of our nations.
>
> How come you live in your own country, and you don't own anything? The only thing is to run to Botswana and South Africa. The tragedy of African governments is that they keep their own people poor, and keep foreigners rich. The key lies in a work-conscious, ownership conscious, skilled populace. Don't think, 'who can give me a job?' Think, 'when can I start a business?' (Otabil addressing a crowd in Lusaka, Zambia, August 1994, quote taken from Gifford 1998: 240, 242)

What we can conclude is that Otabil's triangulation of black pride/Afro-centrism, Pentecostal liberation ideology and a prosperity gospel based on private entrepreneurship provides him with a prism with many sides to show in a variety of contexts. Whereas his messages in the context of Afro-American relations emphasize a break with slave mentality and a unification of purposes across the trans-Atlantic — which global Pentecostalism provides — in Africa black pride is becoming a constitutive element of private enterprise in the face of failing governments and white economic dominance.

Despite his overall success and appeal in Ghana, in many parts of Africa and overseas in Ghanaian and Afro-American communities of the English-speaking world, his ideas have not particularly struck a chord in the Dutch Ghanaian community. A branch of Otabil's church was set up relatively late in the Netherlands when compared to all the other Ghanaian Pentecostal churches that were established from the mid 1980s onwards. Furthermore, it was established in The Hague, one of the smaller concentrations of Ghanaian migrants in the Netherlands, while in fact the largest concentration is found in Amsterdam (Van Dijk 2001c, 2002b). In the meantime 40 different Ghanaian Pentecostal and other congregations had already come into existence, and so the International Central Gospel branch has remained small in membership and dependent on the help and support of one or two 'like-minded' churches in the city (Acts Revival and Rhema Gospel Church). Mensa Otabil has never visited the branch, as far as I am aware, although he has been to the much larger London-based branch of the church. The various magazines related to Otabil's activities (such as *Greener Pastures* or the university-related magazine *Pathfinder*) do not circulate widely in The Hague, nor do his tapes or video recordings. Some church-related musical recordings are an exception, particularly those that feature Ghanaian or American gospel artists, such as Black Heritage or Ron

Kenoli, and their performances on stage in the Christ Temple in the centre of Accra. Many of Otabil's views on black pride and Pentecostal liberation theology, however, remain absent from much of the Pentecostal discourse in the city of The Hague where his branch in located. Given the immense popularity of Otabil in Ghana and the far-reaching influence of much of his Afro-centric and politically critical thinking, this absence and silence is indeed striking.

Conclusion: Interpreting Otabil's absence

The first point to be made is that the growing elitist outlook of Otabil's church and its dominant views have meant that the church has moved away from a more popular and broader-based Pentecostalism in which the ritual practices of 'breaking' and deliverance dominate. The majority of Ghanaian migrants in the Netherlands were unskilled or semi-skilled when they left Ghana to try their luck in this part of Europe, unlike those who migrated to English-speaking countries where training and education were, or became, of dominant importance (see Ter Haar 1998). The Pentecostal churches, which in a sense followed this migration pattern to the Netherlands, were mostly of the type of popular or per force populist orientation in which the practices of breaking and deliverance are considered major elements of their appeal. Many of these churches that have been established in Amsterdam, such as the Resurrection Power Ministries or the Bethel Prayer Ministries, became successful in Ghana and in the diaspora largely because they embraced the practice of deliverance. This is a ritual practice of dealing with evil and misfortune that has become part of the hallmark of Pentecostalism and directly relates to the widely shared concerns of the general public.

On several occasions Otabil has proclaimed to be alarmed by the deliverance hype that hit Ghana in the last decade and which has often led, in his view, to a frenzied search for the occult and dark powers in people's private and social lives (personal communication with Mensa Otabil, but see also Gifford 1998: 108). Gifford writes:

> His concern arose for a characteristic reason: that because in practice deliverance bears on idols, local spirits, ancestors, stools and face markings, it hardly applies to whites and is really tailored for blacks, and is thus one more way of alienating blacks from their culture. (ibid)

What is this practice of deliverance that is so abhorred by Otabil? The practice of deliverance (*ogyee*) has become a common denominator in popular Pentecostalism as it shares and negotiates a fear of how demons, ancestral spirits and the like from the past may haunt a person in the present. The more positions of leadership were taken by Africans and the more Pentecostal churches and breakaway groups were started by Africans, the more the practice of deliverance — a way of dealing with a person's past — came to take a central position in worship and church organization. Its significance has become the subject of extensive study, by scholars from Ghana (see, among others, Atiemo 1993, Adubofuor 1994, Larbi 2001) as well as from elsewhere (Meyer 1995, 1998, Van Dijk 1997, 1999, Gifford 1998: 97-109, Ter Haar 1998: 175-76).

The aim of deliverance is to free people from the powers of Satan that hold them in bondage through demonic forces. These demonic forces are said to reside within society at large but more particularly within the individual's immediate circle of family relationships and descent. Satan is believed to work through ancestral or generational curses (*nnomee*), which can become manifest in specific problems haunting individual family members such as infertility, alcoholism, misfortune or tragic death. Pentecostal believers are, therefore, urged to be aware of such manifestations that may signal the presence of a curse from a past and of which the individual was unaware.

Deliverance is aimed at creating a rift, a clear-cut rupture with the known or, in most cases, unknown past. Deliverance should be preceded by 'breaking' (*obubu*), the spiritual breaking of the bonds that keep people entangled with their past, their former upbringing within the family circle where the ancestors are venerated at the family shrines through the practices of the shrine priests (*okomfoo*). Name-giving, 'outdooring' (an elaborate ritual of bringing a new-born child out into the community), initiation, healing and the pouring of libation to the ancestors performed at important events in a person's life may signal links with the family spirits which in Pentecostal discourses provoke danger and impurity.

Deliverance ministries are established in most churches and provide a break with the past. 'Make a complete break with the past' is a cry often heard in the context of these ministries (see Meyer 1998). Such a break operates on two levels. One is the person's immediate lifestyle, the engagement with present-day society in which the confirmed believer is trapped in moral wrongdoing — drinking, theft, other forms of crime, greed, poverty, rudeness, envy and hatred. These are all redefined in Pentecostal ideology as resulting from evil spirits, or even as spirits manifesting themselves in these forms.[8] Being Born Again is,

[8] As Pastor Ampiah Kwofi proclaimed at a gathering of his Global Revival Outreach Ministries which I attended on 29 October 1995: 'Poverty is a spirit you need to get rid of'.

therefore, often portrayed as a fierce battle between the individual and the powers from the person's immediate past.

At a deeper level, however, deliverance from the ancestral past confronts the bondage of the *longue duree*. The past life of the family is to be inspected for the sins that have been committed in the past. Any person alive today may be haunted by ancestral curses that become manifest through recurrent problems in terms of the blood-line with the past: families and individuals may experience problems with childbirth, with being able to conceive, with chronic diseases, with afflictions from ancestral or evil spirits which become apparent in possession, madness and nightmares. In Pentecostal ideology these ancestral curses all result from blood covenants that in the past have been established through and by the ancestors with devilish powers. The answer to such problems, as is stressed during deliverance rituals, is a complete break with the blood tie that keeps a person trapped within the realm of an ancestral curse. It may imply a subsequent rejection of all those rituals, such as initiation and funerals, that emphasize connections with a family's bounded past.

Most churches operate special hours, meetings places or even entire 'camps' where people can subject themselves to what are sometimes called 'spiritual operations' meant to relieve them of their burdening ancestral influences (Van Dijk 1997). Often taking place in a highly ecstatic and emotional atmosphere, people are 'broken' through prayer healings from these ties and all evil influences are spiritually cast away. Before this takes place, particularly in the context of admittance to prayer camps, people are requested to fill out extensive questionnaires in which every detail of their exposure to ancestral worship, traditional healing practices or 'devil worship' are investigated so as to enhance the spiritual treatment of all of them. As I have shown elsewhere (Van Dijk 1997), the ritual practices at these specialized prayer camps are considered by many aspiring migrants to be essential before moving from Ghana to other parts of the world to partake in all that migration may offer.

While breaking and deliverance are seen as key elements in the Pentecostal ritual structure as they provide a personal reconstruction of an individual's past and heritage, the control of time, history and self-making it prescribes is reinterpreted by Otabil in a different dimension. He, his church and some of the other churches that came later and that followed the inspirational lines he had set out came to perceive of a second wider and cultural domain of controlling the past: the moral supervision of culture. These Pentecostal churches, which for instance include the successful Lighthouse Chapel, are deeply concerned about culture and how the government and other authorities negotiate the call for a preservation of heritage, ritual and symbolic styles. These Pentecostals perceive African rituals as yet another dangerous avenue by which Satan ensures that ancestral and generational curses manifest themselves in present-day society. They tend to provoke a profound contestation in the public realm in terms of a politics of culture and its implied nostalgia (see for violent clashes, Van Dijk 2001e).

In their view, traditional ritual blocks progress not only at an individual level but also at the community level. In other words, social-cultural traditions form an impediment to the community's and even to the nation's progress, and Pentecostal initiative is thus directed at disqualifying such displays of cultural life. Consequently, Pentecostals critically examine efforts, such as those by the state, that are aimed at reviving and rejuvenating certain traditions, and that aim to overcome the ruptures with a cultural heritage which have been brought about by the modern projects of colonialism, missionization, western education, and capitalist market relations. Instead, within much Pentecostal ritual surrounding birth, death, marriage and so forth, we notice an explicit strategy aimed at replacing the cultural forms that are so cherished by those wishing to preserve their heritage.[9]

In Otabil's view therefore, breaking and deliverance require — at a higher level of abstraction — a critical examination of cultural styles and repertoires, of tradition and of the Ghanaian state's cultural policy of re-inscribing a cultural heritage into present-day public life. Black pride must be a Christianized pride, which runs counter to a state that has become complicit in encouraging and preserving certain traditions that are defiling to the nation. Considering this staunch criticism, it is remarkable that Otabil has become an influential member of the National Commission on Culture which, established under Rawlings, has become the patron of much of the state's effort to preserve cultural heritage for national interests (which in practice demonstrates the perplexing intricacies of the courting relationship between religion and politics in the modern developments of state formation in Ghana, an issue which I will leave for further discussion elsewhere).

In the Ghanaian migrant communities in the Netherlands, breaking and deliverance in the perspective of personal healing and fortune have remained the dominant perspective of most of the Pentecostal churches that have been

---

[9] Replacement may take place, for instance, when after childbirth, usually within a period of about three months, a name-giving ceremony for the baby is held. I once witnessed how an ICGC pastor took full 'possession' of the ritual, proclaimed the name of the baby and, instead of the usual alcohol, put water, salt and honey on the lips of the infant 'to make him taste the three essences of life'. At similar rituals, the power of the family and elders is publicly and substantially reduced and detachment proclaimed. While in a non-Pentecostal context the parents themselves, the family elders or the *okomfoo* (the shrine priests) proclaim the name of the baby in public, in what has become known in English as the 'outdooring' ceremony (Akan, *dintoo*), here the church directly asserts its detaching power over new life.

active since the mid 1980s. They did not, by and large, form part of the more intellectual and reflexive Pentecostalism developed by Otabil after the publication of his book in 1992 (since most of the migrants had already arrived in the Netherlands by then) and their relative seclusion from cultural developments in the Netherlands gave them little incentive to be concerned with such issues as the moral supervision of local cultural heritage. Most of the concerns of Ghanaian migrants in the Netherlands have remained highly personal and private and have not seemed to lead to a more structural interpretation of their individual circumstances and predicaments. This dominant orientation towards personal healing was again evidenced by the visit of highly popular Pentecostal healing prophets from Ghana between 1998 and 2000, healing prophets who were able to attract mass audiences at deliverance practices, which turned into veritable spectacles of healing. When these healing prophets showed up in The Hague, they found thousands of Ghanaian migrants waiting to be delivered from whatever was haunting them in their private lives.

While these Ghanaian migrants were unfamiliar with Otabil's thinking as far as the relationship between breaking/deliverance and the quest for black pride in cultural terms, the inverse of this is also true. Otabil's ideas of black pride in relation to self-esteem, one's own initiative and entrepreneurship seem not to be tailored to the specific situation of many Ghanaian migrants living in Dutch society. Otabil's ideas appear to assume too much in terms of freedom to take initiative, to develop entrepreneurial activity, to travel around the world in a cosmopolitan fashion in the pursuit of economic success and independence, as if conditions were the same everywhere and as if everybody had equal access to all sorts of resources to be able to live up to the expectations of these aspects of black pride. His ideas and public statements seem too little attuned to the often harsh political realities of the Ghanaian migrants' predicament in societies such as the Netherlands that are increasingly turning hostile to the presence of foreign labour.

In the Netherlands it has been particularly the presence of large numbers of Ghanaian and other West African migrants that has been a cause of alarm to the authorities with regard to Dutch immigration and identity policies. Around 1992, after the crash of an Israeli plane into a low-cost housing area of Amsterdam that caused an unknown number of Ghanaian deaths in the fire that followed, the commissioner of police sounded alarm bells concerning the allegedly high number of illegal Ghanaian migrants in Dutch cities. The Netherlands came to experience an unprecedented tightening of its identity policies which in the following years specifically targeted five immigrant communities, labelling them officially as 'problem countries'. At the top of that list was Ghana (Van Dijk 2001d, 2002b). The official view came to be that identity documents of any kind from these countries can never be believed to be genuine and that in almost 100 per cent of cases the identity papers of their citizens must be considered fraudulent.

The Ghanaian community became the subject of intense control and investigation by the Dutch authorities. The Dutch government introduced so-called verification procedures in Ghana whereby investigations into a person's true identity would take place in the first instance on Ghanaian soil (see Van Dijk 2001d, 2002b). This has led to feelings of unrest among the migrant community as well as among their families and friends back home in Ghana. Verification in fact soon became the most pressing problem for many Ghanaian migrants as it prevented them from travelling, from accessing resources elsewhere, from marrying spouses from Ghana, from being united with their families and children from and in Ghana and from obtaining tenured jobs in the Dutch labour market. It also led to a situation in which the many Ghanaian Pentecostal churches that had emerged in the meantime came to be seen by some as the only remaining safe haven where illegal migrants could take part in a social life of some kind. Churches are not commonly targeted for identity checks by the authorities, unlike almost all other public places in the city. Contrary to Ghanaian indignation about these identity and taxonomic state policies, the Dutch authorities basically perceived them as ways of dealing with a kind of corruption which in principle could be tackled though technical and administrative solutions.

As a consequence of the many measures the government took to curb what it saw as illegal immigration from Ghana, protests against harsh treatment from within the Ghanaian community soon mounted. Voiced by a number of Ghanaian migrant interest groups in the country, and not so much by the Pentecostal churches, these protests did not adopt a race-related discourse. The groups could not argue that Ghana had become listed as a 'problem-country' on the basis of racist thought, leading Ghanaians to become a disenfranchised people. This listing included non-black countries as well (India, Pakistan and the Dominican Republic). Although racial discrimination undoubtedly has a long and dark record in Dutch labour relations — a problem many Ghanaians have certainly encountered — the implementation of these specific identity procedures that impacted on the community to such a large extent have never developed a clear racial bend (Van Dijk 2001d, 2002b). Nor have issues of race ever really emerged either among the Ghanaian population and the way they felt they were treated or among Dutch officials. An issue of globalization, weakening state borders, parochial identities, yes, but not an issue of racial identities as such.

So, Otabil's ideas seem to have missed their mark in this specific context. While his ideas of black pride appear to resonate in a cosmopolitan world where he, his books and his ideas can have unfettered travel, can foster opportunity-seeking in an entrepreneurial fashion unhindered by borders of any kind and as such seem to fulfil the promise of globalization, Ghanaian migrants instead have begun to face the consequences of the 'fortress called Europe' (Ter Haar 1998). Ideas of black pride and free enterprise appear to have little meaning and appeal in a situation where globalization has come to mean blockades, control and increasing supervision through a state apparatus that extends its investigations into Ghana as well. Hence, breaking and deliverance in a *structural* sense, as proclaimed in Otabil's Pentecostal liberation theology, do not bespeak a situation in which these problems of blockade, control and supervision above all have come to be experienced as a highly personal, private problem; an individual's quest for 'verification' of all sorts of documents and as such a highly individualized conquest of almost Kafkain administrative procedures.

Instead of fighting a (pre-supposed) inferiority complex, many Ghanaians see themselves besieged by such questions as: 'Which force from within my family, my background, my past is responsible for these verification problems I am facing? 'Why is this all happening to me and who is to be held responsible for this particular kind of misfortune?' Breaking and deliverance remain inescapably personal and individual. Due to the lack of leverage in a practical sense, Otabil's ideas come across as irrelevant to a Ghanaian migrant community facing the predicaments of Dutch society where bureaucratic and taxonomic rationales have been able to turn 'identity' into an exclusively individualistic affair of coping and manoeuvring.

Important conclusions can be drawn from this difference in the appeal of Pentecostal Afro-centric ideas with regard to the intellectual ownership of such views, and the world and social groups to which they seem to belong. There is no self-evident relationship between such ownership and belonging, as Otabil's case for black pride and the Africanization of the Bible appear to imply. His claim, after all, is that the ownership of ideas of black pride and Pan-African unity do not belong *a priori* to an intellectual class of people well versed in Western enlightened ideals of scholarship but can and ought to be placed in the hands of the ordinary believer. While Otabil's Pentecostal views display a sense of ownership of specific Pan-African identity and entelechy in what it aims to achieve, the Ghanaian migrants who share this identity do not feel that Pan African ideals are part of their longing and belonging. This chapter has, thus, argued that ownership and belonging cannot be taken together as one great solvent of local identity contesting global marginalization, but that there is a dialogue between the two that requires a contextual understanding for each of the situations in which it emerges.

References

Adubofuor, S.B. 1994, 'Evangelical Parachurch Movements in Ghanaian Christianity: c. 1950-1990s', PhD thesis, University of Edinburgh.

Aluko, O. 1985, 'The Expulsion of Illegal Aliens from Nigeria: A Study in Nigeria's Decision-making', *African Affairs* 84 (337): 539-60.

Appiah, K.A. 1992, *In My Father's House. Africa in the Philosophy of Culture*, Oxford: Oxford University Press.

Atiemo, A.O. 1993, *The Rise of the Charismatic Movement in the Mainline Churches in Ghana*, Accra: Asempa Publishers.

Bruner, E.M. 1996, 'Tourism in Ghana. The Representation of Slavery and the Return of the Black Diaspora', *American Anthropologist* 98 (2): 290-305.

Byfield, J. 2000, 'Introduction: Rethinking the African Diaspora', *African Studies Review*, special issue 'Africa's Diaspora', 43 (1): 1-10.

Darkwah, N.B. 2000, *The Africans who Wrote the Bible. Ancient Secrets Africa and Christianity Have Never Told*, New York: Aduana Publishing Co.

Davies, I. 1998,'Negotiating African Culture: Towards a Decolonization of the Fetish', in: F. Jameson & M. Myoshi (eds), *The Cultures of Globalization*, Durham: Duke University Press.

Davis, O.I. 1997, 'The Door of No Return: Reclaiming the Past Through the Rhetoric of Pilgrimage', *The Western Journal of Black Studies* 21 (3): 156-61.

Ebron, P.A. 2000, 'Tourists as Pilgrims. Commercial Fashioning of Transatlantic Politics', *American Ethnologist* 26 (4): 910-32.

Ellis, S. & G. Ter Haar 1998, 'Religion and Politics in Sub-Saharan Africa', *The Journal of Modern African Studies* 36 (2): 175-201.

Ghana Evangelism Committee 1993, *National Church Survey 1993: Facing the Unfinished Task of the Church in Ghana*, Accra: Assemblies of God Literature Centre.

Gifford, P. 1998, *African Christianity. Its Public Role*, London: Hurst.

Gilroy, P. 1993, *The Black Atlantic: Modernity and Double Consciousness*, Cambridge, Mass: Harvard University Press.

Hackett, R.I.J. 1998, 'Charismatic/Pentecostal Appropriation of Media Technologies in Nigeria and Ghana', *Journal of Religion in Africa* 28 (3): 258-77.

Hanchard, M. 1999, 'Afro-Modernity: Temporality, Politics, and the African Diaspora', *Public Culture* (11): 245-68.

Hasty, J. 2002, 'Tourism, Asante and the Performance of Wealth: National Vulture and Transnational Heritage in Ghana', Paper presented at the conference on 'Performing Culture. The Politics and Aesthetics of Cultural Expression in Contemporary Ghana', Amsterdam, KIT/ASC, 13-14 June.

Larbi, E.K. 2001, *Pentecostalism: The Eddies of Ghanaian Christianity*, Accra: SAPC series.

Lewis, E. 1995, 'To Turn as on a Pivot: Writing African Americans into a History of Overlapping Diasporas', *American Historical Review* (100): 765-87.

Marshall, R. 1998, 'Mediating the Global and the Local in Nigerian Pentecostalism', *Journal of Religion in Africa* 28 (3): 278-315.

Maxwell, D. 1998, '"Delivered from the Spirit of Poverty?" Pentecostalism, Prosperity and Modernity in Zimbabwe', *Journal of Religion in Africa* 28 (3): 350-73.

Maxwell, D. 2001, '"Sacred History, Social History": Traditions and Texts in the Making of a Southern African Transnational Religious Movement', *Society for the Comparative Study of Society and History* 43 (3): 502-24.

Meyer, B. 1995, '"Delivered from the Powers of Darkness": Confessions of Satanic Riches in Christian Ghana', *Africa* 65 (2): 236-55.

Meyer, B. 1998, '"Make a Complete Break with the Past". Time and Modernity in Ghanaian Pentecostalist Discourse', in: R.P. Werbner (ed.), *Memory and the Postcolony. African Anthropology and the Critique of Power*, London: Zed Books, Postcolonial Identities Series.

Meyer, B. 1999, *Translating the Devil. Religion and Modernity Among the Ewe of Ghana*, Edinburgh: Int. African Library.

Meyer, B. 2001, 'Money, Power and Morality: Popular Ghanaian Cinema in the Fourth Republic', in: P. Nugent & B. Meyer (eds), *Religion in the 4th Republic of Ghana*, Thematic Issue, *Ghana Studies* (4): 65-84.

Mudmbe, V.Y. 1994, *The Idea of Africa*, Bloomington: Indiana University Press.

Otabil, M. 1992, *Beyond the Rivers of Ethiopia: A Biblical Revelation on God's Purpose for the Black Race*, Accra: Altar International.

Parsons, Q.N. n.d. 'F.Z.S. Peregrino (1851-1919): An Early Pan-Africanist', Unpublished paper, History Department, University of Botswana.

Peil, M. 1979, 'Host Reactions: Aliens in Ghana', in: W.A. Shack & E.P. Skinner (eds), *Strangers in African Societies*, Berkeley: University of California Press.

Peil, M. 1995, 'Ghanaians Abroad', *African Affairs* (94): 345-67.

Sudarkasa, N. 1979, 'From Stranger to Alien: The Socio-Political History of the Nigerian Yoruba in Ghana, 1900-1970', in: W.A. Shack & E.P. Skinner (eds), *Strangers in African Societies*, Berkeley: University of California Press.

Ter Haar, G. 1994, 'Standing up for Jesus: A Survey of New Developments in Christianity in Ghana', *Exchange* 23 (3): 221-40.

Ter Haar, G. 1998, *Halfway to Paradise. African Christians in Europe*, Cardiff, Cardiff Academic Press.

Van Binsbergen, W. (ed.), 1997 'Black Athena: Ten Years After', *Talanta*, Proceedings of the Dutch Archaeological and Historical Society, vol. 28-29.

Van Dijk, R. 1997, 'From Camp to Encompassment: Discourses of Transsubjectivity in the Ghanaian Pentecostal Diaspora', *Journal of Religion in Africa* 27 (2): 135-69.

Van Dijk, R. 1999, 'The Pentecostal Gift: Ghanaian Charismatic Churches and the Moral Innocence of the Global Economy', in: R. Fardon, W. van Binsbergen & R. van Dijk (eds), *Modernity on a Shoestring*. London & Leiden: SOAS & ASC, Anthony Rowe.

Van Dijk, R. 2001a, 'Time and Transcultural Technologies of the Self in the Ghanaian Pentecostal Diaspora', in: A. Corten & R. Marshall-Fratani (eds), *Between Babel and Pentecost. Transnational Pentecostalism in Africa and Latin America*, London & Bloomington: Hurst Publishers & Indiana University Press.

Van Dijk, R., M. de Bruijn & H. van Dijk 2001b, 'Cultures of Travel: Fulbe Pastoralists in Central Mali and Pentecostalism in Ghana', in: M. de Bruijn, R. van Dijk & D.

Foeken (eds), *Mobile Africa: Changing Patterns of Movement in Africa and Beyond*, Leiden: Brill, African Dynamics Series, no. 1.

Van Dijk, R. 2001c, 'African Pentecostalism in the Netherlands', in: S.D. Glazier (ed.), *Berkshire Encyclopedia of African & African-American Religions*, New York: Routledge.

Van Dijk, R. 2001d, '"Voodoo" on the Doorstep. The Trafficking in Young Nigerian Women for the Dutch Sex Industry and its Moral Panic', *Africa* 71 (4): 558-86.

Van Dijk, R. 2001e, 'Contesting Silence: The Ban on Drumming and the Musical Politics of Pentecostalism in Ghana', in: P. Nugent & B. Meyer (eds), *Religion in the 4th Republic of Ghana*, Thematic Issue, *Ghana Studies* (4): 31-64.

Van Dijk, R. 2002a, 'Localising Anxieties. Ghanaian and Malawian Immigrants, Rising Xenophobia and Social Capital in Botswana', ASC Working Paper no. 49.

Van Dijk, R. 2002b, 'Ghanaian Churches in the Netherlands: Religion Mediating a Tense Relationship', in: I. van Kessel (ed.), *Merchants, Missionaries and Migrants: 300 Years of Dutch-Ghanaian Relations*, Amsterdam: KIT/Sub-Saharan Publishers.

Yeboah, Y.F. 1986, 'The Crisis of International Migration in an Integrating West Africa: A Case Study of Nigeria and Ghana', *Africa Development/Afrique et Développement* 11 (4): 217-56.

7

Global connections, local ruptures: The case of Islam in Senegal

Roy Dilley

This chapter examines the relationship between Islam and caste in Senegal. It investigates how new meanings of caste identity have been negotiated in view of differing conceptions of Islam that have taken hold within the country. Twentieth-century reformist movements have challenged the predominant role of Sufi brotherhoods, bringing about a reassessment of the relationship between caste and Islam. The Nyasiyya brotherhood provides the basis for a brief case study, which shows that the popularity of this Order abroad is not matched by its reception in Senegal. Some of the possible reasons are examined for this disjunction between the global connections the Order establishes and the local ruptures it engenders within the local Muslim community. The chapter traces the dynamics of Sufism and reformist Islam to reveal a double-edged thrust of global connections brought about through an internationalizing Islam, and of local ruptures mediated through caste identities.

Introduction

Certain theories of globalization suggest that we are living through very particular times, in which processes connected with the increasing speed of communication, of movements of goods and people from one part of the world to another make for a unique experience that is driven by connections being forged on a global scale. It is easy to regard this as a unique late-20th-century/early-21st-century phenomenon. This chapter seeks to suggest that in other periods of history movements of people and ideas on a global scale were also in evidence, and arguably one of these was the spread of the religion of

Islam itself from the Middle East across North and Sub-Saharan Africa, through parts of Europe, as well as east into Asia and elsewhere. This movement began as early as the late 7th and 8th centuries CE, and the spread of ideas within the Islamic diaspora has waxed and waned ever since. I attempt to pick up some of the threads of this sense of connectedness with respect to different conceptions of Islam in West Africa, and especially how these varying conceptions of religious thought and practice have been formed within a conversation between Muslims within West Africa and those beyond the region.

These ideas about global connectedness form a backdrop to one of the central issues under investigation in this chapter, namely, the relationship between Islam and caste in Senegal. Islam as a globalizing force has been shaped in its encounter with local conceptions of social and cultural difference — that is 'caste'. This investigation entails the study of how in the contemporary period new meanings of caste identity have been negotiated with respect to the differing conceptions of Islam that have become established in Senegal. The relationship between caste status and the religion of Islam has been historically a matter of local debate in the region and, as is shown below, 20th-century reformist Islamic movements have brought this matter to the fore once again.

Islam in Senegal has been forged historically by a series of global connections: reformist movements from the Almoravids in the 10th century, the influence of Moorish scholars in the 17th and 18th centuries, and the Wahabbist-inspired jihads of the 19th century under the leadership, for example, of El Hajj Omar Taal are all examples of this.[1] This chapter picks up threads of this conversation from the early 20th century, in particular by examining an assault on Sufism by anti-Sufist Muslims as well as by those educated in a Western rationalist tradition. Globalization, however, is not a one-way process. Global connections linking one locality to another are complex and ambiguous, and must be understood by reference to those worlds of meaning in which people find themselves. While the impact of ideas generated in places outside West Africa can be plotted, so too can the attempts by members of a locality who actively seek out new sources of knowledge and authority to meld them into forms that have roots within any particular location. I aim to trace the dynamics within Sufism in Senegal, and this investigation reveals a double-edged thrust of global connections and local ruptures. Two contradictory processes are at work: while some Muslims seek a more internationalist platform for their faith, others are developing conceptions of the Muslim community that address local ruptures. One main form of social distinction that has constituted a rupture within the community of Sufi Muslims in Senegal has been 'caste', a label used to refer to members of occupationally specialized artisan and musician groups

[1] See Willis (1967, 1970) on the Wahabbist influences on Taal.

who have conventionally been excluded from full participation as co-religionists.[2] This chapter examines the relationship between Islam and caste in Senegal with regard to processes connected with colonialism and the post-colony.

The kind of Islam most commonly associated with Senegal in the literature on West African Muslims is that of the Sufi brotherhoods, particularly the Tijaniyya, Qadiriyya and the Muridiyya. One central area of expertise among the marabouts of these orders is the control of Arabic literacy and associated forms of 'book magic' (Goody 1968) that constitute one of the most significant forms of magical operation that marabouts control. But what might be called the 'esoteric construction' of knowledge and the role of literacy within these Sufi orders is under attack. The main protagonists in this contest are Islamic reformers and Islamists who are leading an assault on contemporary forms of Sufi mystical practices in West Africa. Traditional Sufi brotherhoods have been challenged in terms of how their systems of belief and practice represent a departure from 'orthodoxy'. Reformers and Islamists have traced anew where the Muslim community should draw the limits. And their new definitions of this community have entailed the inclusion and the exclusion of specific categories of people. These Islamist critiques of Sufism have proposed replacing what might be seen as 'local' forms of religious belief and practice with more internationalist or global forms. These represent for some observers a modernist vision in Islamic guise.

What seems to be happening today is a bifurcation in the Senegalese Muslim community: Islamists and reformers propose radically new visions of the *jama'a,* the Muslim community, while at the same time, others are reinventing and recasting conventional forms of West African Sufism. There is, therefore, a complex set of shifting patterns of social association and religious identification in Senegal. Indeed, running parallel with the Islamist and reformist developments has been the spread of Sufi brotherhoods outside Senegal. The Murid Order, for example, operates internationally in both Europe and the United States, and the Nyasiyya — an offshoot of the Tijaniyya — is developing a global reach beyond the boundaries of Senegal. While many of these developments are beyond the scope of this chapter, it is the Nyasiyya that forms the focus of this investigation. The popularity of this order abroad, however, is not matched in terms of its standing and reception at home in Senegal. This

[2] See Dilley (2000) for a discussion of the use of the term 'caste' to describe such categories of persons. As employed here, the gloss 'caste' provides a generalized, non-ethnic-specific short cut for a range of social categories that are variously named in local vernaculars. In Pulaar, for instance, they are known as *nyeenybe.* Its use also reflects popular usage by local speakers who use the term 'caste' interchangeably with 'race'.

chapter examines some of the possible reasons for this disjunction between the global connections that the order establishes on the one hand, and the local ruptures it is engendering within the Islamic community on the other. The association between the order and people of 'caste' origin is central, the chapter argues, and this plays a large part in the local understanding of the order's place within a Senegalese Islamic context.

Forms of knowledge and education

The nature of literacy practices and the status of 'book magic' within Sufi brotherhoods have been thrown into relief by virtue of the challenges laid down by opponents of mystical Sufism. Brenner (2000) refers to the 'esoteric episteme' that underpins a variety of forms of West African Sufi mysticism. This episteme also supports their corresponding forms of knowledge and conceptions of power. However, new forms of knowledge and conceptions of power have been used to challenge mystical Sufism, and this challenge comes not only in the form of a secular Western education. It is also derived from within Islam itself, especially from radical reformist movements bent on confronting what they regard in Sufi religious practice as wrongful innovation (*bid'a*), condemnable religious acts (*sihr*), religious mixing (*ikhtilât*), and the sin of association (*shirk*) in the near deification of marabouts. Sufism for them is a degenerate form of worship that has lost sight of Islamic law and custom (*sharia* and *sunna*) and has moved away from the message of the Qur'an and the motivations of the early Muslim community. These critiques must be seen within an historical frame that highlights the changes taking place in the field of education.

The early European-oriented educational system in Senegal, established in the 19th century, aimed at a policy of educating Senegalese for administrative positions in the expanding colonial government. This system established literacy in French as a key skill for the emerging local urban elites and developed in parallel with a system already set in place by local Muslims, namely a network of schools for Qur'anic study. The French colonial authorities attempted to modify their own European system to accommodate Muslims' needs but these attempts met with little success (Bouche 1974). The traditional Qur'anic school (*dudal*) constituted an element within the system of literacy restricted by and large to the children of cleric families. The gulf between education in rural and urban areas became apparent too in wider divisions over the direction of educational policy in the country as a whole. One view advocated a universal education system based on the European tradition and another on the realities of Senegalese social life in the countryside (Colin 1980). In the more recent period

A new mosque, being built with the help of Middle-Eastern finance, in the town of Tivouane, the centre of the Tijaniyya in Senegal
Photo: Roy Dilley

of structural adjustment, characterized by the withdrawal of the arm of the state from rural areas such as Fuuta Toro, there has been a mobilization of self-help schemes (*bamtaare*, mutual-aid groups), most of which have been based upon remittances from emigrant workers in France and elsewhere. These schemes have provided health and educational facilities as well as provision for the construction of new mosques (Knight 1994), a development encouraged by Muslim reformers.

The installation of new European-based schooling did much to encourage what Brenner (2000) has called 'a secular rationalist discourse' in which knowledge and power are differently construed in comparison to West African Sufism. Access to knowledge was no longer effected through an initiatory process linked to a single spiritual and divinely gifted individual but instead learning became a topic of public acquisition and enquiry. Personalized methods of Sufi Islamic apprenticeship were replaced by impersonalized techniques of learning. Brenner (2000: 38) states — in relation to Mali — that 'the grip of the esoteric episteme would begin to erode [with the arrival of European colonial powers], challenged by the imposition of new power structures that ignored and denigrated esoteric claims to knowledge and power'. The emerging system of education was not simply dualistic, however, with European secular rationalism opposing Muslim Sufi mysticism, for within the Islamic community a series of fundamental shifts were taking place.

Muslim reformers, often operating outside the system of Sufi brotherhoods, began a two-pronged attack on education provision from the 1930s onwards in Senegal. Critical of what they considered to be the neglect of Islam in the French system, reformers attempted to establish a broadly based education in which the use of Arabic was central, sometimes alongside French, as the language of instruction; and a wider curriculum was developed beyond strict Qur'anic studies. Subjects such as mathematics, geography and history were introduced into these new Arabic schools, which were called *medersas* (Schmitz 2000b). In Fuuta Toro, Al Hajj Mahmud Ba, for example, on his return from the Hijaz set up a new school during this period in the village of Jowol. Another individual, Ahmad Al-Azhari, university-trained in Egypt, sought to achieve the same status for Arabic that French had attained as a language of study (Ba 1985-86: 250 *et passim*). He encouraged the development of modern Arabic culture in the valley and he himself belonged to the category of young people educated abroad in the Maghreb, the Middle East or Arabia. Fluent in Arabic language and culture and well versed in Islamic theology, they were labelled 'arabisers' or *arabisants* in French.

Developments such as these were part of a wider Islamic revivalist movement in West Africa. Often mistakenly labelled 'Wahhabist' by colonial authorities (Monteil 1980: 274) — a movement drawn from central Arabia and associated with the House of Saud[3] — a host of reformers with a spectrum of Islamic viewpoints launched campaigns for the renewal of Muslim religious beliefs. Not only were they concerned about the imposition of Western education and European-centred models of social, economic and cultural development, they also rallied against what they regarded as religious and moral laxity, condemned the veneration of marabouts, and labelled maraboutic magic as superstition. Book magic, so central to West African Sufism, was disenchanted and its aura of mystique stripped away. While Wahhabis in the strict sense have been few on the ground in Senegal, their presence does indicate the radical impact of 'Arabization' and the severity of the attack on Sufi Islam.[4] Along with French education, reformed Islamic schooling encouraged a rationalist paradigm of thought and spread a functional literacy in Arabic to a much wider section of the population. It propagated literacy skills in the general population to an extent never seen before.[5] This form of schooling also undermined, like its European counterpart, the relationship of apprenticeship and devotion of a disciple to his marabout, and encouraged more impersonal forms of learning. Schmitz (2000b), for example, reports the use of cassette tapes that are circulated among Muslim students eager to hear lectures of Middle Eastern Arabic teachers and Islamic scholars.

The new *medersa* schools contrasted, therefore, with those offering a traditional Qur'anic education. The latter contributed to the development of a narrow literate clerical elite who possessed a competence, albeit often uneven, in Arabic. They also provided the foundation upon which gifted scholars could progress into esoteric sciences and Islamic arts. At the heart of this system of education was what has been called the oral transmission of the written word, and this mode of transmission continued throughout the highly personalized relationship of disciple (*taalibe* or *murid*) and marabout that characterized the higher stages of learning and initiation. The reformed *medersas* developed a broader curriculum comprising a range of subjects and taught a competence in Arabic based less on rote memorization of texts and more focused on the language as a medium of study and communication. As Brenner and Last (1985: 443) point out: 'competent literacy in Arabic is the major factor in West Africa which separates establishment from popular Islam'. But the effect of the

---

[3] It is named after Shaykh Muhammad b. Abd al-Wahhab, born in central Arabia in 1703. He entered into an alliance with the Emir of Dariya in Saudi Arabia that resulted in the establishment of the House of Saud. See Clarke (1982: 216-17).

[4] The anti-Sufi Wahhabi movement was much stronger in Mali and Côte d'Ivoire. See, for example, Brenner (1983a) and Soares (1999).

[5] Adult illiteracy levels were over 70% in the 1988 census but had dropped below that figure in 1995, although it is doubtful whether literacy in Arabic would have been used as a criterion for exclusion from this statistic (*African South of the Sahara* 1999).

development of reformist Muslim schools was to offer new routes to Arabic literacy and to challenge the nature of the literate Islamic establishment.[6]

Islamic reform movements

Within the plural educational context, a challenge was mounted to the institutions that were part of the restricted literacy practices of an earlier period in Fuuta Toro. The result was that the scope and level of access to an expanded literacy programme increased. Alongside this change was a two-pronged attack on the previous 'establishment' Sufi marabouts: French-based education encouraged secularism that charged maraboutism with religious archaism, superstition and unwarranted privilege; and the campaigners for Islamic reform charged maraboutism with the corruption of their religion, moral laxity and degeneracy. Reformers embraced a vision of a revived Muslim faith that was particularly attractive to young urban dwellers in that it was seen as a force for an international and universalist conception of the religion that transcended local boundaries and was identified with a wider Muslim world (Brenner 1983b, Evers Rosander & Westerlund 1997, Soares 1999). This vision also sought to re-establish the sovereignty and uniqueness of God and offered the prospect of a state run according to *Shari'a* principles.

Muslim militants who have held to this latter position have frequently been referred to as 'fundamentalists', although this term is rejected in much of the literature. Instead, the preferred term for those movements calling for a link to be made between the structure of the state and the Muslim religion is 'Islamist', since their members often regard themselves not simply as returning to a fundamental tradition but as representing a contemporary alternative to Western modernity.[7] The Islamist movement took hold in Senegal in the 1970s and 1980s, adding another dimension to, or even replacing, earlier Muslim

---

[6] Brenner and Last make the following comment regarding the situation in the neighbouring country of Mali, and it could well apply to Senegal: 'Educational reformers in Mali, through *medersas*, have virtually managed to establish themselves as a new dominant class of 'neo-'*ulama*'. They not only condemn the French educational system that, they claim, destroys Islamic values, but they have succeeded in portraying the traditional maraboutic and Sufi '*ulama* class as perpetrators of a form of popular Islam, that is, one which is semi-literate and doctrinally aberrant' (Brenner & Last 1985: 442).

[7] See, for example, Evers Rosander (1997) and Gomez-Perez (1991) for a discussion of this issue.

reformists that had begun their activities in the 1930s.[8] Reformism had placed a different emphasis upon Muslim sources such as the Qur'an, the Sunna and *ijma* or consensus, none of which was to be renounced but which could be accommodated within a modern world. Indeed, Islam had to be integrated into this new context but it would accept aspects of Western thought and culture in a modified form.

One of the earliest Senegalese reform groups was *La Fraternité Musulmane*, established in the town of Saint Louis in 1935 (Gomez-Perez 1991). This group, for example, intervened over escalating bridewealth payments in Fuuta Toro in the 1930s, and attempted to cap prestations at affordable levels (Robin 1947). It also complained about the excessive demands of praise-singers at ceremonies, a complaint often heard from a range of more contemporary Muslim leaders. Another influential reformist group, the *Union Culturelle Musulman* (UCM), was founded by Cheikh Touré in 1953.[9] It engaged in a struggle against the effects of French colonialism and opposed the stance of the leading Sufi marabouts who had collaborated with the colonial powers. It criticized the French authorities for interfering with the practice of Islam and railed against the archaism of maraboutism — its mysticism, its talismans and amulets as well as the complete submission of a disciple to a spiritual guide. The tone of the UCM attack on maraboutism can be gleaned from the following rallying call to fight against:

> religious fetishism and exploitation, under the sway of which is the mass population that is the victim of a prefabricated Islam... It is in part a devalued religion with which our populations have been intoxicated and it will be by a renewed faith that detoxification will be brought about. (author's own translation)[10]

The Union also forbade the young from going to cinemas and nightclubs, and from attending French schools, and encouraged cultural 'Arabization', a secular state and a universal fraternity amongst all Muslims.

While voices of the Muslim reformers became muted after independence, a decade or so later the cries of Islamist militants could be clearly heard again.[11]

---

[8] See Loimeier (2000) on the 'two generations' of Islamic reform in Senegal, the first of which he dates as developing in the 1950s, the second from the 1970s onwards.

[9] In Arabic this group was called *'Ittihad ath-Thaqafi al-Islami* (Loimeier 2000).

[10] See Monteil (1980: 274) from whom the quotation is taken: '...fétichisme religieux et l'exploitation dont est victime la masse sous le couvert d'un Islâm préfabriqué... C'est en partie par une religion dévaluée que nos populations ont été intoxiquées et ce sera par une foi rénovée que la désintoxication se fera.'

[11] The account that follows draws heavily on Gomez-Perez (1991). See also Monteil (1980), Clarke (1982), Callaway & Creevy (1994), Evers Rosander & Westerlund (1997) and Schmitz (2000b). Loimeier (2000) notes that, post-independence, President

However, as early as 1956 a movement called *Harakat al-Fallah* ('Movement of Salvation'), as it was later known, influenced by Wahhabism, called for the establishment of an Islamic republic in Senegal. During the 1970s and 1980s, similar kinds of groups flourished: 'Society of Servants of the Merciful', the Jama'at Ibad ar-Rahman or Jamaatou Ibadou Arraham[12] began as an offshoot of the UCM following a breakaway by a group of young dissenters who struck up associations with the al-Fallah movement. Much more politically engaged than either the UCM or al-Fallah, the majority of its members were young urban intellectuals. Another Islamist group was created in 1985 by Cheikh Touré, founder of the moderate UCM that he had deserted due to its pro-government and politically uncritical stance. This group, *L'Organisation pour l'Action Islamique* (OAI), adopted a more virulent and critical anti-European discourse and took as a model of political organization the theocratic state of Iran. These reform movements are part of the second generation of Islamist groups, some of which gained especial social influence in the sphere of education. They developed a critique of maraboutic Sufism, but also adopted a critical stance towards the secular Senegalese state. In this respect they found common cause with the marabouts, and it appears that their public discourse in the 1990s concentrated less on confrontation with Sufi brotherhoods and more on creating a broad-based Muslim alliance against secular politics (Loimeier 2000).

A wide variety of Muslim reformist and Islamist groups in the post-World-War-II period formulated a critique not only of the French-bequeathed political structure and Western modernity, but also attacked Sufi maraboutism, its mysticism and forms of magic. Traditional forms of charisma came under attack. The esoteric episteme of Sufi maraboutic knowledge and power was criticized, and with it by implication the esoteric construction of knowledge and power of the various specialized, hereditary occupational groups.

With respect to these latter groups, the position and status of the members of these hereditary, occupationally specialized craftsmen and musician categories, the 'castes', became contested.[13] Until then, they had by and large been excluded

---

Senghor managed to bring the UCM under state control by integrating its reformers into the political system and into certain professions.

[12] The first title in Arabic is translated by Loimeier (2000) as the 'Society of the Servants of the Merciful', and the second slightly different transcription as 'a group of individuals recognizing the supremacy of their creator and desirous of figuring among his servants' by Clark & Colvin Phillips (1994).

[13] The nature of such social categories across West Africa in particular, but known in other parts of the continent too, has been the subject of much research and scholarly debate. Indeed, the use of the term 'caste' to describe these categories of persons has also been a moot point. For a wider literature on 'caste' groups see, for example, Conrad & Frank (1995), Diop (1981), McNaughton (1988), Richter (1980), Silla (1966), Tamari (1997), Todd (1977) and Vaughan (1970).

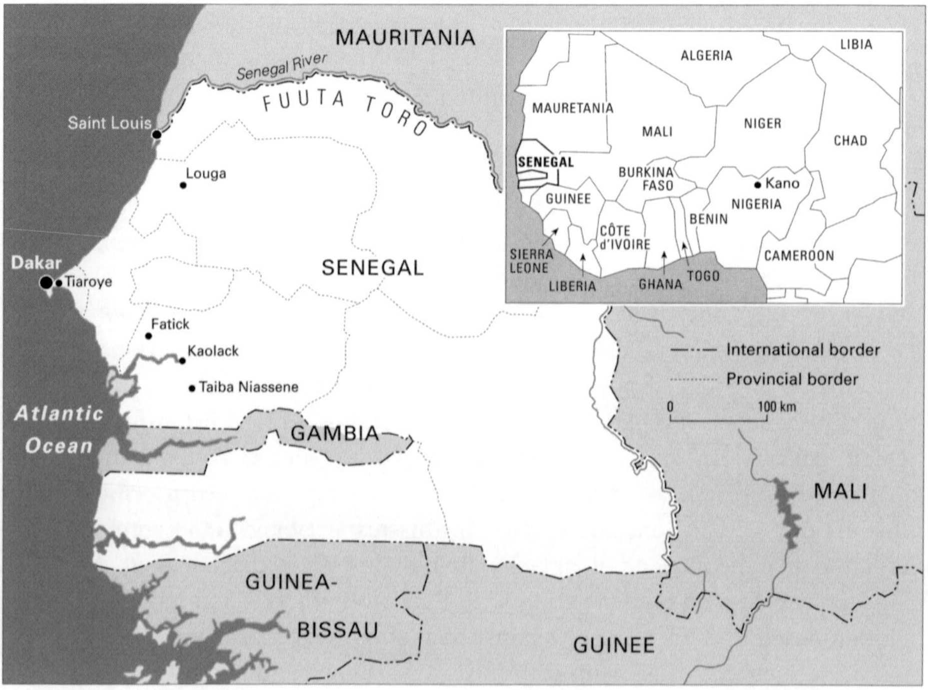

Map 7.1: Senegal

from the central religious offices within Sufi Islam. Reformist and Islamist groups offered new opportunities for previously marginalized members of the Muslim *jama'a* to enter into a more active engagement with the religious community.

The renegotiation of Islam and social exclusion

In the mid 19th century the newly introduced Tijaniyya Order under El-Hajj Umar Taal was more open to individuals of lower social rank than the existing orders. Those members of men-of-skill categories or of slave descent who rose through the ranks of the Sufi brotherhood did so during the militaristic and expansionist phase of Taal's Muslim campaigns. The order appears subsequently to have reverted to an earlier model of social organization in which caste prejudices surfaced again and craftsmen and musicians were once more marginalized and excluded from religious office. By contrast, the Qadiriyya, a much older order in West Africa[14] appears to have been less flexible in assimilating and promoting those of artisan origin; while the uniquely Senegalese Murid Order is generally held to be more open as regards the caste status of its members.[15] The family of the founder of the Murids, Amadu Bamba (1850-1927), is linked through his mother to an important Fuuta Toro family, the Busso clerics who hold village political office in a river valley (Morice 1982: 282). Amadu Bamba's father's patronym, Mbacké, is also thought to be connected to Haalpulaar roots. Bamba promoted praise-singers and smiths to the summit of the Murid hierarchy (Monteil 1980: 362) and in the 1950s a singer called Ali Samba Guêye officially represented the brotherhood at Kaolack, collecting one million FCFA for the 'Grand Serigne' (ibid: 365). Smiths, woodcarvers and other artisans were particularly sought out by the brotherhood for their practical skills, especially during its formative period when it was

[14] The first Islamic brotherhood to be introduced into West Africa, the Qadiriyya traces its origin to a Muslim from Baghdad named Sidi Abd al-Qadir al-Jilani or Gilani (1079-1166 CE). The order spread throughout the region in the late 15th and early 16th centuries, and it is most probable that Abdul Qadir Kan, the founder of the Almamate regime in Fuuta Toro in the late 18th century was one of its leading figures in the area.

[15] Of the three main Sufi brotherhoods in Senegal, the Tijaniyya and Muridiyya represent something in the region of 47% and 30% respectively of the Muslim population, which itself constitutes around 85% of the total number of 7 million Senegalese (see Recensement Général, 1988). The Qadiriyya is a much smaller order than the other two. The Murid brotherhood has its roots in the Qadiriyya, and the Tijaniyya embraces a number of offshoot sects such as: Layeens of Cap Vert, Nyasiyya of Kaolack, and the Hamilliyya which developed in Mali.

settling the new lands (*Terres Neuves*) of Salum and Senegal Oriental to establish their characteristic village organization based around groundnut cultivation.[16] Indeed, the late Khalif Général of the Murids, El-Hajj Falilu Mbacké (d. 1968), second son of Amabdu Bamba, once declared that 'castes' derive in the most part from 'pre-Islamic beliefs', but yet he cited a number of instances of marriage contracted by members of his own freeborn family with persons considered to belong to inferior social ranks (Diouf 1983: 230). Muslim leaders such as him are caught on the horns of a dilemma when they proclaim equality amongst all Muslims regardless of caste and rank, for in trying to gain the sympathy and support of those of inferior status whom they seek to protect, they run the risk of alienating significant numbers of their freeborn members. Indeed, despite the words of the late Khalif Général about caste equality, Murid marabouts continued to seek marriage partners predominantly among freeborn families or within the ancient Wolof ruling families (Diouf 1983).

This example of the Murids throws into relief the complex issue of renegotiation and indeed contestation that has been going on within Sufi brotherhoods over the status of believers of 'caste' origin. To assert that 'the notion of a hierarchical caste system is anathema to the tenets of Islam' does little justice to the complex processes that are being played out.[17] A number of concerns can be raised in this respect. First, such statements elide the distinction between the rhetoric of equality and the social practice of a religion; second, they neglect local debate about the issue; and third, they treat West African Islam as a single undifferentiated whole, a single system of belief and practice.[18] What I call an 'accommodationist' Sufi Islam allowed craftsmen and musicians a marginal but inferior position within it but it also encompassed caste groups within a complex ideological framework. The proclaimed ideology of Sufi brotherhood ignored the question of caste and was rarely used to oppose the social exclusion resting at the heart of these orders. Taal's mid-19th-century reform movement attempted to renegotiate the limits of inclusion but this

[16] See Cruise O'Brien (1971) and Diouf (1983). The former argues that the Murid Order provided a new social framework for displaced Wolof populations, especially craftsmen and musicians who lost their means of patronage after the collapse of the leading families among the Wolof (ibid: 15). He also notes that there were more artisans in Murid villages than in others (ibid: 84).

[17] Villalón (1994: 57) states, for example, '... Islamic theology ... tends to be hostile to any distinction that is incompatible with the notion of the fundamental equality of all men before God'.

[18] Ceerno Bokar Taal, the Haalpulaar cleric who settled in Mali, believed in the 'inevitability of the inequality in society, but also in the equality of all men before God' (Brenner 1983a: 17). This statement suggests different principles are appropriate to different domains of thought and different contexts of action — the secular and the sacred.

eventually met with little success. The orthodox Sufi view on the matter was that while the Holy Book did not sanction caste distinction, it did not forbid it either. The issue was often left to benign neglect. As indicated in the Murid example, one major field of social life and a key area of social reproduction in which caste considerations remained an important determinant was — and still is — marriage.[19] The exclusive matrimonial strategies of leading marabout families, who often sought alliances with high-ranking freeborn families rather than with other social categories, evince the gulf between rhetoric and social action. This exclusivity in marriage, however, was prized as much by members of caste groups as by those of higher social status. Islam in itself did not provide an ideological justification of caste differentiation and did not play the same role as the Hindu religion in relation to Indian caste. Moreover, its muted voice in relation to the question of brotherhood allowed for the possibility of accommodating a broad range of practices in different domains of social life.

A good deal of debate in post-independence Senegal has centred on whether castes would disappear, and on whether they would be assimilated by Islam (see Diop 1981, Diouf 1983, Monteil 1980, Morice 1982). One obvious factor was the changing employment opportunities offered in urban settings, in expanding markets and so forth. Modernization would see an end to such an archaic social structure, or so many commentators thought. The rupture of the connection between caste status and occupation in urban areas did contribute to the loosening of the organization of social groups compared with that in the rural economy. Indeed, economic possibilities for members of lower caste groups offering manual skills might be greater than those for higher status clerics who had few practical talents to offer (see Diop 1965). However, it must be remembered that the social status of men-of-skill categories has never been linked tightly to a unique connection with one occupation. The practice of a trade never constituted the only criterion of caste membership, since notions of descent and inheritance contributed as much, if not more, to the recognition of status.[20] Caste occupations have not been stable over time (see Tamari 1997).

Another dimension to this debate about the continuance of caste concerns the ideological and discursive nature of the relation between social differentiation and the presumed equality of the community of the faithful. Some authors have argued that Islam would come to 'whiten' or bleach the stain of low social status

---

[19] See Diop for a discussion on this issue among Wolof (1981: 94-104).

[20] Panzacchi (1994) reports an interesting observation that among praise-singer families the members of the generation 40-60 years old in the mid 1990s were more self-conscious about their social origins than their children tended to be. This younger generation has embraced the traditional occupation with a new zeal, offering at once a romanticization of an unalienated and 'authentic' construction of the past, as well as a potentially lucrative career as a modern musician in Dakar and Europe.

deriving from membership of a caste.[21] This idiom of 'whitening' gains a significance if it is placed in the context of the opposition between white and black bodies of lore and knowledge that is used to distinguish Islamic from craft expertise respectively. The former was primarily in the hands of the freeborn Islamic cleric social category, and the latter in those of the men-of-skill social categories. From this perspective of the relationship between Islam and caste, the black (as in the 'black lore' of men-of-skill) is not accommodated within nor encompassed by Muslim lore and knowledge but is in fact stripped of colour and transformed by it. Diop (1981) concluded pessimistically about the outcome of this proposed transformation:

> It is to be admitted that Islam has not brought about in a society of castes the revolution that might have been expected of it. Marabouts have shown themselves to be conservative in the face of the force of traditions that they have not dared or wanted to dismantle, being themselves the offspring, in the majority of cases, of the superior caste. (author's own translation of Diop's original French text)[22]

He went on to argue that Islam had adapted itself more to the caste system than the latter had adapted itself to the religion, above all in the area of the equality and fraternity of believers. If certain marabouts made pronouncements condemning the institution of caste difference as contrary to the fraternal spirit of Islam, and if some attempted to abolish it, then even fewer succeeded in making many gains in rolling it back.

Ambiguity and ambivalence surround the issue of caste at various levels of debate: it is in turn denied and subsequently claimed by those inhabitants of the country who live within it; different voices within Islam contest it; and the Senegalese state has contributed in no small way to the contradictory tensions surrounding it. As Morice (1982:99) states: 'the attitude of public powers with regard to castes is marked with a large measure of ambiguity' (author's own translation). Since independence, it has been against the law to make reference to an individual's caste origins or to discriminate against a person in

[21] Diouf (1983: 233), for example, states: 'De nombreux marabouts aujourd'hui encore ont été "blanchis" par l'Islam'.

[22] The original paragraph in French by Diop (1981: 98) is as follows: 'Il est permis d'affirmer donc que l'Islam n'a pas realisé dans la société de castes la révolution qu'on était en droit d'attendre de lui. Les marabouts se sont montrés conservateurs, devant la force des traditions qu'ils n'ont pas osé ou voulu bousculer, étant issus eux-mêmes, dans leur grande majorité, de la caste supérieur. Ils ont justifié leur attitude en affirmant que 'la religion ignore les castes mais ne s'oppose pas à elles'. Ainsi, l'Islam s'est beaucoup plus adapté au système des castes que ce dernier ne s'est conformé à ses principes, surtout en ce qui concerne l'égalité et la fraternité des croyants.'

employment on these grounds. It is also illegal to organize an official political party around the issue of caste or on the basis of religion. A complex and ambiguous situation has arisen which has its roots in colonial times, when a system of European-based law ran in parallel with customary tribunals (*tribunaux indigènes*). In the latter context it was possible to claim divorce on the grounds of one partner withholding or hiding his or her true caste origins. Changes brought about in the legal system, shifting the emphasis away from customary law and towards European-based law, involved the introduction of new codes, especially the Family Code (*Code de la Famille*) of 1972, revised in 1990 (Callaway & Creevy 1994). These codes attempted to establish changes to procedures in marriage, divorce, inheritance and the economic independence of women but were opposed on many fronts by marabouts and Islamists as an attack on the principles of Islamic law. While part of customary practice had been to allow a recognition of caste, changes brought in to modernize and simplify the plurality of legal codes were condemned. Moreover, the implementation of the Family Code was much more effective in urban areas than in rural towns and villages, where issues of caste are more deeply rooted.[23] The issue of the Family Code illustrates a case in which Islamists and Sufi marabouts have buried their theological differences and have worked towards a common cause to protect an Islamic domain.

Under the Family Code, caste was no longer an issue in a legalistic sense, and Islamists opposed the changes to customary law not on the grounds of the advantages they might appear to give caste members in terms of marriage, but as an aspect of law that was previously much more under the control of local Muslims. It is difficult to say, however, whether the adoption of the Family Code has made it any easier for cross-caste marriages to take place, although it might now be less onerous if one were to lie about one's caste origins prior to marriage. Changes that may be detectable in marriage patterns could well be attributable to the conditions of modern urban living rather than to amendments to legal statutes.[24]

---

[23] One of the problems of land development schemes, particularly irrigation systems introduced in Fuuta Toro over the last 20 years or so, has been the challenge they posed to the customary distribution of land among different caste groups in any village. Many schemes have insisted upon private ownership and equal access to land by all members of a community irrespective of caste status, whereas those that have attempted to be more sensitive to local conditions run the risk of maintaining the differential distribution of cultivable land. See Knight (1994) and Adams (1996).

[24] See Panzacchi (1994) on the changing roles of traditional praise-singers, one of whose tasks today in modern urban settings is to investigate the status of potential marriage partners for the sons and daughters of the patron's family.

The Islamic reformist groups that developed between the two World Wars and then after independence have frequently sought to abolish caste distinctions that were a feature of many Sufi brotherhoods. The educational reformer Al Hajj Mahmud Ba, who set up *medersa* schools in Fuuta Toro, called for the abandonment of 'tribal and professional considerations' (a coded reference to caste) in the provision of schooling (Ba 1985-86: 250 *et passim*). Many reformist groups appealed to nouveau-riche traders, to craftsmen, artisans and praise-singers (Schmitz 2000b), for they found in them the opportunity of social elevation and religious advancement previously denied to them. Similarly, Islamist movements attracted individuals of low caste origin. But there were contradictory forces of inclusion and exclusion working within them upon different marginal groups. Generally within Sufi brotherhoods, women were placed in a subordinate position: it was harder for them to receive the same level of Qur'anic education as boys; there were barriers to them becoming disciples to a male marabout, and women seldom held formal religious office or positions of responsibility within Sufi orders. There were, however, instances of women creating 'shadow' or parallel organizations that ran alongside those of the men, but they rarely attained the same public profile as their male counterparts.[25] Despite slight differences among the Sufi brotherhoods regarding this issue, the marginalized position of women was nonetheless never as extreme as that advocated by certain Islamist groups. Members of these radical reform groups called for the seclusion of women, the wearing of the veil and their withdrawal from public life.[26] These demands placed on women by Islamists mark a significant disjuncture with the older Sufi orders, and their exclusionary force suggests an intriguing paradoxical movement within radical reformist groups. While they advocate the differential treatment of followers on the basis of gender, they have attracted followers previously marked out as different on the basis of caste. The position of women within Sufi Islam and the position of craftsmen and musician groups were in some ways comparable: both were marginalized, muted and treated with mistrust regarding the full and proper functioning of the Muslim community. There appears, then, to be evidence to suggest that the educational opportunities, as well as the possibilities for social advancement offered by reformist Muslim organizations have led to a

[25] See Callaway & Creevy (1994) for further discussion of the variations in the position of women in relation to different Sufi brotherhoods.

[26] Callaway & Creevy (1994: 174) suggest that paternalistic, maraboutic Sufism provides a check on the extremes of fundamentalism that is spreading through a young and educated urban elite: 'So far, the continuing political power of the marabouts has acted as a buffer protecting Senegalese women against the extremes of seclusion, veiling, and withdrawal from many facets of public life, all of which the fundamentalists demand'.

significant up-take by those of artisan, craftsman and caste status in their participation within those organizations.

In relation to reformist and especially Islamist groups, the integration or 'whitening' of one category of persons is accompanied by the extreme differential marking or exclusion of the other. Moreover, while a European-educated urban elite militates for Western-style equality of opportunity between genders and among castes, an Arab-educated sector of the urban population seems to militate for one but not the other.

The changing nature of caste and Islam: The Islamic Brotherhood of the Nyasiyya

I now turn to an example of the renegotiation of the connection between caste and Islam to illustrate something of the dynamism of their relationship. It illustrates the way in which exceptional individuals, who became powerful Muslim reformers, have emerged from time to time in West African history. They combine the mystery of Sufism with the potency of traditional artisan status and have harnessed the institutional division of power and knowledge among castes to the driving force of individual charismatic power.

It is necessary first to describe something of the background to this Senegalese Muslim brotherhood and the significance that is read into its development by members of different social categories. This is an example not so much of how Islam might be considered to 'whiten' low status castes but how, from the perspective of some followers of the Nyasiyya, caste status has as it were 'blackened' Islam. In this example an echo will be heard of the earlier Sufi reform movement started in the mid 19th century by El-Hajj Umar Taal, whose exceptional spiritual powers were interpreted by some as evincing a connection to blacksmith stock through his mother's line.

Members of the Nyas family, now based in the town of Kaolack, are part of a relatively new offshoot of the Tijaniyya Sufi Order.[27] The establishment of the order goes back to a late-19th-century forefather of the Nyas line, one Abdoulaye Nyas who died in 1922. The main contemporary branches of the family stem from two of Abdoulaye's sons, the elder son Khalifa who was supposed to succeed his father and his younger brother Ibrahima 'Baye' who developed the

[27] This account is based on a number of sources on the Nyas movement (sometimes spelt Niasse or Niass in the literature). See for example: Abun-Nasr (1965), Brenner (1983a), Clarke (1982), Diouf (1983), Gray (1988), Kane (1997), Klein (1968: 223-24), Marty (1915-16), Monteil (1980: 155-56), Morice (1982), Schmitz (2000b) and Villalón (1995: 140-42).

Nyasiyya Order into the important movement it is today. Two of Khalifa's sons, Ahmed Khalifa and Sidi Lamine, disseminated Islamist ideas, the latter especially through the newspaper *Wal Fadjri*, established in 1983, of which he was the editor. Various calls were made by them for the creation of an Islamic state in Senegal, and Ahmed Khalifa gained the reputation as the 'Ayatollah of Kaolack' following pronouncements that drew on ideas used during the Iranian revolution (Gomez-Perez 1991). It is, however, the Nyas line from Abdoulaye through to Ibrahima 'Baye' that represents the focus of interest here.

Abdoulaye Nyas, a Wolof speaker born in the country's northern region around the town of Louga in 1844 or 1845,[28] was descended from a line of blacksmiths.[29] His father, Mamadou, was nonetheless a marabout and had migrated to the central regions of Senegal around 1865 where he founded the village of Niassene, and later his son Abdoulaye established the settlement of Taiba Niassene. Abdoulaye too became a marabout, having studied in Mauritania under Matar Fal Ndiaye among others, and is said to have received the Tijani *wird* from a companion of Shaykh Umar Taal, the mid-19th-century militant and mystic.[30] In the Tijani tradition, tracing a chain of transmission of knowledge (*silsila*) back to Umar Taal is an important ingredient in establishing authority as a religious leader. Abdoulaye had also fought alongside the Islamic leader Ma Ba in the jihads conducted in Senegal's central regions in the 1860s. The Nyas family thus gained a reputation for leadership in religious affairs: they possessed an erudition in Islamic sciences, advanced expertise in Qur'anic study and Muslim theology, and they were also renowned for their mastery of Arabic.

On Abdoulaye's death in 1922, his eldest son Muhammad, also known as Khalifa, succeeded his father and took over as religious leader within the family. However, it would be Ibrahima, his younger brother (born in 1902), who was to become the more influential of the two sons. Ibrahima, who died in 1975, was a charismatic religious leader who developed a massive international following among Muslims in West Africa,[31] and set up his headquarters (*zawiya*)[32] on the outskirts of the town of Kaolack, the centre of groundnut production in the country's middle belt. Here in Medina he built a mosque and a school, and it is

---

[28] Dates vary concerning his birth: for example, Gray (1988) gives 1840, Marty (1915-1916) 1845, others 1844.

[29] See Seesemann (n.d.) on this claim about his ancestry, first made he argues by French colonialists in the 1950s; but it is one that is held by many Senegalese today.

[30] See Seesemann (n.d.) on the connections between Mauritanian Tijanis and the Nyas family.

[31] Kane (1997) estimates the number of disciples of the movement in West Africa to be in the order of millions, most notably in Mauritania, Niger, Nigeria, Togo, Guinée, Ghana, Burkina Faso and Chad.

[32] It is known as *Zawiya al-Madinat al-Jadi* or 'Retreat of the New City'.

to this religious centre that up to 30,000 pilgrims reportedly flock each year for the annual *ziyara* ceremony in celebration of the Prophet's birthday (*mawlud*).[33] Some Islamist groups are especially critical of the Nyas Order for what they see as excessive veneration of the Prophet's birthday and naming-day.

Ibrahima was hailed by some members of the Muslim Sufi community as the 'Saviour of the Age' (*ghawth al-zaman*) and as the 'pole' or 'axis' (*qutb*) of the saints, one who has reached the summit of spiritual discipline. Both of these titles are time-honoured epithets bestowed throughout the Muslim world, and they are applied exclusively to great Sufi saints. He was also made Khalifa of the Tijaniyya Order by a *shaykh* in Fez in 1937 at the age of about 35. He created important religious alliances with the Emir of Kano in Nigeria, where there is a huge following, and he emerged as a man of remarkable stature in West Africa, being consulted by political leaders such as Nkrumah and Egypt's Nasser. On his death in the mid 1970s, Ibrahima was succeeded by his son Abdoulaye, although the position of Khalifa of the Order was left to Ibrahima's son-in-law, a disciple and imam of the Kaolack Medina mosque, a man named El Hajj Alioune Cissé.[34] This has created tension in the movement between blood relatives and their direct descendents and a line of 'spiritual kinship' and the inheritance of *baraka* established through ties of 'breath or saliva' (Schmitz 2000a). The religious following that has developed around Ibrahima Nyas is drawn from virtually all the countries within West Africa, and has extended most notably into Nigeria and the United States too. Indeed the movement is perhaps better recognized outside of Senegal than within its borders.[35] There are reasons for this large disparity in the number of followers at home and abroad. Schmitz (2000b: 128) sees part of the success of the Nyas religious movement

[33] Schmitz (2000b: 129) reports that each year in the 1980s some 4,000-5,000 Nigerians, many of whom were rich Hausa traders, made their way to Kaolack. The town was connected to Kano by two flights per day, especially during the period of the annual celebrations.

[34] See Villalón (1995: 141) who suggests that this form of succession and the inheritance of charisma by a son-in-law are unusual. Schmitz (2000a) has illustrated, however, that the favouring of a bright and gifted pupil, who is often given the hand of a daughter of a marabout, is one means by which religious authority and charisma in Sufi orders are passed on.

[35] It is difficult to gain an accurate picture of the number of followers of the Nyasiyya in Senegal. The figures that are available regarding religious affiliation usually embrace under the rubric of 'Tijani' an array of such offshoots. Villalón (1995) reports that in the town of Fatick, just 50 miles or so north-west of Kaolack, the centre of the Nyas Order, only one of the 17 *dahiras* or urban cells of a Sufi order belongs to the Nyasiyya. This perhaps gives an indication of its minority status in the country. Kane (1997) notes that one family with the patronym Sakho is especially associated with the order in Fuuta Toro, where it is particularly attractive to the young. Sakho is a patronym associated with the Fishermen social category.

as resulting from the ability of its leaders to slide into the space vacated in the course of rivalry and competition between the Tijaniyya and the Qadiriyya. There are, I suggest, other reasons for this skewed popularity.

The Nyas family background is intriguing given the strength of the claims that the 19th-century marabout Mamadou Nyas and his son Abdoulaye Nyas were of blacksmith stock. It is taken as evidence of the social mobility made possible by the Tijaniyya, in particular, that someone of caste origins could have been elevated to the position of religious leader (Gray 1988). This openness among the Tijaniyya was noted during the mid 19th century under the leadership of Umar Taal. The elevation in status of Nyas, if indeed it was such, must have occurred in the late 18th or at least the early 19th century, and he would probably have been very old, if not dead, by the time Umar Taal's militant Tijani movement got underway. Nyas may have been caught up in a reorganization of members of various social categories that mirrored what was happening in Fuuta Toro in the mid to late 18th century under Abdul Qadir Kan, a member of the Qadiri Order. The period just prior to the Almaamate uprising in Fuuta Toro (the 1790s) was characterized by the possibility of social promotion for those of caste origin who affiliated themselves to the cause of radical reformist cleric Islam. Perhaps a similar situation prevailed around Louga, in the area just south of Fuuta Toro from where the Nyas family hailed prior to their migration south towards Kaolack. Like the Caams (Tyams or Thiams) of Fuuta Toro who are reputed to have blacksmith origins but yet became important in Umar Taal's movement maybe Nyas achieved the same degree of elevation under a liberating and open form of Sufi Islam that was later to close ranks after its initial impetus was lost.

Morice (1982) reports that the evocation of this artisan past is altogether prohibited by the Nyas family. It is likewise the case that it would be seen as a huge insult to accuse the descendents of Taal or Caam lines of having a similar ancestry. The Nyas family today observes a strict form of endogamy among only those of freeborn descent (Morice 1982: 99). Again, there are parallels here with the situation in Fuuta Toro of the newly elevated families, which, having assimilated themselves among the ranks of the *toorobe* clerics, began progressively to marry within that social category to the exclusion of their own cognate kinsmen. The Nyas family have married many times into the old nobility of the Siin and Saloum (Diouf 1983: 229), although these unions were not uncontested by members of those high-ranking families. Silla (1966) reported the following anecdote (also related in Diouf 1983) that tells of how a proposed marriage between Nyas and a woman of freeborn stock stirred up discontentment in the region. Those opposed to the marriage decided to boycott the ceremonies and even planned to abscond with the bride, so preventing the union. However, they were not able to carry out their plan as a serious car accident involving a number of the conspirators put an end to the proposed abduction. The accident was seen by many of those sympathetic to the Nyas cause as a punishment from God and his Prophet on those who wanted to obstruct the desire of one of His representatives on earth.

The hugely successful Muslim proselytiser Ibrahima Nyas, who presided over the enormous expansion of the order into territories beyond the boundaries of Senegal, is an ambiguous and ambivalent figure in the eyes of many Senegalese. There are echoes again of the popular image of the 19th-century figure, Umar Taal, who was likewise seen as charismatic, divinely gifted and spiritually powerful. A similarly charismatic figure, Ibrahima, was reported to have possessed marvellous esoteric abilities and controlled an array of supernatural powers. He is attributed by some educated Senegalese with the power of magically crippling one of the country's politicians who opposed him. Furthermore, he was said to able to talk to trees and summon the spirits who lived there in order to attack his enemies (Gray 1988). These are the powers associated with craftsmen, and woodcutters (*lawbe*) in particular, and bring an image to mind of Umar Taal, who was likewise attributed with such powers that stemmed, as some would have it, from a line of common ancestry with both blacksmiths and tree-fellers. Ibrahima Nyas was also the target of pejorative remarks, defamatory characterizations and attacks upon his moral integrity, not only in official reports but also more generally in popular circulation (Kane 1997). He was described as being a 'dubious' or 'unwholesome Sufi', a person of 'questionable morality' and a person of 'detestable filiation' or ancestry. These reports again echo the kinds of moral evaluation attached to members of craftsman and praise-singer castes.

The 'taint of caste' on the Nyas family history seems to have been an important factor in restricting the spread of the movement within Senegal among freeborn sectors of the population.[36] The fact that these matters of social origin carry very little significance beyond the geographical boundaries of Senegambia might contribute to our understanding of Ibrahima's success in places such as northern Nigeria. There, it is Nyas's high reputation for Islamic erudition, his abilities in esoteric sciences and the Arabic language, and his depth of Qur'anic exegesis that are indexes of his popularity and authority among his following. Kane attributes the attraction of the movement in large measure to the fact that it advocated a much greater 'democratization of the sacred' than other Sufi

[36] Villalón (1995: 68) makes a similar observation: '...Abdoulaye Niasse [Nyas] was a blacksmith, and despite several generations of clerical careers the taint of caste seems to continue to play a role in limiting the family's capacity to draw followers from non-casted people. Perhaps partly as a result, the Niasse have been especially successful in developing a following outside Senegal, most notably in northern Nigeria.'

orders;[37] but with this democratization of the sacred comes the possibility of involvement of members of lower castes in positions of authority within the brotherhood. Those Senegalese who have become attached to the Nyasiyya are attracted by its openness and its lack of restriction on religious promotion to those of low caste origin. Not only have craftsmen and musicians been attracted to and prospered within the order, but women too have been drawn by its spirit of openness. Women have been encouraged to pursue Qur'anic study and Islamic learning, and some have even become *muqaddams* or religious leaders appointed to transmit the *wird* or litany of the brotherhood. A number of Ibrahima's sisters and daughters have achieved renowned scholarly and spiritual reputations (see Callaway & Creevy 1994, Schmitz 2000b). This reformed Sufi order — in many ways no different from other Tijani movements, but in contrast to Sunna militants and Islamists — has embraced and promoted the interests of persons of low caste origin and of women, both of whom were previously marginalized by cleric-dominated brotherhoods.

The last issue to be developed in this discussion is the idea of legitimacy of the Nyas movement in the eyes of those who have joined, especially from the point of view of previously marginalized craftsmen and musicians. While a sense of the conventional cleric freemen perception of the low caste status of Nyas's Islamic brotherhood has already been suggested — namely, it is morally repugnant 'unwholesome Sufisim' led by an individual of 'destestable' ancestry — those who are persuaded of the Nyas family's spiritual mission evaluate it differently.

A *dahira* linked to the Nyas Order operated in a location on the outskirts of Dakar where I conducted fieldwork during the early 1980s and mid 1990s among resettled Haalpulaaren from Fuuta Toro. A *dahira* (or *daaira*) is a cell or 'circle' (from the Arabic) or local unit of a Senegalese Sufi order based in urban areas. Located near Tiaroye a few miles from the capital city, a Haalpulaar community established itself in a *quartier* centred around the household of a *toorodo* cleric, El Hajj Demba Ngaydo. He had been the patron (*njartigi*) to a number of men-of-skill or low caste families, one of whom was the weaver family Gisse that I had worked closely with. In the mid 1960s, during the early stages of settlement of the *quartier*, nineteen families had formed a mutual aid and support group called the *Fedde Sahabaabe*, or the 'Age-set of the Companions of the Prophet'. It organized savings for members, each of whom paid a weekly subscription, and was the focus of rituals and celebrations on the occasion of the births, marriages or deaths of its families' members. It also met each Thursday for entertainment and a meal, and these weekly soirées were held

[37] Kane's words in the original are: 'L'attrait de ce mouvement s'explique en grande partie par le fait qu'il prônait une plus grande démocratisation du sacré' (1997: 316).

Evening prayers at the Nyas *dahira* in Tiaroye
Photo: Roy Dilley

in turn in members' houses. In this context, the specialized roles of each of the social categories represented by its members were played out, such that, for instance, the *maabu* weaver sang songs accompanied by the young *bambaado hoddu* player, or those of servile origin made the preparations and served food during the collective festive or ceremonial gatherings (see Dilley 1984).

By the mid 1990s, the patron cleric Ngaydo was dead, and although the mutual aid group (*Fedde*) continued, a new organization had established itself. This was a Nyas *dahira* or cell of the brotherhood linked to Ceerno Alhusseni Nyas. The local cell was led by an imam who was of Haalpulaar Fisherman origin, a caste that, like craftsmen and musicians, was previously excluded from holding religious office within Islam. For those of men-of-skill origin, the Nyas *dahira* represented a synthesis of the white lore and knowledge of Islam (*gandal danewal*) and the black lore and knowledge (*gandal balewal*) of the caste specialist that is derived from the bush or the wild. This union was evinced, various members pointed out, by the nature of the origins of the Nyas family — namely it was of blacksmithing stock — and by the fact that the imam was a Fisherman (*cubbalo*), a social category associated with the powerful black lore of the river. Moreover, my weaver friend had become the *imam as-salat*, the leader of the group prayers, who chanted the litany and performed the *rakas* that the congregation would follow. This role contrasted with the one he occupied in the *Fedde*, which would also conduct communal prayers for the last two scheduled daily prayer times at dusk and at dark on a Thursday evening. In this context, he would defer to the religious authority of a group member of *jawaando* or Courtier origin. Since joining the Nyas prayer group, the weaver had felt it necessary to give up *cowrie* divination, for on the advice of his new imam his prayers would not be heard for forty days after each divinatory consultation. The weaver had much earlier been persuaded to cease practising *nyengi* magic, since he had been told that it led to eternal damnation. He continued, however, with the practice of herbal medicine and curing with incantations and protective verses. It would seem that what informants meant by the idea that this Muslim order represented a synthesis of white and black lore was not that it entertained a series of ritual practices that might be condemned by other branches of Islam. It did not amalgamate in a novel combination Islamic with non- or pre-Islamic beliefs and practices. Instead, what appears to have been meant by this claim was that the close association between men-of-skill and spiritual powers that derived from the wild did not deflect from the possibility of divine blessing offered by the Muslim religion. It is as though the spiritual expertise that men-of-skill possessed by virtue of their ancestry could be an important ingredient in building a foundation of legitimacy for religious authority in this branch of Islam. The legitimacy of Umar Taal and of Ibrahima

Nyas had been built around precisely this combination in the eyes of certain sectors of their followings.

Discussion

This brief ethnographic example illustrates how, at the grass-roots level of the Nyas brotherhood, the issue of caste, forbidden as a topic of discussion by the family, is a key element in the construction of a religious following amongst members of particular social categories. Whilst this feature works to attract a following from the ranks of lower caste or marginalized sections of the population, it also acts as an obstacle to the members of those social categories previously associated with religious leadership in longer established Sufi brotherhoods. The pattern in these conventional cleric-dominated brotherhoods has been to assimilate the faithful from low caste ancestry, albeit in an inferior position of dependence and not of spiritual leadership. This is a pattern of accommodation and not of integration. The Nyasiyya at grass-roots level has integrated and embraced the powers of caste groups such that it has become in the eyes of some an essential element in its ideological scheme and in the process of legitimising authority. The grass-roots organization of the Nyas Order seems to have succeeded where others have failed, although the extent of that success is tempered by the *toorodo* resistance to non-cleric Islam.

This discussion has led to an appreciation of the sources of power and potency that form part of the contested field of culturally defined realms of mystical force that constitute one of the key dynamics in the social relations of Haalpulaaren and other neighbouring language groups. As Villalón (1995:122) points out, we must recognize the 'very real centrality of the metaphysical' that is 'all too often ignored in secular discussions of Senegalese Islamic organizations'. While the critiques of West African Sufism stemming from Western-educated elites versed in secular rationalism and from *arabisants* and Islamists versed in ideas of Middle Eastern origin have attacked this metaphysical core of brotherhoods, the popular view of legitimate religious authority holds fast to such spiritual considerations. A bifurcation of the Muslim community has occurred around opposition to Sufi mysticism. Western-educated Senegalese intellectuals and Arabic-educated Islamists make odd bedfellows in their stance against mystic Sufi brotherhoods. These attacks on Sufi mysticism and its particular esoteric construction of knowledge and power are also by implication an attack upon the similar construction of knowledge and power among men-of-skill groups. However, these two parties are joined in a common voice of criticism by the conventional freeborn Muslim clerics. The latter denounce reformed brotherhoods such as the Nyasiyya for proposing a form of integration of cultural knowledge and power that should normally, from their point of view, be kept apart. Freeborn clerics, while recognizing the legitimacy of Sufi constructions of knowledge and power, are critical of its assimilation with those forms associated with men-of-skill. The Islamists hold that Sufi mysticism represents a retrograde step in the standing of the Muslim religion. They reject outright the esoteric paradigm of conventional forms of knowledge and power. The cultural dialogue instigated by the cleric-inspired Islamic revolution in the mid 18th century has broadened to become today a conversation involving numerous parties, each with its own view of the composition of the Muslim community.

The Islamic community is perhaps more fractured than at any time in recent history. Islamists are blind to caste but eagle-eyed with regard to gender. Clerics and the followers of the Nyas brotherhood both recognize caste, although with very different consequences. The Nyas Order has also extended religious privileges to women in a way few other orders have done. Moreover, the example of the Nyasiyya is suggestive of a range of sometimes-contradictory forces that operate within the field of globalization. When considered from a pan-West-African perspective, the Nyas Order might be seen as a globalizing force that has transcended ethnic and national boundaries. It has a broad appeal to Muslims right across the region from Côte d'Ivoire to Nigeria and into Chad. Yet, at the same time, the local understanding of what the order embraces within Senegal has given it an appearance that is less appealing to many Muslims, whether these be cleric-led Sufis from one of the older-established brotherhoods or radicals from one of the reformist and Islamist groups that look instead to sources of inspiration of a modernist or internationalist persuasion.

The processes of globalization constitute part of a two-way movement: connections that are made between one place and another across the globe are at the same time shaped by specific local networks of social relations and frameworks of meaning. The numerous conceptions of Islam variously established within Senegal are thus the product of an exchange of ideas and practices between West Africa and elsewhere, and are simultaneously the product of localizing factors. The local ruptures caused by the institution of caste have long composed an element in a dialogue about the religion of Islam in Senegal. The examples of reformist Muslims, Islamist groups and the Nyasiyya presented here suggest that within this matrix of relations between caste and Islam, new senses of identity and belonging are being generated such that being a member of a low caste social category can be integrated in a variety of fashions within the compass of a long-established world religion.

References

Abun-Nasr, J.M. 1965, *The Tijaniyya: A Sufi Order in the Modern World*, London: Oxford University Press.

Adams, A. & J. So 1996, *A Claim to Land by the River: A Household in Senegal 1720-1994*, Oxford: Oxford University Press.

Africa South of the Sahara 1999, London: Europa Publication, (28th ed.).

Ba, O. 1985-1986, 'Le Rôle des Ecoles Islamiques dans le Développement de la Culture Arabo-islamique dans le Bassin du Fleuve Sénégal', Thèse de doctorat de 3ième cycle, Université de Paris IV-Sorbonne.

Bouche, D. 1974, 'L'Ecole Française et les Musulmans au Sénégal de 1850 à 1900', *Revue Française d'Histoire d'Outre-Mer* 61 (223): 218-35.

Brenner, L. 1983a, *West African Sufi: The Religious Heritage and Spiritual Search of Cerno Bokar Salif Taal*, London: Hurst & Co.

Brenner, L. (ed.) 1983b, *Muslim Identity and Social Change in Sub-Saharan Africa*, London: Hurst & Co.

Brenner, L. 2000, *Controlling Knowledge: Religion, Power and Schooling in a West African Muslim Society*, London & Bloomington: C. Hurst & Co./Indiana University Press.

Brenner, L. & M. Last 1985, 'The Role of Language in West African Islam', *Africa* (special issue on 'Popular Islam' South of the Sahara) 55 (4): 432-46.

Callaway, B. & L. Creevy 1994, *The Heritage of Islam: Women, Religion and Politics in West Africa*, Boulder & London: Lynne Rienner Publishers.

Clark, A.F. & L. Colvin Phillips 1994, *Historical Dictionary of Senegal*, Metuchen, NJ & London: The Scarecrow Press, (2nd ed.).

Clarke, P.B. 1982, *West Africa and Islam: A Study of Religious Development from the 8th to the 20th Century*, London: Edward Arnold Ltd.

Colin, R. 1980, *Systèmes d'Education et Mutations Sociales: Continuité et Discontinuité dans les Dynamiques Socio-educatives. Le Cas de Sénégal*, Paris: Librairie Honoré Champion.

Conrad, C. & B.E. Frank (eds) 1995, *Status and Identity in West Africa: Nyamakalaw of Mande*, Bloomington: Indiana University Press.

Cruise O'Brien, D. 1971, *The Mourides of Senegal: The Political and Economic Organisation of an Islamic Brotherhood*, Oxford: Clarendon Press.

Dilley, R.M. 1984, 'Weavers among the Tukolor of the Senegal River Basin: A Study of their Social Position and Economic Organisation', Unpublished D.Phil. thesis, University of Oxford.

Dilley, R.M. 2000, 'The Question of Caste in West Africa, with Special Reference to Tukulor Craftsmen', *Anthropos* 95: 149-65.

Diop, A.B. 1965, 'Société Toucouleur et Migration. Enquête sur l'Immigration Toucouleur à Dakar', *Initiations Africaines* XVIII, Dakar: IFAN.

Diop, A.B. 1981, *La Société Wolof: Tradition et Changement: Les Systèmes d'Inégalité et de Domination*, Paris: Karthala.

Diouf, M.B. 1983, 'Forgerons Wolof du Kajoor; Forgerons Sereer du Siin et du Jegem: De l'Epoque Précoloniale à Nos Jours', Thèse de doctorat de 3ième cycle, EHESS Paris.

Evers Rosander, E. 1997, 'Introduction: The Islamization of "Tradition" and "Modernity"', in: E. Evers Rosander & D. Westerlund (eds), *African Islam and Islam in Africa: Encounters between Sufis and Islamists*, London: Hurst & Co., pp. 1-27.

Evers Rosander, E. & D. Westerlund (eds) 1997, *African Islam and Islam in Africa: Encounters between Sufis and Islamists*, London: Hurst & Co.

Gomez-Perez, M. 1991, 'Associations Islamiques à Dakar', *Islam et Sociétiés au Sud du Sahara* 5: 5-20.

Goody, J. (ed.) 1968, *Literacy in Traditional Societies*, Cambridge: Cambridge University Press.

Gray, C. 1988, 'The Rise of the Niassene Tijanniyya, 1875 to the Present', *Islam et Sociétés au Sud du Sahara* 2: 34-60.

Kane, O. 1997, 'Shaikh al-Islam Al-Hajj Ibrahim Niasse', in: D. Robinson & J.L. Triaud (eds), *Le Temps des Marabouts Itinéraires et Stratégies Islamiques en Afrique Occidentale Française, v. 1880-1960*, Paris: Karthala.

Klein, M.A. 1968, *Islam and Imperialism in Senegal: Sine-Saloum 1847-1914*, Edinburgh: Edinburgh University Press.

Knight, D. 1994, *A Burning Hunger*, London: Panos.

Loimeier, R. 1994. 'Cheikh Toure: Du Reformise à l'Islamisme, Un Musulman Sénégalais dans le Siècle', *Islam et Sociétiés au Sud du Sahara* 8: 55-66.

Loimeier, R. 2000, 'L'Islam Ne Se Vend Plus: The Islamic Reform Movement and the State in Senegal', *Journal of Religion in Africa* XXX (2): 168-90.

Marty, P. 1915-1916, *L'Islam en Mauritanie at au Sénégal*, (Revue du Monde Musulman, t. 31), Paris: E. Leroux.

McNaughton, P.R. 1988, *The Mande Blacksmiths : Knowledge, Power, and Art in West Africa*, Bloomington: Indiana University Press.

Monteil, V. 1980, *L'Islam Noir: Une Religion à la Conquête de l'Afrique*, Paris: Editions du Seuil.

Morice, A. 1982, 'Les Forgerons de Kaolack: Travail Non Salarié et Déploiement d'une Caste au Sénégal', Thèse de doctorat de 3ième cycle, Paris.

Panzacchi, C. 1994, 'The Livelihoods of Traditional Griots in Modern Senegal', *Africa* 64 (2): 190-210.

Recensement Général de la Population 1976 [1982] & 1988 [c. 1992], Dakar: Bureau National du Recensement.

Richter, D. 1980, 'Further Considerations of Caste in West Africa: The Senufo', *Africa* 50 (1): 37-54.

Robin, J. 1947, 'L'Evolution du Mariage Coutumier Chez les Musulmans du Sénégal', *Africa* XVIII: 192-201.

Schmitz, J. 2000a, 'Le Souffle de la Parenté: Mariage et Transmission de la Baraka Chez des Clercs Musulmans de la Vallée du Sénégal', *L'Homme* 154: 241-78.

Schmitz, J. 2000b. 'L'Islam en Afrique de l'Ouest: Les Méridiens et les Parallèles, *Autrepart* (16) (special issue, E. Grégoire & J. Schmitz (ed.), *Afrique Noire et Monde Arabe: Continuités et Ruptures*) pp. 117-37.

Seesemann, R. n.d., 'The *Shurafâ*' and the Blacksmith: The Role of the Idaw 'Alî of Mauritania in the Career of the Senegalese Tijânî Shaykh Ibrâhîm Niasse (1900-75)', Unpublished paper.

Silla, O. 1966, 'Persistence des Castes dans la Société Wolof Contemporaine', *Bulletin de l'IFAN* (série B) XXVIII (3-4): 731-70.

Soares, B.F. 1999, 'Muslim Proseltization as Purification: Religious Pluralism and Conflict in Contemporary Mali', in: Abdullahi Ahmed An-Na'im (ed.), *Proselytization and Communal Self-Determination in Africa*, New York: Orbis Books, pp. 228-45.

Tamari, T. 1997, *Les Castes de l'Afrique Occidentale*, Paris: Société d'Ethnologie.

Todd, D.M. 1977, 'Caste in Africa?', *Africa* 47 (4): 398-412.

Vaughan, J.H. Jr. 1970, 'Caste Systems in the Western Sudan', in A. Tuden & L. Plotincov (eds), *Social Stratification in Africa*, New York: The Free Press, pp. 52-92.

Villalón, L.A. 1994, 'Sufi Rituals as Rallies: Religious Ceremonies in the Politics of Senegalese State-Society Relations', *Comparative Politics* 26 (4): 415-38.

Villalón, L.A. 1995, *Islamic Society and State Power in Senegal: Disciples and Citizens in Fatick*, Cambridge: Cambridge University Press.

Willis, J.R. 1967, '*Jihad fi sabîl Allâh*: Its Doctrinal Basis in Islam and Some Aspects of its Evolution in 19th Century West Africa', *Journal of African History* 3: 395-415.

Willis, J.R. 1970, 'Al-Hâjj 'Umar b. Sa'îd al-Fûtî al-Tûri (c. 1794-1864) and the Doctrinal Basis of his Islamic Reformist Movement in the Western Sudan', PhD thesis, SOAS, University of London.

8

How is a girl to marry without a bed? Weddings, wealth and women's value in an Islamic town of Niger

Adeline Masquelier[1]

In Niger, bridewealth has become the target of Izala, a reformist Muslim organization that condemns ostentatious expenditure and promotes frugality. In the Muslim town of Dogondoutchi, where Mawri residents are increasingly exposed to Western bourgeois values, the Izala ban on excessive bridewealth and conspicuous weddings has angered many for whom gift exchange is inseparable from social worth. Thus, mothers struggling to equip their daughters with the latest trappings of modern domesticity reject Izala expressions of Islamic frugality. For them, prosperity is not antithetical to Islamic piety. This chapter looks at a young woman's insistence on receiving a Formica bed from her impoverished mother and shows how the acquisition of such beds is implicated in the reconfiguration of a domestic lifestyle that owes as much to

[1] Research for this chapter has been carried out since 1988, supported by awards from the National Science Foundation, the Wenner-Gren Foundation for Anthropological Research, the National Institute of Mental Health, and fellowships and grants from Tulane University. I would like to thank everyone who has been generous with their comments and critiques, including Dorothy Hodgson, Sue O'Brien, Steven Pierce, Rosalind Shaw and Pnina Werbner. Special thanks go to Misty Bastian and Brad Weiss for their invaluable comments on a preliminary draft of this chapter. I am indebted to Barbara Cooper whose engaging and imaginative work on Hausa women and marriage has paved the way for my own musings on the subject. As always, the women of Dogondoutchi deserve thanks for their valiant efforts to share with me their concerns, their aspirations, their world. Finally, I am grateful to Wim van Binsbergen and Rijk van Dijk, first, for inviting me to the conference on Globalization and Questions of Ownership and, second, for pointing out key issues in this chapter that needed to be clarified. I alone am responsible for any flaws that remain.

local understandings of matrimony and morality as to Western bourgeois domesticity.

> If her family can afford it, [a Hausa woman] will have a four-poster bed piled high with mattresses, covered with a satin spread adorned with many pillows. This bed is the central decorative piece in the room and she neither sleeps nor sits on it. (Callaway 1987)

> A [Mawri] mother must [...] contribute to the dowry of the young bride who should arrive at her husband's with her calabashes, ladles, basins, mats, water pots, furniture, etc, which will be exhibited for all to see. Fashions change. Today, a mother will burst with pride if, on her wedding day, her daughter can display a metal bed with a mattress in addition to all the conventional utensils. (De Latour 1992)

'Fathers, they have nothing to say about marriage. It is our business,' one Mawri[2] woman interjected as I was discussing matters of bridewealth *(sadaki)* with my neighbour in the rural town of Dogondoutchi, Niger in March 2000. 'If the daughter wants a man for a husband and her mother agrees, *shi ke nan* (that's it)! They "tie" the marriage,' she concluded. By insisting that marriage was women's business, this senior resident was resolutely challenging patriarchal authority and defining wedding prestations as a female arena of power from which men were — or at least, should be — theoretically excluded. She further implied that women should systematically resist Islamic ideologies that had in the last decade or so started to undermine forms of accumulation through which women traditionally created value and generated status for themselves. Her testimony echoed the words of numerous Mawri women similarly anxious to secure some measure of autonomy and preserve their power base at a time when economic forces and religious reforms increasingly appear to be working against women's interests and agendas.

In this chapter, I describe some strategies female Dogondoutchi residents have been employing to challenge patriarchal notions of social order that have emerged through the forum of new Islamic 'traditions'. With a discussion of Mawri women's creative efforts to redefine their roles and responsibilities in the matrimonial economy, I hope to contribute my two cents to an already extensive and growing anthropological debate on globalization. By focusing on the

[2] Traditionally recognizable by their 'ethnic' marks, a double scar that cuts the cheek from the corner of the mouth to the ear on both sides, Hausaphone Mawri are a largely heterogeneous population of 250,000 people. They tend to identify with the more inclusive Hausa ethnic group that mainly occupies southeastern Niger and northern Nigeria. For a detailed political, economic and religious history of Dogondoutchi and the surrounding region (known as Arewa), see Piault (1970).

cultural dynamics of global processes, such debate has made it increasingly clear that globalization can no longer be equated with cultural imperialism and described as a process of homogenization promoting the convergence of cultural style and resulting in a world of sameness (Friedman 1994, Inda & Rosaldo 2002, Meyer & Geschiere 1999). Far from gradually making the world over in the image of the West — a scenario based on the problematic assumption that globalization is synonymous with Westernization — global flows have turned out to presuppose and even promote local fixity. Rather than eroding boundaries, the seeming intensification of flux appears to reaffirm borders and redefine categories. Put another way, globalization is about uprooting as much as it is about belonging. Making sense of this 'paradoxical articulation of flow and closure' (Meyer & Geschiere 1999: 3) means attending to the sometimes highly variable and subtle ways in which people everywhere utilize global capital (consumer goods, foreign symbols, information technology) to reassert local values and re-inscribe cultural identities. For our purposes here, the recognition that global consumption and local transformation are two sides of the same coin translates into an appreciation of the creative strategies through which Mawri women customize imported goods to redefine themselves in resolutely local terms. By embracing emblems of the foreign to reaffirm cultural difference, women in Dogondoutchi are actively resisting the tide of Islamization while at the same time they are participating in local redefinitions of Islamic identity. If they are neither the passive recipients of global cultural imports nor the silent victims of male-centred hegemonic designs, they are nonetheless struggling to respond to the challenges and limitations imposed by the social transformations currently affecting their world. Out of this struggle emerge new forms and spaces of reflexivity. Following Butler (1997) and through a focus on women's preoccupation with bridewealth and wedding gifts, I show how the processes and means that have secured Mawri women's subordination are also the conditions through which these women have become aware of their marginalization and I discuss the growing salience of marriage transactions in their strategic redefinitions of their social worth.

Whenever people discussed bridewealth and marriage in Dogondoutchi in 1994 and 2000, I heard women grumbling about the ridiculously limited quantity of household items they could buy with the small *sadaki* payments many families received now that both the government and Muslim reformists had put a cap on bridewealth transfers. Men, by contrast, often complained bitterly that bridewealth had become such an extravagant expense that no one could afford to marry anymore. In the last decade, weddings and the gift transactions they entail have become a frequent source of controversy among Dogondoutchi residents who are struggling to meet their social obligations in an

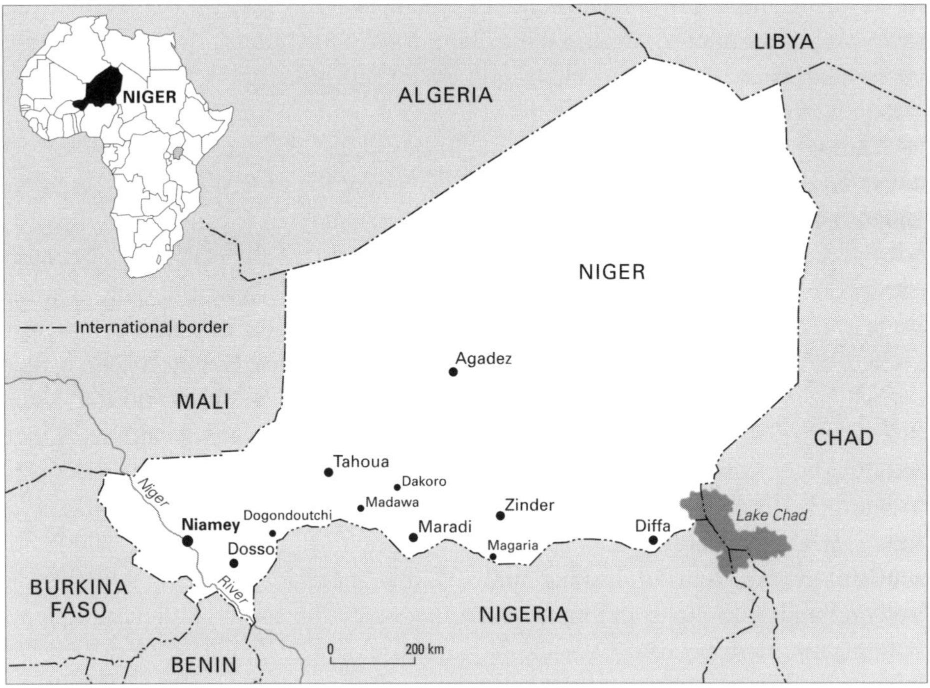
LIBYA
ALGERIA
NIGER
NIGER
International border
Agadez
MALI
CHAD
Tahoua
Dakoro
Madawa
Zinder
Niger
Niamey
Dogondoutchi
Maradi
Diffa
Lake Chad
Dosso
Magaria
River
BURKINA FASO
NIGERIA
0
200 km
BENIN

Map 8.1: Niger

era of dwindling resources and opportunities. Amidst competing visions of how to solve the 'problem' of marriage in contemporary Niger, Mawri women feel increasingly compelled to articulate their own perceptions of what weddings entail and what their own rights and responsibilities are when it comes to arranging the marriage of a daughter.

Throughout the African continent, bridewealth practices are the focus of considerable debate and dispute as the collapse of national or regional economies and the emergence of new markets and new forms of production have forced many to reconsider the nature and content of these often complex transactions. In defiance of Uganda's tradition of bridewealth paid by the bridegroom to the bride's family, a 25-year-old scooter taxi driver recently invited older women to vie for his hand in marriage and to present what they thought would be an acceptable 'dowry' (Fisher 2000). In KwaZulu Natal Province in South Africa where the centrality of cattle in bridewealth exchange has long been eclipsed by the money earned by migrant workers, a man decided to adorn his only daughter with cash and clothes to concretise her value as a future wife and mother (Stengs, White, Lynch & Zimmermann 2000). In southern Sudan, a Nuer brother and his full sister began living together as husband and wife under the assumption that since they were cattleless orphans with no marriage prospects — she having no extended family upon which her in-laws could call in times of need and he having no cattle — they had nothing to lose if they were later killed for having committed incest (Hutchinson 1996). While these three incidents constitute each in their own way fairly unique modes of creatively circumventing what have increasingly become contentious practices, they must nonetheless be seen as part of a larger debate through which ideologies of gender, power and family are brought under heightened scrutiny at a time when the sources and perceptions of prosperity shift easily with the flow of money and markets.

In Niger, women's grievances about low bridewealth and their creative efforts to defy the limitations imposed by a collapsing economy similarly underscore wider concerns about changing definitions of gendered roles and realities. In this chapter, I describe how women are shaping the confines and contours of the debate on bridewealth in a rural town in Niger, where the recent emergence of anti-Sufism has sparked intense questioning about the management of wealth, the status of women and more generally, the relevance of Islam in the lives of ordinary Muslims. By defending what they consider to be their daughters' interests and expectations, senior women often end up contesting local standards of Muslim piety, virtue and civility. While they do not necessarily agree that fathers 'have nothing to say about marriage' and sometimes even challenge each other as they confront husbands, Muslim elites and the Nigerien authorities, most mothers in Dogondoutchi entertain definite ideas about the meaning and purpose of bridewealth exchange and they make their voices heard whenever they can. At the same time, and while they feel pressured to indulge their daughters' dreams of bourgeois domesticity, they are also mindful that respectability has increasingly become indexed through the language of Islam. For an increasing number of conservative Muslims eager to demonstrate their piety and commitment to the faith, the flaunting of wealth during wedding celebrations is now contrary to the maintenance of an Islamic moral order. For the women who devote their resources and energies to filling their daughters' marital homes with furniture, mats and bowls, however, such conservative Islamic values make little sense. Far from being inimical to local concepts of morality, piety and containment upon which marriage and domesticity are ideally based, mass consumption, I argue here, paradoxically becomes for Mawri mothers the instrument through which these values are objectified at a time when the very fabric of society — the integrity of families — and the moral essence of identity have come under increasing scrutiny. How women chose to navigate the shifting terrain of moral identities while retaining access to the sources of wealth in the context of marriage transactions is the focus of this chapter. Amidst the controversies generated by Muslim reformists' denunciation of conspicuous consumption, women's discourses on bridewealth and wedding gift exchange provide a useful commentary on gender relations and the manifold anxieties of consumer culture. They also highlight how contested Islamic visions of gender, power and domesticity have given rise to, as Bernal (1997: 148) puts it in the case of Sudan, 'both new mechanisms for controlling women and new opportunities for women to renegotiate their positions in gender relations'.

Aside and apart from their impact on local religious debates, Dogondoutchi women's resistance to the appeal of conservative Islam and their dynamic engagement in an ever-widening global consumer market underscores the difficulty of trying to predict first, how commodities — be they beds, beads or bicycles — will be put to use by local actors, and second, what understandings of modernity will emerge out of these experiences (Graeber 1996, Hunt 1999, Renne 1999, Weiss 1996). The assumptions of theorists of modernity and globalization notwithstanding, the interface of global and local processes has produced multiple and different ways of 'being modern' and different ways of understanding not only the material but also the moral impact of modernization.[3]

[3] Modernity everywhere is perceived as simultaneously seductive and threatening, yet that hardly means that at the local level people weigh the costs and benefits of modernity in similar, predictable ways. Thus, while Congolese *sapeurs* who spend all their earnings on designer clothes from France and Italy appear to 'consume modernity to strengthen themselves' (Friedman 2002: 242), Ghanaian Pentecostalists, who see the

And while there is widespread agreement that globalization 'is itself a deeply historical, uneven and even *localizing* process' (Appadurai 1996: 17), we cannot ignore the centrality of people's agency in creatively engaging this process. In contexts when people increasingly consume resources that were neither produced in their own societies nor produced for the uses they are now being put to, it becomes crucial to trace the complex ways in which the appropriation of foreignness becomes not simply a strategy of self-production but occasionally also a means of empowerment and self-defence against the perceived hegemonic forces of change. For Dogondoutchi women who are struggling to reinvent themselves in light of both the temptations of the consumer market and newly emerging discourses on marriage and morality, the creative appropriation of globally circulating emblems of domesticity highlights the resiliency of time-honoured local forms of productivity and sociality. It also reminds us that in Niger, as elsewhere in the Islamic world, modernity does not solely or necessarily come from the West.[4] Abu-Lughod (1998), Bernal (1997) and Cooper (2001) have already shown that for urban Egypt, northern Sudan and Hausaphone Niger respectively, Islam has become a crucial source of modernity for members of the Muslim diaspora.[5] By proudly and loudly re-asserting their rootedness in a resilient economy of female-centred practices, Mawri mothers and daughters thus learn to juggle selectively with two competing paradigms of modernity — one Western and one Islamic — and to profit from, rather than fall prey to, their powers.

The contest over *Sadaki* in Islamic discourses

If debates about rising bridewealth and wedding expenses appear to have acquired of late an unprecedented prominence, the concerns they betray are far from new. In fact, the high cost of weddings was already a matter of intense interest in the colonial period. Later, the first post-colonial regime attempted to

---

global market as an abode of invisible satanic forces from which they must protect themselves with the power of religion, occasionally throw away commodities – such as underpants – that are allegedly filled with dangerous diabolic spirits (Meyer 1998).

[4] My intent, here, is not to equate globalization with modernity. Rather, I wish to briefly note that globally circulating goods – be they Formica beds or prayer beads, Tupperware bowls or televisions – become locally identified as modern things precisely because they come from afar, even if elsewhere they might be considered old or out-of-date. To be modern in such a context means being connected to global consumer networks.

[5] I have also written on Mawri perceptions of Islam as a form of modernity and as a means of gaining access to modernity (Masquelier 2001b).

regulate the matrimonial economy, but with little success. In 1975, the Nigerien president Seyni Kountché, troubled by the moral climate resulting from the spiralling inflation of bridewealth in the country, made the following remarks to the women of Niamey:

> Faced with this social and moral chaos, the CMS (*Conseil Militaire de Sécurité*) has decided — I am confirming it — that from now on, we will not tolerate any wedding celebrated with ostentation and extravagance. Wedding expenses cannot exceed 50,000 CFA francs; noisy bridal processions spilling out of the town hall with fake veils and a nouveau-riche look are strictly forbidden. Equally forbidden — I am declaring today — are the one hundred roasts that have surfaced out of who knows which gluttonous tradition. [Forbidden] as well are the collections of outfits for the bride conspicuously exhibited throughout the city's streets and the loud and pretentious baptisms.

In an attempt to curb the moral and material excesses of the first government of independent Niger, Colonel Kountché — who had seized the reins of power in 1974 and instituted military rule following the disastrous famine of the early 1970s — actively promoted discipline, restraint and frugality at work and at home. Though Kountché made no mention of religion in his speech to Nigerien women, Islam — systematically used by the military regime to forge a nationalistic consciousness among disparate ethnic elements — became a building block of this new moral order where ostentatious displays and consumption of wealth had no place. What is remarkable about the formal presidential announcement is that it was addressed exclusively to women. Women, Niger's head of state implied, controlled the means and modes of wealth expenditure associated with wedding celebrations and were responsible for their excesses. They — and apparently no one else — must therefore be the targets of campaigns aimed at ridding Nigerien society of 'gluttonous traditions' and 'moral chaos'. As has been convincingly demonstrated in a growing body of literature on gender in Africa (Allman 2001, Hodgson & McCurdy 2001, Hunt 1991, Vaughan 1991), women often end up being identified as the 'problem' when far-reaching changes in economic relations are translated as moral 'crises' and described in terms of chaos, degeneration and disease. Nigerien society appears to be no exception in this respect.

Some twenty years after Kountché's denunciatory speech — and in a strikingly similar fashion — the followers of Izala, an anti-Sufi movement of Nigerian origin aimed at purifying Islam from a host of sinful accretions, generated considerable interest as well as resentment among Nigeriens for loudly condemning the ostentatious re-distributive practices that had long integrated local communities through complex and enduring socio-economic networks.[6] Among other things, Izala reformists insisted that bridewealth payments should be limited to a token sum that most men would be able to put together fairly rapidly. They also encouraged women to spend wisely and conservatively when it came to acquiring the *kayan 'daki* (things for the room) that mothers traditionally invested in to ensure their daughters' prestige and well-being (see Cooper 1997, Nicolas 1986, Pittin 1979). As I have noted elsewhere (Masquelier 1999), their condemnation of excessive materialism and their pleas for frugality were perceived by many Dogondoutchi residents as intrusive attacks on legitimate and long-standing local traditions through which individuals continually affirmed their social worth. While the assertive individualism of Izala angered those who saw it as a threat to society and family, it nevertheless provided many youths with a publicly sanctioned means of avoiding the costly social obligations (bridewealth, gifts to patrons or clerics, birth celebration expenses) that generally exceeded the average farmer's meagre income in this predominantly agricultural region.

Taking advantage of the moral panic sparked by Westernization, the development of public education, the flood of commodities onto local markets and the dispersal of family and community through migrancy, Izala preachers boldly challenged the authority of the state and of Muslims elites, thereby attracting a number of people frustrated by the government's and the local authorities' failure to deal with their problems. At a time of intense parental preoccupation with the alleged slackening of social control, the disintegration of family ties and the concomitant spread of 'immorality' amongst unmarried youths, the Izala message about bridewealth payment reduction resonated with earlier visions of a pristine moral order unsoiled by modernity and secularization. By insisting that bridewealth could be paid with 10,000 CFA francs (1,000 CFA francs equals €1.5) rather than the customary 200,000 CFA francs, Izala leaders technically enabled young men to marry quickly. More importantly, perhaps, low bridewealth enhanced the marriageability of *budurwoyi* (virgin girls), thereby preventing the dreaded possibility that they could 'spoil' before acquiring a husband.[7] Some mothers complied with the

---

[6] The Izala movement, more properly known as *Jama'atu Izalat al-Bid'a wa Iqamat al-Sunna* (Movement for Suppressing Innovations and Restoring the Sunna), was founded in Jos, Nigeria in 1978 by Malam Ismaila Idris, with the support of Sheikh Abubaakar Gumi, who had close ties with Saudi Arabia and the Muslim Student Society. For a more detailed history of Izala, see Kane (1994), Loimeier (1997), Masquelier (1999) and Umar (1993).

[7] In a society where virtually no young women remain single for any length of time, Callaway (1987: 40) notes of Kano, Nigeria: 'the social advantage of an early marriage outweigh the possibilities of anything else imaginable a daughter might do'. Although more women are now pursuing secondary studies and contemplating careers, they do

reformists' recommendation and gave up their rights to a 'full' *sadaki*. The large majority, however, responded to the Izala campaign for a more frugal and moral society by ever more openly flaunting their daughters' wealth at wedding ceremonies. While senior women's preoccupations with young girls' unbridled sexuality betrays a growing concern with the loose moral standards so aggressively criticized by Izala reformers, few mothers are prepared to readily give up the *sadaki* for the alleged sake of their daughters' virtue. Respectability, in the end, means different things to different women. Mothers' divergent attitudes toward the *sadaki* controversy thus reveals substantial divisions within the female community at a time when religious identity has become ever more central to the ways in which Mawri women constitute themselves as 'respectable' persons.[8]

The changing content and value of bridewealth

C. Piault (1963), M. Piault (1978) and more recently Cooper (1997) have noted how the terms and content of marriage prestations in Hausa-speaking communities have changed dramatically in the last century and, with it, the meaning of marriage as new kinds of material goods and new modes of producing wealth emerged in tandem with the commoditization of services, land and labour. In pre-colonial times, bridewealth payments amounted to over 1500 cowries (Piault 1978: 422). The *kyauta*, which initiated the period of betrothal and enabled the 'wait until the harvest' (*sai hita wuri*) — when beans would be sold to pay the *sadaki* — was a negligible sum. By the 1930s in Dogondoutchi, the *sadaki* varied according to the wealth and status of the groom's family but it generally consisted of two heifers, an ox and the sum of 115 francs[9] (Archives

not see employment as an alternative to marriage and motherhood. Elite young women may postpone the age of marriage to complete their studies but the fact remains that for them as well as for every other woman – and man – marriage remains a social obligation rather than an option.

[8] Despite the rapid spread of Islam since independence in 1960, the indigenous form of spirit worship known as *bori* has remained an integral and influential dimension of Mawri experience even as it appears to be being swept away by a growing Muslim influence (see Masquelier n.d., 2001b, 1996). A large majority of the *bori* membership is comprised of women who can, in theory at least, derive power and prestige from their association with spirits and their status as mediums. Young women increasingly shun *bori*, however. Mindful that most prospective husbands associate *bori* identity with backwardness and rusticity, they prefer to present themselves as 'pious' Muslims – or for a tiny minority, as dedicated Christians.

[9] Piault (1978: 422) notes that around 1935 bridewealth payments could be as low as 20 francs.

Nationales du Niger 1936). In the mid 1970s, the *kyauta arme* (wedding gift) had risen to 2,500 CFA francs in Dogondoutchi and despite the cap of 20,000 CFA francs instituted by the government, bridewealth usually amounted to a considerable sum (Piault 1978: 422). Piault recalls that a young office clerk who could not count on his kin — all distantly located — for support was asked to pay 75,000 CFA francs as *sadaki* — an extravagant sum in those days, all the more so given that neither he nor his future in-laws could boast wealth or claim membership of a chiefly lineage (ibid). In the early 1980s, it was not unusual for families to pay a bridewealth of 60,000 or 70,000 CFA francs while the *kyauta* itself could reach 45,000 CFA francs. Today, the *sadaki* is officially set at 120,000 CFA francs if the bride has never married and is technically a virgin (*burdurwa*). Childless women who have married once before command a *sadaki* of 50,000 CFA francs, while those who marry for the second time and have given birth should expect their future husbands to pay 30,000 CFA francs. At a time when unskilled labourers can rarely hope to make more than 30,000 CFA francs a month, earning the cash necessary to pay bridewealth for a *budurwa* can be quite challenging especially when Dogondoutchi mothers, mindless of the Islamist message, decide the marriage will not be 'tied' unless their financial expectations are met.

In addition to paying *sadaki,* the groom must provide a whole array of gifts for the bride's family. In the past, these gifts were part of an elaborate and complex circuit of exchange which played a crucial role in solidifying the couple's marriage – defined not so much in terms of husband-wife relations but in terms of the cross family linkages that emerged out of the wedding ceremony. Successful marriage transactions today still hinge primarily on the groom's ability to secure the support and patronage of numerous kin and friends who through their *gudummawa* (assistance in the form of gifts) help meet the demands of the bride's family, but the mobilization of these social networks has become harder to achieve. Junior men can no longer systematically call upon the assistance of their families to meet the multiple demands of their future in-laws. They are generally expected to leave their fathers' compounds and to set up their own households when they marry. Thanks to generational divisions, increasing individuation and economic privatization, Mawri men are now free to choose their own brides but they are less able to depend on shared family resources for procuring the cash and goods they need to fulfil their numerous and onerous obligations (De Latour Dejean 1980). The 'problem' with marriage, as junior men see it, is therefore not simply that financial obligations have multiplied and grown more burdensome thereby slowing down the processes culminating in the 'tying' ceremony. It also hinges on the erosion of the complex web of relationships — traditionally forged or strengthened through wedding gift contributions and counter-gifts — that enabled a marriage to occur in the first place. Amid dwindling economic opportunities, increasing land shortages and the loosening of social ties, Islamic campaigns against immorality and profligacy have found eager support amongst a minority of residents for whom the drastic reforms in the management of wealth provide a welcome solution to the exigencies of both modern life and membership in the Islamic community.

Kayan aiki: Female images of industriousness and fertility

While men are struggling to meet their financial obligations at marriage, women scramble to assemble the *kayan 'daki* (things for the room) with which their daughters will carefully decorate their new homes. They invest considerable time, labour and resources to acquire impressive arrays of household goods that will ensure the stable beginnings for a young couples marriage.[10] In the not so distant past, a mother's steady labour — spinning cotton or growing groundnuts — allowed her to acquire some of the gifts her daughter would one day proudly exhibit in her home. A significant portion of the goods was further obtained through the social networks she carefully nurtured by attending and contributing to other wedding and birth celebrations. Old women I interviewed recalled that once the marriage had been 'tied' and the wedding celebration was over, the bride would then leave her parent's compound with her 'things'. Piault (1986: 427), in his account of marriage in Mawri society, similarly notes that when the young woman departed for the marital compound, she would take with her 'all the necessary cooking utensils' given to her by her mother. This is how Malka, a widow of about sixty, described to me the wedding gifts she received:

> When I married, 2,000 francs were paid for *ku'din arme* [bridewealth] and 1,500 francs were paid for *kyauta* [gift]. Cloth was brought, there can't there be a wedding without cloth, you see. Calabashes and cooking pots were brought as well as a *talla* [leather bags to draw water from the well]. How can you bring a bride to her husband without her *kayan aiki* [work things]? It is the mother of the bride who buys everything she [her daughter] needs. I did not get a bed but I brought a *kujera*

[10] In her wonderfully rich and insightful analysis of wedding gifts in the neighbouring Hausa town of Maradi, Niger, Cooper (1997) points out that earlier accounts of marriage in Hausa society have generally described women's investments in *kayan 'daki* as labour-intensive activities from which wives and mothers reap no appreciable benefits because they simply serve the very social system that constrains female opportunities in the first place. What both the Maradi and the Dogondoutchi cases demonstrate, however, is that women generate more than simply material value when they invest in, and display, material goods for the benefit of their newly married daughters.

> *mata* [women's low wooden stool]. I also brought a pestle and my husband brought the mortar.

What is striking in Malka's description of the gifts she received in the early 1950s is the emphasis on 'work things'. In contrast to the *kayan 'daki* (things for the room) which brides receive today primarily to adorn their rooms, Malka stressed that a bride entered her marital home with not so much decorative but practical things, utensils she would use daily to perform the requisite household chores: pounding the grain, cooking millet flour, preparing sauces, drawing water at the well, etc. From this perspective, the little stool she mentions was not a piece of furniture designed 'to look good'. Rather, it was a functional item, something women but never men sat on when they cooked or braided another woman's hair — in short, not a decorative object visitors admired.

'Work things' evoked images of industrious domesticity but, like the ubiquitous pestle and mortar, some of them had further symbolic resonances. Together they represented the fruitful unity of and complementarity between male and female principles, principles which provided the basis for local conceptions of the universe and its reproduction (Last 1979, Nicolas 1975). In Malka's youth, Mawri brides brought the pestle while their new spouses provided the mortar (see also Piault 1963). While the vision of the pestle next to the mortar had potent sexual implications during the wedding, in the daily act of pounding, the woman thereafter symbolically re-enacted the fecund union of complementary elements (mortar=womb/pestle=penis) so crucial to the viability of marriages and the vitality of society because of what it produced (food=child). Nowadays, the mortar and the pestle are purchased together at the market, something which has only faintly weakened their association with sex and reproduction.[11] Calabashes, too, evoke fertility and the life cycle. Grown, collected and carved by the women themselves, they were treated not only as utensils but also as objects of decoration which housewives proudly exhibited in carefully assembled rows. Because they visually resembled the ridges on a farm and the multiple rows of harvested grains — both images of agricultural

[11] One need only hear the self-conscious laughter that erupts among women at the mere mention of 'pestle and mortar' to verify the sexual connotations that are still attached to these objects despite the changing protocol in the acquisition of wedding gifts. Before my very eyes, a young woman once threatened to hit her husband with her pestle in a moment of anger. Appalled by the boldness of her gesture, the husband retaliated by threatening to divorce her. The story of their altercation quickly spread via the grapevine causing shock and outrage. Yet, I believe that these intense reactions – including the husband's – were caused as much by the violence of the young woman's act as by the symbolic message it conveyed – inverting sexual roles as it were and turning her husband into the mortar in which she was planning to thrust her 'phallic' implement.

fecundity — the high columns of stacked calabashes 'bespoke of future fertility and wealth earned through the work of creating and nurturing social ties' (Cooper 1997: 95). At another level, calabashes summon up images of fecundity and reproduction through their common association with the womb. Unadorned calabashes often feature in ceremonies held to promote the fertility of afflicted individuals. Before twin sisters can marry, for instance, they must break a calabash in two to liberate the fertile potential that was locked in their problematic 'oneness'. Only by thus breaking the womb of twinship can they be reborn as single and separate beings, each with her own womb (Masquelier 2001a). As womb-like products of the land and through their various stages of growth and decay, they graphically reproduce critical stages of the human life cycle — in the present context, processes of production and reproduction.

The colourful hand-woven cotton blankets women received during their weddings also evoked fertility and reproduction. Aside from the fact that they were — and still are — only displayed prominently on the walls of their rooms on the birth of a new child to celebrate a mother's fertility, the very manufacture of these multicoloured *sakala* (blankets) metaphorically re-enacted the process through which the social fabric is woven. The basket and the spindle used in spinning cotton respectively symbolized the male and female genitals in their productive coupling (Darrah 1980: 125). In Mawri society, women used to spin while men wove — and dyed cotton threads (Masquelier 1996). Husbands provided women with the raw material for cotton spinning after which the thread would be sold or brought to a weaver and then a dyer before being worn. The cloth she wore thus concretely 'tied' a wife to her husband The rise of the market economy, which made imported cloth readily available during the colonial period, progressively led to the demise of local cotton production (see Cooper 1997) but the act of tying clothing still bears conjugal associations. The verb *darme* (to tie), which describes the action of putting one's clothes on, is also used to refer to the process of contracting a marriage (*darmen arme*: to tie a marriage). This is why, as Malka put it, 'there can't be a wedding without cloth'. When the bride was sent to her new husband's home with her *kayan aiki*, the display of these images of fertility and reproduction in the streets of Dogondoutchi further underscored the sexual symbolism of the wedding ceremony.

Mothers' work: Reconfiguring wealth and worth

In their respective descriptions of the marriage ceremony in Mawri society, neither C. Piault not M. Piault mention the festive and colourful parades through which brides publicly display their *kayan 'daki* as they are themselves ushered to their new homes. This silence over what I found in the late 1980s to be such a conspicuous part of the wedding celebration suggests that prior to the late 1960s or 1970s, bringing the *kayan 'daki* to the bride's marital compound was not as elaborate a process as it has now become. While brides obviously derived a significant amount of prestige from the pots, bowls and calabashes, which promoted their productive and reproductive capacities and effectively launched them in the world of marriage and motherhood, the public act of bearing *kaya* (things) was unremarkable enough to escape the scrutiny of two anthropologists in the early 1960s. In contrast, contemporary public displays of *kayan 'daki* are one of the most visually stunning dimensions of the marriage process and one through which women actively contribute to their self-actualization, as we shall see. Once the 'tying' ceremony and the *semaine* (three-day wedding celebrations sponsored by the groom's friends) are over, the bride's mother assembles in her compound all the *kayan 'daki* she has acquired including the bed, mattress and other furnishings. After a close and drawn-out inspection process that allows everyone in the neighbourhood to admire and comment on the quality and quantity of the goods, female kin or friends each hoist a bundle of gifts on their heads and proceed in a loud and boisterous column towards the bride's marital compound. Known as *kan kaya* (bearing or carrying the things), the joyful procession of ululating women bearing calabashes, cloth and cooking implements convey an image of 'head-borne wealth' that is essential to the prestige women earn as brides, as Cooper (1997: 94) has pointed out. Meanwhile, the bride hides under a heavy woven blanket and, together with a similarly veiled friend, reaches her husband's house inconspicuously and away from the potentially deadly glare of jealous onlookers. Her own invisibility during the *kan kaya* paradoxically enhances the salience of her 'things' while these, in turn, promote her and her mother's worth by providing a concrete measure of their productive abilities and their social network — a vast array of gifts implies both material wealth and a dense web of contributors even if women are increasingly unable to maintain the social ties that once secured access to wedding gift contributions. Once paraded along the streets all the way to their final destination, the goods belong to the bride and, as movable property, they are hers to keep should the union end in divorce.[12]

---

[12] Women similarly pointed out to me that the goats and sheep tethered in their compounds were their exclusive property, and not that of their husbands. Husbands are not simply morally but also legally obliged to support their wives (and children). Because a man has such obligations, the income his wife may derive from her cash-generating activities is considered hers. She can dispose of it in any way she wants (and buy goats, for instance), even if it means, in some cases, lending money to her own husband so that he may support her.

One of the reasons for the increasing prominence of the *kan kaya* is that the content and value of the gifts themselves have shifted in the last fifty years with the changing economic context, the weakening of social ties and the impact of mobility, migration and consumer goods. As imported goods flooded local markets and wealth became increasingly derived from access to cash rather than land, the calabashes women decorated were partially — but not entirely — replaced by enamelled metal pots of varying sizes and shapes, mass-produced carpets of Mecca or of kittens playing with their mothers outnumbered the multicoloured locally woven *sakala* (blankets), and wooden utensils gave way to metal spoons, porcelain teapots and Pyrex cups made in China. Brides are still sent to their new homes with peanut oil, grain, onions and salt — a reminder, perhaps, of the organic basis of traditional forms of wealth in a region still dominated by farming — but the prominent gifts a young woman receives today are neither handmade nor produced locally. Wealth and prestige are increasingly articulated in the language of money, modernity and cosmopolitanism. The fashionable outfits that migrant labourers bring back from Abidjan or Cotonou, the video cassette recorders with which pilgrims return from Mecca, and the shoes or watches which traders smuggle from Nigeria have firmly inserted rural Mawri in the global economy. The best and priciest wax cloth is referred to as 'Java', a term that enhances the appeal of the fabric by designating it as 'foreign'. Similarly, the fact that the elaborate metal beds so prized by housewives in the 1980s and 1990s were known as *gadon Kano* (bed from Kano) is no coincidence, I suggest. Rather than evoking fertility, actualizing ties to the land or reflecting the skills of their makers as they once did, wedding gifts now display a different kind of value, one tied to the complex translocal circuits of migrancy, marketing and smuggling through which Mawri people acquire, exchange and consume mass-produced goods of all sorts.

Because they can no longer count on the support of extensive social networks, farm groundnuts or spin cotton to generate the resources needed for their daughters' *kayan 'daki*, women have responded to this economic challenge by actively reforming the use to which the *sadaki* and other marriage payments are put. In the past, a large part of the money was re-distributed among the bride's kin — in compensation for their contribution to the collection of *kayan 'daki* — and the various individuals who assisted the two families through the various stages of the marriage transactions. Nowadays, the *uban arme*, the two women who wash the bride with henna and the siblings of the bride's parents receive a small gift of money from the groom, but the bulk of the marriage payment automatically becomes the property of the bride's mother who is in turn solely responsible for equipping her daughter with the latest indispensable commodity,

Calabashes filled with millet and covered with hand-woven blankets soon to be transported during the *kan kaya*, while the men haul the furniture and mattress. In the late 1980s, a metal bed was a new bride's most prized possession.
Photo: Adeline Masquelier

namely, a bed — made of pressed wood covered with Formica — with adjoining shelves and drawers for displaying nick-nacks or storing clothes. Aside from the mattress, the sheets, pillows and coverlet she must also purchase to set her daughter up, the bride's mother is sometimes pressured by her daughter into buying a matching Formica armoire in which the young woman will store her ample collection of metal bowls, plastic containers and Pyrex dishes in neat vertical rows. A decade or so ago, it was the canopy metal bed 'from Kano' with its innumerable mirrors and alarm clocks that was a 'must' for any self-respecting bride. So indispensable was it to the wedding that its absence could provoke the postponement of the ceremony, Fala (1988) notes.

Like the bowls, blankets and calabashes that are conspicuously paraded through town to convey prosperity and confer value, the imposing bed acquired nowadays by the bride's mother will be carried through the streets for all to see. When beds consisted of a simple wooden structure or could be divided into separate metal pieces, a maternal cousin of the bride was traditionally assigned to haul the bulky structure — or the metal headboard — to the bride's new home. If the bed had been purchased by the father instead of the mother, a paternal cousin of the bride would carry it on his head. The sheet or hand-woven blanket he had used as buffer during the transport would be his to keep after the wedding. Today, women happily and noisily parade with head-borne calabashes overflowing with grains or bundles of enamel bowls tied in chequered cloth but the bed, due to its massive weight, arrives on a truck, and more rarely by donkey cart. Before returning home, each participants in the *kan kaya* will be rewarded by the groom with a *tukuici* (gift of appreciation to bearer of another gift) of 1,000 or 1,500 CFA francs.

Because it so visibly indexes a mother's wealth as well as her capacity to produce that wealth, the *kan kaya* must dazzle onlookers with the sheer quantity of the items displayed. The more, the better. As Cooper (1997: 95) notes, profusion and repetition, not the originality of each piece, are key because they create an image of *arziki*, or prosperity (see also Smith 1955). Failure to express satisfactorily one's (and one's daughter's) worth is worse than no *kayan 'daki* at all because it lodges itself permanently in the social memory to 'mark' a woman's reputation. It is, therefore, not uncommon for a mothers who has little or no savings and limited means of raising funds at the time of her daughter's wedding to postpone the *kan kaya* altogether for two or three years until she can adequately impress the community with a belated, but nonetheless, sufficient display of wealth, and by extension, self-worth.

So crucial is the ceremony that publicly demonstrates a mother's productivity and value that when a father negotiates a 'marriage of alms' (*armen sadaka*) for his daughter to demonstrate piety and reap divine reward, it is generally understood in Dogondoutchi that he must reimburse his own wife for the 'loss' of *sadaki*. Women, I was told, do not generally oppose their husbands' plans to give their daughters 'for nothing' provided that they receive from their husbands the 120,000 CFA francs or more they need for the bride's bed and mattress. In addition, a father should give his wife the *kyauta arme* of 40,000 or 50,000 CFA francs so that, as one woman explained, 'she can start the work of acquiring bowls for her daughter'. Piety, in a woman's view, is a good thing to have and to display because it might ensure one's entry into paradise. But even *lada* (divine reward), it appears, should not come at the expense of one's earthly honour. For the majority of local women who cannot count on a salaried kin or a profitable business to provide easy access to cash, the *sadaki* that they now receive in its quasi entirety when a daughter marries has become an inalienable right that they are unwilling to sacrifice even for the assurance of eternal salvation. For some, this inalienability further translates as a right to dispose of the money for whatever use they see fit. As a mother of eight bluntly put it: 'you know, the wife of that prophet Boubacar (sic) who returned the *sadaki* to her husband, she was a fool. Me, I would have kept the money and started a trading business.' In this mother's eyes, bridewealth, once it was paid, became a woman's property no matter what the circumstances, even in extreme cases when it did not ultimately serve to purchase things for the room.

A bed for Hadiza

I started this essay by noting that Mawri women's struggles to be valued have been played out in the controversial arena of marriage where their understanding of wealth, prestige and social capital now often clashes with more conservative ideologies of gender, family and society. I now turn to a conversation that took place between a young migrant and a senior woman to illustrate the extent to which women are provisionally carving out their own spaces for self-determination in a society that militates increasingly against them despite the recent liberalization of national politics and the concomitant proliferation of religious discourses.[13] 'So, where is the bridewealth you are going to bring so I can buy Hadiza the fine bed she wants for her wedding?' Bebe asked Boubacar in a provocative tone. Tired of finding my assistant Boubacar hanging around

[13] The *décrispation* (liberalization) promoted by former Nigerien president Ali Shaibou in the late 1980s to facilitate the country's transition to a civilian regime ushered in an era of unprecedented public debate and also fostered the emergence of new forms of social protests. Nigeriens throughout the country started organizing in specific groups to express and defend their own interests. It was during this period of democratization that the Izala association emerged in broad daylight.

her daughter, a long-time friend Bebe was demanding that he start seriously thinking about *sadaki*. It was April 2000, everyone in town was hoping that the coming rainy season would offset the catastrophic losses of the previous year and Boubacar, who had just returned to Dogondoutchi after a three-year absence, had recently learned that his wife had divorced him because he had sent her no money from abroad. He was now courting Bebe's oldest daughter Hadiza, hoping that she would consider marrying him. Hadiza had recently divorced her own husband because he could not provide for her and their young daughter.[14]

> 'Women, that's all you think about, things you can show off to your friends,' Boubacar responded warily.
>
> 'But you know Hadiza will not consider you otherwise. She already has a suitor, a rich *commerçant*, who brings her gifts every Friday [market day in Dogondoutchi],' Bebe teased.
>
> 'Even if she got a bed worth one million CFA francs, would it ensure that she is happy with her husband and that the marriage will last?' an exasperated Boubacar retorted.
>
> 'No, of course not,' Bebe said.
>
> 'Well, there,' Boubacar countered. 'So why always think about the bed? There are more important things in a marriage.'
>
> 'Yes,' Bebe responded. 'But Boubacar, listen! What is going to happen if your wife comes to your house with a *karaga* [traditional wooden bed]? Aren't all her friends going to make fun of her and you? You, yourself, will feel shame for your wife.'
>
> 'Of course,' Boubacar reluctantly agreed. 'I wouldn't let her come home with a wooden bed. But there's a difference between a *gadon kara* [bed made of millet stalk] and a 100,000 CFA franc bed! One must be reasonable and not live above one's means.'

Burdened by the need to take care of her daughter as any respectable mother would, Bebe refused to entertain Boubacar's plea for moderation on the matter of wedding expenses. Despite the serious financial difficulties she had faced ever since her husband had gone 'mad' and been unable to earn a regular income in the early 1990s, she felt that her honour and prestige were at stake if she did

---

14. In addition to providing food and shelter for his wife and children, a husband should buy them new clothes (see Masquelier 1996). Bebe angrily pointed out to me that Hadiza's husband had not bought his wife even one *complet* (a custom-made blouse, ankle-length wrapper and shawl/veil of matching fabric) during their short marriage. Even worse, Hadiza occasionally came to her mother for food because her husband's family would not feed her.

not send her daughter off with an impressive array of *kayan 'daki* if and when the young woman eventually settled on a suitor.

Bebe's attitude towards wedding gifts illustrates a widespread female concern with changing definitions of marriage, sexuality and respectability. On several occasions, my friend had confided in me her worries about her daughters' dissipated lifestyles and her frustrations at not being able to curtail their freedom. She was anxious to marry them off but she also knew that times had changed and that modern girls now freely hung out with their boyfriends before settling into married life. Yet, like other Nigerien mothers forced to acknowledge the rise of premarital sexual encounters and the concomitant proliferation of unwed mothers, Bebe lent a deaf ear to the exhortations of Izala preachers who aggressively promoted the virtues of low bridewealth, thereby hoping to increase the marriageability of young women in this era of economic uncertainty and growing public anxiety about 'wayward' youths. While she grappled with the sexuality of her unwed daughters and concurred with her peers that illegitimate pregnancies brought nothing but shame upon families, she was not ready to concede that doing away with high bridewealth and ostentatious *kan kaya* would solve the 'problem' of marriage and help young girls achieve matrimonial respectability. It was precisely the transfer of *sadaki* and the performance of *kan kaya* that created value, something that, in Bebe's view, was essential to the production of a vital kind of female respectability.

Boubacar, on the other hand, felt that Bebe was simply too interested in Hadiza's material comfort and that her obsession with beds and other pricey items blinded her to far more important issues, such as the fragility of the marital bond. Several years before, he had experienced first-hand the greed of his in-laws when, after paying the *sadaki*, sponsoring the *semaine* (three-day wedding celebrations) and giving his new wife an impressive *valise* (a supplemental gift consisting of several three-piece wrappers, pairs of shoes, soap, perfume and jewellery) to demonstrate his generous intentions, they had insisted he provide further gifts of cash to several individuals not traditionally designated as recipients of the groom's largesse. Yet despite all his efforts — at least initially — to satisfy his affines' expectations and to provide generously for his wife, he was now wifeless. Though he wanted to remarry and was attracted to Hadiza, he had no intention of handing over to his future mother-in-law the equivalent of several months' wages so that she could buy a bed too bulky to fit in what would become in all probability his new wife's quarters in the family compound. In the end, and while everyone still speculated as to whether or not she would marry the young Izala trader who brought her such extravagant gifts every week, Hadiza married a bush taxi driver. Bebe, in a letter to me, recounted a couple of months after my departure how disappointed she had been with her daughter's choice of husband. She had approved of the Izala merchant because he was kind and patient, worked hard, and had honourable intentions despite the fact that he already had a wife. He was an active member of the Izala association but displayed none of its devotees' proverbial parsimony: he regularly brought gifts to all of Bebe's children and had showered Hadiza with expensive clothes and jewellery for nine months in an effort to win her heart.

After Hadiza announced her imminent wedding, Bebe worked feverishly to earn the money she would need to purchase wedding gifts. For almost a year she had already participated in an *adashi* (a rotating credit association) to save enough cash to be able to buy a mattress for Hadiza. In addition to the money I had given her as compensation for her invaluable help during my field study, she was slowly earning money through petty trade but as a secluded wife, she relied upon her younger daughters to buy at rural markets the condiments and vegetables which would be later resold at a profit in Dogondoutchi. Despite her multiple income-generating strategies, she could not save money fast enough. With her husband out of work and the family field in the hands of unscrupulous brothers-in-law, her regular resources were already stretched to the limit. On good days, Bebe earned enough cash braiding women's hair — or having her daughters hawk food door to door — to buy a new ladle or a pair of flip-flops for one of her eight children, while on other days, she had to scrimp to feed her large family. Only weeks before, some of her hard-earned cash had gone to fix the family's crumbling thatched house, which threatened to fall apart even further with the coming rains. Despite these obstacles, Hadiza eventually left her parents' home with the assortment of bowls, the new Formica bed and the mattress her mother had managed to purchase. In her frenzied search for money (*neman ku'di*), Bebe tapped into all her cash reserves and exhausted every available resource: Hadiza even took the family's only pair of sheets, those I had given her mother as a parting gift. Bebe's honour was safe.

The bed of marriage and the mother-daughter bond

Originally, mother and daughter had disagreed as to what kind of bed would be purchased: Bebe felt that 50,000 CFA francs would buy a very nice bed but Hadiza had set her sights on a bed twice as expensive. Despite their differences, both knew long before Hadiza had chosen a husband that the young woman would eventually own a fine looking *gado* (bed) designed to elicit the admiration of her female visitors. Bebe, like many of her peers, was determined to not let her own poverty limit the reputation she was carving out for herself as mother of, and provider for, the bride. I want to ponder briefly on senior women's preoccupations with *kan kaya* for what they tell us about Mawri mothers' attempts to define themselves as creators and providers of value. Women's worth, as I have already noted, is inscribed publicly through the performance of *kan kaya* which testifies to their capacity to assemble and display wealth (see also Cooper 1997). By amassing things that their daughters will then store in their own 'room', women forge intergenerational female bonds and compensate for their transience in a society where marriage is virilocal. Moreover, the wealth a young wife stores in her room in the form of beds and bowls may one day be used to acquire the things for the room her own daughter will expect to bring to her marital home. In this respect, and despite changing tastes and fashions, *kayan 'daki* may literally and figuratively tie generations together. When members of the Izala association started forbidding high bridewealth and the ostentatious consumption and display of *kayan 'daki,* they effectively prevented women from symbolically stating the wealth of brides and the productive capacities of senior women — thereby negating the latter's social contributions and revoking their status as providers.

By regularly 'banning', or at least discouraging traditional forms of *kan kaya*, *'yan* Izala are also disrupting the mother-daughter bond that women work so assiduously to create through gift giving. The *kan kaya* loudly and colourfully concretises the lasting connection between a mother and her daughter through the physical link the long parade of head-borne *kaya* (things) creates between the two compounds. In delineating through a graphic trail of moving things both the departure of the transient daughter and her attachment to her mother, the *kan kaya* weaves together two places and two people through what De Certeau (1984: 99) calls a form of 'pedestrian enunciation'. When they complain that Izala marriage reforms are foolish and absurd, women who decry the ban on costly weddings are also indirectly lamenting the erasure of the mother-daughter connection so vividly inscribed through the 'rhetoric of walking' (ibid: 100) of the *kan kaya.*[15] *'Yan* Izala are notorious for rushing things and insisting that the bride be brought to the groom's home five days after the 'tying' ceremony. Such a short interval leaves little time for the bride's mother to acquire the *kayan 'daki* once the bridewealth has been paid. 'What kind of work can a mother do in five days?' Maimouna, a savvy trader and mother of six, once asked rhetorically to underscore the lengthy and painstaking labour of women who, I was often told, traditionally started 'working' for their daughters long before the

[15] Furthermore, Izala restrictions on *sadaki* and gift exchange have potent implications for not simply the creation but also the circulation of women's wealth if we consider how a mother's own material property may ultimately be used to finance her daughter's *kayan 'daki*. Though it is at this point too soon to tell, it may well be that women are also bemoaning changing patterns of inheritance which, under Izala influence, have become more male-centred.

latter reached the age of marriage. Aside from cheating her of the wealth and the time she requires to fulfil her responsibilities as provider properly, Izala marriage practices also render the bride's mother literally invisible: in Izala households, the *kan kaya* occurs at night so that no one can watch and assess how much the bride has received. Ostentation, here, becomes irrelevant because one's worth is expressed through frugality and piety rather than through images of *arziki*. It is precisely such invisibility that women are resisting when, in total defiance of Izala rules, they loudly parade through the streets of Dogondoutchi at midday with *kayan 'daki* on their heads.

Of beds and other modern things: Making value and marking difference

To my question about what wedding gifts a young girl had received upon marrying an Izala devotee, my neighbour Rakiya answered succinctly, 'What can you buy with 30,000 CFA francs? Not even a good mattress.' Rakiya's response, like other complaints I heard about 'unaffordable' wedding gifts, must be understood in terms of both the material and symbolic losses that senior women experience when they can no longer be publicly honoured for their wealth-producing capacities. It is as much the absence of social capital as the lack of material wealth that women decry when they criticize the stinginess of *'yan* Izala and complain about the transformations affecting marriage. While many of them agree implicitly with reformist Muslims that an early marriage is the most effective prevention against the shame of single motherhood, they nonetheless actively resist Izala's calls to facilitate weddings by doing away with needless and burdensome expenditure. Besides openly manifesting their disapproval by simply declining low bridewealth offers, women further resist their gradual exclusion from the local economy by feverishly working to equip their daughters with *kayan 'daki* whose value resides not in their practical utility or in their evocations of fertility — as they once did — so much as in their association with national and transnational circuits of wealth and information.

When wealth in things is held as the last bastion against the marginalizing impact of an increasingly male-centred economy, ensuring one's daughter's well-being now means acquiring household furnishings whose comfort and characteristics owe more to Western ideas of bourgeois lifestyle than to an Islamist vision of frugal domesticity.[16] Aside from the fact that beds and

[16] If I have drawn a sharp distinction between Western bourgeois ideology and reformist Muslim notions of restraint and asceticism, I do not want to imply that all Izala devotees live austere lives away from the temptations of consumer culture. Local members of the

armoires remain items of prestige in households where, up until a few decades ago, mats — and women's stools — provided the essential furnishings, their value further resides in their exchangeability: during hard times, a woman may opt to sell some of her furnishings to obtain the cash necessary for vital goods such as food or medicine (see Schildkrout 1982). As shameful as it might be, selling one's *kayan 'daki* is sometimes the only option for women whose access to scarce resources is becoming increasingly challenged by the worsening of the Nigerien economy and the normalization of reformist Islam. Bebe herself was forced sell her bed when her husband fell sick and lost his job at the car park. Her insistence that Hadiza be provided with a costly bed before settling into a new marriage must perhaps be seen against the backdrop of her own history of poverty and deprivation. From this perspective, Hadiza's 50,000 CFA franc bed was not simply a form of insurance against hard times but also served to actualize Bebe's personal victory against adversity: she had lost *her* bed in a desperate struggle for economic survival but she could now buy it back, so to speak, and use her daughter's *kan kaya* to ensure there would be multiple witnesses to her triumphant display of *arziki* (prosperity). Hadiza's marriage thus afforded her a unique opportunity to transcend the crippling limitations of poverty and dependency: through it, she could simultaneously recreate herself in the image of a young *wealthy* bride (her daughter) and polish her image as an industrious and resourceful mother who could afford to marry off her daughter in lavish style.

In demonstrating how Mawri women have fought Islam and the state's efforts 'to "moralize" the matrimonial economy' (De Latour 1992: 71), I have so far focused on senior women's roles, activities and preoccupations. Even if they contemplate marriage and dream of prosperous homes have their own concerns and aspirations that do not always accord with those of their elders. I want to consider briefly the frustrations and ambitions of this group of women to tease out another dimension of the complex value-making process associated with the consumption of Formica beds. During my last visit to Dogondoutchi in 2000, the perceived shortage of not-yet-married, educated civil servants was a routine subject of conversation among schoolgirls and young school leavers eager to escape the rusticity of their mother's lifestyle and embrace bourgeois values. Mindful that many of them 'offered' themselves to professional men in the hope of securing marriage,[17] Muslim preachers regularly admonished parents to keep

---

Izala association include very wealthy merchants who live in two-storey houses (the ultimate expression of wealth in Dogondoutchi), own cars and provide their wives with luxurious beds, armoires, televisions and refrigerators.

[17] A similar situation has been described for Nigerian elite women by Bastian (2002: 3), who points out that though educated young women aspire to marriage, they often 'find themselves wrestling with the multiple failures of nationalist political and Western-

their daughters 'at home', while they advised junior women to lower their matrimonial expectations and marry hardworking and honourable farmers. While very few junior women wedded educated men whose salary allowed them to fully indulge in the comforts of bourgeois domesticity, owning a modern bed covered with Formica (rather than the metal canopy bed so popular only a decade ago) was on the minds of many future brides. Aside from the fact that they come with their own display shelves, these new beds are coveted precisely because they differ so starkly from the metal beds women brought to their marital homes a generation ago. By insisting on Formica beds, junior women are demarcating themselves from their mothers and creating the generational differences that enable them to carve their own spaces for definition and agency as they settle into matrimony. In contemporary Mawri society, wedding beds are not simply emblematic of consumer culture and bourgeois values. Through their imposing presence, first, in the *kan kaya* and then, in the marital home, they become objects of female pride and central repositories of value, simultaneously enabling senior women to forge enduring bonds with their married daughters and allowing brides to create their own generational distinctions.

Aesthetics and interiority

In his work on modernity and mass consumption in Trinidad, Miller (1994) describes how the hanging out of curtains, the trimming of cakes and other decorative tasks associated with Christmas celebrations reassert the physical interiority of the home for family members in a manner which changes their relationship to it. In this festive reawakening and celebration of domesticity, he suggests that 'the physical environment is inseparable from the social values to which it is host' (ibid: 89). Whether Trinidadians decorate their windows or their cakes, what is significant to these various aesthetic tasks, Miller argues, is that they highlight the centrality of the notion of enclosure. Celebrating Christmas, in this context, becomes a means of focusing on what is 'inside' from an aesthetic and social as well as spatial perspective. Creating or reasserting interiority through a focus on physical enclosure is an equally important concern among Mawri women, I would argue, and it is precisely in the context of birth and wedding celebrations that such a concern can be appreciated. Just as the Trinidadian family 'strives towards a sense of quiet solidity' (ibid: 101) once new or newly cleaned curtains have been hung days before Christmas, so new

based economic ideologies' in a society whose marital and sexual practices remain essentially patriarchal.

Women nowadays proudly display decorative items on the shelves that come with their Formica beds.
Photo: Adeline Masquelier

naming ceremony of their newborns. By hanging hand-woven, colourful wedding blankets on each and every wall of the room in such a manner that even the doors and windows are covered, they create a warm, dark and comfortable environment in which their child can be 're-born' as a named, and therefore fully human, individual — a true person. Hospital births — whereby children do not come into the world in their mother's natal compound as was traditionally the case but in an impersonal white-walled and brightly lit 'public' space (from which they depart a few days later to return to the family compound) — have altered the significance of these aesthetic preparations. Despite such modifications in the extended 'birth' process, however, 'interiorization' (ibid: 217) remains a central concern for mothers who welcome both their new child and their kin and friends into their homes on the day of the *biki* (birth celebration). By literally re-building the boundaries of her room with heavy blankets that prevent dust, breeze and even light from entering, the new mother constructs an 'ideal of intensive sociality' (Miller 1994: 216) as well as a space of rootedness in which all — including the newborn — can 'belong'.

If naming ceremonies provide a compelling example of enclosing practice, they are hardly exceptional, I would point out. Taking my cues from Miller once again, I want to suggest that the labour-intensive and now increasingly controversial task of 'filling up' a home with beds, carpets and armoires must be similarly seen as part of the 'centripetal aesthetic' (ibid: 144) through which women in Dogondoutchi anchor their sense of family and morality. By working, at times feverishly, to equip their daughters with cumbersome pieces of furniture, some of which barely fit into the small spaces they are destined to embellish, mothers are effectively reasserting the dichotomy between 'inside' and 'outside'. Once the bride's room is furnished, it becomes a potent expression of beauty and prosperity, not simply because of the sheer quantity of *kayan daki*, but also because by literally filling up the place (until there is hardly a patch of uncovered wall or space to walk around), the conspicuous wedding gifts (and the surrounding space) reaffirm the sense of interiority that is so central to women's moral and sexual identities. Because their bodies are perceived as containers, women must strive to preserve their personal integrity and prevent external forces from contaminating them despite their inherent openness (see Masquelier 2001b). Accumulating stuff in one's marital room is thus a step in the process of progressive incorporation through which, as Miller puts it in the Trinidadian context, 'the domestic becomes not merely an enclosed space but a kind of centripetal force striving to incorporate as much of the outside world as possible into itself' (ibid: 101). Far from being antithetical to the moral values preached by conservative Islam and enforced through such practices as veiling and seclusion, *kan kaya* and the congested rooms it produces appear to reinforce the notion of enclosure so vital to female productivity and respectability, thereby becoming the very means through which such qualities are displayed and objectified aesthetically. Let me also add that while the beds that teenage girls and prospective brides yearn for may be coming from Kano or from an equally distant place, in the end, they are more than mere symbols of the modern and the foreign. Through their incorporation into the cramped rooms they adorn, they not only bring in the outside world but also become transformed by the context. By saturating the inside space with their solidity and beauty after having been prominently displayed through town, they enable the kind of enclosing and incorporative aesthetic that ultimately reaffirms local ideals of female domesticity. From this perspective, *kan kaya* is hardly a morally reprehensible practice that requires banning. On the contrary, it acts to visibly insert and root new brides into the very space from which they will derive their social place and identity as wives, mothers and mistresses of their homes.

Conclusion: Marriage, identity and agency in Dogondoutchi

Even if Islam, in its multiple and antagonistic expressions, increasingly focuses on women as the instruments of its reforms, Muslim women in Dogondoutchi are not powerless pawns in the ideological battles through which Sufi and anti-Sufi factions advance competing visions of gender, domesticity and social control. Rather, and despite the erosion of certain income-generating strategies through which wives traditionally secured autonomy and heightened their visibility, women for the most part now appear to be gaining greater control over the terms of marriage and the sources of prestige derived from conspicuous wedding ceremonies. Of late, their efforts to resist marginalization in an increasingly male-centred economy have taken on a more aggressive form since many of them started to openly denounce marriage reforms that threatened to undermine their own networks of wealth and value. Hence, when they criticize the stinginess of Izala grooms, insist on the defective quality of wedding gifts in some households,[18] or, in direct contradiction with reformist norms, stage ever

[18] As I was talking with a friend about wedding gifts, her sister interjected that an Izala bride had received a very small metal bed purchased by the groom, one that, she stressed, no mother would ever buy for her daughter today. My friend, who because she knew the young woman's mother, had had a chance to inspect the wedding gifts, further pointed out that the *matelas* (mattress) was of such poor quality that it would probably get ruined very fast. More than a reproach of the mother's inability to generate wealth for her daughter, the two women's critical evaluation of the bed and mattress this bride had received was an indirect condemnation of the marriage reforms that forced local women to undermine their own and their daughter's access to wealth and status.

more impressive *kan kaya,* mothers (and daughters) are striving to preserve, or even enhance, their control over material wealth and, through it, their capacity to generate social capital, affective bonds, self-identity, as well as the sense of enclosure so vital to their well-being and productivity. More generally, women's active engagement with the redefinition of marriage as a traditional female-centred process highlights the complex ways in which globalization and belonging work to simultaneously encompass and reject imported forms as they transform them. Put another way, women's engagement and the transformations it produces provide a striking example of how, far from simply leading to an erasure of local traditions or a seamless blending of different pre-existing cultural traditions, globalization is directly implicated in the 'production of locality' (Appadurai 1996: 178) through the promotion of new boundaries and the 'parochialization' of traditions.

When Malam Awal, the self-declared Shehu who settled in Dogondoutchi in 1997, presented himself as a Sufi liberator who could put an end to both the corrupt exactions of orthodox Muslim elites and the egalitarian excesses of Izala leaders, local residents flocked to attend his sermons. Predictably, *sadaki* was one of the contentious issues the charismatic leader initially raised in his campaign against greed and immorality. Arguing that few girls would marry if their parents kept on requiring bridewealth payments nobody could afford, Malam Awal soon convinced many that a small *sadaki* payment was better than none at all. In a matter of months, the Sufi preacher allegedly facilitated the marriage of some three hundred young women by negotiating for each a bridewealth payment of 30,000 CFA francs. At first, Malam Awal's 'progressive' policies appeared to have broken new ground, for instance, by convincing senior women that they could require the groom to pay for the bed and mattress or that the *kayan 'daki* could always be brought later. By mid 2000 however, it had become abundantly clear that women's initial enthusiasm for his campaign for purity and piety was fading as they came to terms with the social implications of these marriage reforms. Women, who had originally not dared to speak up against their husbands, were now finding the courage to resist Malam Awal's marriage initiatives and defend their own interests. I was told that some junior women had allegedly threatened to spoil their own wedding ceremonies by refusing to enter their new marital compound if they only received a *karaga*, the traditional wooden bed their grandmothers had and which Izala preachers were promoting as an alternative to the pricier Formica models. If marriage in Hausaphone communities 'has served as a central institutional and discursive locus for the mediation of change' as Cooper (1997: xlviii) rightfully notes, it has also provided a fertile terrain for women's self-actualization as modern brides and respectable mothers.

In considering the growing popularity of Formica beds among Mawri brides, I have shown that we must re-evaluate the conventional assumption made by both anthropologists and reformist leaders that, when women buy wedding gifts for their daughters, they tend to channel their resources into unproductive and impractical investments.[19] Far from being burdensome or useless property, the beds that future brides admire in their friends' homes before eventually acquiring their own have become vital means of creating wealth, social and moral value and generational difference for women whose social aspirations are being increasingly thwarted by the combined effects of economic collapse and religious intolerance. Whether they are poor or rich, pious or indifferent Muslims, loud or shy critics of marriage reforms, Dogondoutchi women have actively contributed to the means and terms through which they are valued as wives and mothers. In this respect, reformist Islam has both successfully limited women's powers of autonomy and self-expression and exacerbated their discontent with these limitations. Through what Butler (1997) calls the paradox of *subjectivation,* the very structures Izala established for securing women's subordination have become the means through which women can regain control over their own lives. By attempting to regain control over the terms of their lives, women are also actively shaping what it means to be both modern and grounded in the secure interiority of their domestic world.

References

Abu-Lughod, L. 1998, The Marriage of Feminism and Islamism in Egypt: Selective Repudiation as a Dynamic of Postcolonial Cultural Politics, in: L. Abu-Lughod (ed.), *Remaking Women: Feminism and Modernity in the Middle East*, pp. 243-69.

Allman, J. 2001, 'Rounding Up Spinsters: Gender Chaos and Unmarried Women in Colonial Asante', in: D.L. Hodgson & S.A. McCurdy (eds), *Wicked Women and the Reconfiguration of Gender in Africa*, Portsmouth, NH: Heinemann, pp.130-48.

Appadurai, A. 1996, *Modernity at Large: Cultural Dimensions of Globalization*, Minneapolis: University of Minnesota Press.

Archives Nationales du Niger 1936, Etude sur les Coutumes Fétishistes Maouris (Signée par le Chef de Sub-division à Doutchi, le 25 juillet). Cercle de Dosso 5.1.1.

[19] Because it ties capital into property that, while transferable, does not generate further income, women's investment into *kayan 'daki* has not generally been critically analysed. Save for Cooper's (1997) masterful account of Maradi women's contribution to the local economy, the literature on Hausa women's income-generating strategies has been remarkably gender biased (Callaway 1987, Raynaut 1977, Schildkrout 1982). Ironically, Izala male-centred discourses about marriage and wealth appear to be replicating these very same biases.

Bastian, M.L. 2002, 'Acadas and Fertilizer Girls: Young Nigerian Women and the Romance of Modernity', in: D.L. Hodgson (ed.), *Gendered Modernities: Ethnographic Perspectives*, New York: Palgrave, pp. 53-76.

Bernal, V. 1997, 'Islam, Transnational Culture and Modernity in Rural Sudan', in: M. Grosz-Ngate & O.H. Kokole (eds), *Gendered Encounters: Challenging Cultural Boundaries and Social Hierarchies in Africa*, New York: Routledge, pp. 131-51.

Butler, J. 1997, *The Psychic Life of Power: Theories in Subjection*, Stanford: Stanford University Press.

Callaway, B. 1987, *Muslim Hausa Women in Nigeria: Tradition and Change*, New York: Syracuse University Press.

Cooper, B.M. 1997, *Marriage in Maradi: Gender and Culture in a Hausa Society in Niger, 1900-1989*, Portsmouth, NH: Heinneman.

Cooper, B.M. 2001, 'The Strength in the Song: Muslim Personhood, Audible Capital, and Hausa Women's Performance of the Hajj', in: D.L. Hodgson (ed.), *Gendered Modernities: Ethnographic Perspectives*, New York: Palgrave, pp. 79-104.

Darrah, A.C. 1980, 'A Hermeneutic Approach to Hausa Therapeutics: The Allegory of the Living Fire', PhD thesis, Department of Anthropology, Northwestern University.

De Certeau, M. 1984, *The Practice of Everyday Life*, trans. S.F. Rendall, Berkeley: University of California Press.

De Latour Dejean, E. 1980, 'Shadows Nourished by the Sun: Rural Social Differentiation among the Mawri of Niger', in: M. Klein (ed.), *Peasants in Africa: Historical and Contemporary Perspectives*, Beverly Hills: Sage Publications, pp.104-41.

De Latour, E. 1992, *Les Temps du Pouvoir*, Paris: Editions de l'Ecole des Hautes Etudes en Sciences Sociales.

Fala Habi Aboubacar, G. 1988, 'L'Art Traditionnel de Décorer l'Habitat chez la Femme Haoussa dans l'Ader à Tahoua au Niger. Mémoire de Fin d'Etude', (C.A.E.M.T.P.), Ecole Normale Supérieure d'Enseignment Technique et Professionel, Université Cheikh Anta Diop, Dakar, Senegal.

Fisher, I. 2000, 'Young Man Decides to Wive It Wealthily in Uganda', *Wobulenzi Journal* http://www.nytimes.com/library/world/africa/070500uganda-marriage.html.

Friedman, J. 1994, *Cultural Identity and Global Process*, London: Sage.

Friedman, J. 2002, 'Globalization and Localization', in: J.X. Inda & R. Rosaldo (eds), *The Anthropology of Globalization: A Reader*, Malden, MA: Blackwell Publishers Ltd, pp. 233-46.

Graeber, D. 1996, 'Beads and Money: Notes Towards a Theory of Wealth and Power', *American Ethnologist* 23 (1): 4-24.

Hodgson, D.L. & S.A. McCurdy 2001, 'Introduction: Wicked Women and the Reconfiguration of Gender in Africa', in: D.l. Hodgson & S.A. McCurdy (eds), *Wicked Women and the Reconfiguration of Gender in Africa*, Portsmouth, NH: Heinemann, pp. 1-24.

Hunt N.R. 1991, 'Noise over Camouflaged Polygamy, Colonial Morality Taxation and a Woman-Naming Crisis in Belgian Africa', *Journal of African History* (32): 471-94.

Hunt, N.R. 1999, *A Colonial Lexicon: Of Birth Ritual, Medicalization, and Mobility in the Congo*, Durham, NC: Duke University Press.

Hutchinson, S. 1996, *Nuer Dilemmas: Coping with Money, War, and the State*, Berkeley: University of California Press.

Inda, J.X. & R. Rosaldo 2002, *The Anthropology of Globalization: A Reader*, Malden, MA: Blackwell Publishers.

Kane, O. 1994, 'Izala: The Rise of Muslim Reformism in Northern Nigeria', in: M.E. Marty & R.S. Appleby (eds), *Accounting for Fundamentalisms*, Chicago: University of Chicago Press, pp. 488-510.

Last, M. 1979, 'Strategies Against Time', *Sociology of Health and Illness* 1 (3): 306-17.

Loimeier, R. 1997, 'Islamic Reform and Political Change: The Example of Abubakar Gumi and the 'Yan Izala Movement in Nigeria', in: E.E. Rosander & D. Westerlund (eds), *African Islam and Islam in Africa: Encounters between Sufis and Islamists*, Athens, OH: Ohio University Press, pp. 286-307.

Masquelier, A. 1996, 'Mediating Threads: Clothing and the Texture of Spirit/Medium Relations in Bori', in: A.A. Hendrickson (ed.), *Clothing and Difference: Embodied Identities in Colonial and Post-Colonial Africa*, Raleigh Durham, NC: Duke University Press, pp. 66-93.

Masquelier, A. 1999, 'Debating Muslims, Disputed Practices: Struggles for the Realization of an Alternative Moral Order in Niger', in: J.L. & J. Comaroff (eds), *Civil Society and the Political Imagination in Africa: Critical Perspectives*, Chicago: University of Chicago Press, pp. 219-50.

Masquelier, A. 2001a, 'Powers, Problems, and Paradoxes of Twinship in Niger', *Ethnology* 40 (1): 45-62.

Masquelier, A. 2001b, *Prayer Has Spoiled Everything: Possession, Power, and Identity in an Islamic Town of Niger*, Durham, NC: Duke University Press.

Masquelier, A. n.d. 'The Naked Spirit: Disrobing, Deviancy, and Dissent in *Bori* Possession', in: A. Masquelier (ed.), *Transgressive Surfaces: Dirt, Undress, and Difference in Comparative Perspective*, manuscript in preparation.

Meyer, B. 1998, 'Commodities and the Power of Prayer', *Development and Change* 29 (4): 751-76.

Meyer, B. & P. Geschiere 1999, *Globalization and Identity: Dialectics of Flow and Closure*, Malden, MA: Blackwell Publishers.

Miller, D. 1994, *Modernity, An Ethnographic Approach: Dualism and Mass Consumption in Trinidad*, New York: Berg Publishers.

Nicolas, G. 1975, *Dynamique Sociale et Appréhension du Monde au Sein d'une Société Hausa*, Paris: Institut d'Ethnologie.

Nicolas, G. 1986, *Don Rituel et Echange Marchand dans une Société Sahelienne*, Paris: Institut d'Ethnologie.

Piault, C. 1963, 'Contribution à l'Etude de la Vie Quotidienne de la Femme Mawri', *Etudes Nigériennes* 10 IFAN-CNRS.

Piault, M.H. 1970, *Histoire Mawri: Introduction à l'Etude des Processus Constitutifs d'un Etat*, Paris: Editions du Centre National de la Recherche Scientifique.

Piault, M.H. 1978, 'Mariage en Pays Hausa', in: A. Adler, M. Cartry, M. Izard, M.H. Piault & J. Rouch (eds), *Systèmes de Signes*, Paris: Hermann, pp. 419-33.

Pittin, R. 1979, 'Marriage and Alternative Strategies: Career Patterns of Hausa Women in Katsina City', PhD thesis, Department of Anthropology, University of London.

Raynaut, C. 1977, Aspects Socio-économiques de la Préparation et de la Circulation de la Nourriture dans un Village Haoussa (Niger), *Cahiers d'Etudes Africaines* 68 (17): 569-97.

Renne, E. & D.S. Usman 1999, 'Bicycle Decoration and Everyday Aesthetics in Northern Nigeria', *African Arts* 32 (2): 46-51.

Schildkrout, E. 1982, 'Dependence and Autonomy: The Economic Activities of Secluded Hausa Women in Kano, Nigeria', in: E. Bay (ed.), *Women and Work in Africa*, Boulder: Westview Press, pp. 55-83.

Smith, M.F. 1955, *Baba of Karo: A Woman of the Muslim Hausa*, London: Faber & Faber.

Steng, I., H. White, C. Lynch & J.A. Zimmermann 2000, 'Millennial Transitions', *Public Culture* 12 (2): 344-50.

Umar, M.S. 1993, 'Changing Islamic Identity in Nigeria from the 1960s to the 1980s: From Sufism to Anti-Sufism', in: L. Brenner (ed.), *Muslim Identity and Social Change in Sub-Saharan Africa*, Bloomington: Indiana University Press, pp. 154-78.

Vaughan, M. 1991, *Curing their Ills: Colonial Power and African Illness*, Stanford: Stanford University Press.

Weiss, B. 1996, *The Making and Unmaking of the Haya Lived World: Consumption, Commoditization and Everyday Practice*, Durham, NC: Duke University Press.

PART IV: GLOBALITY AND AFRICAN HISTORIC RELIGIONS

9

The social life of secrets

Ferdinand de Jong

By looking at initiation rituals it is possible to arrive at a better understanding of secrets in a given society in a globalizing world. This chapter, however, suggests that the secret emerges in a performance in which initiates and non-initiates are complicit. Secrecy produces a shared subjectivity between initiate and non-initiate. Such complicity is often denied in ethnographic texts that claim authority for a subject penetrating the secret of the Other. This chapter holds that these ethnographic poetics make a distinction between subject and object, which, in the case of secrecy, seems untenable. To acknowledge this implies recognition of the co-ownership of secrets. The secrets performed in a globalizing world can no longer be localized properties. As ethnographic cases in the chapter demonstrate, secrecy creates a translocal intersubjectivity that requires recognition in ethnographic texts.

'The Field', seen as a place of writing, leaks. (Clifford 1990: 64)

A widespread paradigm holds that secrets represent the core of culture. Moreover, many ethnographic texts assert that secrets are the inalienable property of those who hold them. In my experience in south Senegal, this impression was largely confirmed. Those who hold secrets consider them essential to the definition of their self-definition. Secrets are 'owned' by those who hold them. The ethics of anthropology therefore require that anthropologists do not expose the secrets they have traced in their research, as they are the property of the researched. Secrets appear in the ethnographic text as signs of alterity.

After a long period of intense interest in issues of ethnographic writing, the question of how authority is established in ethnographic texts remains acute (Clifford & Marcus 1986, Clifford 1988, Geertz 1988, James *et al.* 1997). We need to re-examine every aspect of the way in which we make representations. Here, I examine how secrecy structures the production of knowledge. I argue that the metaphor of secrecy contributes to the making of both ethnographic subject and object. This chapter deals with the politics and poetics of secrecy. Rather than assuming that a focus on the poetics of ethnography leads us away from its politics (Said 1989), it works on the assumption that poetics and politics are intricately intertwined. Concealment and revelation are part and parcel of the fieldwork experience. Secrecy often produces ambiguity (Piot 1993) but in spite of this, secrets are often represented in unambiguous terms in ethnographic texts. The metaphor of revelation is frequently used in anthropological rhetoric and, in ethnographic texts, fieldwork often appears as the gradual penetration of hitherto hidden knowledge (Clifford 1988, Gable 1997). Anthropology reveals the innermost cultural essence of the 'Other'. The rhetoric of secrecy reinforces the notion that culture is located in secrets and that cultural knowledge can only be obtained by a penetrating subject.

Secrecy as a metaphor in the construction of ethnographic authority contributes to our paradigmatic assumption that cultures are bounded. The metaphor of secrecy creates cores of culture that are set apart and require revelation through ethnography. The trope of secrecy in anthropological texts *posits* boundaries and should be exposed as instrumental in the production of boundaries. That alterity should be spatially distributed is problematic, and it becomes even more problematic in the age of globalization. If we can no longer think of culture as territorialized (Gupta & Ferguson 1992, Malkki 1995), then we need to acknowledge that the anthropological 'field', in Africa or elsewhere, can no longer be spatially defined. It is no longer productive to posit impermeable cultural boundaries. This is a serious challenge to anthropology, as the discipline has always relied on the spatialization of cultural difference. Here, I hope to demonstrate that secrecy engages anthropological subject and object, rendering this categorical distinction problematic. I demonstrate that secrecy is, in fact, an intersubjective performance enmeshed in historically contingent power relations.

Secrets as boundaries

It is not hard to establish that secrecy serves to establish boundaries (Barth 1969). In the most general sense, a secret establishes a boundary between those 'in the know' and those excluded from the secret knowledge. When conducting fieldwork in south Senegal I noticed that secrecy worked in precisely that way. To what effect secrecy is used, however, depends very much on the context. For instance, it can be argued that Jola male initiation primarily serves to demarcate a realm of male ritual activity from which women should be excluded. Such a realm allows the construction of a particular masculinity based on ritual separation and instruction into male esoteric lore. Male initiation, arguably, not only structures the male population into a hierarchy of age-sets, it also differentiates the entire population into separate genders (De Jong 2001a).

The male initiates are instructed into the secret knowledge transmitted in the ritual process. While they become fully entitled to this knowledge by virtue of their initiation, women are deliberately excluded from it, never expecting to be initiated into male secret lore, just like men would never expect to be initiated into the female secret lore as transmitted through female initiation rites. In other words, the performance of secrecy should not be understood as a power struggle between those who know and those who want to know. The excluded are expected to play the role of the excluded and they usually do so. In that sense, secrecy is a performance that requires the cooperation of the members of the excluded sex. Secrecy includes those who are *de facto* excluded. When those who are excluded do not object to their exclusion, they become complicit in the performance of secrecy that excludes them. The construction of boundaries through secrecy is not a simple matter but a highly complex form of interaction in which the excluded are fully aware of their necessary presence.

In the light of this, it is not surprising that the actual secret lore is often known to the excluded. As mothers, wives or girlfriends, women do access parts of the secret lore from which they are actively excluded in ritual contexts. Even outsiders can sometimes access the secret lore denied to them in other contexts. The boundary of the secret can be permeable. While doing fieldwork in Casamance, it took a while before I realized that secrecy was pervasive in this region and that it was mostly performed in connection with the secrets of initiation. The Kankurang masquerade, for instance, is predominantly performed in contexts of initiation (De Jong 2000, 2001b). Such initiations are regularly performed in Ziguinchor, the regional capital, and blacksmiths have a particular responsibility in these ceremonies. I went to see one blacksmith who had been organizing a number of these events and who, besides having such heavy ritual responsibilities, was a gardener at a local *lycée*. He kindly consented to talk about circumcision, initiation and masquerading, and we had various conversations at his home and in the school playground. During one of our meetings he told me the myth of origin of circumcision and Kankurang. He solemnly concluded his story by saying: 'This is the story I tell the initiates in the sacred grove', implying that this was the *secret* knowledge transmitted to the novices in the sacred grove. Secret knowledge can apparently be transmitted without the formal initiation of the anthropologist.

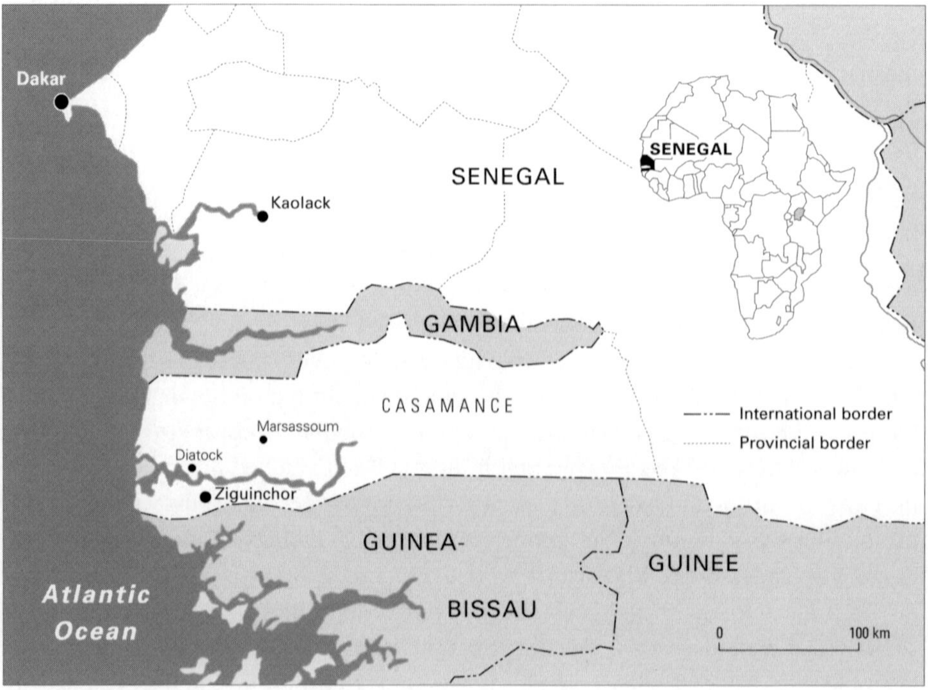

Map 9.1: Southern Senegal

This is not surprising, as Bellman (1984) established that secrecy does not depend on the contents of the secret but on the 'speech environment' that defines the status of knowledge. In other words, the blacksmith defined the knowledge he had just transmitted to me as typically transmitted to novices (and therefore secret for non-initiates). However, he did not explicitly refer to me as a non-initiate, and thereby defined the knowledge as accessible to me.

At other times, however, I was deliberately excluded. The most salient example relates to an embarrassing moment in my fieldwork when I wanted to explore the social dynamics that had led to the execution of two men by the Kankurang secret society. In Marsassoum, a town in mid Casamance, the Kankurang mask had once been desecrated by one of its inhabitants. The man had partially undressed the Kankurang and thereby exposed the secret of the mask. The man and his uncle, who had come to his assistance, were then executed by the mask and its companions (De Jong 2000, 2001b). When my assistant and I settled in the town with the intention of examining this event, the prosecution of the perpetrators was still under way and the judicial process had not yet been concluded. We were not aware of this. However, our inquiries into the matter were quickly noticed and our presence was identified as being of possible harm to the perpetrators. At one point, a young man came to see us and explained the delicacy of the topic of our research, adding that any person willing to give us information would face a verdict similar to those men who had disclosed the mask's secret. We had no alternative but to leave the town. Imposed silence prevented us from revealing the knowledge that, the culprits imagined, might have an impact on the judicial process.

Mandinko men consider the Kankurang masquerade the core secret of male initiation. They can be swiftly mobilized to defend the secret or, if it has been divulged, to avenge its desecration. In that sense it may be argued that the Kankurang masquerade represents the core of Mandinko culture (although we should not dismiss the feelings of women about this masquerade, that is first and foremost used to inculcate values associated with 'appropriate' female behaviour). However, in the case of my obstructed research in Marsassoum, secrecy did not pertain so much to the masquerade itself but to the executions allegedly perpetrated by the masquerade. The secrecy with regard to the executions can hardly pertain to the core of Mandinko culture. It was performed to protect the culprits from persecution. This performance of secrecy was part of an established mode of cultural performance, but the conditions under which it was re-enacted were not those of a pristine, bounded culture. Indeed, secrecy was performed to create an impermeable boundary *vis-à-vis* the State and the Court. What can be conceived as the core of culture is in fact a cultural mode of performance to negotiate external relations (cf. De Jong 1999b, 2002).

Core of culture

Anthropologists use a variety of metaphors to establish ethnographic authority. One of the best-known textual strategies describes the arrival of the anthropologist among the people to be studied, his or her initial confusion, the separation between the ethnographer and the Other, and the gradual rapprochement through the establishment of rapport. Geertz's arrival among the Balinese is the most frequently quoted example (Geertz 1973). Another textual strategy relates to the anthropologist's initiation. The initiation of the anthropologist into the secrets of the tribe authorizes the ethnographic text. Clifford (1988: 53) made this argument with regard to the work of Marcel Griaule. What was to become a classic ethnography was entirely framed in terms of an initiation. Griaule's magnum opus *Dieu d'eau* (1948) is allegedly based on revelations made to the author, and whether Griaule was indeed initiated into secret cultural knowledge or had simply been told a number of intricate improvisations by his principal informant and master, Ogotemmêli, is beside the point. What matters is the rhetoric used by Griaule. His ethnographic authority rests upon his alleged initiation into the deep cultural knowledge of the Dogon. Initiation provides the organizing metaphor and evokes the deepening of understanding that accrues to long-term field research (Clifford 1988: 81).[1] Many monographs relate how the researcher gradually learns about the secrets of the Other. The ethnographer undergoes a 'parallel' initiation: 'As an initiate, the researcher receives and interprets revelations' (Clifford 1988: 84). The metaphor of initiation in Griaule's work has been fully documented but is not restricted to his ethnography. In fact, Marxist anthropologists have just as artfully employed the trope. Let me quote from Maurice Godelier's *The Making of Great Men* (1986: xiii) on male domination among the New Guinea Baruya:

> One may easily imagine, on reading these pages, just how much time and confidence it must have taken on the part of the Baruya to introduce me to their way of thinking and allow me to see (as they have expressed it) not only the leaves, branches, and the trunk, but also some of the most secretly buried roots of their thought.

---

[1] Van Beek's field evaluation of the work of Marcel Griaule (Van Beek 1991) questions the recognizability of his ethnography. Van Beek suggests that Griaule's ethnography is not an accurate representation of Dogon culture and that the ethnography is not based on a direct revelation of secrets but on complex interactions between the anthropologist and his informants. The secrets revealed in Griaule's ethnography are not 'deep' secrets but result from collaboration between Griaule and his informants.

Godelier confidently asserts that he was trusted by the Baruya — a precondition for successful fieldwork. He suggests that, due to the appropriate conduct of fieldwork, the Baruya themselves took the initiative to part with their secret knowledge and allowed him to see 'the most secretly buried roots of their thought'.

Ethnographies often portray fieldwork as 'a gradual penetration in which surface appearances — facades — give way to deeper truths' (Gable 1997: 227). These deeper truths are understood to constitute the core of culture. Indeed, when ethnographers talk about male initiation, secrecy and secret societies, they assume they are dealing with the hard core of culture. In a parallel initiation, the ethnographer accesses the deep, hidden truths of the Other. As Clifford (1988: 158) states, a classic topography assumes barriers and thresholds surrounding a 'secret' to be penetrated by the explorer, researcher or ethnographer. The deep truths of the Other are revealed to us by the ethnographer. Let us return to Godelier's preface:

> I must ask the reader who may sometimes be tempted, according to the lights of his or her own philosophy or mood, to regard the secrets confided to me by the Baruya as derisory, grotesque, or even obscene, to remember that for them they are an essential part of their identity, a vital, sacred force inherited from the past, on which they depend in order to withstand all those voluntary or involuntary pressures that our world brings to bear upon them, often enough in perfectly good faith, but more often still deliberately. (Godelier 1986: xiii)

This is a complex sentence in which negative evaluations of Baruya secrets are projected onto the reader who is not initiated and as yet unaware of the real meanings of the secrets. The author, by contrast, recognizes the importance of secrets to the Baruya: they constitute an essential part of their identity, even a sacred force inherited from the past. Godelier defines the secrets as the core of Baruya culture, an essential core that remains in times of turmoil, on which the Baruya depend in order to withstand change. Change, however, comes to the Baruya from outside, from 'our world'. Change cannot be a Baruya invention since the core of their culture is made up of secrets. Godelier is sympathetic towards the Baruya and the allegory of redemption voluntarily offered to the Baruya is clearly noticeable (Clifford 1986). But it seems the Baruya stand little chance of surviving in a world where pressures are deliberately brought to bear upon them.

Godelier's preface, to which we will return later, is not idiosyncratic. Secrets are often portrayed as the hard core of culture, which anthropologists have set themselves the task of revealing. While my argument only relates to the metaphors of secrecy and revelation, I hypothesize that a good deal of narrative anthropology, even if it does not use the trope of initiation in a literal sense, still displays a similar rhetorical structure. We expect monographs to make a cumulative argument and we always hope for a final, deep ethnographic 'plot' that will make the parts of the monograph fit. In other words, ethnography often takes the form of a narrative of gradual revelation, whereby facades give way to deeper truths. In fact, Geertzian 'thick description' casts the anthropological narrative into a mould that privileges gradual revelation (Geertz 1973). As a form of layered description, it suggests that a cultural core is only accessible through a series of revelations. 'Thick description' may be a model for, and of, ethnography in which a core of culture is revealed to the reader.

Secrets of fieldwork

To understand why secrets have come to represent the core of culture, we need to look at the practice of fieldwork. The idea that the core of culture can be accessed through fieldwork is essential to the history of anthropology. The discipline claims to have developed the methodology — fieldwork — through which such cultural knowledge can be obtained. It forms a necessary stage in every anthropologist's initiation into the profession. Bronislaw Malinowski was the first scholar to declare fieldwork an appropriate method for the collection of ethnographic data. Remember that question in the first chapter of *Argonauts of the Western Pacific*: 'What is then this ethnographer's magic, by which he is able to evoke the real spirit of the natives, the true picture of tribal life?' (Malinowski 1999: 6). The ethnographer's magic, Malinowski answers, lies in the patient and systematic application of a number of rules, the most elementary of which is 'to live without other white men, right among the natives' (ibid: 6). This has been recognized as the methodological innovation that revolutionized anthropology. Malinowski was conscious of the revolutionary nature of his charter and claimed that the method of fieldwork was entirely his discovery: 'At any rate, I found out where lay the secret of effective fieldwork' (ibid: 6). The metaphor of secrecy highlights a breakthrough when Malinowski reveals to anthropology its proper method.[2]

Malinowski established extended fieldwork as *the* method of anthropological investigation. Through observation of the natives and participation among them, data were generated. Experience in the field became a requirement for the establishment of ethnographic authority. Its most essential elements were, first of all, a protracted sojourn in the field to attend all the events associated with the seasonal cycle and, secondly, near-proficiency in a local language. Not all

[2] Although he was not the first ethnographer to do fieldwork, he has to be credited with producing a charter for this method of investigation (Stocking 1983a).

anthropologists met these standards. In fact, one of the classic monographs, *The Nuer*, makes no secret of the constraints on the research that the author conducted (Clifford 1988: 32). *The Nuer* is based on eleven months of fieldwork in almost impossible conditions, as the following testifies:

> As every effort was made to prevent me from entering the cattle camps and it was seldom that I had visitors I was almost entirely cut off from communication with the people. My attempts to prosecute inquiries were persistently obstructed. (Evans-Pritchard 1940: 12)

At various points the author acknowledges that fieldwork was not conducted in ideal conditions. In other words, after rapport and language proficiency had been defined as the quintessential requirements for successful fieldwork, Evans-Pritchard had to acknowledge that these requirements had not been met in his fieldwork. *The Nuer* transgressed anthropology's central values. However, his confession did not make much of a difference in terms of the monograph's reception, which became a classic in the field. Evans-Pritchard's failure to live up to professional expectations was apparently not critical. The fact that field researchers sometimes fail in their professed methodology was acknowledged and may be considered anthropology's public secret. This is reflected in the general consensus that field notes are not to be treated as public evidence (Sanjek 1990). We do not require that field notes should become accessible to others, and they are often surrounded by a measure of secrecy (Jackson 1990: 22, Clifford 1990: 52). The discipline of anthropology resembles a secret society whose members do not publicly question matters of evidence.

Aspiring anthropologists nevertheless continued to be initiated into the profession by means of a protracted stint of fieldwork, the techniques of which were usually learnt in the field by means of a sink-or-swim method. Fieldwork remained curiously unanalysed for as long as functionalism was the dominant paradigm and remained the subject of considerable mythic elaboration (Stocking 1983b: 8). Although the publication of Malinowski's *Diary* (1967) probably only added to this elaboration, it also instigated profound doubts about fieldwork as a methodology. The deliberate deconstruction of fieldwork, however, only seriously began with the publication of Rabinow's *Reflections on Fieldwork in Morocco* (1977). Fieldwork, he had been told as an undergraduate, constitutes the essential rite of passage for the aspiring anthropologist, and he was eager to undergo the experience: 'At the time, this intrigued me. The promise of initiation into the clan secrets was seductive. I fully accepted the dogma' (ibid: 3). But when returning from the field, it was made clear to him that the experience of fieldwork was not what made him an initiate. What was required instead was 'objective data' (ibid: 4). Frustrated by this positivist approach, Rabinow decided to describe his actual experiences and how these constituted the data, no longer to be understood as 'objective'. Rabinow demonstrates that the method of fieldwork cannot yield scientific data in the way Malinowski claims it does. While he acknowledges that fieldwork constitutes a rite of passage, he asks how the data generated through fieldwork can be separated from the experience that generates them. Initiations are meant to make the initiates 'see' things and Rabinow, after his initiation, saw things differently (cf. Poppi 1993). He exposed fieldwork – the secret of anthropology – as an experience that contradicts the dogma: reflection was required.

When the dogma of fieldwork as a scientific method for the production of ethnographic data had been shattered, anthropology became increasingly self-reflexive. The literary turn in anthropology emphasized the fact that ethnography is first of all an exercise in writing (Clifford & Marcus 1986, Geertz 1988, Sanjek 1990). The literary turn also established that cultural knowledge is created in conversations between fieldworkers and informants. Anthropological texts, it was asserted, need to be self-reflexive about the process of writing culture, from the first field note to the final postface. To me, this implies that anthropology has to be self-reflexive about the measure in which fieldwork can still be represented as an initiation into the secrets of the Other.

My initiation

Many monographs that explicitly analyse initiation ceremonies give an account of how the author (usually a man) was initiated into the secrets of the tribe.[3] As already suggested, the description of an initiation into secrets should be understood as an assertion of ethnographic authority. A good example from the field of Casamance studies is the recent book by Robert Baum (1999), in which the author claims to have been allowed to attend 'secret' rituals. It is part of the same rhetoric to suggest that such permission can only be obtained as a result of established rapport. Reading such sections makes me envious. For one reason or another, I never established such good relations or, if I did, my introduction to the 'secret' proved disappointing. What had been concealed from me proved to be of very limited relevance once it was revealed. Or the revelation of the secret happened in such an irregular way that my access to the esoteric lore was immediately framed as illegitimate. Invariably, my presence at secret places was taken as a violation of established modes of revelation (cf. Taussig 1999).

[3] Is there, as Clifford (1988) and Van Beek (1991) suggest, an affinity with the conception of research as a military operation?

At no point during my fieldwork in Casamance did I undergo one of the local initiation ceremonies. It must be said, however, that my initiation would certainly have compromised my academic career since the secrecy imposed on the initiates would have limited me in my writing. I was not prepared to go all the way towards creating intersubjective knowledge on initiation as my initiation would have prevented the production of academic knowledge. Others, however, have been initiated and have acquired a full command of esoteric lore. Van Binsbergen (1991) gives a particularly dramatic and moving account of his initiation as a *sangoma* healer, describing his initiation as a painful process towards an experience of intersubjective healing. His journey was largely triggered by the exclusion that he experienced in the 'field'. Indeed, power relations remain central to the performance of secrecy (Fabian 1998: 55). Although I never submitted myself to formal procedures of initiation in order to establish rapport and 'productive' relationships, exclusion certainly made me eager to learn more about the secret (cf. Simmel 1967: 333). This is apparent, for instance, from the following description of my experiences in a particular initiation ceremony, which I was able to attend because the sons of my host were participating in it. I travelled with my host and his family to his natal village where several of his sons were to be initiated by means of a week of seclusion in the bush. During this week I heard rumours about discussions being held in the sacred grove. The sons of my host who had already been initiated, and therefore were allowed to enter and exit the initiation camp, informed me about what was going on. They complained about the bad organization of the entire ceremony and, remarkably, shared their misgivings with me. Again, the secrecy pertaining to matters of the sacred grove was not so carefully observed. Although I was informed about the proceedings in the sacred grove I also felt terribly excluded when, after a week of seclusion, the initiates were taken to the river for a ritual bath and I was the only man in the village not allowed to accompany them, being left in the company of women who took advantage of the men's absence to mock them and their religious piety.

Surprisingly, after the ritual bath of the initiates my host invited me to visit the sacred grove and suggested that I make a gift to the initiates, who would then pray for me. I was eager enough to accept such a *mise-en-scène*. So we set out for the sacred grove, going past the bend in the path that had for days marked the forbidden. While heading for the grove, we met a number of men returning from it and some politely asked where I was going. All seemed satisfied with the explanations provided by my host, but when we finally got to the place where the initiates were gathered, I felt uneasy. The initiates were gathered in the shade of some mango trees, while their guardians and elders oversaw them. My host informed the elders about the reasons for my presence. There was some confusion. My host showed the 1,000 francs, explaining that I wanted to offer the money to the initiates. One man replied: 'Youssouf, what you have done, no one has ever done before!' The men started a heated discussion and I wanted to leave, but my assistant said that the harm had already been done. Then people calmed down and actually started praying. All of them sank to their knees and raised their hands. Dozing boys were woken up to join the prayer. I was in utter confusion. Luckily, the whole affair lasted for only half a minute, and everyone got up. My host then suggested I take some pictures, and although I had been told at numerous occasions that there is no worse sacrilege than a photograph of the secret, I could not resist the temptation. Some men explicitly asked to be photographed. Having taken a few pictures, I left, complaining to my host about the awkward position he had put me in. Most of the photographs did not turn out well. (There is a widely held belief in Casamance that pictures of the secret never turn out well.)

This set of transactions was utterly complex. While my curiosity drove me to accepting the offer of my host, I was from the outset most hesitant. I had become sensitive to the rules of secrecy. When we approached the sacred grove, I felt excitement and angst about the intrusion I was about to make. My intrusion into the realm of the secret did not fail to produce the expected results. However, once the men had calmed down there seemed to be no real issue. I continued to feel ill at ease, especially when taking pictures. In other words, I was still under the spell of the secret. This may be taken as indicative of the empathy conventionally required of the anthropologist. I had indeed made the secrecy of my interlocutors my own. Yet how and when to perform secrecy remained an unresolved question to which, I realize, no predetermined answers exist.

The mask of secrecy

As anthropology has moved away from structural functionalism, the old assumptions about patterns of culture have been abandoned. Roles and rules have given way to research on the invention and inventedness of culture. In a similar vein, it may be argued that secrecy is not laid down in a set of carefully observed rules, as if written in stone. Secrecy is instead a cultural performance, the eventualities of which cannot be predicted in some kind of ethnographic inventory. How and when secrecy is performed is highly dependent on the context. Secrecy is situationally defined (Bellman 1984). I found this confirmed in my own fieldwork in the Casamance region. The first time I went to do fieldwork my aim was to study masquerades and in order to examine the history of the Ekumpo masquerade I was going to live in Diatock, a Jola village. My teacher Jos van der Klei, who had conducted fieldwork in this village (Van der Klei 1989), introduced me to a young man who was presumably involved in the masquerade and he recommended me as a student of the performance. Van der Klei was careful to point out that I 'had not come to discover secrets'. The man nodded: he had already understood. My teacher had apparently found a way of speaking the language of secrecy. To me his words remained an enigma. Had I come to discover secrets?

I had not come to discover secrets. At the time I knew very little about masquerading, and next to nothing about secrecy. I was still unaware of how secrecy structures communication. Witness, for instance, my naivety in confronting my research assistant Jimmy Carter with a question that had long been on my mind. Suspecting the secret but tempted by my good relations with my assistant, I asked him who was in fact dressed in the Ekumpo costume when the mask performed in the village square. Feigning surprise, he replied: 'What makes you think that a *man* stages Ekumpo?' My curiosity was countered with a performance of secrecy. Although his smile revealed that my question was well taken, Jimmy Carter clearly did not want to divulge secrets and suggested that the mask was not actually a human being. I was left with a mystery. But I noticed that other men — notably elders — were not so reticent and freely discussed the intricacies of the masquerade. I learnt that the young men had a vested interest in the masquerade and were not willing to share their knowledge of it, whereas the elders, whose interests were not promoted by the masquerade, freely talked about backstage matters. The extent to which knowledge is secret, I learnt, depends on the context.

While I was living in Diatock, I tried as far as possible to participate in the Ekumpo masquerade. My friends welcomed my participation, especially my performance in the nightly Ekumpo dance. As I felt I was a very incompetent dancer, I preferred instead to attend the meetings that the Ekumpo society occasionally held in one of the village squares. Only initiated men were allowed to participate in these meetings and I am grateful that I, a non-initiate, was allowed to attend some of them. However I learnt that in addition to these semi-secret meetings in the village clearing, other more exclusive meetings, to which I was never invited, were held in sacred groves. In other words, my participation was limited, as befitting a non-initiate. Although I was never in a position to discuss the intricacies of the masquerade with the members of the Ekumpo society freely, the interaction between me and my informants increasingly relied on the mutual understanding that young men staged the masquerade. The Ekumpo became a shared secret.

The Ekumpo masquerade consists of a number of masks, the central figure of which is called Ekumpo, a mask that looks very much like a haystack as it is made out of the leaves of palm trees that extend from the head to cover the entire body, including the arms, legs and feet. A pole projects upwards from the head. However, Ekumpo's companion, Jarimamma, is dressed in black cloth and wears a carved facemask. Having studied the masquerade, I wanted to acquire such a carved mask. I raised the issue with my assistant who, surprisingly, told me that this could be arranged. One day, I accompanied the young men and women of Diatock on an excursion to a neighbouring village where an Ekumpo feast was to be celebrated. For two days, the young men and women of Diatock and the hosting village indulged in singing, dancing and feasting on the chickens that the girls had to present to the Ekumpo as a penalty for a transgression committed by one of them (De Jong 1999a). In this village Jimmy Carter introduced me to a carver who was allegedly capable of producing the carved mask I hoped for. We negotiated a price and agreed that the mask would be finished before I was to leave Diatock. The entire conversation was conducted in the man's compound, although my interlocutors made sure the carver's wife was out of earshot. I returned to Diatock anxiously anticipating the mask's arrival. It duly arrived a few weeks later and my assistant instructed me to bring a bag to his compound. In the seclusion of his room, he uncovered the mask for me to inspect, hid it in my bag and told me to take it out of the village without letting anyone see it. Some of my host's sons, however, noticed me walking down the road with the bag and made polite inquiries regarding its contents. Versed in the language of secrecy, they accepted my vague answers and made no further enquiries about the bag's contents. Then I left and smuggled the mask out of the village.[4]

At no point during my sojourn in the village or in any conversation, did the young men tell me that Ekumpo was a man in disguise. Although information about Ekumpo was made available to me, the transmission of this knowledge never took the form of an initiation. I gathered bits and pieces of information. While 'in the know', I remained a non-initiate. As my fieldwork progressed, I gradually came to understand that the Ekumpo masquerade is indeed shrouded in secrecy (De Jong 1999a). Although I never swore an oath on the secrets of the Ekumpo mask, I became complicit in the secrecy surrounding it. I smuggled the mask out of the village, as if I had a responsibility to keep the mask a secret *vis-à-vis* non-initiates. But was I not a non-initiate myself?

---

[4] I now realize that my purchase of the mask may have set a precedent in the commodification of the mask, the performance of which was already being commodified (De Jong 1999a). Interestingly, the commodification of both mask and masquerade occurs in secret. Although the mask and masquerade acquire monetary value and are nowadays removed from their original context and use value, secrecy is such a powerful and flexible form of social intercourse that it can even encompass the commodification of the secret.

Translocal secrecy

As Bellman notes, the content of the secret is not important. Rather, it is the context of the communication of secrets that matters. As the case of my intrusion demonstrates, one can become proficient in the performance of secrecy without learning the secret, or without being authorized to talk about secrets. Secrecy is to a large extent performed and is not restricted to the communication of knowledge. In any case, I became particularly sensitive to secrecy as a performance. Every time the novices were led into the sacred grove I was denied access to that mysterious place. A young man would walk up to me and say: 'Whites are not allowed to go any further'. Women would tease me, asking me why I was denied access. Although they would not expect a white European to be initiated, they suggested that I remained somehow inept. In an ironic way, the women identified with a ritual that was designed to exclude them. Others did not really appreciate the irony of their exclusion. A Frenchman married to a girl born in a Jola village where I attended a male initiation ceremony was not at all amused by his exclusion. He had once spent a year in the village and had now come to visit his relatives for the initiation celebration. The man was outraged about his exclusion from the sacred grove and was determined to seek 'revenge'. His excitement need not surprise us. After all, he considered himself a member of the local community. But he was obviously not familiar with the rules of access to the sacred grove. His case demonstrates how much the denial of access contributes to the idea that the most important of all activities takes place at the sacred grove. Secrecy is indeed important for the establishment of boundaries, especially *vis-à-vis* the descendants of the former colonizers. Secrecy can take on translocal dimensions.

Secrecy creates solidarity among the initiates. An initiate is expected to remain silent about the activities at the sacred grove and, as long as he obeys this rule, he will be respected as a man capable of keeping a secret. The resulting solidarity among the initiates travels with them wherever they go. However, the social miracle secrecy produces is that it also creates a bond between those excluded from the secret, and it is in this sense that secrecy produces an intersubjectivity that can engage the excluded. Women are *de facto* excluded from the secret. However, by expressing their allegiance to the rules of male secrecy, women are included in the ritual congregation. The next case illustrates the secret's ability to include women in the congregation. A young Jola woman in Amsterdam has a copy of an anthropological study on the Jola's male initiation written by a Dutch anthropologist. Although she perfectly understands the language the study is written in, she refrains from reading it. She is afraid of learning secrets that are the prerogative of initiated men. Moreover, she does not want the secret to be exposed for fear of it losing its mystery. The power of secrecy can extend even to include a female migrant in the diaspora.

Secrecy includes the male and female members of a community but may also extend to include others who have long been exposed to the secret. The following case demonstrates the secret's capacity to reach outsiders. A young man, born in a Jola village and married to a Dutch woman, has settled in the Netherlands. At the time of the village's initiation ritual, the couple had two children, one of them a two-year-old boy. The father was determined to initiate his son at the sacred grove. His wife, an anthropologist, did not know what initiation was about and feared that her son would be circumcised at the sacred grove. She was concerned about her child and did not want him exposed to unhygienic conditions that might endanger his health. Her husband refused to tell her about the proceedings at the sacred grove, saying it was a male affair. When I met her a few days before her son was to be taken into the sacred grove, she was worried about the consequences of the ritual on her son. I tried to comfort her and gave her a copy of the ethnography written by the Dutch anthropologist to read. Soon afterwards she had to leave the village and took the book with her to the Netherlands. After I returned to the Netherlands, I called to ask her for the book. A few days later her husband showed up and handed over a parcel. After he had left, I opened the tightly wrapped parcel that contained the secret knowledge: the ethnography on Jola initiation. The woman had wrapped up the book so as not to reveal to her husband that she had learned the knowledge forbidden to her.

Interestingly, in this particular case the secrets included in the ethnography have been reincorporated in the domain of secrecy. While the anthropologists committed several transgressions, these can never be openly revealed. I had, for sure, transmitted esoteric lore to a woman (secrets that I myself was not entitled to know). However, the woman and I had been so much exposed to secrecy that we ourselves had become equally secretive. The secret, I dare say, is contagious. Secrecy among initiates generates secrecy among the non-initiated too. Secrecy creates a shared subjectivity that, eventually, incorporates the objectified secrets of ethnography.

Conclusion

In the field I noticed a wide variety of reactions to my professed aim of studying 'local traditions'. Some people showed outright hostility to my research and were not prepared to transmit secret knowledge. One sacred grove officiant refused to talk to me, saying, 'Whites only want to discover our secrets and disclose them in their books'. Fieldwork is not always a matter of dialogue. I frequently found myself excluded as men and women denied me access to certain places and performances. My dissertation was a result of intersubjective dialogue *and* its negation, secretive silence (De Jong 2001a). However, there were times when secret knowledge was transmitted to me. On such occasions this knowledge was not defined as secret and it is, therefore, hard to establish what knowledge was actually framed as 'secret' on other occasions. Strictly speaking, I cannot be accused of revealing secrets since knowledge was never defined as secret to me anyway. Although I cannot reveal secrets, I am aware of the rules of secrecy that prevail in 'the field'. 'The field', however, leaks and the secret has cast its spell on me and others who live beyond the field in the strict sense of the term, in France, the Netherlands, Canada and the United States.

In this chapter I have made an attempt to demonstrate that secret knowledge is accessible, even to non-initiates. The important thing about secrecy is not the content of the secret but the way in which it is performed. Secrecy is performed wherever the initiates or those excluded from the secret go. In the case of anthropologists, the secret travels with them in their field notes. Eventually, the anthropologist has to decide whether to write down secrets or to refrain from writing about secrecy. In practice, many anthropologists use the rhetoric of secrecy to establish ethnographic authority, suggesting that penetration of the secret equals a true understanding of the Other. The secret produces locality (cf. Appadurai 1995). Anthropology has been complicit in the production of such locality, suggesting that alterity is located in a secret core. Secrecy has been used as a rhetorical device to demonstrate the successful penetration of a cultural core (whether or not the secrets thus penetrated are actually exposed in the ethnography). However, while secrecy may create boundaries, it also engages those excluded from the secret. The anthropologist may be excluded, but s/he may nevertheless share the performance of secrecy. The secret is contagious. Secrecy produces a moral binding. As a result of this, the presentation of secret lore in ethnography is often presented as a moral issue. Anthropologists have always been cautious about revealing what they consider to be secret information. As Godelier (1986: xiii) says:

> Knowledge is not a game without consequences. Every society has secrets that it protects and that protect it. To hand them carelessly over to the public without debate or precaution would not merely be treacherous or irresponsible, but would actually pervert the work of scientific investigation into a force of aggression and domination.

Godelier suggests that secrets of the Other should not be divulged. While the ethnographer's rapport enables him to penetrate secrets, his moral obligations prohibit him from bringing secret knowledge into the public domain. The disclosure of secrets is a morally ambiguous area.

While the issue of disclosure may be presented as a moral dilemma — and many anthropologists do present the publication of secrets as a moral issue — references to secrecy always convey authority to the ethnographer as subject. The anthropologist who 'reveals' secret lore and the anthropologist who conceals it use a similar rhetoric: the representation of a cultural core as secret. As Clifford suggests (1988: 158-59): 'Countless stories of concealment, revelation, and initiation are structured by a similar desire that posits secrets in order to reveal them, imagines an other with a true "within"'. Instead of conceptualising culture as an ongoing and inventive process, the metaphor of secrecy presents the core of culture as being unavoidably weakened by the destructive impact of foreign influences. Only when we recognize the resilience of secrecy will we be able to acknowledge secrecy as a mode of performance reproducing itself in a globalizing world. The secrets publicized in monographs are eventually reincorporated in performances of secrecy. The case of the carefully wrapped book demonstrates that published secrets are reframed as secret by initiates and non-initiates alike. This suggests that the performance of secrecy renders ownership of the secret problematic. The secret emerges in a performance between initiate and non-initiate. Although the initiates claim ownership of the secret, the presence of the uninitiated remains a condition for their claim. The globalization of initiates and non-initiates in a worldwide diaspora implies that this ownership is increasingly delocalized.

References

Appadurai, A. 1995, 'The Production of Locality', in: R. Fardon (ed.), *Counterworks: Managing the Diversity of Knowledge*, London & New York: Routledge, pp. 204-25.

Barth, F. (ed.) 1969, *Ethnic Groups and Boundaries: The Social Organization of Culture Difference*, Oslo: Universitets Forlaget.

Baum, R. 1999, *Shrines of the Slave Trade: Diola Religion and Society in Precolonial Senegambia*, New York & Oxford: Oxford University Press.

Bellman, B.L. 1984, *The Language of Secrecy: Symbols and Metaphors in Poro Ritual*, New Brunswick: Rutgers University Press.

Clifford, J. 1986, 'Introduction: Partial Truths', in: J. Clifford & G.E. Marcus (eds), *Writing Culture: The Poetics and Politics of Ethnography*, Berkeley & Los Angeles: University of California Press, pp. 1-26.

Clifford, J. 1988, *The Predicament of Culture: Twentieth-Century Ethnography, Literature, and Art*, Cambridge & London: Harvard University Press.

Clifford, J. 1990, 'Notes on (Field)notes', in: R. Sanjek (ed.), *Fieldnotes: The Makings of Anthropology*, Ithaca & London: Cornell University Press, pp. 47-70.

Clifford, J. & G.E. Marcus 1986, *Writing Culture: The Poetics and Politics of Ethnography*, Berkeley & Los Angeles: University of California Press.

Cohen, A.P. 1989, *The Symbolic Construction of Community*, London: Routledge (first published 1985).

De Jong, F. 1999a, 'Trajectories of a Mask Performance: The Case of the Senegalese *Kumpo*', *Cahiers d'Etudes Africaines* 153: 49-71.

De Jong, F. 1999b, 'The Production of Translocality: Initiation in the Sacred Grove in Southern Senegal', in: R. Fardon, W. van Binsbergen & R. van Dijk (eds), *Modernity on a Shoestring: Dimensions of Globalization, Consumption and Development in Africa and Beyond*, Leiden & London: EIDOS in association with the African Studies Centre Leiden and the Centre of African Studies London, pp. 315-40.

De Jong, F. 2000, 'Secrecy and the State: The Kankurang Masquerade in Senegal', *Mande Studies* 2: 153-73.

De Jong, F. 2001a, *Modern Secrets: The Power of Locality in Casamance, Senegal*, PhD thesis, University of Amsterdam.

De Jong, F. 2001b, 'Démasqué', *Etnofoor* 14 (2): 7-22.

De Jong, F. 2002, 'Politicians of the Sacred Grove: Citizenship and Ethnicity in Southern Senegal', *Africa* 72 (2): 203-20.

Evans-Pritchard, E.E. 1940, *The Nuer: A Description of the Livelihood and Political Institutions of a Nilotic People*, New York & Oxford: Oxford University Press.

Fabian, J. 1998, *Moments of Freedom: Anthropology and Popular Culture*, Charlottesville & London: University Press of Virginia.

Gable, E. 1997, 'A Secret Shared: Fieldwork and the Sinister in a West African Village', *Cultural Anthropology* 12 (2): 213-33.

Geertz, C. 1973, *The Interpretation of Cultures*, London: Fontana Press.

Geertz, C. 1988, *Works and Lives: The Anthropologist as Author*, Cambridge: Polity Press.

Godelier, M. 1986, *The Making of Great Men: Male Domination and Power among the New Guinea Baruya*, Cambridge: Cambridge University Press.

Griaule, M. 1948, *Dieu d'Eau. Entretiens avec Ogotemmêli*, Paris: Editions du Chêne.

Gupta, A. & J. Ferguson 1992, 'Beyond "Culture": Space, Identity and the Politics of Difference', *Cultural Anthropology* 7 (1): 6-23.

Jackson, J. 1990, '"I am a Fieldnote': Fieldnotes as a Symbol of Professional Identity', in: R. Sanjek (ed.), *Fieldnotes: The Makings of Anthropology*, Ithaca & London: Cornell University Press, pp. 3-33.

James, A., J. Hockey & A. Dawson (eds) 1997, *After Writing Culture: Epistemology and Praxis in Contemporary Anthropology*, London & New York: Routledge.

Malinowski, B. 1999 [1922], *Argonauts of the Western Pacific*, London: Routledge.

Malinowski, B. 1967, *A Diary in the Strict Sense of the Term*, London: Routledge & Kegan Paul.

Malkki, L.H. 1995, *Purity and Exile: Violence, Memory and National Cosmology among Hutu Refugees in Tanzania*, Chicago: Chicago University Press.

Piot, C. 1993, 'Secrecy, Ambiguity, and the Everyday in Kabre Culture', *American Anthropologist* 95 (2): 353-70.

Poppi, C. 1993, 'Sigma! The Pilgrim's Progress and the Logic of Secrecy', in: M.H. Nooter (ed.), *Secrecy: African Art that Conceals and Reveals*, New York & Munich: The Museum for African Art & Prestel, pp. 197-203.

Rabinow, P. 1977, *Reflections on Fieldwork in Morocco*, Berkeley, Los Angeles & London: University of California Press.

Said, E. 1989, 'Representing the Colonized: Anthropology's Interlocutors', *Critical Inquiry* 15: 205-27.

Sanjek, R. (ed.) 1990, *Fieldnotes: The Makings of Anthropology*, Ithaca & London: Cornell University Press.

Simmel, G. 1967, 'The Secret and the Secret Society', in: K.H. Wolff (ed.), *The Sociology of Georg Simmel*, New York: The Free Press (first printed 1950), pp. 307-76.

Stocking, G.W. 1983a, 'The Ethnographer's Magic: Fieldwork in British Anthropology from Tylor to Malinowski', in: G.W. Stocking (ed.), *Observers Observed: Essays on Ethnographic Fieldwork*, Madison: University of Wisconsin Press, pp. 70-120.

Stocking, G.W. 1983b, *Observers Observed: Essays on Ethnographic Fieldwork*, Madison: University of Wisconsin Press.

Taussig, M. 1999, *Defacement: Public Secrecy and the Labor of the Negative*, Stanford: Stanford University Press.

Van Beek, W.E.A. 1991, 'Dogon Restudied: A Field Evaluation of the Work of Marcel Griaule', *Current Anthropology* 32 (2): 139-67.

Van Binsbergen, W. 1991, 'Becoming a *Sangoma*: Religious Anthropological Fieldwork in Francistown, Botswana', *Journal of Religion in Africa* XXI (4): 309-44.

Van der Klei, J. 1989, *Trekarbeid en de Roep van het Heilige Bos: Het Gezag van de Oudste en Moderne Veranderingen bij de Diola van Zuid-Senegal*, Nijmegen: Iken.

10

The persistence of female initiation rites: Reflexivity and resilience of women in Zambia

Thera Rasing

This chapter focuses on female initiation rites in Zambia today and shows how Zambian women, in the context of a globalized environment, reflect on their culture and religion. It examines how initiation rites as part of their culture and religion are resilient to such an extent that they can still be performed in the same format as centuries ago. Despite many changes in society, the female initiation rite is a major institution that has remained important for women even in towns in present-day globalized and Christianized Zambia. The initiation rights are considered primordial and valuable for all women, not only for those who are soon to be getting married but also even for religious sisters. Women are showing reflexivity and resilience in their performance of these rites and in adapting them to modern urban life.

Introduction

Recent discussions on globalization have opened up perspectives upon the reflexivity of local people and the resilience of cultures. This chapter focuses on female initiation rites in Zambia today and seeks to make a point about the reflexivity of Zambian women and the resilience of culture in this region. It is based on fieldwork in the Zambian Copperbelt and Northern Province, regions that are predominantly occupied by people identifying themselves as belonging to the Bemba ethnic group. This is considered a dominant ethnic group and consists today of Bemba and Bemba-related groups that have spread over many parts of Zambia.

Female initiation rites (*cisungu*) are an intrinsic part of traditional culture and society. They have existed for many centuries in this region of matrilineal cultures[1] and have always been performed by ritual specialists (*banacimbusa*) who instruct and guide girls into womanhood and marriage.

Initiation rites remain important for women today despite the many social, religious, political and economic changes that have significantly altered Zambian society. Initially the slave trade, pre-colonial state formation, the introduction of Christianity and colonization brought about changes in society, predominantly in the sense of a shift in power — from locals to Westerners — and between men and women, centralizing men and marginalizing women. Both implied a cosmological change (Van Binsbergen 1992, Rasing 2001). More recently, urbanization and economic problems such as massive unemployment, reduced household incomes, a lack of medical care, and the rapid spread of diseases such as HIV/AIDS have brought about changes predominantly in the economic and health spheres (Ferguson 1999, Rasing 2001). One of the changes in Zambian society that this chapter focuses on is the Christianization of the majority of the population and the influence of the Catholic Church. Many Zambians adhere to the Catholic Church, primarily because the first and most important Catholic mission organization that came to Zambia in the late 19th century, popularly called the White Fathers, focused predominantly and successfully on the Bemba in their efforts to christianize the people (Werner 1991, Oger 1991). This has resulted in the Catholic Church becoming the largest church in Zambia, and one to which many women attach themselves for different reasons (Hinfelaar 1989, Rasing 2001).

The Catholic Church has raised the question of whether initiation rites can still be expressed in a traditional way, and whether they are being experienced in this way by urbanized and 'modern' women. The Church is trying to alter these rites as part of their policy of inculturation, in which several traditional customs are being christianized (Rasing 1995, 2001).

This chapter considers how the reflexivity and resilience of Zambian people are being shown in initiation rites for young girls and religious sisters so that they are still performed. All young girls have to experience an initiation rite, also those who want to become a religious sister. Initiation rites for religious sisters show the reflexivity and resilience of Zambians even more than initiation

---

[1] To a certain extent female initiation rites exist at a national level: in 1989 a picture of President Kaunda's daughter at her initiation rite was published in Zambian newspapers.

rites for ordinary girls do. By reflexivity I refer to how people consider their culture and traditions, while resilience is defined as the ways people adapt their cultural customs to new local conditions, and manage to continue these cultural customs despite pressure from institutions such as the Catholic Church. In addition this chapter analyses the tensions between women and the Catholic Church, and discusses how the Church is dealing with these rites. It starts with a description of initiation rites, which is followed by a section on traditional culture and religion. Next, the policy of the Catholic Church on culture in general and initiation rites in particular is examined, with details about the initiation rites for religious sisters. This is followed by a section on the changes in Zambian society, highlighting the reflexivity of Zambian women and the resilience of their culture to these rites.

Female initiation rites

Girls' initiation rites mark their passage from childhood to womanhood. Initiation emphasizes reproductive roles within marriage, domestic and agricultural duties, respect for elders and the novice's future husband, sexuality, and food taboos. Initiation is a rite of transition and sets out the basis for adult life by constructing a new identity for a woman (Richards 1956, La Fontaine 1986, Kratz 1994, Lutkehaus & Roscoe 1995). Initiation equips maturing individuals with the social attributes that a woman is supposed to have and deal with throughout her life. During initiation, boundaries between the genders, and between the initiated and uninitiated, are both constructed and deconstructed, and relationships with her lineage and her *nacimbusa* are established and confirmed. The novice is secluded and receives instructions during the rites that are performed by singing, dancing and displaying clay models (*mbusa*) that express traditional values.

In Zambia, as in many other societies, girls' initiation rites take place just after a girl starts menstruating for the first time. The novice moves from a passive to an active state. This also concerns her sexual life, although young girls are told not to indulge in sexual activity before marriage. Nevertheless, they learn that adulthood includes the joy of sexuality and that they can take the initiative in sexual relations with their husbands and participate actively during intercourse.

The rites include practical and religious or supernatural aspects as well. Spirits are thought to provide the novice with the menarche, the sign that she is fertile, and conception is related to the supernatural world, in particular to the ancestral spirits. During the rites, prayers are said to honour them. Furthermore, there is another type of spirit, whose name the novice is told at her initiation and which is also the name of her ritual specialist and her ancestral spirit. This spirit is thought to be present at other initiation rites and is honoured then. All women initiated by a particular ritual specialist have the name of that specialist and the spirit, and are considered the children of the ritual specialist and of her spirit. In this way, the name of the spirit is spread among a group of women initiated by the same ritual specialist or their kin. They are related to the land (region, country) of origin.

In analysing and interpreting initiation rites, classic anthropology affirmed a functionalist approach, while there is now a move towards a more diverse and eclectic approach, although the functionalist interpretation cannot be fully ignored. Turner's studies (1957, 1967, 1969), which negotiate functionalist and transactionalist views, have greatly influenced the scientific views of initiation rites. From a functionalist point of view, 'initiation is a patterned performance whose purpose is action to achieve transformed individuals but whose effect it is to demonstrate the power of knowledge and legitimize a continuing social order' (La Fontaine 1986: 179). Initiation rites express and confirm solidarity and unity among women. Norms and values concerning gender, production and reproduction, and cosmological ideas are passed on. Symbols and ritual contribute to the creation and maintenance of an inclusive cosmology and to the preservation of a social system through repetition. This does not mean that rites are conservative or ignore new elements, but the general world view expressed in them seems to be maintained. This is elaborated on in the section on reflexivity.

Critiques of the functionalist views have been expressed, among others, by Moore (1999), Lutkehaus and Roscoe (1995) and Simonsen (2000). Roscoe (1995) stated that in the development of the anthropological theory of initiation rites, analytical concepts have largely been developed on the basis of comparative studies rather than on one of the categories of those who practice them, implying that theories have incorporated 'etic' instead of 'emic' ideas of childhood and adulthood that may not coincide with these concepts in the local societies studied. In analysing urban initiation rites, Van Binsbergen (1998) uses the concept of virtuality. Virtuality is obtained when a certain socio-cultural item, for example a ritual, is transferred outside the context in which it originally functioned and from which it originally derived its meaning. The socio-cultural item has come to function in a new context so totally dissimilar to the original that it becomes effectively meaningless in its new context, except for some new meaning that it may acquire in this new context in ways totally unrelated to the original. 'Virtuality then is about disconnectivity, broken reference, de-contextualisation, through which yet formal continuity shimmers through' (Van Binsbergen 1998: 878). Although virtuality is an interesting concept, I do not fully agree with this analysis. Urban initiation may deal with disconnectivity as Van Binsbergen suggests, but the old meaning still applies in the urban setting, even though it was not invented there in the first place. In the rite the transformation of a girl into a woman, the novice's fertility, relations between fertility and agriculture, relations between the novice, her ancestral spirits, the 'blood spirit' and her future husband, all of whom are needed for procreation, and the ancient world view and the *mbusa* with their meanings, are affirmed. These are still relevant. The rites are not detached from socio-economic conditions. Rites contribute to structure by (re-)installing the boundaries between young and old, initiated and uninitiated. The creation of boundaries assists in the acceptance of new situations. These boundaries are conceptual collective ways of seeing reality and of classifying, for example, fashion, sexual and marital roles, ideas about law and order, and about cosmology and causality in terms of 'old fashioned' as opposed to 'modern'. Rites create order in exchange for obeisance to the ancestors.

Grimes (2000) takes a symbolic perspective to examine initiation rites. He stresses the role of power in rituals and emphasizes that initiation rites are just as important for the person concerned as for the community. He extends this point of view not only to small-scale societies but also to Western societies.

In this chapter, however, I focus on the reflexivity of the people who perform these rites and examine how resilience is shown in these rites in the context of globalization. In particular, attention will be paid to traditional leaders and church leaders of the Zambian Roman Catholic Church who seek to have a say in these rites. Studies by Jules-Rosette (1979) on female initiation rites for Independent Churches and those in the United Church of Zambia (UCZ) by Kangwa (1990) have shown that in both churches, rites are performed in a Christian way, emphasizing women's domestic role. Although initiation rites among Catholic women are unavoidably influenced by Christianity, these rites are performed in a quite traditional way, and seem to be almost unaffected by Christianity. This can be explained by the concept of reflexivity, as will be seen later.

The position of ritual leaders, *banacimbusa* in religion and culture

Initiation rites deal with cosmological views. These ideas have been scrutinized by Audrey Richards (1956) who studied and described the cosmological and sexual views of the Bemba in the 1930s. The ideas are similar to the views of neighbouring peoples, and we may perhaps speak of a Northern or Eastern Zambian cosmological view. Many of these ideas are still relevant in urban areas, albeit in a fragmented state.

The instructions in initiation rites are given by a tutor, a *nacimbusa* (pl. *banacimbusa*). This is sometimes translated as a 'traditional midwife' or 'mentrix'. However, these terms do not fit her role and function since her office is a combination of midwifery, mediation and teaching. She is a ritual specialist and well known for her knowledge of herbs, the spiritual world and midwifery, and she guides the young woman during the first few years of her married life. Many are traditional healers as well. For the lack of an appropriate translation, I use the Bemba word *nacimbusa*.

The *banacimbusa* claim to have inherited their skills from their paternal or maternal (classificatory) grandmother, whose spirit (*mupashi*) guides them.[2] Traditionally, *banacimbusa* were regarded as priestesses and as healers, *ng'anga* (Labreque 1931). Indeed, today many *banacimbusa* are still recognized as healers.

The *banacimbusa* are the transformers in rites: they transform and make the novice aware of what it means to be transformed. The *nacimbusa* has to take care of the proper rituals and is knowledgeable about everything concerning fertility, delivery, spirits and all the herbs, roots and medicines used during pregnancy. She is called the 'blood chief' (*mfumu wa mulopa*) and is thought to communicate with the 'blood spirit', which starts a girl's menstruation and, consequently, her fertility. The *nacimbusa* is the mediatrix between the spirit and the novice. The spirit appears to be of a certain category of spirits, perhaps higher than ancestral spirits, who people the land and monitor human fertility.

The position of the *banacimbusa* is related to religious ideas in the matrilineal society such as that of the Bemba. Before the 16th century, women had a central political and religious role and there was equality between men and women (Van Binsbergen 1992, Ahmed 1996). Women did not depend on men and were relatively autonomous. In the 16th century, when political and religious leadership was claimed by male chiefs, the social, economic, political and religious position of women altered but women continued to have important religious roles and could execute their functions to a large extent (Rasing 2001, see also Van Binsbergen 1992).

---

[2] Richards (1956) did not mention anything about spirits in connection with initiation rites. She stated that there were rumours that the skills of *banacimbusa* were inherited but having no evidence, she left this out of her reports. Etienne (White Fathers' archives, undated, but presumably from the 1930s), however, mentioned the involvement of spirits in initiation rites. Being a Catholic priest, he had a negative view of both these rites and spirits and although it is unlikely that he ever attended a rite, he mentioned that during these rites women often became possessed.

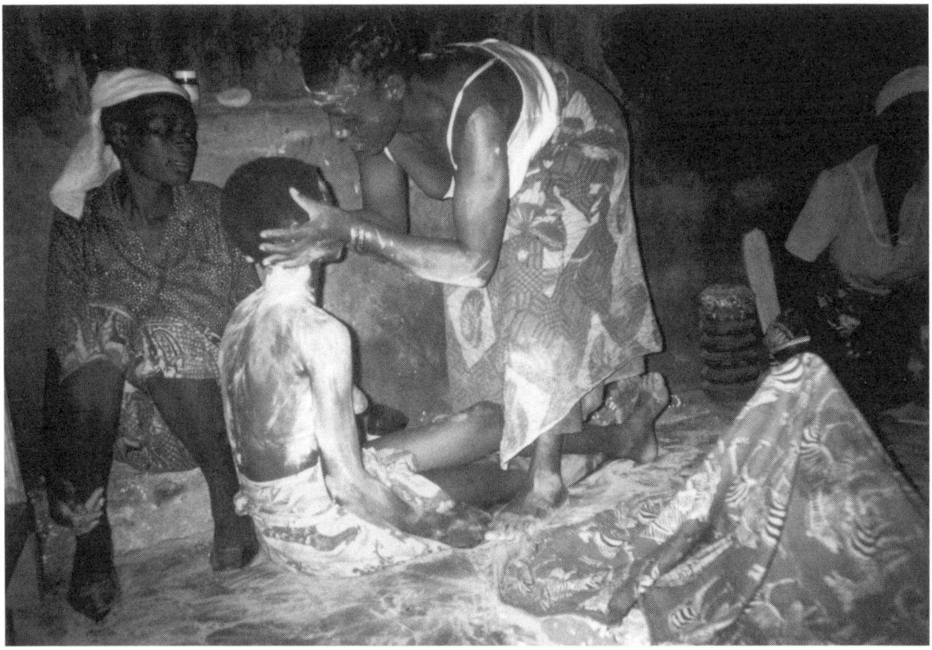

A *nacimbusa* applying *mpemba* (white chalk) to a novice's body to denote her relationship with the spiritual world
Photo: Thera Rasing

The women's central position was derived from the important role they played in this matrilineal society and their role in agricultural production. Women had a firm grip on the cosmic and symbolic order and had a central role in procreation and, therefore, in humankind. They were considered to have contacts with ancestral spirits and were holders of the domestic shrine. The *banacimbusa* were the main shrine-holders of the domestic ancestral shrines and of the *ngulu* (natural spirits) shrines, and hence were priestesses. The *banacimbusa* were strong women who had a mission through their inherited skills and their duty to initiate girls into womanhood. Their religious instructions, mainly given during initiation rites, were at the same time preparation for a girl's married life.

The *banacimbusa* also have political power. For instance, in the 1950s a European priest, who was thought to have too much inside information about initiation rites, was ordered by a *nacimbusa* to leave the country (see Rasing 2001) and she worked — using her political power — together with officials to ensure that the priest did in fact leave.

Women have a unique authority in this matter. While women were marginalized in terms of political power and could only claim the religious domain, they can still operate in political areas, emphasizing their important religious position and confirming the link between religion and political authority, as was the case before Christianity took root and before colonial rule. However, certain religious aspects remained in the hands of women. The initiation rite remained a female institution, performed by *banacimbusa* who kept their authority in the fields of these rites and human fertility.

Christianity takes root in Zambia

In the late 19th century, the first missionaries[3] arrived in Zambia with the specific aim of christianizing and civilizing the African people. They spread the gospel and taught mores that were common in Europe at that time, wanting to imprint these values on the local people and abolish indigenous customs and rituals that they considered pagan and immoral. The sisters of the Missionaries' Society of Our Lady of Africa (MSOLA), popularly called the White Sisters, arrived in the country in 1902. They were mainly occupied with teaching girls household tasks, childcare and hygiene, and worked as nurses.

The Catholic Church, as part of the global institution of Catholicism that aims at spreading a homogenizing Christian faith all over the world, has become

---

[3] Most Catholic missionaries belonged to the White Fathers, originally a French missionary organization that later included missionaries from all over Europe.

the largest church in Zambia. During the 20th century, local people adopted Christian ideas in addition to their cultural ideas. Christianity is a world religion that recently arrived locally as an aspect of globalization, with adherence to it, implying a belonging to the modern globalized world. Christianity has become part of a meaningful world view of Zambians.[4]

Christianity changed gender relations, tipping the balance in favour of men. The missionaries marginalized women and undermined women's positions in the home and in the villages. Even in church circles, women were pushed into the background and the missionaries imposed Western concepts of domesticity on Africans. They saw men as the essential elements of labour, while women were regarded as the wives and servants of their husbands (cf. Comaroff & Comaroff 1991, 1992, Hastings 1989). This resulted in the loss of traditional values and in a deterioration in the position of women.

The missionaries had a negative attitude towards sexuality in general and women in particular. Many offences against church discipline were of a sexual nature, with initiation rites *(cisungu)* considered as one of the main culprits.[5] Expressions of explicit (female) sexuality were considered to be potentially dangerous.[6] The missionaries, however, did not have access to initiation rites because the uninitiated — and particularly single men — were not allowed to attend. The White Sisters were also denied access to these rites since they too lived celibate lives. Nevertheless, when the missionaries gained more knowledge of what happened during the rites,[7] they tried to abolish them. Punishments such as exclusion from Holy Communion, excommunication or the withholding of baptism were stipulated. The missionaries considered the role of the *banacimbusa* to be evil. The *banacimbusa,* who were related to spirits, could not openly claim their position as priestess *vis-à-vis* the Christian

[4] Reasons for adhering to Christianity included access to education and the goods brought by the missionaries. The Catholic Church particularly appealed to the local people because it used statues and images of saints that resembled the images of mythical figures. Moreover, Catholic priests used certain rituals that resembled local ones, for instance, baptism in times of danger of death (*lubatisho lwa pa kufwa*). Women were also attracted by the image of Mary, the mother of Jesus (cf. Hinfelaar 1989; and for other parts of Africa: Green 1999, Notermans 1999).

[5] The other cultural practices the church severely opposed were succession by ritual intercourse (*bupyani*) and the use of the nuptial vessel (*akanweno, inweno*) for ritual ablutions throughout married life. The local people considered it a sacred symbol and a means of ensuring fidelity. The missionaries, however, considered the link between this vessel and the ancestors as ancestral worship, and therefore condemned its use.

[6] Cf. Comaroff & Comaroff (1991) who describe this for Botswana.

[7] The Catholic missionary Labreque (1931) wrote a book in which he painted a reasonably accurate picture of traditional culture, including a section on initiation rites. He described these without imposing any personal judgment.

missionaries. As a consequence of Christianity, the traditional religion and the office of traditional female priests were forbidden or at least marginalized.

However, many of the cultural activities forbidden by the missionaries continued to be performed, often in secret. Richards (1956) mentioned that, near mission stations, rites were curtailed due to punishments by the missionaries but the elaborate rite she described was in fact performed near a mission station, so their power may not have been as great as she suggested. They failed to convince people to withdraw from 'pagan' practices and the women continued to perform initiation rites.

The Church's changed policy on initiation rites

Today, many Catholic priests recognize that initiation rites are painful for the church. Priests and religious sisters admit that during initiation women teach certain admirable values. But although priests acknowledge that they were wrong in trying to abolish these rites, and claim that they see positive aspects in them, many said that the rites should be changed and christianized.[8] From the late 1950s onwards, a shift towards greater appreciation of initiation and a changing attitude towards traditional religions emerged.[9] Traditional cultures and values were re-evaluated (cf. Dondeyne 1967) and required thorough study to see if and how they could be combined with Christianity (Gundani 1994).

In the 1980s the Catholic Church stipulated a policy of enculturaltion,[10] a Catholic term that refers to the adoption of the Christian message in a certain

[8] This is not really new. In 1928 women, together with a missionary from the Dutch Reformed Church in the eastern part of Zambia, suggested that the church consider organizing a Christian initiation rite, *cilangizo*. Initially this rite was only performed for girls belonging to Protestant churches but it was later also extended to other Christians. The combination of Christian and traditional aspects made the rite attractive (Verstraelen-Gilhuis 1982: 184). Following this example, Catholics tried to organize Christian initiation rites (see also Phiri 1998). In 1936, a Catholic *nacimbusa* constructed a Christian initiation rite but it was not adopted by priests. In 1940, Catholics tried again to organize a Christian rite in Zambia but failed (Rasing 2001).

[9] In the late 1950s, the policy of bringing initiation rites more in line with the Christian faith was taken up by certain Catholic priests (Hinfelaar 1989: 199). This was the prelude to the Second Vatican Council (1962-1965) that aimed, among many other things, at more freedom in adapting the liturgy to African culture.

[10] Enculturation started a long time ago (although the word was not used) with the question of African music in church. Oger (1991: 122) wrote that African music was introduced into public worship in the cathedral in Ilondola in 1923. The question of Africanizing church music has been widely discussed since the 1931 General Missionary Conference. Enculturation came to be emphasized and encouraged during and after the Second Vatican Council. A synod on enculturation was set up entitled

culture.[11] This term has recently been replaced by 'dialogue'. Enculturation or dialogue is encouraged by the church as a way of meeting local people and is considered a method of learning more about local culture, but it may be assumed that this 'locality' is constructed by lay people in ways agreed to by priests. In fact, it is a means of facilitating the adoption of the Christian faith and of gaining access to, and control over, cultural aspects in order to use or alter them. Through enculturation, the church can exert power and influence.[12] As part of enculturation, European priests also want initiation rites to be christianized.

In my interviews with European priests, they claimed that they were not against initiation *per se*, but only against the certain parts of it they regarded as uncivilized or brutal. An initiation would be acceptable for priests if the (ritual) beating of the novice, which sometimes happen during the rites, and the emphasis on her lowly position towards elders and her future husband were omitted, if the novice were fully dressed, Christian prayers could be said, parts of the Bible could be read and the thanking of the ancestors by clapping and rolling on the floor were omitted. African priests, however, consider these rites as the correct teaching of values and good preparation for marriage, which should thus be preserved. There is a definite gap in appreciation between African and European priests.

The Zambian priests I interviewed said that initiation rites are not oppressive for women. According to them, christianizing initiation rites means that the actual sense of initiation is lost, and the rites are destroyed. When some parts of the rite are omitted and Christian aspects are added, the meaning is believed to change. This is important and helps clarify the problems of christianizing initiation rites.

Despite the generally more tolerant attitude of priests, European priests still consider the rite pagan (Chakanza 1998), immoral, and oppressive for women (Rasing 2001). Traditional customs are considered a hindrance to genuine advancement.

'Walking with Christ towards the year 2000', starting in 1993 and ending in 1998. The subjects discussed included family life, initiation, anointing, the parish structure, justice and peace.

[11] Protestant churches use the word 'conceptualization' for the same process.

[12] For some, the dancing group *buomba* (minstrels), which sings and dances at special masses in church, is an example of enculturation. This group started in the early 1990s and has spread to different parts of Zambia. The groups are considered 'traditional Bemba' and refer to the people who used to perform songs and dances at the chief's palace. There is much discussion about these groups. Some also perform initiation rites

The church wants to have a say, not only because it seeks more Christians with a profound faith but also because it wishes to influence people in a moral way. The church condemns many aspects that have to do with sexuality, such as initiation rites. Morality and sexuality are part of all religions. Jansen (1993: 159) stated that religions are moral systems, and as such are preoccupied with controlling morality and sexuality (see also Neuhaus 1990). People's moral behaviour influences the community but not all religious systems define sex as a moral issue in the way Christianity does. Besides extramarital relationships, an age-old phenomenon, new issues arose in the 20th century: contraception, abortion[13] and HIV/AIDS.

Some European priests suggest that initiation can be useful for informing girls about HIV/AIDS and they regard initiation as a way of reducing its spread. However, while the *banacimbusa* see the need to minimize the number of new HIV/AIDS cases, only a few reported instructing girls directly about HIV/AIDS. They teach about the dangers of illicit sex, emphasizing that one can contract diseases from extramarital relationships. According to these *banacimbusa,* the specific illness concerned is not important — the girls have been warned that HIV/AIDS does not belong to the repertoire of initiation rites.[14]

Tensions between priests and women over initiation rites

Some priests have taken the initiative to stimulate a dialogue with women on initiation rites as a way of changing the rites. Today priests recognize that *banacimbusa* are important and seek their collaboration to gain more information about the topic.

Individual priests who were interested in initiation looked for ways to combine initiation rites with confirmation or baptism, or to bless girls in church towards the end of the rite. But these efforts failed for various reasons. In many parishes priests are trying to take the initiative by setting up groups of women to teach girls because of the assumed immoral behaviour of the youth and the

since they are supposed to be traditional and claim they should teach traditional matters. They also initiate priests.

[13] For instance, see Bishop Mpundu's claim that abortion is shameful, *Zambia Daily Mail*, 1 February 1998.

[14] According to Zambians, the concept of illness after sexual infidelity is very old and is called *icifuba*. It is said to have the same characteristics as AIDS and cannot be cured. This illness is caused by the breaking of a taboo concerning sexuality. This idea that improper sex is dangerous dates back some centuries.

increasing number of divorces.[15] These groups are taught by a *nacimbusa* who is supposed to teach from a booklet containing texts from the Bible (St John's and St Matthew's gospels, Acts) and are supposed to integrate Christian aspects into traditional rites. However in these groups, rites are also performed in traditional ways using clay models and songs, and missionaries still complain that they have no control over them. The church is trying to create an infrastructure but has failed to implement this policy. In only a few rites can Christian aspects be observed, usually a Christian prayer that is said at the start or when food is served.

The majority of women, on the other hand, do not want to reveal much to priests and do not want them to influence the ways the rites are performed.[16] For many, the idea that a priest attend a rite is unacceptable. Initiation should be secret and private, and no man, and certainly no celibate (European) man, is supposed to be involved. If it were merged with Christian issues and brought into the church, the rite would be publicly performed and would lose its meaning. There are three aspects at stake here: a religious aspect, namely that of Christianity as opposed to traditional religion in which priests and women each defend and support their own religion, the gender aspect, and the aspect of secrecy, as women consider the rites secret and private, while the priests want them to be more open.[17]

Initiation rites deal with secrets and secrecy. What happens in the rites should not be heard beyond their confines to prevent uninitiated persons from knowing or hearing anything. One should not speak about it, particularly not when uninitiated people (men or young people) are within earshot. Also, what is

---

[15] Whether the percentage of marriage break-ups is increasing is a matter of debate, as statistics are not available. The claim that divorce is on the increase is often made by clergy, laity and in the literature. See, for instance, Chondoka (1988). Two points must be made here, however. Firstly, the number of divorces has no doubt increased but that does not say anything about the number of divorces per 100 weddings conducted. Moreover, in (pre-)colonial times marriages were not registered, let alone divorces. The claims are not based on statistics. See also Larsson (1991).

[16] This can be concluded from the following event that happened during my fieldwork. At a meeting of a Nazareth group, the women discussed the fact that in a neighbouring town a Nazareth group had invited a priest to attend an initiation rite. The women present at the meeting protested strongly, repeatedly saying: 'Initiation rites and wedding ceremonies are for women only' (*cisungu no bwinga ca banamayo beka beka fye*), and 'It is a case for women' *(mulandu wa banamayo*), implying that they might claim their right in court.

[17] Occasionally, individual priests were, and still are, invited to attend parts of initiation rites, but apparently most of the clay models and sexual aspects are not revealed to them (see Rasing 1995). In 1992 I attended a rite in an urban area, part of which the parish priest was allowed to attend. In 1995 I attended a rite in a village every night for four weeks. Here a priest was allowed to be present on only one night.

taught during the rite is considered secret, concerning mainly knowledge about sexuality and marriage. This is something between a husband and wife, and should not be talked about with others. It is visualized and symbolized in various ways during the rites. Hence the secret knowledge demarcates a border, both in initiation rites and in marriage.

Women consider the rites as a primordial fact, as a custom that they have to perform. They are thought to be given by the ancestors, and have to be continued. In this way the rites are linked to the past but also to the present and future. They are thought to be related to spirits, something the church opposes. Moreover, according to women, the rites should be performed in a particular, traditional way, otherwise they would be misleading and would not teach the novice the right things. So even though they are Christians, many women continue to adhere to their traditional religion.

The rites concern the construction of womanhood, menstruation and female sexuality, and should be kept away from the male-dominated church, for these are subjects to be discussed neither in church nor with men. Their daughters have to be taught about adult life but in this respect membership of any one church is irrelevant. Women stressed that even in a modern, urban context, they have to perform these rites because a woman's role in sexuality is as important in marriage today as it was in the past. This is shown by the symbols, rituals and taboos concerning sexuality that are taught in the rites in the same way as they were in the past. They are still valuable. The construction of female identity, as imprinted by the rites, remains central but in new ways.

Thus the missionaries and the women have different and contradicting interests. The church seeks to incorporate ideas on initiation into the church while women refuse to have the rites as part of church matters. They have a sub-discourse within the hegemony of the church that is provoking tensions between priests and women. Women have a diplomatic and diffuse attitude and operate in a way that is beneficial to them. They overtly adhere to Christianity, while at the same time they perform rituals that belong to the traditional religion. In their performances of initiation rites they stick to the old format and keep the rites away from the missionaries. In this regard, women have 'won the battle', while missionaries are giving up the fight at a time when the Roman Catholic Church is still seeking ways to christianize initiation rites and discuss the topic as part of its Synod.

Ritual leaders in the context of globalization

In the 1960s, when the churches were more positive about initiation rites and tried to chrisitanize them, Catholic women in church lay groups appointed other women to teach their daughters. These women, called *mamakalale* (grandmother from the town), are Catholic women who are considered to be similar to *banacimbusa*, even though they did not inherit their skills from their grandmothers. Since they are Christian, one would expect them to teach in a Christian way but in fact their teaching is performed in a traditional way. So within the hegemony of the church, women find their own personal space in which they celebrate their own religion.

Although among Christians the ideal is that *banacimbusa* are Christian, and Catholic among Catholic people, in practice many Christians prefer famous *banacimbusa* for their daughters, and always look for a *nacimbusa* who comes from the same region as the novice. Traditional aspects are important and are incorporated in Christian rites. The *banacimbusa*, as traditional priestesses, accept the Christian perspective but continue their own religion at the same time. So these two types of religion are parallel and *banacimbusa* use both. In this way the *banacimbusa* remain priestesses and mediate across boundaries. Thus, apart from Christianity, which is shown publicly by attending mass and membership of a lay group, aspects of traditional religion continue.

There is rivalry between these *banacimbusa* and *mamakalale*: both perform initiation rites but the rivalry tends to be over payments.[18] The one who teaches has to be paid handsomely because of her important job. In addition, the payment is a sign of honour to the *nacimbusa* and to the spirit whose skills she has inherited. Since the *mamakalale* has not inherited her skills from a spirit, she is usually paid less. Competition between the *banacimbusa* and *mamakalale* about money is understandable when considered in the Zambian context of economic decline, debasement and humiliation. Zambians used to be part of the modern world but have become marginalized (Ferguson 1999, Rasing 2001). Ferguson sees this as disconnectivity and uses the word 'abjection' to describe the process of being thrown aside, expelled or discarded.

However, everyone recognizes that the real *banacimbusa* are the best ones when it comes to performing a rite. They are considered to be knowledgeable, to perform better and explain the *mbusa* more clearly because they have inherited these skills and are guided by their ancestral spirit. Real knowledge is

---

[18] It is unclear how much money is paid for a rite. Generally, women claimed that real *banacimbusa* do not ask for money but leave it up to the parents of the girls concerned to decide how much importance they attribute to the initiation of their daughters and consequently how much they want to pay. The *bamamakalale* may ask little beforehand but are often disappointed afterwards and ask for more money and presents to be given, such as a *citenge* (a cloth), a chicken, beer and sometimes other items. This frequently creates bad feelings. It is also a reason why some people do not ask the woman who initiated their first daughter to perform the rite for their second daughter. This never happens when the rites are performed by a *nacimbusa*.

the central dispensation one receives through inheriting the spirit of a *nacimbusa*. Such a *nacimbusa* has much more power and authority. The experience and knowledge of the *banacimbusa* gives them the authority that is incorporated into ritual structure and recreated by their ritual roles. The *mbusa* are thought to convey knowledge and it is believed that only a *nacimbusa* who has inherited the skill from her (classificatory) grandmother can make these *mbusa* and explain their meanings. These sacred objects are believed to be given by the ancestor and to be related to the ancestral spirit and the 'blood spirit'. The majority of the rites are, therefore, performed by *banacimbusa*.

The *banacimbusa*'s claim of contact with a spirit refers to a claim on tradition, on the past, on the continuation of the rites performed in the same way as they have always been and in the way the ancestral spirits tell them. In addition, for women, *banacimbusa* are still important people to be consulted in the event of marital or sexual problems. Women usually ask advice from a *nacimbusa* instead of from someone from the church, even though the churches have groups in which marital problems are discussed.

In addition, initiation rites performed by *banacimbusa* who come from the same area as the novice can play an important role in the reproduction of ethnic identities, in particular in urban contexts. This is shown by the competition over cultural claims by other women.

Youth opinions about initiation rites

Let us now turn to young girls who were raised in town in a modernized and Christian environment, to see how they experienced their initiation.

Before being initiated, young girls do not know — or at least are not supposed to know — about the initiation rites. It is, therefore, difficult to get information from them beforehand. Young girls have no say about participating in these rites: they are ordered by their (grand)mothers to experience the rite and during it the *nacimbusa* has the power and authority to order the novice to do and undergo certain acts. This authority and power, based on hierarchy and knowledge, is an aspect of the rite.

The girls I interviewed after their initiation rites all claimed that they had learned to take responsibility, which is good preparation for their future lives and marriage, mainly because the teachings are about hardship in life. 'They teach you that life isn't easy. So it is mainly about perseverance.' Also, some girls said: 'It gives you an identity. Somehow it gives you a sense of belonging.' The claim that it gives an identity and a sense of belonging points to the changes in identity, from child to adult, and more precisely, what it means to be a woman and to become part of the world of women. Girls said they considered themselves different from those who have not been initiated. In the rite they felt that a change in female self-understanding is evinced. Generally, people claim that the behaviour of initiated girls is different from that of uninitiated girls.

Girls claim to have learned a lot, such as taking responsibility, feeling grown up, and are considered adults by others. The knowledge they get is different from what they are taught at school: the school curriculum covers human biology and procreation but they all consider most of the knowledge taught in the initiation rites as valuable. Although it may seem backward or to conflict with Western knowledge that is taught in school, girls always seem to appreciate the fact that the knowledge revealed during the rite offers lessons for life and imprints a new and adult identity. In addition to any knowledge received, the experience of the rite and the fact of becoming a full member of society are equally or even more important to the girls.

Initiation rites for sisters

Among the people who adher to Catholicism, a minority of young women become religious sisters. Two religious congregations that were set up by two Zambian Catholic bishops with the assistance of Western religious sisters have included traditional initiation rites at a certain stage in the novices' curriculum before they fully become a sister, in addition to the church rites they experience when they take their vows.[19]

Surprisingly, these rites are performed with the consent of Zambian bishops and follow the same format as the rites for lay women. This has been condemned by missionaries and priests since the early 20th century onwards, as we have seen. The issue of traditional initiation rites among religious sisters raises questions about the appropriateness of these rites for religious sisterhood.

Some sisters did not experience an initiation rite at their menarche because they were being educated in institutional environments where the rites were not practised, but the majority of the sisters I interviewed had experienced the ritual of the *ukusolwele*, the ritual in the bush, as part of the initiation rite.[20] Thus a lot

---

[19] The congregations that perform these rites are the Sisters of the Child Jesus, founded in Mbala-Mpika Diocese in Northern Province, a predominantly Bemba and Bemba-related area but spread all over Zambia, and among the Sisters of Mercy in Mansa Diocese in Luapula Province, an area that is occupied by Aushi, Ngombo and others but who claim to be related to the Bemba, and often refer to themselves as Bemba. The initiation rites for the Sisters of the Child Jesus take place just before they take their final vows. Among the Sisters of Mercy this takes place at the time of their first vows but they are considering changing this to the time of the final vows.

[20] In this ritual they are anointed with medicine and are told about menstruation.

A novice dancing during the coming-out part of the initiation rite
Photo: Thera Rasing

of religious sisters experience two initiation rites — one at their menarche before they start living in a convent, and another at the time of their vows. There is a parallel with lay Bemba girls: they have the ritual of *ukusolwele* in the bush when they first menstruate, while other parts of the initiation rites are postponed until their wedding, which is similar to the initiation rite they experienced at their menarche. A 'wedding ceremony' for religious sisters is performed when they take their vows and hence are 'married' to God.

The initiation is performed in a non-Christian way, using clay models. The same ritual acts are performed as in the initiation rite (*cisungu*).[21] A sister explained: 'It is to be taught about our tradition. To be taught by experience, instead of by hearing it, like in school, and to become responsible women.'

Religious sisters experience the same initiation rites as lay girls but in initiation rites for sisters reference is made to the Bible, mainly to Genesis. Religious sisters as well as lay women claim that these rites are performed as part of the traditional culture in which they were raised. The sisters explained that they should know these traditional values about sexuality and traditional norms because in their lives as sisters they may come across people who have problems due to a lack of or improper performance of traditional rituals. 'It is good preparation for life: they learn about hardship, that is what they experience, also in the community. We are respected more since we know more about these things.' However, it can be concluded that experiencing such a rite is important for the novice herself, whether she is a religious sister or a lay girl.

Cultural aspects are important. As one sister explained: 'We want sisters in their full cultural background, we want to bring the real Zambian women into Christianity, into sisterhood'. Consequently, after experiencing a rite, religious

[21] In these rites the novice is taken to the bush where the same rituals as in an ordinary initiation ceremony are performed around certain trees. During these rites a novice only wears a slip of cloth, she has to crawl on the ground and is hidden under a *citenge*. She is taught about the beads (that are given to a woman at her wedding ceremony and used to attract a husband). The novice's mother is symbolized by the mother superior. She has to welcome her daughter from the bush at the end of the rite. The ritual of taking fire (*ukutekensho*) is performed to remove the ban on fire because during her initiation she is not allowed to come near a fire. During the rite the novice frequently has to thank (*ukushikulo*) the ancestors in a traditional way by rolling on the ground and clapping. The novice has to perform the ritual cleansing that is supposed to be performed after sexual intercourse. In this rite it is explained as: 'This means that one has to be good to the community' (a couple that is not cleansed after sexual intercourse can endanger the community). At the coming out, the novice has to dance with rattles around her ankles and wrists, an act that is always performed during the final stage of the rite. The novice is taught household tasks, about marriage and family life with the emphasis on social living, and other traditional values and norms on how to behave, how to dress, about hygiene, how to treat visitors, how to serve food, and show respect, in particular towards elders.

sisters feel more complete and more accepted by the community. They perceive themselves as adults and subsequently feel more responsible. They are considered adults both by themselves and by others, and they gain wisdom from their culture. They also consider themselves more female, as one sister said: 'You appreciate your gender more'.

Through initiation, religious sisters may be made to perceive themselves as real women but may also be considered asexual and genderless. While sisters claim they consider themselves as adult women, they are, sociologically, seen as neither men nor women. The rites seem to confirm the genderless identity of sisters. Their initiation rites appear to be a culturally accepted way of becoming a ritual woman. By showing them aspects of marital life, represented by *mbusa*, and the sexual act related to the cosmological view, *banacimbusa* transform sisters into ritual women since they cannot be considered women (wives or mothers) in the cultural and sociological sense. They have a ritual status higher than ordinary women. Cosmologically, sisters are nearer to God or Lesa than common people.

For some parents it is problematic when their daughter wishes to become a religious sister, especially if they have only one daughter.[22] This may also be a reason why initiation rites for sisters are performed because after they have been properly initiated they are considered close to 'real' women.

As a consequence of their voluntarily chosen profession, sisters do not reproduce. This remains a problem for many religious sisters and their parents, and constitutes the main reason why sisters leave religious sisterhood. A sister who had been initiated explained: 'We are women, we are fertile, so we have to thank the ancestors for our fertility.' During their initiation rites, sisters also perform the ritual honouring of the spirits in the bush. This is an important part of the initiation rite that cannot be left out and is performed in all initiation rites, also for lay girls, since through this ritual, the spirit of fertility, the so-called 'blood spirit' is honoured. It is the spirit that is thought to provide women with fertility. Through this ritual one becomes the child of the blood spirit. Although in the rite for sisters this ritual may also be seen as asking the ancestors for forgiveness for the fact that she has voluntarily given up her gift of parenthood, I suggest the most important meaning is that she becomes a 'child of the spirit', and is subsequently recognized as belonging to a specific group of women.

It is the superiors in the congregation who want sisters to be initiated, and these rites are favoured by the local laity, African priests and some African

[22] Parents have to give their consent if their daughter wishes to become a religious sister. Sometimes sisters want to leave the sisterhood but in most cases fellow sisters know this is because the parents do not want their daughter to become a sister.

bishops. They are organized and performed by *banacimbusa* and lay women.[23] It may be explained as a way for the *banacimbusa* to reclaim their previous religious role as priestesses of traditional religion.

Yet the performance of initiation rites for religious sisters and the need to teach them about sexuality in detail remains debatable and is a multifaceted matter that raises questions hinging on traditional issues as well as on issues of church authority. In Zambian society, women have authority and are the owners of their body and of their sexuality. For sisters, the question of sexuality and the human body is complex. They are taught sexual points, for example, how to 'dance' moving their pelvis in a way that attracts men, and other aspects concerning sexuality. While learning this by experiencing these rites, it appears that religious sisters also have authority over their own body and sexuality and learn to have sexual control over their body. But they are supposed to refrain from sexual life. Moreover, religious sisters belong to a religious congregation and to the bishop of the specific diocese where they are working and have to obey the bishop. As such, they are 'owned' by the hierarchy of the Catholic Church but because initiation rites for religious sisters are performed by traditional female religious leaders, in the same format as initiation rites for lay women, sisters become a child of the traditional religious leaders. In these rites, relationships with the sister's lineage and her *nacimbusa* are established and confirmed. Hence they are also 'owned' by their *nacimbusa* and her spirit. This may lead to personal conflicts.

Furthermore, the fact that initiation rites are compulsory for religious sisters reveals that experiencing an initiation rite — including being shown the *mbusa,* the sexual act and the knowledge that is revealed — is important for a woman regardless of whether she voluntarily chooses to refrain from sexual relationships and motherhood. Since she is a Bemba woman, she has to experience this rite and become a child of a *nacimbusa*, and know the traditional knowledge that is passed on through the generations. She has to know her ancestors, the spiritual world, and be part of it. So, the rites are a symbolic way of becoming an adult and being Bemba, irrespective of whether one is a Christian as well.

---

[23] Other people attending these rites included the novice's grandmother and father's sister (or a representative). Also for rites for religious sisters it is important that the *nacimbusa* is from the same area as the novice. All the sisters who have been initiated attend the rites and drink traditional beer. The novices do not know or at least are not supposed to know about this initiation rite beforehand.

Women's changed socio-economic position

Female initiation rites can be traced back to at least 400 AD (cf. Roberts 1976: 32, Ahmed 1996: 12) but before analysing the continuing performance of urban initiation rites in present-day Zambia, we first have to understand the many changes that have taken place in Zambian society over the past few centuries, partly due to (proto)globalization, and the context in which the rites are performed today. I have already described the influence of Christianity on Zambian culture but many other changes have also taken place.

From the 1960s onwards, due to urbanization, initiation rites were more often performed in towns, where about half of the Zambian population lived. The urban population is composed of various ethnic groups and many of these groups perform female initiation rites. Subsequently, women from different ethnic groups get together to attend a rite.

Further in the past and over the last few centuries, women have moved from having a central role in the villages and in religion and politics to a more marginalized position due to the *bena ngandu* rule of male chiefs and subsequent pre-colonial state formation, colonialism, Christianity and migration to urban areas. Before the colonial time, and particularly before the 16th century, *banacimbusa* had both political and religious power, with the position probably of chief. With the coming of the chiefs of the *bena ngandu* who belonged to a particular ethnic group that started to rule the Bemba area and whose name they have taken over, these predominantly male chiefs took over political and religious power.

Furthermore, women are no longer attracted to the traditional system of agriculture in which they used to have an important role. Formal education for girls, changing family patterns in urban areas and rapid urban class formation have all served to disengage an increasing number of women from farming. Yet even in urban areas, the role of women in farming is important to families, albeit at a reduced level, either for household consumption or for generating income. Women still tend to be identified with their role in agriculture as food producers, in particular with hoeing. This implies, at least in their own eyes, a certain autonomy *vis-à-vis* their own labour and produce. 'Women tend to think of their labour effort in terms of being part of a natural order to ensure adequate food production and basic survival of their dependants and themselves' (Bryceson 1995: 8, cf. Richards 1939). Obviously, the natural order Bryceson appeals to is socially constructed. Yet, I think it is precisely this construction of the natural order that emphasizes the role of women in agriculture and that is expressed in daily narratives and in initiation rites.

Men dominate the formal economy due to Western colonial ideas, to the introduction of capitalism and the exploitation of the copper mines in the late

1920s. The informal sector was occupied by urban women in the early days of the towns in the late 1920s, and it is still dominated by women but, as a result of class formation and formal education, women have also gained access to the formal sector. Due to the current economic situation, men have started to lose their jobs, and incomes are insecure for those still in employment. Women continue to generate income from other activities. At present, women can increasingly be seen engaging in trade, often across impressive distances. Women used to be the mainstay of the traditional economy based on agriculture but they are currently forming the backbone of the Zambian economy by having paid jobs and engaging in trade, a vital sector of the country's economy in today's uncertain economic situation.

The importance of kinship structures is dwindling. Women are experiencing increasing difficulty in successfully appealing to traditional kinship structures in which they had a prominent role under the matrilineal system. Kinship lines are negotiated and offset against economic benefits. The matrilineal system still exists but is vanishing and the matrilocal setting has disappeared.

The state, which has come to be an important institution, has a predominantly male bias. Women have little access to political functions and power (except for issues concerning initiation rites, as already mentioned). Christianity, another important institution, is also dominated by men. On the one hand it has been a liberalizing force for women, while on the other it has been oppressive. Women are being marginalized in the political, religious and social spheres.

These socio-economic and political changes have led to an imprinting of Western concepts of womanhood. This has amounted to a certain deconstruction of womanhood for Zambian women: their important role as the centre of the matrilineal extended family has decreased, men are supposed to be the breadwinners, and their significant role in religion has vanished. Changes in society, such as urbanization, modernity, a declining economy and globalization, are triggering a search for fixed orientation points and action frames, as well as determined efforts to affirm old boundaries and construct new ones. In this, ethnic identity is a central concept (Meyer 1998, Meyer & Geschiere 1998, Inda & Rosaldo 2002). This may explain the importance ascribed to the fact that the *nacimbusa* and the novice have to originate from the same area and to belong to the same ethnic group to which the spirit is thought to be related.

Resilience of culture and religion, and the reflexivity of women concerning initiation rites

To analyse the persistence of initiation rites in urban Zambia today, the concept of reflexivity is useful. Reflexivity in this sense does not mean the awareness of the background and position of the social researcher (cf. Hammersley & Atkinson 1995). Instead, the concept refers here to an understanding of how Zambians create specific forms and domains as arenas of reflexivity. The positive and negative aspects, the marginalization as well as the creativity of globalization are debated, lived and experienced. Forms and domains of such reflexivity are both cultural and historical, shaped by prevalent sociological and economic circumstances and by aspirations and imaginations of certain groups. Reflexivity on cultural and religious aspects has always existed but through the process of globalization the form and domain of reflexivity may change in nature and in quality more rapidly than before. Interesting questions to now consider are how, in the globalization process in which many changes in society have taken place, women reflect on their culture and how culture is resilient to such an extent that initiation rites can still be performed and experienced.

For Zambian women, the performance of initiation rites is a form and domain of reflexivity. Initiation rites are related to the private and concealed domain of the inner quarters of family life, and this rite is an intimate issue as well as an intimate experience. Large parts of it are performed secluded from the 'normal' social world, in the bush and in a room inside the house separated from other daily activities. Moreover, the rite mainly deals with issues that are private and concern the home, husband-and-wife relationships and sexuality, while in a sense these private issues may also affect the whole community.

Zambians maintain relationships with other parts and aspects of the world. They keep links open and do not create boundaries but are looking for ways to open them up. They adhere easily to Christianity, have adapted to a quite Western lifestyle, and use many items that are alien to their own culture. They reflect on how globalization is or should be transformed to local circumstances and imaginations. Local discourses, debates and discussions revolve around the question of whether and which elements of globalization can fruitfully be used. They deliberately adopt new items and dismiss what they consider useless.[24]

---

[24] This can be seen for instance in the organization and performance of kitchen parties, which are common among working-class women in urban Zambia today. These parties are based on and have the format of an ancient ritual performed as the final part of the wedding ceremony, but are combined with what Zambians believe are elements of bridal showers as performed in the United States, at which Western kitchen utensils are given to the bride (Rasing 1999).

Concerning initiation rites, however, women stick as far as possible to the format in which these rites are supposed to be performed, since this is the way it should be done, according to them. Changes due to compression and curtailment or as a result of omitting or adding small parts do not change a basic centuries-old symbolic structure but are responses to the modernization of daily life. Despite minor changes, the rites' central message and meaning have remained the same over the course of time. Major alterations of ideological content, like those stressed by priests from Christian churches, however, would change the symbolism and ideology of the rites. For this reason, women prefer to keep them separate from church matters and certainly away from any interference by priests, even though the church's lay organizations may provide a ready setting for the mobilization of women. Moreover, transformations in the performance of these rites may occur rapidly as they shift from the private to the public sphere. This is what the Catholic Church seeks to reach in its policy of opening up these rites to bring them more into the open, and to add Christian elements while certain traditional aspects are omitted.

Zambian people, like people in all societies responding to globalization, show resilience. This resilience emphasizes not a return but a continuation of a proud consciousness of their own time-honoured resources of norms and values, world views, religion and forms of social and political organization. The resilience seems to restore the balance against the overwhelming and rather dominating effects of globalization and favours a view according to which Zambian people, in the globalization process, are eminently capable of creative responses. They adapt their tradition and cultural practices to the urban environment. This form of resilience is successful not only in so far as the appropriation of alien aspects is concerned, such as Christianity, modern lifestyles and urbanization, but also in so far as the affirmation is concerned of the importance of female initiation rites, which have been owned by Zambian women for many centuries, and which, after a few centuries of colonial and post-colonial suppression and exclusion, and the marginalization of women, now prove capable of once more showing their values and importance. Despite suppression, women have continued to perform these rites, showing their reflexivity. As conditions and circumstances change, resilience also changes. For instance, when the church tried to abolish the rites, they were performed more or less secretly. In the urban environment, they have been curtailed and adapted to urban conditions.

Urban initiation rites mediate deeply-felt tensions between local and global influences, which in turn are constituting gendered notions about what being Zambian or being Bemba means at present (Hansen 1997). Experiencing an initiation rite provides women with a sense of being female, a sense of belonging, of humanity, and of adulthood: it continues to establish women's identity, adulthood and womanhood. Initiation is performed and experienced at a local level, and deals with local ideas of womanhood and adulthood. Other items derived from modern urban life, including Christianity, are added to their identity of being a person.

Initiation is about being incorporated into society but also about individual personhood. It indicates and provides knowledge about a certain type of individual personhood, that of being female and adult in a Zambian society and related to others in that society, in particular parents, ancestors, elders, a husband, and future children. Women articulate themselves as women and adults, in full personhood, experiencing personhood through the rites and in their lives after the rites. To reach this stage of full personhood and gain knowledge about the spiritual world, one needs to be humiliated, to be brought back to zero and reborn with a new status (see Turner 1967, 1969). This can only be reached by initiation rites.

Initiation rites denote a sense of belonging to a community of women and create a gender identity. In urban areas, in social interaction in daily life and through inter-ethnic marriages, the lines between ethnic groups have become blurred. Women attending the rites can be from different ethnic groups and are constructing a community based on the urban situation and on womanhood, instead of one based on ethnicity and kinship, as was the case in the villages. Urban rites have created new patterns of solidarity among women. Yet, the *nacimbusa* because she is guided by the 'blood spirit' that is related to the land of origin has to be from the same ethnic group and area as the novice. This points to the fact that women perceive themselves not only as urbanites taking part in the modern world but also as members of a specific ethnic group.

The initiation rite denotes important gender roles and clarifies a central tension in gender relations, one between complementarity and interdependence in households. Although respect for the husband is emphasized in the rites, a man should equally respect his wife. Moreover, the novice is taught to be independent. The need for independence is stressed due to the present economic situation in which men are losing their jobs and women are being forced to rely on themselves. Women enjoy a considerable measure of power and authority, not only regarding female and sexual matters, but also in family life, gender relations and food production.

During initiation, symbols are used which originally derive from village life. The cosmology peculiar to a certain region with a specific form of socio-economic organization (the village) is not strictly tied to this region and forms of socio-economic organization, but may also spread to other places like urban areas with other economic and social structures, and can even survive there. Initiation, although initially a rural institution, does not exclusively belong to the village but is related to a way of life, to life itself as defined in that way of life. Initiation rites may be enacted wherever that way of life is being pursued. At the same time, there is the suggestion that, even when still tied to the village, a girl's initiation is not entirely a merely local and particularistic cultural item. On the contrary, universal themes emerge in that specific rural form. These themes include the universal human life-cycle, gender oppositions and the need to transfer cultural knowledge from one generation to the next.

In constructing initiation rites as meaningful because they are authentic and handed down from the remote ancestors, Zambian participants in their verbal expressions depend heavily on the notion of tradition, which in Bemba is called *ntambi* or *ifishalano*. No doubt contemporary use of this local concept is somewhat influenced by the circulation of the word tradition in modern media, and its frequent use in the idiom of enculturation by which the Roman Catholic Church seeks to affirm its presence in contemporary Zambia. However, for Zambians, *ntambi* refers to time-honoured ways of social valuation that are not primarily due to the inroads of globalization.

The notion of tradition may be applied to the initiation rites in two interrelated ways. First, cultural identity is expressed by performing the rites. The link with the ancestors is revived in a general, abstract way regardless of the specific form and content of the actions performed. But secondly, in the performance of these initiation rites, specific, now obsolescent and typically rural aspects of the life of the ancestors are being enacted, for example, how they used to pour libations at ancestral shrines, how they used to apply the agricultural system of *citemene*, and how essential aspects of their everyday life were represented in the *mbusa* clay figures shown at important moments during the initiation rite. The *mbusa* themselves contain traditional items such as a pestle and mortar, a hoe, and symbols that refer to animals no longer seen in urban areas.

This process of selectively representing the past in the present in an attempt to build an identity and to give form and meaning to life is perhaps inherent in every ritual or culture. It allows people to recreate their sense of themselves and to deal with changing circumstances. The image of tradition emerges from a dialectic between similarity and difference and between past and present. Known practices become original practices, and current memory becomes primordial (Kratz 1994: 321-24). Thus the way people speak about ritual creates an image of tradition that supports the assertion of continuity. This sense of continuity is produced both in practice and in discourse about practice. Past becomes present, in part through a projection of present practice into the past. 'The past becomes present in different ways as people have multiple images of both, commenting on and framing current practice, politics, and their sense of identity through history' (ibid: 320). The people on the Zambian Copperbelt refer to the continuity of tradition as both explanation and justification for doing things in a certain manner. Imagining tradition also presupposes a sense of cultural identity, the continuity of tradition and a sense of being a member of a group of people who follow similar traditions.

Yet there is a striking similarity between current initiation rites in towns and villages and those that Richards (1956) noted in the 1930s. The ideas surrounding them, their format, ritual actions and *mbusa* remain the same. Their persistence today demonstrates the permanence of ceremonial tradition. Although certain new songs have been added and old ones have disappeared, the themes in the songs are identical and the rite still has the same structure and meaning.

The rite is a representation of continuity. Descent continues because the ancestors are able to manage the life of the living, and in turn are able to produce and control the next generation. Descent implies obeisance, honouring the ancestors and elders. Thus the rite represents two sides of life: that of the ancestors and that of 'this world'. The continuation of the rite explains cultural continuity, and symbolizes the reproduction of society and of the cosmos (Lutkehaus 1995: 28). Initiation points to the individual autonomy of maturing persons. Elders confer on them the trust that they will continue the reproduction of the community. Reproduction refers to more than the female body and biological procreation. It incorporates ideas about social relations, the exchange of resources, power and cosmology. According to this cultural schema, reproduction is a biological, political and economic process (Lutkehaus 1995: 27). The continuity of initiation rites ensures the continuity of female self-understanding (Grohs 1989: 202), in other words female identity. Once this is realized, it can be seen why these rites, regardless of their origins in a distant rural context and (presumably) in the remote past, are not stray flotsam that has accidentally ended up in town. Female self-understanding or identity in South Central Africa has been under attack ever since the arrival of Europeans over a hundred years ago. This has created a situation where the ritual technology of self-understanding through initiation is all the more indispensable. While this observation applies throughout modern Zambia, it is particularly pertinent in town. Here there is unmistakably an environment inimical to women, marked by male control over the state and the economy, and supported in this power position by the patriarchal orientation of Christianity. Experiencing an initiation rite provides the basis and knowledge that construct a woman's identity and create solidarity among women.

Conclusion

This chapter has tried to discover how Zambian women, in the context of a globalized environment, reflect on their culture and religion and how initiation rites as part of their culture and religion are resilient to such an extent that they can still be performed in the same format as centuries ago. As conditions and circumstances change, so may resilience.

Female initiation has not become obsolete or diminished by globalization. Despite the influence of Christianity, urbanization, changed gender roles and the decreasing role of women in agriculture, the female initiation rite is a major institution that has remained important for women even in towns in present-day globalized and Christianized Zambia. They are considered primordial and for all women, not only for those who will soon be getting married, but also for religious sisters who need to experience such a rite.

In male-dominated Christianity, women are marginalized. Tensions between missionaries and local lay women have evolved around womanhood in general and initiation rites in particular. Missionaries have made several attempts to christianize initiation rites but have failed to alter them. Women consider Christian initiation rites insufficient to impart the knowledge a young woman is supposed to receive. The rites remain important for women as a means of constructing their identity and celebrating their culture. Women prefer and manage to keep initiation rites separate from priests, and show their authority in the rites.

The performance of initiation rites in today's urban Zambia should not be seen as a longing for the past that is forcibly being maintained in a globalized world, but as a local institution that is part of a religion. The perpetuation of these rites cannot be considered a way of holding back on religion but is one of the explanations of traditional religion. In this religion woman's power is shown in the sense of continuing life, giving birth, having contact with spirits that have power over fertility and life and death. In the rite, the most important features of religion, spirituality, fertility, adulthood and womanhood are taught and clarified. This is not only for the girl who is being initiated but is a repetition for all women who attend a rite. They celebrate their procreation together and at the same time honour the spirit of fertility. They also show and clarify belonging to a community of women related to the spiritual world and fertility. In addition, it is also a profound model of transcendence and adulthood. Even in a global context, this concept is valued by Zambians.

Imitation rites emphasize traditional knowledge, mainly about procreation, human relationships and relationships with the spirits, topics that remain important in a globalized formal economy. The performance of initiation rites in modern urban Zambia reveals that women consider these rites as their own: it is their institution that was first, that has always existed and always will exist, no matter what comes later and is added or adapted to society.

Experiencing an initiation rite gives a sense of being female among females, in a world that is divided into males and females. This gender division and strict gender roles can be seen in many aspects of daily life. Women and men have different tasks in the household, in agriculture, in child raising, and men and women are expected to occupy different spaces: the house is the domain of women, while the public sphere is that of men. Although both men and women are expected to earn a living, in practice more women than men have jobs or are generating income.

Initiation rites emphasize female power and autonomy. This power and autonomy are related to women's dominant role in sexual activities, such as how to please a man, how to attract a man and maintain a good relationship, and the woman's role in rituals surrounding sexuality that are connected with the ancestral spirits and the spirit of initiation rites. Women's power and autonomy are also related to procreation. Fertility is a person's most important gift — particularly for women — according to matrilineal cosmological ideas.

In these rites and in this concept, the *banacimbusa* play an important role, having knowledge about fertility and contacts with the spirits that provide human fertility and fertility of the land. They guide young women into this world of fertility and the spirits that provide fertility. In this regard, women, and more specifically *banacimbusa*, have a privileged role in and knowledge of society. The knowledge they have can be regarded as intellectual knowledge of culture, religion, fertility, illness and health in Zambia, and probably in the larger area.

Women show reflexivity and resilience in their performance of the rites and in adapting them to modern urban life. With this, they demonstrate their authority in this matter, and in society. Women remain a powerful group. Through their reflexivity on their culture and religion, and through their continuing performance of initiation rites they pass on important values.

References

Ahmed, C.C. 1996, 'Before Eve Was Eve: 2200 Years of Gendered History in East-Central Africa', Unpublished thesis, University of California, Los Angeles.

Bryceson, D.F. 1995, 'African Women Hoe Cultivators: Speculative Origins and Current Enigmas', in: D.F. Bryceson (ed.), *Women Wielding the Hoe: Lessons from Rural Africa to Feminist Theory and Development Practice*, Oxford & Washington DC: Berg Publishers.

Chakanza, J.C. 1998, 'Unfinished Agenda: Puberty Rites and the Response of the Roman Catholic Church in Southern Malawi 1901-1904', in: J.L. Cox (ed.), *Rites of Passage in Contemporary Africa*, pp. 175-168.

Chondoka, Y.A. 1988, *Traditional Marriages in Zambia: A Study in Cultural History*, Ndola (Zambia): Mission Press.

Comaroff, J. & J. Comaroff 1991, *Of Revelation and Revolution: Christianity, Colonialism, and Consciousness in South Africa*, Chicago: University of Chicago Press.

Comaroff, J. & J. Comaroff 1992, 'Home-made Hegemony: Modernity, Domesticity, and Colonialism in South Africa', in: K. Hansen (ed.), *African Encounters with Domesticity*, New Brunswick, NJ: Rutgers University Press, pp. 37-74.

Dondeyne, D. 1967, 'De Juiste Bevordering van de Culturele Vooruitgang', in: *Vaticanum 2: De Kerk in de Wereld van Deze Tijd, Schema Dertien, Tekst en Commentaar*, Hilversum: Uitgeverij Paul Brand, pp. 148-99.

Ferguson, J. 1999, *Expectations of Modernity: Myths and Meanings of Urban Life on the Zambian Copperbelt*, Berkeley, Los Angeles & London: University of California Press.

Green, M. 1999, 'Women's Work is Weeping: Constructions of Gender in a Catholic Community', in: H.L. Moore, T. Sanders & B. Kaare (eds), *Those who Play with Fire: Gender, Fertility and Transformation in East and Southern Africa,* London & New Brunswick, NJ: The Athlone Press, pp. 255-80.

Grimes, R. 2000, *Deeply into the Bone: Re-inventing Rites of Passage*, Berkeley, Los Angeles & London: University of California Press.

Grohs, E. 1989, 'Traditional Rearing of Young Girls among the Zigua and Ngulu: Problems of Identity Change', in: E. Linnebuhr (ed.), *Transition and Continuity of Identity in East Africa and Beyond: In Memoriam David Miller*, Bayreuth: Bayreuth University, pp.178-205.

Gundani, P. 1994, 'The Roman Catholic Church and the *Kurova Guva* Ritual in Zimbabwe', *Zambezia* XXl (ll): 123-146.

Hammerslay. M & P. Atkinson 1995, *Ethnography: Principles and Practices*, London: Routledge.

Hansen, K.T. 1997, *Keeping House in Lusaka*, New York: Columbia University Press.

Hastings, A. 1989, *African Catholicism: Essays in Discovery,* London: SCM Press.

Hinfelaar, H.F. 1989, 'Religious Change among Bemba-speaking Women of Zambia', PhD thesis, University of London.

Inda, J.X. & R. Rosaldo 2002, 'Introduction: A World in Motion', in: J.X. Inda & R. Rosaldo (eds), *The Anthropology of Globalization: A Reader*, Oxford & Massachusetts: Blackwell, pp. 1-35.

Jansen, W. 1993, 'Creating Identities: Gender, Religion and Women's Property in Jordan', in: M. Brügmann, S. Heebing, D. Long & M. Michielsens (eds), *Who's Afraid of Femininity?: Questions of Identity*, Amsterdam & Atlanta, GA: Editions Rodopi, pp. 157-69.

Jules-Rosette, B. 1979, 'Changing Aspects of Women's Initiation in Southern Africa: An Exploring Study', *Canadian Journal of African Studies* 13 (3): 389-405.

Kangwa, M.M. 1990, 'The Chisungu Initiation Rite among the Bemba of Zambia', in: C.A.B. Zigira (ed.), *Occasional Research Papers,* vol. 34, December 1990, pp. 49-73. Makery University, Dept. of Religious Studies. Nairobi: City Printed Works Ltd.

Kratz, C.A. 1994, *Affecting Performance: Meaning, Movement and Experience in Okiek Women's Initiation*, Washington & London: Smithsonian Institution Press.

La Fontaine, J.S. 1986, *Initiation*, Manchester: Manchester University Press.

Labreque, E. 1931 (1982), *Beliefs and Rituals of the Bemba and Neighbouring Tribes,* Ilondola/Chinsali (Zambia): Language Centre. (first printed in 1931-1934).

Larsson, B. 1991, *Conversion to Greater Freedom? Women, Church and Social Change in North-Western Tanzania Under Colonial Rule*, Stockholm: Almqvist & Wiksell International.

Lutkehaus, N.C. 1995, 'Feminist Anthropology and Female Initiation in Melanesia', in: N.C. Lutkehaus & P.B. Roscoe, *Gender Rituals: Female Initiation in Melanesia*, London & New York: Routledge, pp. 1-33.

Lutkehaus, N.C. & P.B. Roscoe 1995, *Gender Rituals: Female Initiation in Melanesia*, London & New York: Routledge.

Meyer, B. 1998, 'Een Visie op de Antropologie Nu en in de Toekomst', in: A. Gevers (ed.), *Uit de Zevende: Vijftig Jaar Politieke en Sociale Wetenschappen aan de Universiteit van Amsterdam*, Amsterdam: Het Spinhuis, pp. 172-86.

Meyer, B. & P. Geschiere 1998, 'Globalization and Identity: Dialectics of Flow and Closure', *Development and Change* 29 (4): 601-16.

Moore, H.L. 1999, 'Gender, Symbolism and Praxis: Theoretical Approaches', in: H.L. Moore, T. Sanders & B. Kaare (eds), *Those who Play with Fire: Gender, Fertility and Transformation in East and Southern Africa,* London & New Brunswick, NJ: The Athlone Press, pp. 3-38.

Neuhaus, R.J. 1990, *The Catholic Moment: The Paradox of the Church in the Postmodern World*, San Francisco: Harper and Row.

Notermans, C. 1999, *Verhalen in Veelvoud: Vrouwen in Kameroen over Polygynie en Christendom,* Nijmegen: Valkhof Pers.

Oger, L. 1991, *Where a Scattered Flock Gathered*, Ilondola, Ndola (Zambia): Mission Press

Phiri, I.A. 1998, 'The Initiation of Chewa Women in Malawi. A Presbyterian Women's Perspective', in: J.L. Cox (ed.), *Rites of Passage in Contemporary Africa*, pp. 129-46.

Rasing, T.S.A. 1995, *Passing on the Rtes of Passage: Girls' Initiation Rites in the Context of an Urban Roman Catholic Community*, London & Leiden: Avebury & Africa Studies Centre.

Rasing, T.S.A. 1999, 'Globalization and the Making of Consumers: Zambian Kitchen Parties', in: R. Fardon, W.M.J. van Binsbergen & R. van Dijk (eds), *Modernity on a Shoestring: Dimensions of Globalization, Consumption and Development in Africa and Beyond*, Leiden/London: EIDOS, pp. 227-47.

Rasing, T.S.A. 2001, *The Bush Burnt, the Stones Remain: Female Initiation Rites in Urban Zambia*, PhD thesis, Leiden & Munster/Hamburg: Africa Studies Centre & Lit Verlag.

Richards, A.I. 1939, *Land, Labour and Diet in Northern Rhodesia: An Economic Study of the Bemba Tribe*, London: Oxford University Press.

Richards, A.I. 1956 (1982), *Chisungu; A Girl's Initiation Ceremony Among the Bemba of Zambia*, London: Tavistock Publications Ltd, Faber & Faber.

Roberts, A.D. 1976, *A History of Zambia*, New York: African Publishing Company, Holmes and Meier Publishers.

Roscoe, P.B. 1995, 'Initiation in Cross-Cultural Perspective', in: N.C. Lutkehaus & P.B. Roscoe, *Gender Rituals: Female Initiation in Melanesia*, London & New York: Routledge, pp. 219-38.

Simonsen, J.K. 2000, 'Webs of Life: An Ethnographic Account of Cisungu Female Initiation Rituals among Mambwe-speaking Women in Zambia', Unpublished PhD thesis, Faculty of Social Science, University of Oslo.

Turner, V.W. 1957, *Schism and Continuity in an African Society: A Study of Ndembu Village Life*, Manchester: Manchester University Press.

Turner, V.W. 1967, *The Forest of Symbols*, New York: Cornell University Press.

Turner, V.W. 1969, *The Ritual Process*, New York: Cornell University Press.

Van Binsbergen, W.M.J. 1992, *Tears of Rain: Ethnicity and History in Central Western Zambia*, London & New York: Kegan Paul International Ltd.

Van Binsbergen, W.M.J. 1998, 'Globalization and Virtuality: Analytical Problems Posed by the Contemporary Transformations of African Societies', *Development and Change* 29 (4): 873-904.

Verstraelen-Gilhuis, G. 1982, *From Dutch Mission Church to Reformed Church in Zambia: The Scope for African Leadership and Initiative in the History of a Zambian Mission Church*, Franeker: T. Wever.

Werner, D. 1971, 'Some Developments in Bemba Religious History', *Journal of Religion in Africa* 4 (1): 1-24.

List of authors

Ferdinand de Jong trained as a historian at Erasmus University, Rotterdam and was awarded his PhD at the University of Amsterdam in 2001. He has published extensively on masquerading and initiation practices among the Jola and Mandinko of South Senegal in, for example, *African Arts*, *Cahiers d'Etudes Africaines* and *Africa*. His present research interests are focused on issues of art and cultural property, memory, and cultural heritage. Ferdinand de Jong is currently teaching anthropology at the School of World Art Studies and Museology at the University of East Anglia, UK.
email: f.jong@uea.ac.uk

Roy Dilley is a senior lecturer in the Department of Social Anthropology, University of St Andrews, Scotland. He has conducted extensive fieldwork in Senegal, most recently in 1995-96 and 2003, and has published widely on hereditary, occupationally specialized artisan groups (castes). Related material on apprenticeship and knowledge among weavers appeared in *Cultural Dynamics* (1999), on caste and social identity in *Anthropos* (2000), and on time, experience and agency in W. James & D. Mills (eds) *The Qualities of Time* (Routledge, in press). An ethnographic monograph entitled *Between the Mosque and the Termite Mound* on the historical relationship between caste and Islam in Senegal is in press with the International Africa Institute, London.
email: rmd@st-andrews.ac.uk

Jan-Bart Gewald is a social historian of Africa at the African Studies Centre, Leiden. He has lived, studied and worked in a number of African countries and is currently establishing a research project dealing with the socio-economic implications of the internal combustion engine in African history. His publications include *Herero Heroes: A Socio-political History of the Herero of Namibia 1890-1923* (James Currey/David Philip/Ohio University Press, 1999), *'We Thought We Would be Free': Socio-cultural Aspects of Herero History in Namibia 1915-1940* (Köppe, 2000) and, together with Jeremy Silvester, *Words Cannot be Found: German Colonial Rule in Namibia, An Annotated Reprint of the 1918 Blue Book* (Brill, 2003).
email: gewald@fsw.leidenuniv.nl

Adeline Masquelier is an associate professor of anthropology at Tulane University, New Orleans. Her current research explores issues of gender and Islamic revival in Niger. She has done extensive fieldwork in Niger focusing on *bori* spirit possession and the connection between modernity and mystical practices and her research on possession, medicine, memory, modernity and the historical imagination has been published in journals such as *American Ethnologist*, *Cultural Anthropology*, *Public Culture*, *Journal of Religion in Africa*, *Anthropological Quarterly*, *Ethos* and *Ethnology*. Her book entitled *Prayer Has Spoiled Everything: Possession, Power, and Identity in an Islamic Town of Niger* (Duke University Press) was published in 2001.
email: amasquel@tulane.edu

Francis B. Nyamnjoh was an associate professor in the Department of Sociology at the University of Botswana from 1999 until July 2003 when he joined CODESRIA in Dakar, Senegal, as Head of Publications and Communication. He has researched and written extensively on Cameroon, where he taught for several years. He is co-author with Piet Konings of *Negotiating an Anglophone Identity* (Brill, 2003), joint editor with Harri Englund of *Rights and the Politics of Recognition in Africa* (Zed, 2004), and has recently contributed chapters to *Magical Interpretations, Material Realities* by H. Moore & T. Sanders (eds) (Routledge, 2001) and *Postcolonial Subjectivities in Africa* by R. Werbner (ed.) (Zed, 2002). Nyamnjoh is currently researching globalization, citizenship, belonging and xenophobia in Botswana and Southern Africa.
email: Francis.Nyamnjoh@Codesria.sn or Nyamnjoh@yahoo.com

Sanya Osha has a PhD in philosophy and has been teaching at universities in Nigeria for the last ten years. His current research interests revolve around personal and collective conditions of life in the African post-colony, and also questions of gender and sexuality in Africa. He is a fellow of the Centre for Rhetoric Studies, University of Cape Town, South Africa and was a visiting scholar at Smith College, Massachusetts, United States in the fall of 2003. His article 'Theorizing the Postcolony or the Force of the Commandement: Meditations on Achille Mbembe's *On the Postcolony*' appeared in *Quest*: *An International Journal of Philosophy* (vol. XIV, no. 1-2, 2000), and 'Anthropology at the Limits: A Genealogical Re-Appraisal of Colonialism in the Time of Globalization' was published in *Research in African Literatures* (vol. 34, no. 1, 2003).
email: babaosha@yahoo.com

Thera Rasing is a cultural anthropologist. She specializes in gender studies and has conducted wide-ranging research on female initiation rites in Zambia. She is affiliated to the Department of Culture, Health and Illness at the Leiden University Medical Centre (LUMC) and has recently been researching levels of knowledge about HIV/AIDS among Zambian youth. Among her publications are *The Bush Burnt, the Stones Remain: Female Initiation Rites in Urban Zambia,* (African Studies Centre/Lit Verlag, 2001), and 'Globalization and the Making of Consumers: Zambian Kitchen Parties' in *Modernity on a Shoestring: Dimensions of Globalization, Consumption and Development in Africa and Beyond* by R. Fardon, W. van Binsbergen & R. van Dijk (eds) (EIDOS, 1999: 227-46).
email: thera@rasing.demon.nl

Wim van Binsbergen is Professor of Intercultural Philosophy at Erasmus University, Rotterdam, and a senior researcher at the African Studies Centre in Leiden. He is presently working on the theory and method of research into cultural globalization in connection with virtuality, Information and Communication Technology, ethnicity and religion. Another of his projects is 'Africa's Contribution to Global Systems of Knowledge: An Epistemology for African Studies in the Twenty-First Century'. His most recent publications include *Trajectoires de Libération en Afrique Contemporaine* with Piet Konings & Gerti Hesseling (Karthala, 2000) and *The Dynamics of Power and the Rule of Law* (African Studies Centre/Lit Verlag, 2003). His book entitled *Intercultural Encounters: African and Anthropological Lessons towards a Philosophy of Interculturality* is currently in press. Wim van Binsbergen is also the editor of *Quest: An African Journal of Philosophy*.
email: binsbergen@chello.nl

Rijk van Dijk is an anthropologist at the African Studies Centre, Leiden. He has done extensive research on the rise of Pentecostal movements in urban areas of Malawi and Ghana and is the author of *Young Malawian Puritans* (ISOR Press, 1993). He has co-edited *Modernity on a Shoestring* with Richard Fardon & Wim van Binsbergen (EIDOS, 1999), *The Quest for Fruition through Ngoma* with Ria Reis & Marja Spierenburg (James Currey, 2000) and *Mobile Africa* with Mirjam de Bruijn & Dick Foeken (Brill, 2001). He has recently contributed articles to, among others, *Magical Interpretations, Material Realities* by H. Moore & T. Sanders (eds) (Routledge, 2001) and *Religion in the Process of Globalization* by Peter Beyer (ed.) (Ergon Verlag, 2001). His current research

focuses on the transnational dimensions of Ghanaian Pentecostalism, in particular in relation to the migration of Ghanaians to the Netherlands and Botswana.
email: dijkr@fsw.leidenuniv.nl

AFRICAN DYNAMICS

ISSN 1568-1777

1. Bruijn, M. de, R. van Dijk and D. Foeken (eds.) *Mobile Africa.* Changing Patterns of Movement in Africa and Beyond. 2001. ISBN 90 04 12072 6
2. Abbink, J., M. de Bruijn and K. van Walraven. *Rethinking Resistance.* Revolt and Violence in African History. 2003. ISBN 90 04 12624 4
3. Van Binsbergen, W. and R. van Dijk. *Situating Globality.* African Agency in the Appropriation of Global Culture. 2004. ISBN 90 04 13133 7